COGNITIVE STRATEGIES AND EDUCATIONAL PERFORMANCE

EDUCATIONAL PSYCHOLOGY

Allen J. Edwards, Series Editor
Department of Psychology
Southwest Missouri State University
Springfield, Missouri

In preparation

Charles D. Holley and Donald F. Dansereau (eds.). Spatial Learning Strategies: Techniques, Applications, and Related Issues

Published

John R. Kirby (ed.). Cognitive Strategies and Educational Performance

Penelope L. Peterson, Louise C. Wilkinson, and Maureen Hallinan (eds.). The Social Context of Instruction: Group Organization and Group Processes

Michael J. A. Howe (ed.). Learning from Television: Psychological and Educational Research

Ursula Kirk (ed.). Neuropsychology of Language, Reading, and Spelling

Judith Worell (ed.). Psychological Development in the Elementary Years

Wayne Otto and Sandra White (eds.). Reading Expository Material

John B. Biggs and Kevin F. Collis. Evaluating the Quality of Learning: The Solo Taxonomy (Structure of the Observed Learning Outcome)

Gilbert R. Austin and Herbert Garber (eds.). The Rise and Fall of National Test Scores

Lynne Feagans and Dale C. Farran (eds.). The Language of Children Reared in Poverty: Implications for Evaluation and Intervention

Patricia A. Schmuck, W. W. Charters, Jr., and Richard O. Carlson (eds.). Educational Policy and Management: Sex Differentials

Phillip S. Strain and Mary Margaret Kerr. Mainstreaming of Children in Schools: Research and Programmatic Issues

Maureen L-Pope and Terence R. Keen. Personal Construct Psychology and Education

The list of titles in this series continues on the last page of this volume.

COGNITIVE STRATEGIES AND EDUCATIONAL PERFORMANCE

Edited by

John R. Kirby

Department of Education
The University of Newcastle
New South Wales, Australia

1984
ACADEMIC PRESS, INC.
(Harcourt Brace Jovanovich, Publishers)
Orlando   San Diego   San Francisco   New York   London
Toronto   Montreal   São Paulo   Sydney   Tokyo

ACADEMIC PRESS, INC.
Orlando, Florida 32887

United Kingdom Edition published by
ACADEMIC PRESS, INC. (LONDON) LTD.
24/28 Oval Road, London NW1 7DX

Library of Congress Cataloging in Publication Data
Main entry under title:

Cognitive strategies and educational performance.

(Educational psychology)
Based on a conference held at the University of
Newcastle in 1981.
Includes bibliographical references and indexes.
1. Cognition in children--Congresses. 2. Learning
--Congresses. 3. Academic achievement--Congresses.
I. Kirby, John R. II. Series.
LB1067.C568 1983 370.15'2 83-7050
ISBN 0-12-409580-1

PRINTED IN THE UNITED STATES OF AMERICA

84 85 86 87 9 8 7 6 5 4 3 2 1

Contents

PART II
BASIC CONCEPTS AND RESEARCH

3
Aspects of Planning   35
J. P. Das

4
Educational Roles of Cognitive Plans and Strategies   51
John R. Kirby

5
Being Executive about Metacognition   89
Michael J. Lawson

6

Learning Strategies, Student Motivation Patterns, and Subjectively Perceived Success 111
John B. Biggs

PART III
CROSS-CULTURAL STUDIES

7

Ethnography, Cognitive Processes, and Instructional Procedures 137
Graham R. Davidson and L. Z. Klich

8

Toward a Recognition of Australian Aboriginal Competence in Cognitive Functions 155
L. Z. Klich and Graham R. Davidson

9

Indigenous Games and the Development of Memory Strategies in Children 203
Graham R. Davidson and Nand Kishor

PART IV
STUDIES OF THE COGNITIVELY DISABLED

10
Some Thoughts on Research in Learning Disabilities and Attention 217
Judy Lupart and Robert Mulcahy

11
The Cognitive Abilities of the Moderately and Severely Retarded 249
A. F. Ashman

12
The Effects of Intervention on Deep and Surface Approaches to Learning 279
John B. Biggs and Bernard A. Rihn

Contributors

Numbers in parentheses indicate the pages on which the authors' contributions begin.

A. F. Ashman (249), Department of Education, The University of Newcastle, New South Wales 2308, Australia

John B. Biggs (111, 279), Department of Education, The University of Newcastle, New South Wales 2308, Australia

J. P. Das (13, 35), Department of Educational Psychology, University of Alberta, Edmonton, Alberta, Canada

Graham R. Davidson[1] (137, 155, 203), Centre for Behavioural Studies in Education, The University of New England, Armidale, New South Wales 2351, Australia

John R. Kirby (3, 51), Department of Education, The University of Newcastle, New South Wales 2308, Australia

Nand Kishor (217), School of Education, The University of the South Pacific, Suva, Fiji

L. Z. Klich[2] (137, 155), Centre for Behavioural Studies in Education, The University of New England, Armidale, New South Wales 2351, Australia

[1]Present address: Department of Humanities and Social Sciences, Darwin Community College, P. O. Box 38221, Winnellie, Darwin, New Tasmania 5789, Australia.

[2]Present address: Australian Institute of Aboriginal Studies, P. O. Box 553, Canberra City 2601, Australia.

Michael J. Lawson (89), School of Education, Flinders University, Bedford Park, South Australia 5042, Australia

Judy Lupart[3] (217), Department of Education, Mount St. Vincent University, Halifax, Nova Scotia, Canada

Robert Mulcahy (217), Department of Educational Psychology, University of Alberta, Edmonton, Alberta, Canada

Bernard A. Rihn (279), Stanford Learning Assistance Center, Stanford University, Stanford, California 94305

[3]Present address: Department of Educational Psychology, Faculty of Education, The University of Calgary, Calgary, Alberta T2N 1N4, Canada.

Preface

This book is about strategies and how they can affect educational performance. It represents a continuation of the effort to link information-processing theory from psychology to a variety of educational achievement problems. Like previous volumes of this informal series,[1,2] this one is motivated by the belief that both psychology and education can benefit from this linking process. The hope is partly to answer specific questions (for instance, How can one teach certain strategies?) and partly to learn how to ask better questions (for instance, What is a strategy?).

The contributions to this volume come from a number of different researchers, who are pursuing different research questions but who share a common theoretical framework. The chapters are arranged into four parts. Part I consists of two chapters that introduce the basic concepts and some of the ideas that follow. Part II presents four different research approaches to the strategy question. In Part III, strategies are investigated from a cross-cultural point of view, and in Part IV the focus is on remediation of cognitive disabilities.

[1]J. P. Das, John R. Kirby, and Ronald F. Jarmon, *Simultaneous and Successive Cognitive Processes* (New York: Academic Press, 1979).

[2]John R. Kirby and John B. Biggs, *Cognition, Development, and Instruction* (New York: Academic Press, 1980).

This book is based on a conference that was held at The University of Newcastle in 1981. Appreciation is due to The University of Newcastle's Internal Research Assessment Committee and Department of Education for underwriting some of the costs involved in that conference. More substantive gratitude is expressed to the contributors and participants, whose mutual constructive criticism and enthusiasm encouraged the publication of this volume.

COGNITIVE STRATEGIES AND
EDUCATIONAL PERFORMANCE

PART I

INTRODUCTION

1

Strategies and Processes

JOHN R. KIRBY

In recent years, cognitive psychology has become so complex that it is difficult to know which parts of it (or even which views of which parts) to apply to educational problems. In one sense, there is an increasing consensus over the broad outline of a model of cognition and its basic nature, but in other senses, there are real disagreements about the functioning of the components of that model and about which components are most involved in educational problems. In fact, the closer we approach those educational problems, the more it becomes apparent that they themselves are in need of further definition and clarification.

This book aims to contribute to bridging the gap between cognitive theory and educational problems: As in all good bridge building, this involves work at both ends of the gap, in cognition and in education. It is hoped that this process produces developments in both fields.

The purpose of this initial chapter is to act as an advance organizer for those that follow. This will involve primarily the introduction of the major themes of the remainder of the book. In addition, some attempt will be made to describe the commonality of theoretical and practical viewpoint

Cognitive Strategies
and Educational Performance

that the author sees in the work of those represented in this volume.[1] There is, I believe, a broad basis of agreement, which should not be surprising, as the authors were selected to represent at least complementary points of view. A final purpose of the present chapter is to clarify some very confusing terminology, or at least to clarify the nature of that confusion.

WHAT THIS BOOK IS ABOUT

Put simply, this book is about the educational relevance of cognitive strategies. Strategies refer to one of two categories of cognitive processes, those concerned with the control of cognitive operations rather than with the operations themselves (see also the next section, "Strategies and Processes"). Most of the authors of the chapters of this book would agree that strategies may play a key role in understanding some educational/ psychological phenomena (e.g., cross-cultural differences, differences between ability groups) and in solving some educational problems (e.g., remediating learning disabilities).

STRATEGIES AND PROCESSES

Process, as in information processing, cognitive *processes,* and so forth, is a leading contributor to terminological confusion (or at least vagueness) in modern psychology. The basic problem is that *processes* sometimes refers to the general category of cognitive[2] or mental functions and sometimes only to a subset of those functions. The second, subset meaning is the one that will be used in this chapter.

The distinction that most authors in this book would accept is between one class of cognitive functions that are involved in the actual encoding, transforming, and storing of information (I would call these *processes,* or performance components) and a second class of functions that are responsible for controlling or planning the use of these processes (called *strategies,* or plans, or control components). This is by no means a radical departure from recent tradition, as much the same distinction is made by many writers. For instance (I will refrain from attempting an exhaustive list), Atkinson and Shiffrin (1968) contrasted *structural features of memory* with *control pro-*

---

[1]Obviously, the commonalities described are my opinion. I believe that most of the authors would agree, but I cannot bind them to that.

[2]A good argument could be made that *cognitive* is in second place in generating terminological confusion (see Kirby, 1980, p. 121).

cesses, Perfetti and Lesgold (1977) distinguish *procedures* from *strategies,* and Sternberg (1980) has *performance components* and *metacomponents.* Despite minor quibbles about definition and major disagreements over measurement, these and other distinctions are isomorphic with the one proposed here. An issue that remains is the status of metacognition, which may have both process and strategy aspects (see Chapter 5).

What is difficult about the process–strategy distinction? I have elaborated upon my confusion in Chapter 4. The basic problem as I see it is that strategies have process aspects, and vice versa. Furthermore, when the cognitive system begins to perform a realistic task, the distinction is hard to maintain.

A strategy is essentially a method for approaching a task, or more generally attaining a goal. Each strategy would call upon a variety of processes in the course of its operation. It is not difficult to see that in a true hierarchical system, with more than two levels, there will be higher-level processes, or lower-level strategies, that will be intermediate in nature. For instance, one might adopt a reproducing strategy (see Biggs, Chapter 6) in approaching a college course, and that general strategy might call primarily upon a lower-level rehearsal strategy in some tasks or upon other strategies in other tasks. In this case, the rehearsal strategy has been well learned and, like all learned strategies, is stored in memory; in this sense, it can function as a process.

Is the proposed distinction between strategies and processes wrong? I do not think so; rather the distinction is a slightly blurred one, and it would be wrong to try to impose a strict dichotomy upon it (see Chapter 4 for more on this).

Further difficulties emerge in examining the strategies domain by itself. As Lawson points out in Chapter 5, one should distinguish between the control aspects of this domain and the knowledge aspects (i.e., metacognitive knowledge). The problem is compounded when we consider that much of the metacognitive knowledge is a result of control functions and that some metacognitive knowledge concerns the use of strategies.

Finally, consider what can happen when a strategy is employed. The strategy can be well established and even habitual in a given situation, and therefore merely has to be called up. Alternatively, one might have to generate or construct a new strategy for a given task: Clearly, more of something is needed in the second case. Das (Chapters 2 and 3) and I (Chapter 4) would refer to this as planning ability, the individual differences skill required in strategic behavior. The key distinction between established and to-be-constructed strategies concerns *automaticity* (e.g., Case, 1980). The category of strategies (or plans, etc.) only makes sense if one accepts its breakdown along a dimension of automaticity. Other divisions, along qualitative–quantitative and micro–macro lines, will be considered later.

OUTLINE OF A CONSENSUS MODEL OF COGNITION

The authors represented in this volume would basically agree that cognition can be usefully analyzed into two interdependent systems—one concerned with the control of processing and the other with processing, corresponding to the strategy–process distinction made in the previous section.

The processing system includes various encoding and storage components, primarily working memory and long-term memory. Working memory is particularly important in the present context, as it appears to be the space that is taken up by strategies (even though they are constructed or selected elsewhere) in addition to data. This emphasizes the interdependence of the processing and strategy systems: A good strategy can compensate for a lack of working memory space, but insufficient working memory space almost guarantees an ineffective strategy.

The strategy system is responsible for setting goals, selecting or constructing strategies, and monitoring performance. Strategies can be narrow and situation specific (e.g., a rehearsal strategy) or as broad and generalized as a cognitive style. By emphasizing strategies, it should not be inferred that we think that processes are unimportant.

When an individual behaves in a certain way, it is difficult to ascribe that behavior to one or the other of the systems. This is particularly true when qualitatively different groups of subjects are being compared (ability groups: Chapters 10, 11, 12; cultural groups: Chapters 7, 8, 9).

The two-system model is deliberately called a model: It functions as a framework guiding our thinking, not as a theory generating predictions testing its validity. Theoretical predictions can be generated within the context of the model, but these concern more specific aspects and do not challenge the model itself.

Individual differences. Although it no longer sounds radical or innovative to say so, the present group of authors do support the unification of cognitive psychology with individual differences psychology. In this book, we could be described as using the theories of cognitive psychology to explain the data of individual differences psychology.

Simultaneous and successive processing theory. Das and I have been identified with the proposal of what has been referred to as "simultaneous and successive processing theory" (Das, Kirby, & Jarman, 1975, 1979; Kirby & Das, 1978), about which many of the other authors in this book have written, although not all would agree with it.

The theory itself was derived conceptually from the work of Luria (see Das's account in Chapter 2), and we elaborated its relations to cognitive theory, psychometrics, and education. Although Luria emphasized three functional cognitive systems (*arousal, processing, planning*) and we adopted them, our early work concentrated upon the processing system and two forms of processing (*simultaneous* and *successive*) that take place in it. Ashman (1978) really began work on the planning system, and Chapters 2, 3, 4, and 5 of the present book constitute developments of that system, in somewhat divergent directions.

The *planning–processing* distinction is exactly the same as the *strategies–processes* distinction proposed here. For that reason, it should not be surprising if the terms are used interchangeably. All the same, I would not want to imply that by talking of strategies an author is necessarily accepting any other aspect of the simultaneous–successive theory (which as Das implies is more properly termed *information integration theory*).

Whatever it is called, a problem that has vexed the theory has been how to describe between-group performance differences. For instance, Krywaniuk (1974) showed that Canadian native Indian children performed less well on measures of successive processing than did white children. A remedial program improved their scores on successive processing tests, as well as on measures theoretically related to successive processing (i.e., reading). Had the native children previously had low successive processing ability, and had the remedial program increased that ability, or had they had normal ability but not known how or when to use it? In the former case, the problem and solution concerned only processing; in the second, planning or strategies are clearly implicated. Whether discussing cultural group differences (Chapters 7, 8, and 9) or ability group differences (Chapter 11), this question remains important for educational planning. As with many such either–or questions, of course, the answer is likely to involve a little of each.

In Chapter 2, Das gives a statement of the basic theory, reviews what evidence does exist for it, and proposes ways to validate his hypotheses. In Chapter 3, Das reviews recent research by him and his students about the planning system in particular. My Chapter 4 is in a sense a response to that research, investigating whether there are aspects of planning beyond those considered by Das (this volume) and Ashman (1978).

Davidson and Klich (Chapters 7 and 8) apply the simultaneous– successive model cross-culturally, and Ashman (Chapter 11) uses it to study the severely mentally retarded. Both of these applications demonstrate the difficulty of applying a framework derived in one context to a fundamentally different context, but both also illustrate the potential of the attempt.

This book is not primarily about the simultaneous–successive processing theory, though much of the research reported here has been conceptualized in its context. That theory is only one perspective upon cognitive strategies, and others are certainly needed (e.g., Chapters 5 and 6). As Das indicates in Chapter 2, our theories will have served their purpose if they generate interesting research and application, advance our understanding even slightly, and ultimately sow the seeds of their own obsolescence.

IS THERE A PLANNING ABILITY?

Much of the research reported in this book has been guided by an interest in individual differences. Accordingly, it is not surprising that when various manifestations of cognitive strategies are studied, it becomes tempting to think of their composite as some sort of strategic or planning ability. Investigating this issue is fundamentally the same as inquiring whether there is a single intelligence factor, and it suffers from all the same pitfalls. Ashman (1978, 1979) and Das (this volume, 1980; Ashman & Das, 1980) have begun by considering a set of planning measures that correlate highly enough with each other to legitimize the postulation of a single factor. As Das shows in Chapter 3, this single factor is very useful as a between-subjects individual differences variable in experimental studies.

On the other hand, the research reviewed by Lawson and myself in Chapters 5 and 4 demonstrates that various aspects of planning (or meta-cognition, etc.) can be separated. This is not surprising, given the situation specificity of that sort of skill. Furthermore, even the unitary planning factor does not emerge in the severely retarded (Ashman, Chapter 11). It would appear that planning acts like other mental abilities: It develops with experience and can be studied at various levels of analysis. The question of whether or not there is a single planning factor is not a good question. The more important question is what aspects of planning, at which level of analysis, should be considered in a particular context.

How is planning ability, in either its uni- or multifactorial guises, related to intelligence? Theoretically, intelligence should be a general index of the functioning of the entire cognitive system. From this perspective, the planning system is one contributor to intelligence. However, it does not require a great deal of scepticism to conclude that most commonly used intelligence tests are not designed to test planning ability. If planning and strategies are as important as the authors of this book suggest, this is an obvious direction for future research.

DIFFERENCES AMONG STRATEGIES

Qualitative versus Quantitative

If the task at hand is to memorize some words, and the people we want to memorize these words are normal members of our Western society, we have little hesitation in recognizing an order of "goodness" to the type of strategy used. "Bad" strategies involve not looking at the words, not listening to the task instructions, etc. A better approach is to apply rote-memory-relevant strategies, such as overt naming and cumulative rehearsal. Better strategies still, especially if the words are concrete or conceptually related, involve semantic or imaginal coding. While some of the "less good" strategies may be more effective in certain situations, there would be little disagreement that, in general, strategies that are meaning oriented are better than those that are rote oriented. It is similarly noncontroversial to conclude that the strategies employed by the retarded (Chapter 11) or the learning disabled (Chapter 10) are less good than those chosen by normal children, at least in academic tasks.

When the focus is shifted to a cross-cultural context, however, the hierarchical ordering of strategies becomes less acceptable. Davidson and Klich (Chapter 7) discuss how a cultural context (including language, ecology, and values) can shape the preferred cognitive strategies of a culturally defined group. From an ethnographically pure point of view, the transfer of one culture's frame of reference onto another is wrong and can be quite vicious (see Klich and Davidson, Chapter 8, for an analysis of such studies of Australian Aborigines). It would be unfortunate, however, if this resulted in some phenomenological hands-off imperative. Chapters 7, 8, and 9 demonstrate that it is possible to deal with cultural differences sensitively and sympathetically, without losing sight of the important practical goals of educational attainment and even survival.

It would be wrong to deny that there are quantitative differences between strategies, that some strategies are simply better for certain purposes. It would be equally wrong and perhaps more pernicious to deny qualitative differences in strategies. Can methods of instruction be designed that promote academic achievement (perhaps as defined by the particular culture) but protect the cultural identity of the learners? If this is to be done, greater understanding of the nature of strategies and their relation to performance is required.

Micro versus Macro

One distinction among strategies that emerges from the chapters that follow is that between microstrategies (or microplans) and macrostrategies. The former are conceived as more task specific, more related to particular knowledge and abilities, closer to performance, and more responsive to instruction. Macrostrategies are more pervasive, sometimes more intertwined with emotional and motivational factors, more related to cultural and stylistic differences, and more difficult to change by instruction. The micro–macro distinction can be seen as a dichotomy or as a continuum; Biggs (Chapter 6) includes the middle category of mesostrategies.

One fascinating aspect of macrostrategies is the intertwining of cognitive and affective (motivational) factors (cf. Lupart & Mulcahy, Chapter 10). It has been a persistent criticism of cognitive psychology that it is relatively affectless; this may be because recent work has been primarily at the microstrategy level, where affect is either not necessarily involved or is involved in a way in which it can be clearly separated from cognitive factors.

Two areas of research have commonly linked cognitive and affective variables: psychometric studies of ability and personality variables, and research concerned with cognitive styles. Curiously, both of these areas seem to have receded in prominence in recent years.[3] From the current perspective, especially that supplied by Biggs in Chapter 6, this may have occurred because of the lack of an adequate conceptual framework.

The basic issue that emerges from this distinction is transfer: As several authors mention, much research is disappointing in showing relatively little transfer of training when strategies are taught. One could forgive a critic for being more surprised and skeptical when transfer does occur. Just saying that transfer does not occur when training is at the micro level does not solve the problem, but it does provide a sensible way of discussing the problem and may lead to solutions. One implication is that rather massive changes may have to be made to some very fundamental personological traits (macrostrategies): In the case of abilities, such changes may not be possible (e.g., mental retardation); in some cross-cultural settings, such changes may not be desirable. Perhaps greatest effect will be had at some middle level of trait–task noncongruence, legitimizing Biggs's meso level.

Examples of meso level noncongruences between subjects' strategies and the tasks they have to perform could include the following:

1. *Learning disabled children.* As Lupart and Mulcahy discuss in Chapter 10, these children approach some academic tasks in a vague or distractible manner; not surprisingly, several years of school failure gives rise to an antiacademic cognitive–motivational–social syndrome that is very difficult to tackle. Teaching highly task-specific strategies (micro) is unlikely to be the solution; a more top-down, metacognition-oriented approach, such as that recommended by Lupart and Mulcahy, may be the answer.
2. *Educating children from different cultures.* As Davidson and Klich observe in Chapter 7, a difference in basic values can be an obstacle to applying our educational system to non-Western or nonmajority children. Changing such values may involve work at the macro level, which is likely to be difficult and may be ethically hard to justify.

---

[3]There is a clear cognitive bias to this observation, but I do think that there is some objective reality to it as well. See the work of Messick (e.g., 1979) for more information regarding the interaction of cognitive and noncognitive measures in education.

Instead, such value conflicts can be avoided by changing our educational methods to make use of culturally acceptable values or approaches; essentially, this is working at the meso level, changing students' middle-level strategies while attempting to leave macro level ones alone, and changing tasks to match existing macro and meso level strategies.

3. *Students who are otherwise perfect.* Biggs and Rihn (Chapter 12) present the interesting case of university students who are high in intelligence and, unlike the learning disabled, high in basic academic skills. They are even highly motivated! What they seem unable to do is to use all of this macro level advantage to generate an appropriate strategy–motivational mixture.

OVERVIEW

The chapters that follow are about cognitive strategies and their various impacts upon educational performance. Das, myself, Lawson, and Biggs each present research-based theoretical analyses of strategies and the forms they can take. Important themes that are raised in these chapters include: the dimensionality of the planning domain, whether strategies can be usefully divided along a micro–macro continuum, and how planning or strategies are related to traditional mental abilities and more modern concepts, such as metacognition. Davidson, Klich, and Kishor deal with cross-cultural issues, which also involve many of the substantive themes raised in the basic research studies. Their perspective broadens the scope of these themes and shows how many conceptually thorny problems have practical consequence. Finally, Lupart, Mulcahy, Ashman, Biggs, and Rihn provide examples of how strategy-oriented research can be applied to the cognitively disabled: In these cases, "cognitively disabled" includes mentally retarded persons, learning disabled children, and highly intelligent university students.

One final comment about a bias shown in the chapters that follow: All are concerned with practical educational problems. As such, all are concerned with understanding what *does* work, in addition to understanding many things that could work. This mixture of theory and practice, of psychology and education, can be said to bridge a gap between the two, but it also defines a subdiscipline—"applied cognitive educational psychology," if you will—that exists between the two.

REFERENCES

Ashman, A. F. The relationship between planning and simultaneous and successive synthesis. Unpublished doctoral dissertation, University of Alberta, 1978.

Ashman, A. F. Planning—the integrative function of the brain: Empirical evidence and speculation. *Educational Enquiry*, 1979, 2, 78–94.

Ashman, A. F., & Das, J. P. Relation between planning and simultaneous and successive processing. *Perceptual and Motor Skills*, 1980, 51, 371–382.

Atkinson, R. C., & Shiffrin, R. M. Human memory: A proposed system and its control processes. In K. W. Spence & J. T. Spence (Eds.), *The psychology of learning and motivation* (Vol. 2). New York: Academic Press, 1968.

Case, R. The underlying mechanism of intellectual development. *In J. R. Kirby & J. B. Biggs (Eds.), Cognition, development, and instruction*. New York: Academic Press, 1980.

Das, J. P. Planning: Theoretical considerations and empirical evidence. *Psychological Research*, 1980, 41, 141–151.

Das, J. P., Kirby, J., & Jarman, R. F. Simultaneous and successive syntheses: An alternative model for cognitive abilities. *Psychological Bulletin*, 1975, 82, 87–103.

Das, J. P., Kirby, J. R., & Jarman, R. F. *Simultaneous and successive cognitive processes*. New York: Academic Press, 1979.

Kirby, J. R. Individual differences and cognitive processes: Instructional application and methodological difficulties. In J. R. Kirby & J. B. Biggs (Eds.), *Cognition, development, and instruction*. New York: Academic Press, 1980.

Kirby, J. R., & Das, J. P. Information processing and human abilities. *Journal of Educational Psychology*, 1978, 70, 58–66.

Krywaniuk, L. W. Patterns of cognitive abilities of high and low achieving school children. Unpublished doctoral dissertation, University of Alberta, 1974.

Messick, S. Potential uses of noncognitive measurement in education. *Journal of Educational Psychology*, 1979, 71, 281–292.

Perfetti, C. A., & Lesgold, A. M. Discourse comprehension and sources of individual differences. In M. A. Just & P. A. Carpenter (Eds.), *Cognitive processes in comprehension*. Hillsdale, N.J.: Erlbaum, 1977.

Sternberg, R. J. Sketch of a componential subtheory of human intelligence. *Behavioral and Brain Sciences*, 1980, 3, 573–584.

2

Intelligence and Information Integration

J. P. DAS

BACKGROUND

Intelligence is a construct. It is not an object out there. One might ask, then, what the meaning of such a construct is. In fact, the term has many different connotations depending on the orientation of the person who uses it and the use to which such a construct is put. For Cyril Burt, intelligence was an innate general cognitive ability. If you do not agree with any one of the terms in this definition, it does not mean that you do not accept intelligence as a valid construct. For instance, the extreme environmentalists believe that intelligence is not innate. Many factor analysts believe that it is not a general ability but consists of many specific abilities. Some would quarrel with the characterization of intelligence as purely cognitive because of the obvious personality and motivational influences that interact with the manifestation of intelligent behavior. And lastly, there are those who take issue with the definition of intelligence as an ability, preferring to describe intelligence as processes underlying behavior. Contemporary theorists of intelligence often assume its connotation without explicitly stating it. For instance, Robert Sternberg considers it mostly in terms of problem solving. Under other contexts, he views intelligence as a macrocomponent that

13

Cognitive Strategies
and Educational Performance

includes general, academic, practical, crystalized, and fluid intelligence, as well as motivation (Sternberg, 1980).

There has been quite a trend recently toward describing intelligence as close to a biological entity, whose manifestation is reflected in reaction time. For Jensen (1981), it is the speed in choice reaction time—especially, the variability in speed—that could be considered as a single important index of intelligence. Eysenck (1981) goes a step further and looks for signs of intelligence in the complexity of event-related potentials.

A construct is created because of a necessity to order disparate bits of knowledge. It has either theoretical or practical utility, or both. Psychometric tests of intelligence, therefore, fulfilled the needs of the time when large numbers of people had to be screened to work in the Army. When vast numbers of children had to be screened into distinct programs in school, so that their ability matched the difficulty of the curriculum, the Binet and Terman–Merrill tests were constructed and used. These psychometric measures of intelligence are essentially measures of competence. Most of them are correlated substantially with academic performance, especially in early school years, since their purpose was to sort out children in elementary school.

However a shift to processes from abilities was inevitable. IQ tests ceased to serve a practical purpose, and IQ became a pejorative label for minority children and mentally handicapped individuals. This happened in the United States in the late 1960s and early 1970s. There was such a resentment against psychometric tests of intelligence that some states prohibited the general use of IQ testing in schools. As an aside, it is curious to note that under similar circumstances psychometric testing was banned in the Soviet Union shortly after the socialist revolution. A vast majority of working-class children were found to be poor in IQ testing, which persuaded the new egalitarian leaders of the Socialist Republic to ban IQ testing altogether. In the United States, where intelligence testing had become an enormously large industry, the opposition to testing often assumed a political force against the establishment. Some curious adjustments have since taken place in the field of testing. One of these allows a handicap score to minority children, which is added to standardized intelligence test scores (Mercer, 1973). A healthier approach is illustrated by criterion-referenced testing, or testing based on specific competencies rather than on global competence.

Apart from the social and political problems arising out of a change in the zeitgeist that made psychometric tests of intelligence unpopular, some serious theoretical flaws were also pointed out. The psychometric test industry did not reflect current progress in the fields of learning, memory, and thinking, and essentially operated as a parallel movement to mainstream psychological research. Deploring the existence of two psychologies, Cronbach (1957) and McNemar (1964) gave the signal for a paradigm shift in the field of intelligence. But the effect of this shift has become visible only very recently, along with the emergence of information processing theories within the framework of artificial intelligence.

Thus, the American approach to mental processes was influenced by the computer. So strong was the influence that for a time "information processing model" meant nothing else than the simulation of mental processes in computer terminology. However, since then, typically human intelligent behavior has gained popularity as a topic among those who work on computer models. For instance, Earl Hunt (1980) wrote an integrative paper on intelligence as an information processing concept. The three key concepts in intelligence presented in the paper were structure, process, and knowledge base, all of which are compatible with computer models but wide enough to be interpreted outside the context of computers. Information processing, then, is not a model by itself but a framework that can accommodate other systems besides the computer. It is a generic term that can subsume any model of mental processes and strategies.

In the contemporary American psychology of intelligence, or intelligent behavior, information processing models either have attempted to explain mental processes in terms of perception and short-term memory or have concerned themselves with the manner in which problems are solved. Such a dichotomy between explanations in terms of high- and lower-level processes has arisen because of the nature of the performance that is the object of explanation. Saul Sternberg (1966) has advanced a model to explain memory search and reaction time response. A sequential model is proposed starting with a presentation of the stimulus, which leads to stimulus encoding, which then leads to serial comparison, binary decision, translation, and response organization, and finally to the activation of response.

Problem solving models, in contrast to the sequential linear chain of boxes exemplified in Sternberg's model, are naturally complex; in some of these models, such as in the "missionaries and cannibals" problem (Glass, Holyoak, & Santa, 1979), the roles of perception and short-term memory are not explicitly mentioned. Ernst and Newell's (see Glass *et al.,* 1979) General Problem Solver computer model can be applied to solve the above problem, after collecting the following basic information: (*a*) information on the initial state, goal state, and operations; (*b*) information on all possible differences between these states; and (*c*) information on specific operations that will be required to reduce each possible difference.

Although computer models may describe the orderly stepwise procedure, in a reaction time or problem solving task, could we be certain that an individual follows the same procedure? Take the example of deductive inferences—do we as individuals always arrive at the conclusion by deliberately examining the major and minor premises? To take the example further, solving a mathematical theorem may involve 100 sequential steps, but an individual may not follow most of these logical steps. In fact, some mathematicians cannot work out the procedure, although they can arrive at its solution. One must entertain the possibility that thinking up a solution may not be knowable, and thought appears to be logical only when it needs to be communicated. Even that much cannot always be claimed. Consider an intuitive statement: "Then I realized that in God everything is possible."

Why should we be interested in studying cognitive processes? Theories of how the mind works gain importance when they seem to be parsimonious in comparison with their competitors, but perhaps that is not enough to prolong their longevity. They must be ultimately applied to predict, and more importantly to correct, faults in cognitive processing of a class of individuals.

A good measure of cognitive processes must have three aspects, as Figure 2.1 shows. Since measuring competence is sometimes quite essential, one of the aspects of a comprehensive cognitive measure must include competence. Current intelligence tests certainly fulfill this need, but they exclude measures of the two other aspects in the cognitive cube. Beyond competence are the processes that underlie the level of competence achieved by an individual. We have proposed essentially two major processes; coding and planning. These will be described later in this chapter. But no instrument or measure of cognitive functions is complete without the third aspect indicated in the figure—prescription, which includes training and remediation. It is of little use to a clinical psychologist, or a school counselor, to know that a certain child has a specific IQ. The psychologist is

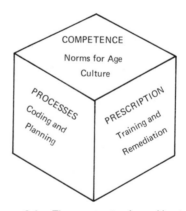

Figure 2.1. Three aspects of cognitive testing.

left with very little information to plan further action unless (*a*) the test describes exactly the processes in which the child might have a defect or might be experiencing a developmental delay; and (*b*) what is perhaps of primary concern in clinical situations, the test gives a rationale for training, remediation, or therapy. We would like to suggest that the information integration model to be described here has all three aspects; it provides the user with an index of the subject's competence in relation to other individuals of his or her age and culture, while pointing out the psychological processes adopted by the individual in approaching the tasks, and finally, it provides a rational basis for removing the deficiencies revealed by a process analysis of the child's competence.

The information integration model views information processing as a function of the brain. If we wish to understand how information is processed by human beings, it follows logically that we must comprehend how processing occurs in the brain rather than in a computer. To follow Earl Hunt's three concepts, the structure for the model is the brain, the processes are neuropsychological, and the knowledge base is provided as always by the experience and education of the information processor.

The remainder of this chapter first describes the development of a neuropsychological model, based on the clinical observations of Luria. Then a schematic diagram of our model is provided and delineated. This is followed by a section on basic statements and supporting evidence for the model.

NEUROPSYCHOLOGY AND
INFORMATION INTEGRATION

Luria observed behavioral dysfunctions following lesions in the brain for several years before he came upon three main functional divisions of the brain. He conceptualized these as Block 1, which is involved in arousal; Block 2, which controls coding; and Block 3, which is concerned with planning and decision making (Luria, 1966, 1973). Since these functional systems have been described in detail by Das, Kirby, and Jarman (1975, 1979), only a brief discussion of the blocks will be provided here.

The essence of Luria's distinctive theory is his notion of functional organization. Prior to Luria's research, many attempts were made to localize brain functions punctiliously at certain microscopic areas of the brain. However, it was soon discovered that an attempt at relating, for instance, injury to 1 mm of brain tissue with a specific and limited form of behavioral disorder is subject to both logical and neuroanatomical fallacy. A function may be disturbed in many ways, not necessarily by the presence of a lesion in a particular part of the brain. In other words, the injury in the brain may not be of central importance to the dysfunction observed at the level of behavior. Pathways in the brain form a pattern, a complex network, rather than a specific connection of fibers. Thus, a lesion in a certain region of the brain may cause pathological behavior because it may tangentially affect functional pathways by injuring adjacent neurons that are not central to the damaged function. Similarly, a function might be spread out in a wide part of the brain, and the lesion may disrupt only some part of that function. By doing so, however, it may create a weakness in the total network of functions, which in turn may cause a general disruption. Such arguments have been put forth much more succinctly and with neurophysiological evidence in several contemporary books on neuropsychology (cf. Hécaen & Albert, 1978; Gazzaniga & Le Doux, 1978).

Another point to be kept in mind while associating functional disorder with a lesion is as follows. Even if there is consistent evidence linking a lesion to a dysfunction, one may not posit a strong relationship between the damage and the function unless such an assumption would explain, not only abnormal, but also normal behavior. In other words, a functional explanation should be useful for intact as well as deranged functions. For instance, patients with frontal lobe lesions show derangement in programming their behavior. Luria (1966) observed that such patients experience difficulties in regulating their various activities according to a plan. The role of the frontal lobes in normal individuals is recognized to be the generation of plans, selecting appropriate plans from among others as well as executing them (Das, 1980). In this way, we realize that behavioral abnormalities ascribed to frontal lobe damage are but the negative consequences of disrupting the normal functions of the frontal lobes.

One is often faced with the problem of distinguishing between structure and function. The same question takes another form when one differentiates between structure and process. The structure in neuropsychology of course refers to the neurophysiological and neuroanatomical base of the brain. Function, on the other hand, is dynamic, changeable, and adaptive. Luria (1973) also distinguishes a functional system from a static notion of abilities as follows: "The presence of a constant task, performed by variable (variative) mechanisms, bringing the process to a consistent (invariant) result is one of the basic features distinguishing the work of every functional system [p. 28]."

The functional systems, according to Luria, have both depth as well as spread. Processing of information in simultaneous quasi-spatial arrays, for example, is spread over a large area comprising the occipital and parietal lobes. Successive information processing—that is, ordering information temporally—likewise is widely located in the temporal and the frontotemporal areas of the brain. Planning and making decisions may inhere in the whole of the frontal lobes. Considering depth, any kind of coding, such as coding of visual information, passes through three hierarchical levels of the brain consistent with its topography. These can be described in a rather simplistic manner, as the projection area where the modality characteristic of the information is intact. Above the projection area lies the projection-cum-association area. As information reaches this area, it loses part of its modality tag. Above this area is the tertiary area or zones of overlapping where information is typically amodal. This enables information to be integrated from different sensory organs without any restriction due to modality.

Our model, described elsewhere (Das *et al.*, 1975), can be essentially characterized as an information processing model (see Figure 2.2). It as-

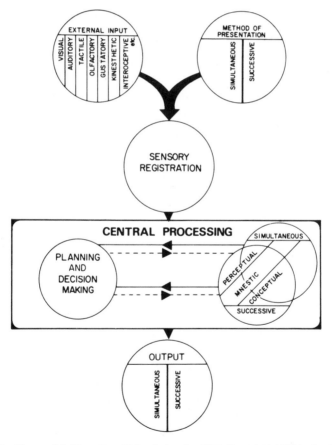

Figure 2.2. The model. [From Das, Kirby, & Jarmin, 1975. Copyright 1975 by the American Psychological Association.]

sumes the very same basic stages of information processing as all models within this framework do. First, information is received by receptors. It can be presented to the receptors either all at once (i.e., simultaneously) or in a sequential fashion, whereupon information enters the sensory register. The concept of a sensory buffer can be brought in at this point in order to explain how information can be held in the sensory register for a little while. The length of time it can be held of course varies from modality to modality. Then information proceeds to the central processing unit, which is responsible for sorting information and synthesizing it according to a goal or a purpose. The central processing unit, thus, is conceived to have two major functions. One is the analysis and synthesis of information; the other is planning and decision making based on coded information. The third unit of the model is concerned with output, which could be simultaneous, as in recognition of old from new items in a memory experiment, or successive if recall is required. We have not worked at all on the output unit itself, but it is conceivable that such a unit will be essential for planning motor activity.

Luria's (1966) notions have thus been represented in the schematic diagram and operationalized in terms of a battery of tasks that can be approached either simultaneously or successively depending on the characteristics of the sample. Thus, unlike psychometric tasks, which are fixed measures of one specific ability, a simultaneous task, such as Raven's Coloured Progressive Matrices, was approached successively as well as simultaneously by a sample in India.

Any model becomes easier to verify if deductions and corollaries from it are specifically stated. The more general the statements are that emanate from the model, the harder they are to check, and for that reason, they become less useful. An attempt has been made in the following section to state the various aspects of the model; review evidence, where it exists, in their support; and indicate what needs to be proved and verified in regard to the implications of a statement. I do this with the full realization of the inadequacies of such an attempt. I present only positive evidence; this is the method of agreement in inductive logic. An adequate procedure should also include the method of difference, and jointly through these opposite methods, do we ensure the validity of inductive statements. Part of the reason for my one-sided presentation is the relative paucity of research into simultaneous, successive, and planning processes outside our laboratory. Some research has been carried out by the authors of other chapters in this book and by a few in the United States (A. S. Kaufman, 1979: Ryckman, 1981); but without a fair body of investigations by others who try to verify the major statements as well as their derivatives, one's attempt to formalize the model will remain tentative, although I would not describe it as premature. If I waited until enough researchers had gathered enough data on the model before I proceeded, no theory could be published. My purpose, then, for presenting the next section is to allow the reader to take stock of what has been done and what needs to be accomplished.

BASIC STATEMENTS AND SUPPORTING EVIDENCE FOR SIMULTANEOUS–SUCCESSIVE AND PLANNING PROCESSES

A. Basic Statements

> A.1. *Stimultaneous–successive and planning processes occur at all three levels of cognition: perceptual, mnestic, and conceptual.*

For the purpose of demonstrating *simultaneous* processing at the perceptual level, Figure Copying has been used as a task. At the mnestic level, the task is Memory-for-Designs, and at the symbolic or conceptual level, it is Raven's Coloured Progressive Matrices. In addition to these, certain verbal tasks have been shown to predominantly require simultaneous processing. Concrete paired-associate learning loads on the simultaneous factor (Das *et al.*, 1975). This is a mnestic task and is verbal. Lexical ambiguity correlates with simultaneous processing (Das, Cummins, Kirby, & Jarman, 1979). It involves perception of ambiguity. The task may be classified as both perceptual and symbolic, and it is verbal.

Piaget's tasks comprising conservation of liquid, transitive inference, and class inclusion require simultaneous and not successive processing. The high simultaneous, low successive and the high simultaneous, high successive do better than the low simultaneous, high successive and the low simultaneous, low successive groups, as shown in a doctoral thesis from our center (Mwamwenda, 1980).

A representative battery of verbal tasks for measuring simultaneous processing in children needs to be constructed. Good candidates are tests of a logicogrammatical nature (Luria, 1966). A specific example of one of the several logicogrammatical structure tasks is to ask the subject to say as quickly as possible whether or not the following two sentences are the same or different: *Be less brief or beautiful. Be less beautiful or brief.* Another verbal task is comprehension, when vocabulary is high (seventieth percentile and above); it correlates with Memory-for-Designs, a simultaneous task as observed by McLeod (1978). McLeod's research was a sequel to Kirby's (1976), who found that, in average readers, both simultaneous and successive processes contribute to or are used in vocabulary and comprehension.

Successive processing tasks as used in many studies (see Das, Kirby & Jarman, 1979) belong to the category of mnestic or memorial ones. Examples of these are digit span and serial recall of words auditorily presented or of numbers visually presented in a matrix. In regard to instances of perceptual and symbolic categories, it is not difficult to find them. Consider decoding: Schoolchildren are asked to judge if pairs of pseudowords, such as *spert* and *srept,* are the same or different. This task involves detection of the transposition of the letters *p* and *r.* As children engage in comparison, some of them will sound out the words, by applying rules of phonological coding. The task is successive in so far as ordering of the letters is necessary. One of Luria's examples for dysfunction of successive processing was the inability to understand syntax. Thus, one would expect individual differences in appreciation of syntax to be related to successive processing. Cummins (Das, Kirby, & Jarman, 1979) has discussed the relationship between the two; the tasks consisted of perception of ambiguous sentences. It was shown that surface-structure ambiguity (e.g., *He told her baby stories*) as well as deep-structure ambiguity (e.g., *The eating of the chicken was sloppy*) were related to the successive processing factor.

Nonverbal measures of successive processing have not been frequently tried out in our research. Cross-modal Coding (Das, 1973) is in fact the only one in our standard battery, but this task has loadings on both simultaneous and successive factors. In this task, the subject is required first to listen to patterns of taps or tones separated by a short or a long duration and then to recognize visually the pattern from among two others presented as dots separated by relatively short and long gaps. It will not be difficult to devise a variation of this task that will be a measure of item order and will involve only one modality.

A visual and nonverbal successive task would be as follows. Consider a transparent chute through which marbles are dropped, one at a time at two different intervals, short and long. The subject is required to copy the experimenter's pattern by dropping the marbles through the chute.

Planning tasks, as used in our battery, represent perceptual (Visual Search), mnestic (Trail Making), and the symbolic (Planned Composition) aspects of cognitive functions. We have added mostly symbolic tasks to the battery, such as time to solve three-term syllogisms in a learning-to-learn condition, and a game of strategies, such as *Master Mind,* in which the subject is asked to break a code that the experimenter has set up (Heemsbergen, 1980).

   A.2. *Simultaneous and successive processes are not hierarchical.*

Consider decoding and comprehension in reading (Das, Cummins, Kirby, & Jarman, 1979). At an early stage of reading, decoding depends more on successive than on simultaneous processes, but both are involved in decoding as well as in comprehension. In reading, decoding of words in print must precede comprehension, and therefore successive processes are needed earlier than simultaneous processes. However, the opposite may be true for other cognitive tasks where a scheme or a picture of the whole is needed to understand the parts correctly.

One may think that comprehension is much more complex than decoding, hence simultaneous processing is higher. But consider the next example. Perception of lexical ambiguity is related to simultaneous processing, whereas the perception of surface- and deep-structure ambiguity seems to be related to successive processing (Das, Kirby, & Jarman, 1979; see chapter by Cummins). Obviously, lexical ambiguity is simpler to detect than the other two. It cannot be argued, then, that simultaneous processing is at a higher level than successive processing.

A.3. *However, either simultaneous or successive processing may appear earlier than the other and have a distinct pattern of development that is not shared by the other.*

The question of which process appears earlier is still mainly unresolved. Obviously, potential for both processes is present from an early age, but which one is employed earlier than the other? Does simultaneous appear earlier and develop faster than successive during the early childhood years?

The answer that may be given in terms of the development of paradigmatic and syntagmatic association is as follows: Syntagmatic associations develop before paradigmatic associations according to Luria (1966, 1973). That paradigmatic association is a variation of simultaneous coding appears to be a reasonable assumption (Das, Kirby, & Jarman, 1979). Thus, it may be concluded that, at least in this specific linguistic function, successive processes are utilized earlier.

But there are serious methodological problems if one wishes to determine which of the two processes develops *faster*. First of all, the representative tasks of each process must be equal in difficulty; but then by choosing such tasks for both processes at a particular chronological age, we would have destroyed the very effect we wish to study. The following strategies, however, can provide an answer to the question of which process is employed first in regard to a specific task.

Let us take a task that has a split loading on simultaneous and successive factors (or alternatively a task that has both components that can be specified). Cross-modal Coding (CMC) is known to load on both simultaneous and successive factors. Let us assume that these loadings will indicate a positive correlation between this task and two marker tasks of each coding process (e.g., Memory-for-Designs and Auditory Serial Recall). We have obtained the split loadings in samples of Grade 3 and 4 children (Das *et al.,* 1975).

It may be argued, then, that in observing the relationship in younger and older children, one may find that meaningful loadings (or r_s) on successive factors may increase in the younger age group but diminish for the older age group. The rate with which the processes increase or decrease as judged from an anchoring point (suppose CMC loads almost entirely on the successive factor at age 5) should indicate the initial point of appearance of one or both processes. If more and more tasks are shown to require successive processing earlier than simultaneous processing, evidence in favor of successive processing will be strengthened.

> A.4. *The same task (test) may be approached either simultaneously or successively (and within each mode of encoding, there may be variation in strategies for solution). This would be determined by the interaction of the subject's (a) competence in one mode of encoding; (b) habitual mode of encoding when he or she is competent in both modes; and (c) task demands that can be modified by instructions.*

This proposition is basic to a process approach. Invariant task and invariant outcome (or solution) leave room for different processes that can be used to arrive at the same end result.

> A.5. *Simultaneous like successive processing operates on verbal as well as on nonverbal information.*

As elaborated in A.1., a set of verbal simultaneous tasks and nonverbal successive ones should be included in the battery of tasks we have used repeatedly.

There are basic questions regarding the dichotomies verbal–nonverbal and auditory–visual. Both verbal and nonverbal representations use symbols to represent ideas or objects. In the case of objects, the symbols are to be treated as representative of primary signals or of sensory and perceptual stimuli. This is the sense in which Pavlov (1941/1978) used the term *second-signal system* for verbally mediated stimuli as well as for those mediated by nonverbal symbols, such as pictures. Thus, verbal and nonverbal representations are instances of symbolic operations.

Vygotsky (1963) likewise relates thought to language and observes that, at the early stage of children's development, thinking is nonverbal and language is irrational. The gap closes as there is increasing overlap between the two during the course of the child's development. Here, Vygotsky must have used *language* in the broader sense of symbols—words, numbers, and mathematical representations (e.g., sigma, cosine, sine). Thus, adult thought is mostly verbal. But *verbal* has been used in a narrow sense in the context of abilities. Psychometrically speaking, verbal and nonverbal abilities have been distinguished, for instance, in intelligence tests; in some tests, such as the Wechsler Intelligence Scale for Children (WISC), verbal and nonverbal IQs can be scored separately. However, a good deal of verbally mediated thinking goes on in doing a nonverbal item, such as picture completion.

Since one can describe an idea in terms of words, numbers, or pictures, and even in such typical nonverbal tasks as block design or the progressive matrices verbal mediation is utilized in solving the problem, what should be the correct view or attitude in regard to maintaining a distinction between verbal and nonverbal? What are some of the typical verbal responses?

Probably, one of the major characteristics of verbal processes is naming or labeling. When a child is asked to name objects in pictures, verbal processes can be assumed to be engaged. Naming an object that is familiar to the child is a relatively simple task. But even in this simple activity, those who are backward in reading are slower in naming pictures than are those who are average readers (Denckla & Rudel, 1976).

Another distinctly verbal activity is the understanding of rules that govern language—both spoken and written. It entails not only phonological and syntactical rules but also factors that enable one to comprehend verbal discourse. Examples of the latter could be found in top-down and bottom-up processes in comprehension. Lexical access and similar psycholinguistic features are to be included within language comprehension. Therefore, *verbal* in large part will refer to the preceding components and processes that are involved in reading and spelling (see Frith, 1980).

The relevance to simultaneous and successive processes of these two characteristics of verbal material can be made specific at this point. Apart from the general demonstration that both processes are operative for nonverbal as well as verbal material, it will be necessary to analyze the basic processes underlying the two major features of verbal ability as stated here. For instance, what aspect of naming, lexical access, articulation, or physical identity of the item would be correlated with individual differences in simultaneous and/or successive processing?

A.6. *Simultaneous and successive processes operate on information presented through any receptor.*

The method of presentation of the information can be successive or simultaneous, but the processing of such information should not be determined by the mode of presentation.

However, an interaction between the sensory modality of presentation, method, and the form of processing may be obtained under certain task and subject characteristics (i.e., diagnostic groups, such as the mentally retarded and the dyslexics).

A.7. *Planning subsumes* (a) *the generation and selection of plans and strategies;* (b) *decision making; and* (c) *execution of decisions and plans.*

As such, a wide range of processes involved in these activities will have a commonality, although the correlations between any two of these activities may vary from small to substantial, depending on the degree of similarity between the two subprocesses represented by the task.

A.8. *Planning and coding are interdependent.*

Planning depends on coded material; on the other hand, the gathering, sorting, and storage of information must be planned if a problem is to be solved.

This gives rise to the following corollaries:

1. Planning will emerge as an independent factor only when the coding requirements of a task have reached an adequate level. That is, for complex tasks to be solved by average subjects, or relatively less complex ones to be solved by intellectually subaverage subjects, planning will not be an independent process if the demand on coding is experienced by the subjects to be overwhelming.
2. There may be a developmental threshold for some planning tasks, below which planning will not appear.

B. Validity of Simultaneous, Successive, and Planning Processes as General Cognitive Processes

There are problems in validating a neuropsychological model as a model of general cognitive functioning. First, the tests that are used as measures of the latter are often different. Clinical tests are seldom appropriate for exploring the wide range of functions of nonclinical populations. Since the tests will have been changed to adapt to the needs for tapping into normal cognitive processes, they would be unsuitable for administration to the clinical population for the purpose of validation.

Even if some of the tests can be given to clinical populations, there remains a rather knotty problem for validation that is considered in the following discussion.

Suppose we have determined that one of the stable marker tasks for simultaneous processing is Memory-for-Designs, and for planning, it is Trail Making. Indeed, these tasks have high loadings on the simultaneous and planning factors, respectively. But no task is a "pure" instance of the processing attributed to it. In Memory-for-Designs, there is an element of temporal ordering or successive processing, as there is in Trail Making. The need to use information stored in memory is a minor requirement for a normal population, but not so for temporal-lobe-damaged patients. The temporal coding demand in both tasks assumes unusual importance, perhaps overshadowing simultaneous processes in the first test or planning processes in the second. Therefore, one cannot adopt a validation strategy that entails the selection of, say, a "simultaneous" task and administration to patients with occipitoparietal damage and to temporal-lobe-damaged patients, hypothesizing that the former group of patients will perform significantly worse than the latter group *because* the task taps into simultaneous processing.

There is another complication in this approach to validation. Patients with occipitoparietal damage may develop alternative means of solving a task in Memory-for-Designs. For instance, they may attend to the successive component of Memory-for-Designs and thus compensate for their incompetence to a certain extent. We simply would not know whether or not the present performance of the patients reflects their use of compensatory coding strategies. Because of these complications, patients with temporal lobe damage may be as weak as those with occipitoparietal damage in a certain task, giving the impression that the task is an indicator of general brain damage. Hypotheses regarding the neuropsychological basis of cognitive functions are easy to make, but they need cautious verification.

The methods of validation to be described here do not include brain-damaged patients, partly because of the concerns stated here and partly because we do not as yet have empirical data from our laboratory to validate the information-integration model using clinical cases.

Mainly three strategies have been suggested for validation.

B.1. *Dividing subjects as proficient or deficient in the use of a specific cognitive process.*

It is assumed that subjects so divided will retain their distinctive processing characteristics on any task that requires the use of that process. There may be several ways of testing this, two of which are given here:

1. Divide subjects on the basis of factor scores into high or low on simultaneous, successive, or planning processes, and examine their performance on a task that predominantly requires that process. If more than one process is involved, such as in comprehension, appropriate hypotheses should be provided for testing.
2. Identify a marker task of the specific process, divide subjects in terms of competence on that task, and then examine their performance on a separate task that purports to require the specific process.

B.2. *Task analysis and experimental manipulation.*

1. The general approach for validation of the constructs of simultaneous, successive, and planning processes is to select tasks whose parameters are well known and subsequently to identify components of simultaneous, successive, and planning processes among these parameters. The components in the task can be manipulated instructionally or otherwise to increase their involvement in simultaneous, successive, or planning processes. Finally, performance in the task can be related to individual differences in the three processes.

2. A mixed design of task and subject variables entails the following: Select initially those who have a deficit in successive (or simultaneous) processing, and predict that their performance in the successive (simultaneous) components of the task will be poor, whereas their performance in other components that do not require successive (simultaneous) processing will be unaffected. Similar procedures for planning can be suggested. Furthermore, any combination of the three processes can be used to study the interaction between task and subject variables.

3. A third strategy for validation within the task-analysis approach would be to take a task that has a split loading on simultaneous and successive factors. Then increase the simultaneous component of the task and examine the extent to which performance on the modified task correlates with marker tasks for simultaneous processing. Similar studies can be conducted for successive processing and for planning.

B.3. *Remedial training (or the proof of the pudding is in the eating) is the last major method of validation suggested.*

It is a somewhat indirect method of construct validation. It comprises (*a*) the selection of a disability (e.g., reading) that is related to one of the three basic processes (e.g., successive); (*b*) the construction of a training program for teaching that process; and (*c*) the testing of the effectiveness of the program by examining the trainee's improvement in that process *and* on the skill (e.g., reading) in which he or she was inadequate. The argument here is that if the training procedure improves the basic process and also the skill that is mediated by that process, the process itself is validated as a construct.

This approach has been adopted by Krywaniuk, D. Kaufman, and Brailsford in their dissertation research and has been published. Krywaniuk (1974) used a predominantly successive training procedure with native Canadian children who were poor readers. Kaufman's training was a combination of successive with verbalization activities; he encouraged his low-achieving poor readers to articulate the reasons for doing the training tasks in one way rather than in another (D. Kaufman, 1978). Brailsford (1981) was particularly interested in improving comprehension. Her method of remediation drew upon the two previous ones but included equal parts of simultaneous and successive training with verbalization (Brailsford, Snart, & Das, in press). All obtained significant gains in processing and in reading performance for the treated group over the untreated control group.

CONCLUDING REMARKS

What is the future of the information-integration model? Where do we proceed from a factor analytic verification of the neuropsychological notions of the functional organization of the brain? The major organizations were arousal, coding, and planning; of these, arousal has been left out of our research program. Although in considering hyperactivity or the attentional deficits of retarded children the role of arousal has been acknowledged (Das & Bower, 1971; Williams & Das, 1979), a systematic development of the concept in the model has not been attempted. Personality and motivational factors interact with cognitive processes; a methodical study of the manner in which these processes interact within a neuropsychological framework should be pursued.

Factor analysis provides a heuristic device for initial exploration of an uncharted territory. It may give rise to hypotheses, but it is seldom adequate to verify them. The latter must depend on experimental manipulation or observation. One way to proceed with manipulation is to consider the tasks in the simultaneous, successive, and planning battery and to determine the manner in which the designated process operates. Digit Span, to take one instance, entails two processes: identification and ordering. The salient aspect of successive processing here is ordering, not identification. Group differences in Digit Span are known for the backward and normal readers. But do the backward readers perform poorly because of deficient ordering? Perhaps not, because individual differences in Digit Span are being increasingly attributed to identification (Dempster, 1981).

The model of information integration is, then, a blueprint that is to be tested, tried, and modified. Ultimately, it will be superceded, but one hopes it will have generated some insights into how the mind works before it becomes obsolete.

REFERENCES

Brailsford, A. The relationship between cognitive strategy training and performance on tasks of reading comprehension within a learning disabled group of children. Unpublished master's thesis, University of Alberta, 1981.

Brailsford, A., Snart, F., & Das, J. P. Strategy training and reading comprehension. *Journal of Learning Disabilities*, 1983, in press.

Cronbach, L. J. The two disciplines of scientific psychology. *American Psychologist*, 1957, *12*, 671–683.

Das, J. P. Cultural deprivation and cognitive competence. In N. R. Ellis (Ed.), *International review of research in mental retardation*. (Vol. 6). New York: Academic Press, 1973.

Das, J. P. Planning: Theoretical considerations and empirical evidence. *Psychological Research* (W. Germany), 1980, *41*, 141–151.

Das, J. P., & Bower, A. C. Orienting responses of mentally retarded and normal children to word signals. *British Journal of Psychology*, 1971, *62*, 86–96.

Das, J. P., Cummins, J. P., Kirby J. R., & Jarman, R. F. Simultaneous and successive processes, language and mental abilities. *Canadian Psychological Review*, 1979, *20*, 1–11.

Das, J. P., Kirby, J. R., & Jarman, R. F. Simultaneous and successive synthesis: An alternative model for cognitive abilities. *Psychological Bulletin*, 1975, *82*, 87–103.

Das, J. P., Kirby, J. R., & Jarman, R. F. *Simultaneous and successive cognitive processes*. New York: Academic Press, 1979.

Dempster, F. N. Memory span: Sources of individual and developmental differences. *Psychological Bulletin*, 1981, *89*, 63–100.

Denckla, M. B., & Rudel, R. G. Rapid automatized naming (R.A.N.): Dyslexia differentiated from other learning disabilities. *Neuropsychologia*, 1976, *14*, 471–479.

Eysenck, H, J. The nature of intelligence. In M. P. Friedman, J. P. Das, & N. O'Connor (Eds.), *Intelligence and learning*. New York: Plenum, 1981.

Frith, U. *Cognitive processes in spelling*. New York: Academic Press, 1980.

Gazzaniga, M. S., & Le Doux, J. E. *The integrated mind*. New York: Plenum, 1978.

Glass, A. L., Holyoak, F. J., & Santa, J. L. *Cognition, reading*. Reading, Mass.: Addison-Wesley, 1979.

Hecaen, H., & Albert, M. *Human neuropsychology*. New York: Wiley, 1978.

Heemsbergen, D. B. Planning as a cognitive process: An empirical investigation. Unpublished doctoral dissertation, University of Alberta, 1980.

Hunt, E. Intelligence as an information-processing concept. *British Journal of Psychology*, 1980, *71*, 449–474.

Jensen, A. R. Reaction time and intelligence. In M. P. Friedman, J. P. Das, & N. O'Connor (Eds.), *Intelligence and learning*. New York: Plenum, 1981.

Kaufman, A. S. *Intelligent testing with the WISC-R*. New York: Wiley, 1979.

Kaufman, D. The relation of academic performance to strategy training and remedial techniques. Unpublished doctoral dissertation, University of Alberta, 1978.

Kirby, J. R. Information processing and human abilities. Unpublished doctoral dissertation, University of Alberta, 1976.

Krywaniuk, L. W. Patterns of cognitive abilities of high and low achieving school children. Unpublished doctoral dissertation, University of Alberta, 1974.

Luria, A. R. *Human brain and psychological processes*. New York: Harper, 1966.

Luria, A. R. *The working brain*. Hammondsworth, Great Britain: Penguin, 1973.

McLeod, R. W. An exploratory study of inference, and cognitive synthesis in reading comprehension with selected Grade 4 readers. Unpublished doctoral dissertation, University of Alberta, 1978.

McNemar, Q. Lost: Our intelligence? Why? *American Psychologist*, 1964, *19*, 871–882.

Mercer, J. R. *Labelling the mentally retarded*. Berkeley: Univ. of California Press, 1973.

Mwamwenda, T. S. A relationship between successive–simultaneous synthesis and concrete operational thought. Unpublished doctoral dissertation, University of Alberta, 1981.

Pavlov, I. P. [*Lectures on conditioned reflex*] (W. H. Gantt, Trans.). New York: International Publishers, 1978. (Originally published, 1941.)

Ryckman, D. B. Reading achievement, IQ, and simultaneous–successive processing among normal and learning-disabled children. *Alberta Journal of Educational Research,* 1981, *27,* 74–83.

Sternberg, R. J. Toward a unified componential theory of human intelligence. In M. Friedman, J. P. Das & N. O'Connor (Eds.), *Intelligence and learning.* New York: Plenum, 1980.

Sternberg, S. High-speed scanning in human memory. *Science,* 1966, *153,* 652–654.

Vygotsky, L. S. *Thought and language.* Cambridge, Mass.: MIT Press, 1963.

Williams, N., & Das, J. P. Variations of the orienting response in learning-disabled children. In H. D. Kimmel, E. H. Van Olst, & J. F. Orlebeke (Eds.), *The orienting reflex in humans.* Hillsdale, N.J.: Erlbaum, 1979.

PART II

BASIC CONCEPTS AND RESEARCH

3

Aspects of Planning

J. P. DAS

My grandfather was illiterate, but he was often called to sit by the magistrate of the district when the magistrate came to resolve some conflict in the village. I have asked my father what distinguished him from others. Essentially, he had an uncommon ability to plan, to make decisions. If intelligence is a cultural universal, it must be characterized by the ability to plan and structure one's behavior with an end in view. The more efficient and parsimonious the plan is, the more "intelligent" the resulting behavior (Das, 1973).

Planning as a uniquely human cognitive function can have three aspects: structure, process, and knowledge base. Hunt (1980) has mentioned these aspects for considering intelligence. *Structure* for the purpose of the present chapter will refer to the cortical structure for planning. The process of planning will underlie such activities as the generation, selection, and execution of a plan or program, evaluation of one's own behavior and that of others, and the response tendency to act on the basis of such evaluation. Plans are made, problems are posed, strategies are selected and followed on the basis of available information.

A knowledge base that is broad is likely to yield sophisticated plans and facilitate the emergence of superior decisions. Plans operate on information that has been coded—that is, properly analyzed, synthesized, and stored for

Cognitive Strategies
and Educational Performance

quick retrieval. The interdependence between coding and planning is readily apparent (Das, 1980). Without coded information, planning is empty, and in the absence of a plan, information coding is blind.

The structural base for planning, broadly defined, is the frontal lobes (cf. Luria, 1966). The frontal lobes "regulate the 'active state' of the organism, control the essential elements of the subject's intentions, programme complex forms of activity and constantly monitor all aspects of activity [Hécaen & Albert, 1978, p. 376]." Luria (1969) had observed that injury to the frontal lobes disturbs impulse control, regulation of voluntary action, and perception as in visual search. It has an adverse effect on memory that requires the adoption of strategies, and, above all, on symbolic functions, because it leads to incorrect choice of programs and lack of the ability to restrain premature operations.

There seems to be good neurophysiological reason to justify the role of frontal lobes in planning, which is preeminently a human characteristic. As Luria wrote:

The frontal lobes of the brain are the last acquisition of the evolutionary process and occupy nearly one third of the human hemispheres. . . . They are intimately related to the reticular formation of the brain stem, being densely supplied with ascending and descending fibers. . . . They have intimate connections with the motor cortex and with the structures of the second block[1] . . . their structures become mature only during the 4th to 5th year of life, and their development makes a rapid leap during the period which is of decisive significance for the first forms of conscious control of behavior. [Sapir & Nitzburg, 1973, p. 118].

OPERATIONALIZING PLANNING

The neuropsychological basis of planning in the frontal lobes is thus well recognized and has been so for about a century. As long ago as 1895, Bianchi had enough evidence in the literature to review studies that favor the localization of planning in the frontal lobes. More recently, Shallice and Evans (1978) have concluded that the major function of the frontal lobes is the selection and regulation of cognitive planning. The problem now is to operationalize planning as a component of basic cognitive functions, as was done for simultaneous and successive coding processes (Das, 1973). Specific marker tests for these coding processes have been identified and mean-

---

[1]See Chapter 2 in this book for a description of the three functional blocks of the brain.

ingfully related to such psychometric tests as Thurstone's tests for primary mental abilities (Kirby & Das, 1978) and to such academic activities as arithmetic and reading (Das, Kirby, & Jarman, 1979). A similar effort should be made for the process of planning in order to operationalize the concept, as a first step in establishing it as a process that is separate from coding. One could proceed to choose tasks for defining planning as a factor by identifying those clinicial neuropsychological tasks that indicate frontal lobe dysfunction and subsequently adapting them for use on nonclinical populations. But planful behavior and decision making is demonstrated in quite a different set of tasks, which belong to the field of artificial intelligence and problem solving (cf. Hayes-Roth & Hayes-Roth, 1979). We prefer to stay with neuropsychological tasks, partly because of our inclination to stay within Luria's system of functional organization of the brain. Within that framework, plans and strategies are conceived to be involved at the lower levels of cognition, such as attention, perception, and memory, as much as they are in problem solving. Elaboration of this line of thinking has been made in my earlier chapter in this book. Thus, we have searched and located a set of tasks for measuring planning that is similar in principle to clinical tasks that discriminate between frontal and nonfrontal patients and span the entire range of cognitive function—that is, from attention to reasoning and problem solving.

SUMMARY OF STUDIES ON PLANNING

Initially, Ashman (1978) in our laboratory selected and used Visual Search, Trail Making, Verbal Fluency, and Planned Composition of a story. The tasks are briefly described here.

Visual Search. This test is a typical example of neuropsychological tests that are used to identify deficits in organized search behavior following cerebral lesion (Teuber, Battersby, & Bender, 1949). The test was adapted for general use by preparing overhead transparencies that consist of 48 geometric shapes, letters, and numbers. A circle in the center of each transparency contains a copy of the target. The subject is required to point to the 1 among the 48 shapes that matches the encircled target. Each transparency is viewed through an apparatus that incorporates two electronic timers in order to measure search time and movement time. Typically, the subject starts a trial by pressing a switch that lights the transparency; the switch is to be held down as long as the subject has not detected the target from among the stimuli in the field. As soon as detection occurs, the subject takes his or her finger off the switch and presses on the target. The time taken for detection is search time; the time taken for the execution of the response is movement or reaction time. Search time is expected to reflect planning.

Trail Making. This test has been used as a neurological screening test for brain damage. The test has an intermediate level for ages 5–14, which we have used in our research (Das, 1980). It is divided into two parts. In Part A, the subject connects encircled numbers in the correct numerical order; the numbers are distributed randomly over the page. In Part B, letters and numbers are presented and the subject is required to connect letters and numbers in the correct increasing sequence—for example, 1–A–2–B–3–C. The test is administered individually to all subjects; time to completion is recorded.

Verbal Fluency. Thurstone and Thurstone (1941) defined *word fluency* as a clear primary mental ability. However, Milner (1964) and McFie (1975) disregarded the notion of a primary mental ability and demonstrated that the test discriminated frontal lobe patients. Christensen (1974), who described Luria's neurological tests for brain-damaged patients observed the weakness of frontal lobe patients to produce words, sentences, and phrases spontaneously.

The test is divided into two parts, each prepared in an individual booklet form. In the first part, the subject is required to write as many words beginning with *S* as possible in 2 min; in the second part, as many four-letter words beginning with *C* as possible are to be written within 2 min. Total number of words written minus repeated, meaningless, or foreign words are counted and recorded as the subject's score.

Planned Composition. Luria (1973) observed that frontal lobe patients described events impulsively, and Christensen (1974) found similar difficulties. Perseveration and inability to maintain an overall plan in writing characterized such patients' productive language. It is assumed that the composition of a short narrative would indicate the capacity to structure material and to plan. In order to obtain written composition, Picture 2 of the Thematic Apperception Test (Murray, 1943) is shown on a screen for 20 min. Subjects in groups are asked to write a one-page story about the picture. Each composition is then rated by raters who are often selected from teachers who ordinarily judge compositions. They assess the composition according to the perceived quality of the underlying plan and logical sequence on a seven-point Likert-type scale (1 is the best; 7 the worst).

Simultaneous and successive tasks. In addition to the four tests of planning described, the following five marker tests for simultaneous–successive processing are usually administered in order to delineate the relation between coding and planning. Since these tests have been used in several studies (Das, Kirby, & Jarman, 1975) in the past, and a rationale for their use has been provided in my other chapter in this book, only a brief description will be given here. The tests are Figure Copying and Memory-for-Designs, which measure simultaneous processing, and Auditory Serial Recall, Visual Short-Term Memory, and Forward Digit Span, which measure successive processing. Briefly, the Figure Copying test requires the subject to reproduce geometric figures while the figure is in view. In Memory-for-Designs (Graham & Kendall, 1960), the subject views each design for 5 sec and then reproduces it from memory. Both of these are tests of simultaneous processing.

Auditory Serial Recall consists of 16 lists of words—4 of the lists having four words, the next 4 having five words, progressing continuously to a seven-word series. The subject is required to recall immediately after the list is presented. In the Visual Short-Term Memory test, the subject is presented with 20 slides, each containing a five-digit grid projected onto a screen for 5 sec. When the slide is removed, the subject is required to read off color names presented on a buffer slide for 2 sec. Upon removal of the color slide, the subject writes down as many digits as he or she can recall in their correct position in an empty grid. The test usually loads on the successive factor, although in a few studies it has shown an independent loading on a factor that has been labeled visualization (Leong, 1974). The third test for successive processing, Forward Digit Span, is taken directly from Wechsler (1974).

All the above tests were used in Ashman's (1978) study, although subsequent studies have used some of these tests and have added some new ones. The tests were given to children in Grade 8. As the principal components analysis in Table 3.1 shows, a Planning factor can be clearly identified. The planning factor is defined by Visual Search, Trail Making, and Planned Composition, with a small loading from Verbal Fluency. The latter seems to have equal loadings on the Simultaneous and Successive factors as on planning. An oblique rotation did not change the pattern of loadings appreciably, and the correlations between the factors were very small indeed.

It is possible that Verbal Fluency requires the use of all three processes in the Grade 8 sample in Ashman's study. In his next study, adult workers who were mildly mentally retarded were administered all the tests. But since the retardates could not write or make an oral presentation of the narrative composition, that test was eliminated from the principal components analysis. As Table 3.2 shows, a Planning factor emerges. This time, however, one of the planning tasks, Verbal Fluency, had a substantial loading only on the Planning factor. The factor structure is in fact clearer, confirming the emergence of the two coding and one planning component, accounting for 77.7% of variance.

The uniqueness and stability of the Planning factor has been shown in two subsequent analyses of data from groups of borderline retarded and moderately retarded (mean IQ = 50) subjects (Snart, O'Grady, & Das, 1982; Snart & Swann, 1982). The factor structures in these studies were

TABLE 3.1

Orthogonal (Varimax) Rotation of Four Factors Following Principal Components Analysis ($N = 104$)[a]

Variable	Factors				
	1 Successive	2 Planning	3 Simultaneous	4 Visual	h^2
Figure Copying			673		569
Memory-for-Designs			814		682
Auditory Serial Recall	887				796
Digit Span	835				729
Visual Short-term Memory				682	588
Porteus Maze Test[a]			346	705	625
Trail Making (latency)[b]		−613			425
Visual Search (latency)[b]		−795			653
Verbal Fluency		397	360		538
Planned Composition[b]		−596			407
Variance	1.75	1.64	1.45	1.15	6.01
Percentage of total variance	17.6	16.4	14.5	11.6	60.1

[a] Decimals omitted in loadings. Loadings below 300 have been omitted.
[b] A high score indicates poor performance.

TABLE 3.2

Orthogonal (Varimax) Rotation of Three Factors Following Principal Components Analysis for the Retarded Group ($N = 46$)[a]

Variable	Factors			
	Planning	Successive	Simultaneous	h^2
Figure Copying			−873	793
Memory-for-Designs (errors)[b]			866	815
Auditory Serial Recall		925		860
Digit Span		931		885
Trail Making (latency)[b]	833			741
Visual Search (latency)[b]	658		420	629
Verbal Fluency	−803			717
Variance	1.858	1.848	1.733	5.439
Percentage of total variance	26.545	26.400	24.761	77.706

[a] Decimals omitted in loadings. Factor loadings under 300 have been eliminated.
[b] A high score indicates poor performance.

consistent with that shown in Table 3.2. To give some examples, first from the analysis of mildly retarded workers in a sheltered workshop, the two successive, two simultaneous, and two planning tasks had the following high loadings on their respective factors: .90 and .83 for Auditory Serial Recall and Digit Span; .83 and .85 for Memory-for-Designs and Figure Copying; and .84 and .82 for Trail Making and Visual Search. These loadings were comparable to the high loadings obtained for a moderately retarded population.

Encouraged by the results on the mentally retarded, especially the moderately retarded sample, whose mental age was around 7–8, we tried the tasks on Grade 3 children from regular classrooms. The battery of tasks for the Grade 3 sample included two tasks each from planning, simultaneous, successive, and speed categories (see Table 3.3). *Speed* had been defined in terms of reading time in a Stroop chart for names of colors in words (*red, green, yellow,* and *blue*) and naming color patches (red, green, yellow, and blue). The factor had been conceptualized as speed of processing in our previous research (Das *et al.,* 1975).

SEPARATION OF PLANNING FROM SPEED

Results shown in Table 3.3 have separated the speed aspect in the planning tasks from that in the color word reading and color naming tasks. This

TABLE 3.3
Principal Components Analysis of Measures for Simultaneous, Successive, Planning, and Speed (Varimax Rotation)[a]

	Factors				
Variable	1 Successive	2 Simultaneous	3 Speed	4 Planning	h^2
Figure Copying		−884			823
Memory-for-Designs (errors)[b]		865			806
Auditory Serial Recall	891				839
Digit Span (auditory)	891				812
Color Reading[b]			810		735
Color Naming[b]			835		706
Trail Making (A)[b]				801	736
Visual Search (number target picture background)[b]				802	727
Variance	1.713	1.599	1.550	1.319	
Percentage of total variance	21.418	19.992	19.374	16.489	

[a] Decimals omitted in loadings. Loadings below 300 have been omitted.
[b] A high score indicates poor performance.

is important because the two tests of planning happen to be latency measures; without such tasks as composition, the planning tasks could be mistaken to be merely speed tasks. In any case, we had data on several speedlike tests available on the same Grade 3 subjects as were used in Table 3.3. These were put through a principal components analysis in order to see if one obtains a general Speed factor or separate ones that could be distinguished in terms of their underlying processes. Results are presented in Table 3.4. Three orthogonal factors could be extracted, until eigenvalues were less than 1, as in all of the analyses reported before. These showed clear clusterings of reaction time scores of visual search in the first factor, the Stroop chart Color Reading and Color Naming times in the second, and Trail Making and Visual Search times on the third factor—altogether, explaining about 65% of the variance. It is important to note that the third factor, Planning, retained its identity in the midst of several other measures of speed. The marker indices of Planning in this study did not include composition; yet that does not seem to create any problems for identifying the Planning factor. We have, then, a case here of so-called speed measures clustering together with such nonspeed measures as composition to constitute a Planning factor.

PLANNING AND SCHOLASTIC TESTS

Quite a different approach to establishing the uniqueness of planning, and consequently its relative independence from the two coding processes would be to demonstrate that coding and planning may relate to other

TABLE 3.4
Principal Components Analysis of Measures of Speed of Reaction (Varimax Rotation)[a]

Variable	1	2	3	h^2
Color Reading		837		708
Color Naming		799		656
Trail Making (A)	346	339	563	551
Trail Making (B)	369	359	470	486
Visual Search time (number–picture)			736	603
Visual Search time (picture–picture)			649	452
Reaction time (number–picture)	916			840
Reaction time (picture–picture)	926			872
Variance	2.023	1.636	1.509	
Percentage of total variance	25.292	20.445	18.867	

[a]Decimals omitted in loadings. Loadings below 300 have been omitted. High scores represent poor performance for all variables.

intellectual activities differently. Thus, in the study of the Grade 3 children reported here, we examined the correlations between the coding and planning measures on the one hand and scholastic tasks on the other, as shown in Table 3.5. First of all, no correlations were significant for the factor of Speed; therefore, these have not been reported. Going through the table, it is evident that the correlations with reading are completely according to expectation. The decoding score in reading correlates with both Simultaneous and Successive factors, as does comprehension. The correlations for decoding are higher than those for comprehension. We had obtained very similar results previously (Kirby & Das, 1977).

The next set of correlations are with the Canadian Cognitive Abilities Test. Verbal, nonverbal, and quantitative tasks all correlate highly with simultaneous factor scores. Their correlations with Successive factor scores are also high, but not as high as those for Simultaneous factor scores. Apart from the obvious implication that both simultaneous and successive processing are involved in an achievement test, these results are open to a wider interpretation. First, the nature of the Simultaneous–Successive factor vis-à-vis a nonverbal–verbal dichotomy is clarified. Simultaneous tasks making up the Simultaneous factor are apparently nonverbal (Figure Copying and Memory-for-Designs), and successive tasks (Digit Span and Serial Recall) are verbal in the psychometric classification of instruments that measure abilities. In our previous research on this issue, such a distinction has been considered and found to be inappropriate to a process in contrast to an ability approach. For instance, recall of pairs of concrete words loads on the Simultaneous factor, whereas the recall of abstract word pairs loads on the Successive factor. Comprehension of lexically ambiguous sentences

TABLE 3.5
Product-Moment r_s between Factor Scores of Simultaneous, Successive and Planning, and Other Tasks ($N = 70$)

Variable	Simultaneous	Successive	Planning[a]
Reading—decoding	.330***	.314**	−.236*
Reading—comprehension	.259*	.278*	−.242*
Canadian Cognitive Abilities Test			
Verbal	.439***	.308**	−.08
Quantitative	.555***	.265*	.09
Nonverbal	.585***	.301**	−.12

[a]Defined by tests representing poor performance, and thus the negative correlations with the reading measures are not unexpected.
*$p < .05$.
**$p < .01$.
***$p < .005$.

loads on the Simultaneous factor (Das, Cummins, Kirby, & Jarman, 1979). Memory for words processed for meaning rather than for physical characteristics loads on the Simultaneous factor (Snart, 1979). The present results show that both verbal and nonverbal achievements are related to Simultaneous *and* Successive factor scores, lending further support to our contention that the two coding processes need not be classified in terms of these categories of abilities. We had no basis to expect that the planning tasks should relate to reading achievement or the Canadian Cognitive Abilities Test. As the results show, none of the correlations with planning reached significance.

EXTENDING THE VALIDITY OF THE PLANNING FACTOR

One may still argue that the Planning factor is subject to all the known weaknesses of factor analysis and that the stability of this factor observed in the several principal components analyses could be an artifact of the specific tests chosen. How did we name the factor Planning anyway? These criticisms can be easily handled, although that may not exonerate the use of factor analysis. First of all, the analyses have been confirmatory in nature rather than exploratory. We did not set out with a large number of tests in a look-and-see expedition. Rather, the procedure was to identify tasks that have a history of distinguishing frontal from nonfrontal cases. The naming of the factor, then, is dictated by the choice of the tasks. We had evidence that these tasks did indicate planning deficiencies, and when they clustered together in one factor, it was named Planning.

The validity of these tests as measures of planning has been strengthened in two ways by subsequent research from our laboratory: (*a*) relating the marker tests of planning to a task that involves strategies; and (*b*) selecting individuals who are good versus poor on a marker task in order to observe their behavior in a game of strategy.

In order to see the relation between a new task that can be designed to involve strategies and the planning tasks, Heemsbergen (1980) chose Syllogistic Reasoning. The task consisted of four sets of three-term syllogisms. Specifically, 32 categorical syllogisms (see Sternberg, 1979) were included in the task. In this type of syllogism, the subject received two premises—Tina is smaller than Sally; Sally is smaller than Ann—and a conclusion, Tina is smaller than Ann. The subject was required to indicate whether the conclusion followed logically from the premises by encircling the word *true* or *false.*

The test was given on four separate sheets in the following manner: On the first sheet, eight syllogisms were presented in their natural order—that is, in a forward chain requiring no conversions or reordering by the subject. The second sheet also included a set of eight syllogisms, but in order to come to solution, the subject had to reorder one premise. For example, Susan is taller than Ann; Jane is taller than Susan; conclusion: Ann is taller than Jane. The third set of syllogisms required one premise to be converted. For example, Ann is taller than Alice; Susan is shorter than Alice; conclusion: Susan is taller than Ann. Finally, the fourth set included eight syllogisms in which the subject was required to reorder and convert the premises in order to correctly indicate whether the conclusion follows logically from the premise. For each subject two measures were recorded: the number of errors made and the total time taken to complete the set of eight syllogisms. Subjects were assigned each sheet in an order established by a randomized table of numbers to avoid order effect.

The subjects were community college students who had been administered the battery of simultaneous, successive, and planning tasks. The latter, which is of interest to us here, comprised Planned Composition, Trail Making, and Visual Search. It was hypothesized that, as the college students go through the syllogisms set by set, they will realize that (a) the problems within each set are homogeneous, and (b) each set is different from others in terms of the operations needed to solve the problems. Both of these conditions should facilitate speed of solution. Therefore, it was argued that individual differences in solution time for all four sets will reflect the speed with which the subject has caught on to these conditions. Errors in solution of these simple syllogisms were expected to be small. But in any case, errors were not supposed to indicate planning, at least not nearly to the same extent as solution time. Correlations between the planning tasks and the two measures of syllogisms are given in Table 3.6. As expected, solution time was indeed highly related ($p < .01$) to measures of planning, but the accuracy measure does not have a significant r with solution time.

In the next study by Heemsbergen, *Master Mind,* a commercially avail-

TABLE 3.6
Intercorrelations between Planning Tests (N = 55)[a]

Variable	PC	TM	VS	SR	SRT
Planned Composition (PC)	1.000				
Trail Making (TM)	.311	1.000			
Visual Search (VS)	.218	.503	1.000		
Syllogistic Reasoning (number correct) (SR)	−.135	−.268	−.298	1.000	
Syllogistic Reasoning Time (SRT)	.483	.527	.485	−.174	1.000

r (.05) = .225.
[a]Except in SR, a high score represents poor performance in all other tests.

able game of strategies, was chosen to test the validity of one of the strong marker tests of planning, which is Visual Search. Sixty community college students were first administered the Visual Search task. On the basis of their total search time, they were ranked and the top 15 and the bottom 15 identified. The mean search times for these groups were of course found to be significantly different (8.86 sec and 17.35 sec, respectively; t significant below .001 level). It was argued that if Visual Search time is a representative task of planful behavior, then those who are good at it should be better in using efficient strategies in *Master Mind* than those who are poor. The argument was advanced in spite of the fact that only one of the planning tasks was utilized to divide the sample into good and poor planners and that the strategies required for doing Visual Search were quite distinct from those required for breaking the code in *Master Mind*.

In the game of *Master Mind,* the experimenter set up a linear arrangement of four colored pegs, which was the code; the subject's task was to break the code within the 12 rows on the game board. The score was the number of rows taken by the subject to break the code. Each subject was given three games to play and thus had to break three different codes. The results supported our expectation: Whereas the top subjects in Visual Search could break the code in 5.7 rows, the bottom subjects needed 3 additional rows. Use of appropriate strategies thus seems to be a stable individual differences variable. One also suspects that the bottom group of subjects may have maladaptive behaviors in planning while solving new tasks. Some clues in this regard were obtained by monitoring their spontaneous speech.

The records suggest a distinct set of personality and cognitive differences between these two groups. A case in point is the *superstitious behavior* that was shown by the poor planners:

"Red was good to me last time."
"People usually prefer brighter colors."
"I don't like dull colors."

The poor planners, again, did not appreciate the *value of reasoning.* Bloom and Broeder (1974), in examining lower aptitude students, had observed that these students seemed to hold the view that, in solving problems, reasoning was of little value; one either knew the answer to a problem at once or one did not. A similar attitude was in evidence in the bottom group, or the poor planners; many among them made the following responses:

"There must be a trick to this."
"I can't do this kind of thing; it doesn't make any sense."
"I've just about tried every one of these colors already."

Use of feedback was found to be quite inadequate among these subjects, as illustrated by their placement of pegs during the game. Some subjects would appear to be fixated on a certain color and would continue using it in spite of the negative feedback. Similarly, subjects used the identical color combinations and positions several times within one game, even when the code they had made was not correct. They did not employ effective monitoring and checking strategies.

What limits the ability to perform a task requiring prior planning? Barron (1978) identifies three of these limitations: (*a*) a failure to use appropriate strategy; (*b*) inadequate proficiency; and (*c*) limited capacity. It is unlikely that college students had difficulty in the game of strategy because of limited capacity. Neither was proficiency in question, as the task was new to all of them. However, they certainly exhibited inappropriate and, at times, a sheer absence of strategic behavior. Although feedback from the experimenter was given after each row was completed in the game, subjects who were low in planning did not adequately recognize or utilize the feedback. Planning is certainly involved in the selection of strategies. In this particular task, the effective strategies could be organized in a logical sequence: Formulate hypotheses, explore alternatives, monitor feedback, and finally, verify hypotheses, rejecting those that did not work. There was very little evidence from observation or from the verbal reports of poor players in *Master Mind* to suggest the presence of such a planned sequence.

CONCLUDING REMARKS

The notion of planning as a typically human expression of intelligence is consistent with the zeitgeist of contemporary psychology. Psychology has suddenly become cognitive. The advent of Piaget in developmental and educational psychology has contributed much to the recent interest in cognition, as has Chomsky's aggressive advocacy of the cause of cognitivism as opposed to behaviorism. Even outside the immediate adherents of Piaget or Chomsky, planning or strategic behavior has flourished. Discourse processes use schema frequently. Memory has its executive or control processes. Artificial intelligence refers to scripts and goals. In fact, one wonders how the simple fact that psychology should concern itself with thoughts, knowledge, and goals had been masked by the darkness that shrouds the gap between stimulus and response.

Plans, decisions, and goals are certainly some of the prized products of mental activities. These need not be articulated, nor even break into the realm of awareness. We decide without always being able to justify our decision by verbal elaborations. Many plans indeed function like a hidden agenda determining an individual's activity. In fact, I suspect that the higher forms of thinking are relatively inarticulate. There is no mystery to this. For instance, at the point of understanding a paragraph in psychological literature, I am not aware of the cumulative and interacting bits of information in psychology that make my understanding possible; neither am I aware of the nuances of English language, its orthographic and phonological rules, and their exceptions. We have to accept that although planful behavior can be subjected to psychological study and testing, all planful behavior may not be available for this purpose. A paradox, but only a apparent one, exists here, which is that the highest forms of cognitive activities may be inaccessible for the purpose of conscious reflection.

Perhaps in recognition of such an inevitability, the frontal lobes have developed as silent integrative organs; they do not contain speech areas, nor are they directly responsible for coding sensory information. They are responsible for macrocharacteristics of humans—personality, motivation, plans, and purposive behavior. They start functioning fully around 7 years of age, as neurophysiological evidence indicates. But then are we supporting a biological view of planning, in that the planning function evolves according to a neurophysiological blueprint?

Two types of questions can be asked in regard to a biological basis of planning:

1. How insular is the development and operation of planning to experience and education; do the latter serve merely a triggering function rather than being causal agents?
2. Is it inherited?

The origins of our model of planning and coding functions are in Luria (1966) and Vygotsky (1962). Their view of human beings is essentially social. An individual's plans are dictated by his or her life's circumstances; much of these are social. Enduring goals of an individual are social in origin. In another culture, in another part of the history of humankind, it would be perfectly defensible to posit divine goals, people being merely instruments to fulfill them. A strictly biological attribution will lead to the same conclusion—that goals and purposes are blueprinted; they manifest themselves appropriately in keeping with local conditions. The three competing views share the common belief that the superstructure of goals that regulates a person's major activities in life seems to have its origin outside that person.

On reflection, one could find good reasons to support every one of the three points of view. Universal goals of human beings in most societies transcend the immediate environment and are often described as human ideals. Even the desire to transcend the limits of one's environment has been expressed repeatedly.

> *The desire of the moth for the star*
> *of the night for the 'morrow*

expresses this human longing. Spiritual cravings as voiced here are as real as physical ones in most societies. Hence, one wonders if the universal goals are to a large extent species-specific characteristics of human beings!

The issue of inheritance of planful behavior, both the process of planning and the resulting level of competence, cannot be easily resolved. Intelligence as measured by psychometric tests entails mostly coding and little planning. The utilization of coded information according to a plan is one step removed from coding; over and above this, the generation of the plan itself is further removed from the immediacy of utilization. Is the competence for planning or making good judgments inherited to the same extent as intelligence is? There is no compelling evidence to support that it is. Perhaps the issue of heritability is not an important one for understanding planful behavior. In fact, it is of less theoretical value than the first issue— the origin of plans and goals.

REFERENCES

Ashman, A. F. The relationship between planning and simultaneous and successive synthesis. Unpublished doctoral dissertation, University of Alberta, 1978.

Barron, J. Intelligence and general strategies. In G. Underwood (Ed.), *Strategies of information processing*. London: Academic Press, 1978.

Bianchi, L. The functions of the frontal lobes. *Brian*, 1895, *18*, 497–522.

Bloom, B. S., & Broeder, L. J. *Problem solving processes of college students*. Chicago: Univ. of Chicago Press, 1974.

Christensen, A. L. *Luria's neuropsychological investigation*. Copenhagen, Denmark: Munksgaard, 1974.

Das, J. P. Structure of cognitive abilities: Evidence for simultaneous and successive processing. *Journal of Educational Psychology*, 1973, *65*, 103–108.

Das, J. P. Planning: Theoretical considerations and empirical evidence. *Psychological Research*, 1980, *41*, 141–151.

Das, J. P., Cummins, J. P., Kirby, J. R., & Jarman, R. F. Simultaneous and successive processes, language and mental abilities. *Canadian Psychological Review*, 1979, *20*, 1–11.

Das, J. P., Kirby, J. R., & Jarman, R. F. Simultaneous and successive syntheses: An alternative model for cognitive abilities. *Psychological Bulletin*, 1975, *82*, 87–103.

Das, J. P., Kirby, J. R., & Jarman, R. F. *Simultaneous and successive cognitive processes*. New York: Academic Press, 1979.

Graham, F. K., & Kendall, B. S. Memory-for-Designs test: Revised general manual. *Perceptual and Motor Skills*, 1960, *11*, 147–188. (Monograph Suppl. 2-V11)

Hayes-Roth, B., & Hayes-Roth, F. A cognitive model of planning. *Cognitive Science*, 1979, *3*, 275–310.

Hécaen, H., & Albert, M. *Human neuropsychology*. New York: Wiley, 1978.

Heemsbergen, D. B. Planning as a cognitive process: An empirical investigation. Unpublished doctoral dissertation, University of Alberta, 1980.

Hunt, E. Intelligence as an information-processing concept. *British Journal of Psychology*, 1980, *71*, 449–474.

Kirby, J. R., & Das, J. P. Reading achievement, IQ and simultaneous–successive processing. *Journal of Educational Psychology*, 1977, *69*, 564–570.

Kirby, J. R., & Das, J. P. Information processing and human abilities. *Journal of Educational Psychology*, 1978, *70*, 58–66.

Leong, C. K. Spatial-temporal information processing in disabled readers. Unpublished doctoral dissertation, University of Alberta, 1974.

Luria, A. R. *Human brain and psychological processes*. New York: Harper, 1966.

Luria, A. R. Frontal lobe syndromes. In P. J. Vinken & G. W. Bruyn (Eds.), *Handbook of clinical neurology* (Vol. 2). New York: Amer. Elsevier, 1969.

Luria, A. R. *The working brain*. Hammondsworth, Great Britain: Penguin, 1973.

McFie, J. *Assessment of organic intellectual impairment*. London: Academic Press, 1975.

Milner, B. Some effects of frontal lobectomy in man In J. W. Warren & K. Akert (Eds.), *The frontal granular cortex and behavior*. New York: McGraw-Hill, 1964.

Murray, H. A. *Thematic Apperception Test manual*. Cambridge, Mass.: Harvard Univ. Press, 1943.

Sapir, S. G., & Nitzburg, A. C. *Children with learning problems*. New York: Brunner/Mazel, 1973.

Shallice, T., & Evans, M. E. The involvement of the frontal lobes in cognitive estimation. *Cortex*, 1978, *14*, 294–303.

Snart, F. D. Levels of processing and memory. A developmental approach. Unpublished doctoral dissertation, University of Alberta, 1979.

Snart, F. D., O'Grady, M., & Das, J. P. Cognitive processing by subgroups of moderately mentally retarded children. *American Journal of Mental Deficiency*, 1982, *86*, 465–472.

Snart, F. D., & Swann, V. Assessment of intellectually handicapped adults: A cognitive processing model. *Applied Research in Mental Retardation*, 1982, *3*, 201–212.

Sternberg, R. J. A review of six authors in search of a character. A play about intelligence tests in the year 2000. In R. J. Sternberg & D. K. Detterman (Eds.), *Human intelligence*. Norwood, N.J.: Ablex, 1979.

Teuber, H. L., Battersby, W. S., & Bender, M. B. Changes in visual searching performance following cerebral lesions. *American Journal of Psychology*, 1949, *159*, 592.

Thurstone, L. L., & Thurstone, T. G. *Factorial studies of intelligence*. Chicago: Univ. of Chicago Press, 1941.

Wechsler, D. *Wechsler Intelligence Scale for Children*—Revised. New York: Psychological Corp., 1974.

4

Educational Roles of
Cognitive Plans and Strategies[1]

JOHN R. KIRBY

As cognitive psychology develops more and more elaborate models of how human beings process information, it becomes increasingly appealing to apply these models in real-world, educationally relevant settings. For this application to be successful, the models must be amplified to include developmental or, more generally, individual differences features. Perhaps more challenging is the task for the curriculum specialists, to explicitly define educational performances in terms that are amenable to cognitive process analysis. Should both of these tasks be accomplished, the educator must then design instruction to enhance cognitive process skills that will lead to greater educational attainments. The process approach is by no means a panacea; at best it provides a more realistic and coherent framework with which to attack educational problems.

In this chapter, I will attempt to elaborate one aspect of cognitive models, that concerned with planning. As is the case for all the chapters of this volume, planning will be specifically related to educational performance. Throughout, the concern will be not only for cognitive processes that are

[1]The research reported in this chapter was supported by Educational Research and Development Committee grants to the author, and to P. J. Moore and the author, and by an Australian Research Grants Committee grant to A. F. Ashman and the author. This chapter was written while the author was a visiting fellow at Yale University.

Cognitive Strategies
and Educational Performance

correlated with achievement but also for processes that can be improved in order to *increase* achievement.

It is important to note that an individual differences perspective is being explicitly applied to the planning concept. Planning or control processes seem to be well accepted in information processing models, usually without reference to individual differences. It remains to be seen whether they can be usefully examined from an individual differences point of view. While it is very likely that there exist gross individual differences in planning (e.g., between retarded and normal children, or between 7- and 14-year-olds), it is less certain that stable individual differences can be found within more homogeneous groups (e.g., normal 9-year-olds). It is less certain still that those differences, if they exist, are importantly related to educational phenomena.

This chapter is divided into three sections. Following a brief consideration of the relationships between individual differences and cognitive processes, the first section will present a theoretical analysis of planning. This section will discuss several of the research areas that are relevant to the nature of planning and elaborate upon different methods of characterizing plans. The second section will review a number of recent research studies, under three topics: the structural nature of planning, correlations between planning skills and achievement, and educational benefits of improving planning skills. The final section will present a model for conceptualizing planning and will also discuss several broader issues.

INDIVIDUAL DIFFERENCES AND COGNITIVE PROCESSES

Let us begin by considering a simple diagram, which illustrates the rationale for much of the traditional work that has been done in the area of individual differences. Figure 4.1 shows the hypothetical relationships be-

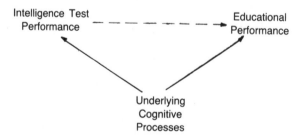

Figure 4.1. Relationships among intelligence test performance, school performance, and underlying cognitive processes.

tween intelligence test performance and educational performance. Briefly, both intelligence test and educational performances are seen to be the result of common, underlying cognitive processes. Thus, while a reasonably strong correlation might exist between intelligence test and educational performances, it would be wrong to say that one had *caused* the other; for this reason, too, it would not be sensible to try to improve real-world (educational) performance by training individuals to do better on intelligence tests. From this norm-referenced point of view, we are not really interested in items; their only value is the degree to which they correlate with school performance.

Unless one adopts a position of mindless prediction, however, any attempt to explain the correlation between intelligence test and educational performances must postulate a set of underlying cognitive processes, skills, components, strategies, etc. that are involved in both types of performances. Theoretically, at least, these are the things that *cause* performance.

With that as a background, we could excuse the naive educator for concluding that the next two steps are '(*a*) defining those underlying cognitive processes, and (*b*) seeking ways to improve them, since from those improvements should flow improvements in school performance. Until recently, however, this direction has not been a dominant concern within individual differences psychology.

Although this is not the purpose of the present chapter, it is possible to mention two reasons for the lack of research in this area. A very basic cause has been the often unstated assumption that the underlying skills, etc. are to a large degree unimprovable; whether innate or shaped by early preschool experience, these underlying factors have been seen as fixed potentials, as upper limits of performance by the time that the child is in school. The second, related explanation for the lack of research in this area is the absence until recently of cognitive process constructs within individual differences psychology (see Kirby, 1980). When the constructs underlying performance are seen as capacities or abilities, it seems to be difficult to conceptualize them as responsive to instruction (there are exceptions, e.g., Ferguson, 1954).

A great deal of research seeks to redefine those underlying constructs in cognitive process terms (e.g., Carroll, 1976; Das, Kirby, & Jarman, 1979; Hunt, 1980; Sternberg, 1977), working toward a reconciliation between cognitive experimental psychology and the traditionally less cognitive individual differences psychology. This research has not yet had much impact upon educational intervention, although it would seem to provide the most logical foundation for instructional design. One difficulty has been that many of the cognitive processes or components that have been identified are quite remote from the instructional situation. For example, Hunt (1980) has consistently found a relationship between verbal ability and the speed with which information can be manipulated in short-term memory; how would the educator go about improving the speed of information manipulation in short-term memory? Clearly, not all cognitive constructs will be equally useful as instructional goals, although all may continue to have an influence upon the effects of instruction. This chapter will examine a cluster of cognitive constructs that can be grouped within the category of "planning abilities" and that in turn appear to play important educational roles.

THE NATURE OF PLANNING ABILITY

The concept of planning ability (or abilities) is based upon a distinction between cognitive processes that act upon information and cognitive processes that act to *control* information processing. In other words, a set of control or executive functions is being postulated that acts to regulate or plan the encoding of information, the transformation and manipulation of memory codes, and the production of a response.These control processes began to appear in memory models (e.g., Atkinson & Shiffrin, 1968) in order to explain the effects that subjects' strategies, mental sets, or goals had upon the ways in which a task was performed. Planning thus refers to individual differences in the effectiveness of those control processes. If the effectiveness of various control processes is a stable characteristic across tasks, and if those control processes covary, then a single planning ability might be said to exist; if, on the one hand, planning in one task domain is not very well correlated with planning in other domains, then several planning abilities might exist. Furthermore, these distinct abilities might be truly independent, or they might be hierarchically related (i.e., lower order factors could be correlated, giving rise to higher order factors), or they might be functionally related (in the sense that a certain amount of one might be needed before another can be effective).

Literature Sources

Extensive reviews of the literature that is relevant to planning ability are available elsewhere (Das, Chapter 3, this volume; Kirby & Ashman, 1981). For the purposes of the present chapter, it will suffice to enumerate some of the domains of planning-relevant research:

(a) *Brain function research.* Many neuropsychologists have investigated planning skills, usually with reference to the frontal lobes of the brain. Luria (e.g., 1966, 1973) in particular has relied upon the controlling or regulatory functions of planning in his theory of brain function. Das, Kirby, and Jarman (1975, 1979) have in turn used Luria's conceptions in their work. In general, it has been shown that frontal lobe damage disrupts visual search skills, maze- and trail-following performance, and selective attention control.

(b) *Memory and cognition research*. While the general concept of planning ability has not really been used in this literature, there is an abundance of more specific instances of planning, usually described as strategies. Some of the strategies that have been shown to affect performance are verbalization (naming of to-be-remembered items), rehearsal, semantic categorization, elaboration (both imaginal and verbal), and semantic integration. Use of these strategies can be studied developmentally or across achievement groups. For instance, it is now clear that the mentally retarded and the learning disabled use such strategies less often and less efficiently than do normal children. Strategy instruction is currently a popular topic for research.

(c) *Metacognition research*. Although questionable whether really separate from the foregoing, a literature has grown up under the rubric metacognition. Essentially, this refers to subjects' awareness of how task, subject, and strategy factors can influence performance. Unlike the memory and cognition research, in which strategies are inferred from patterns of performance, metacognitive research tends to rely upon interviews with subjects concerning their knowledge and strategies. The self-report basis of the data is probably the weakest feature of the matacognition research, although arguably a necessary one as long as awareness is the crucial characteristic. More generally, metacognition can be seen to be involved in performance evaluation or monitoring, strategy switching, and plan or strategy selection. With the inclusion of these characteristics, metacognition begins to resemble the more usual category of control processes.

(d) *Psychometric research*. The traditional multifactor ability theories did not isolate planning abilities specifically, but it is possible to reexamine their postulated abilities for planning emphasis. For example, with reference to the Educational Testing Service's Kit of Factor-Referenced Cognitive Tests (Ekstrom, French, Harman, & Derman, Note 1), the Spatial Scanning, Word Fluency, and Perception factors would seem to share the "visual search" or "selective attention" nature of the measures used by the neuropsychologists. Flexibility of Use and Ideational Fluency appear to be related to metacognition, although the latter also involves "flexibility of method."

(e) *Other research*. Many other areas of research can be seen to involve planning skills—for instance, that concerned with problem solving. Often it becomes difficult to distinguish these from those already listed. A somewhat different area would be that of personnel selection: There probably exist many measures, some perhaps informal, that are designed to tap the planning or problem solving skills required by business executives. Some of these might involve work samples, in which planning is judged in the context of a real problem, not a paper-and-pencil test.

These are only some of the possible literature sources concerning planning. It is one of the purposes of the present chapter to indicate how an integration of this information might proceed, although a complete integration is not yet possible.

Characterization of Plans

Plans are analogous to computer programs, being sequences of actions, evaluations, and conditional actions. Plans are also goal related, so that actions are carried on until a desired goal state is attained (or some criterion of trying is passed). They are undoubtedly hierarchical, in that one plan may call for the execution of a subplan, which could also be a part of other plans. Plans can be seen to involve what have otherwise been called strategies, styles, processes, and abilities. In this context, an *ability* is a skill that, through learning, etc., has reached an asymptotic level of performance; plans can call for the implementation of a certain ability in a certain situation. *Process* is a more vague term, but it can be taken to refer to a more generalized skill that is less task specific (thus, rote memory is an ability, but sequencing is a process); plans can call for processes to be applied. A *strategy* in this view would be a subplan, although since plans are hierarchical in nature, at some level of analysis a strategy could be seen as a plan. If anything, a plan is more suggestive of an evaluative component and is probably at a greater level of generality (thus, we might have a strategy for remembering some numbers, but a plan for the day's activities; plan could have been used for the former, but not strategy for the latter). Finally, *styles* refer to habitual use of qualitatively distinct plans, with the expectation that there would be considerable generalization across task contents.

Level of Generality

In discussing plans, it is important to keep the level-of-generality issue in mind; while it is often frustrating to use the same word to describe entities of greatly different level (e.g., a plan for picking up objects from a desk, a plan for one's life), there are no acceptable alternatives, nor is there a convenient level at which to draw a dividing line. It is useful to remember that planning level is a continuum, not a dichotomy.

Given that, however, and with the appropriate amount of trepidation about coining new terms, it will be useful to think of plans of greater generality as *macroplans* and those of lesser generality as *microplans*. Microplans are clearly more specific in nature, ultimately being specific to certain stimuli and responses. At their more general levels, microplans resemble strategies. At less general levels, it is difficult to distinguish between microplans and *schemes;* the latter are usually used to refer to knowledge structures, whereas the former have more to do with action. The point is that in a very fundamental sense, knowledge is indistinguishable from action, a point with which Piaget and others would agree. These relationships are outlined schematically in Figure 4.2. There is a danger of triviality when discussing microplans in the educational context, in that certain microplans are necessarily required for certain achievements (e.g., various word-recognizing plans are necessary for reading). There should be no surprise that planning ability in that sense is related to achievement or that teaching a particular plan improves achievement. Similarly, if a rehearsal plan is related to rote memory for numbers, the interest is in whether use of that plan will spontaneously generalize to a different context, such as reading, not in whether number memory can be improved.

Within an educational context, it is likely that the more micro plans will be easier to teach, whereas the more macro will be more resistant to change. At their greatest level of generality, the latter correspond to cognitive styles or even personality types, so that conclusion is not surprising. If highly general plans are to be changed, it is likely that this will have to be done by

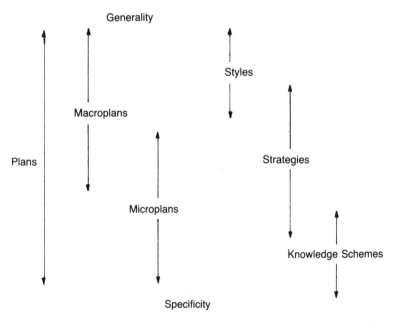

Figure 4.2. Plans, strategies, styles, and schemes. Note that categories overlap.

changing lower level plans, working gradually up the hierarchy (see Biggs, Chapter 6, this volume; Kirby & Biggs, 1981).

Automaticity

A second complicating issue concerns how well established or automatic plans are. A plan that has to be constructed for a particular situation will take up more processing resources than one that is well learned and needs only to be applied (cf. Case, 1980a). Take, for example, the task of driving a car; early in one's driving career, the various dimensions of the task (steering, controlling speed, making signals, looking out for other traffic) absorb all the available resources, to the point that it is difficult or impossible to carry on a conversation. Later, hopefully, that same driver will be able to do all the above, plus perhaps think about something quite different.

The difference is that the driver in the first case had to assemble a "driving plan" on the spot. Even though the component skills (steering, etc.) may have been well learned, their coordination had not been. In this type of situation, a great deal of planning can be said to be required. Contrast that with the second case, in which a well-established plan already existed; although planning was involved in the prior construction of the plan, and some planning may be required in its execution, none is involved in present construction. Unlike the first situation, the plan in the second can be expected to be executed smoothly, efficiently, and automatically, requiring little planning. In such cases, the automatized plan is functioning in much the same way as a knowledge scheme and would consequently be placed lower in Figure 4.2's hierarchy. This may appear to produce a contradiction, in that styles are located high in the hierarchy, even though they are well established. The seeming contradiction is resolvable because styles, although well established, are very general in nature, whereas automatized plans tend to be more task specific. Thus, generality is not necessarily associated with automaticity, and it is the latter that determines the amount of processing resources consumed.

Differences among Plans

If individuals of the same or of different developmental or skill levels are compared, their plans can be seen to differ in at least three ways: (a) the number of independent units of information (chunks) that have to be held simultaneously; (b) the degree to which there are sequential relationships between plan steps; and (c) the depth or structural complexity of the information chunks involved.

The first of these dimensions of difference has been investigated by Case (e.g., 1980a), who has developed a methodology for identifying the separate chunks of information an individual is using. Take for instance a typical ratio problem: On each of two trays, we have a number of glasses of water and of orange juice. The subject's task is to determine which tray of glasses, when mixed together, will taste the more "orangey." Case has analyzed this task, identifying various strategies and their chunk requirements. A primitive strategy is to count the orange juice glasses on tray A (one chunk), then count the orange juice glasses on tray B (two chunks), and select the tray with the larger number. A much more advanced strategy is to count the orange juice glasses on A (one chunk), count the water glasses on A (two chunks), divide forming a ratio (back to one chunk), count the orange juice glasses on B (two chunks), count the water glasses on B (three chunks), divide forming a ratio (back to two chunks), and select the tray with the greater ratio. Similar analyses can be performed for most tasks, although perhaps not as neatly; for example, Biggs (e.g., 1980) has used a similar approach to analyze children's creative writing. This dimension of difference is related to availability of working memory space, which has been shown to increase with developmental level (e.g., Case, 1980a).

The second dimension of difference among plans has been less explicitly investigated.[2] Neisser (1967) distinguished between serial processing, in which a number of actions that are essentially unrelated to each other take place in temporal order, and sequential processing, in which each action in a temporal series is dependent upon the outcome of preceding actions. Working memory space is most easily related to serial processing, as in the example given in the previous paragraph; the only relationship between chunks or actions is a characteristic temporal order. Sequential processing is different, however, and in a way that is important for planning. The processing becomes more sequential as more evaluations and state-contingent actions take place—in other words, as decision making increases. Temporal order is even more crucial in sequential processing.

The third dimension of difference is related to chunk complexity, or more simply chunk size. Since Miller's (1956) pioneering work, it has been known that working memory (or short-term memory) is limited in the number of unrelated chunks that can be maintained, although chunks themselves are not limited in principle in the amount of information that they can contain. Whereas the older research usually measured chunk size in terms of numerical recoding (e.g., the binary digits 101 were recoded as the octal digit 5, etc.; see Miller, 1956), more recent research has benefited from the concept of a scheme (or schema). Thus, chunks can now be conceived of generally as activated knowledge structures. These structures can be quite simple (e.g., the digit 5), or they can be complex (e.g., the concept "democracy"). More relevant to plans, a chunk can be considered as a

---

[2]The importance of this dimension was pointed out to me by Samuel Messick.

subunit of a plan that has not been integrated into a larger structure. In executing a plan, each step usually consists of two chunks; for example, in "If x, then do y," "If x" and "then do y" are the two chunks. If either of these chunks has not been unitized, then more space will be required. If the two have been executed often enough together to have become jointly unitized, then less processing space would be required.

From Theory to Data

The aspects of plans and planning ability have been discussed so far at a very theoretical level. Most of what has been presented has relied upon rational analysis more than empirical evidence. This is not surprising in a new area, but it must also be admitted that many of the details would be difficult to verify experimentally, primarily because of the difficulty in observing subjects' plans. It is certainly the case that the foregoing theoretical framework has outstripped the data that will be presented in the following section.

RECENT RESEARCH IN PLANNING AND STRATEGIES

As outlined at the beginning of this chapter, three questions will be addressed in the research studies to be presented in this section:

1. What are the relationships among the various domains of planning and strategies?
2. Are planning abilities related to educational achievement?
3. Can planning abilities be improved through training so that school achievement also increases?

In each case, reference will be made to studies that have been described more completely elsewhere; the interested reader should examine those sources for greater detail concerning each study.

Domains of Planning and Strategies

Kirby–Ashman Study

The first study to be described was done in conjunction with Adrian Ashman (Kirby & Ashman, 1981). We were interested in the relationships that would emerge among several domains of planning. Of the various domains listed in the previous section, we chose three to include: brain function, memory and cognition, and metacognition. Our procedure was to select from each of these domains a representative sample of measures that could be argued to assess some form of planning ability, to examine the relationships among these measures factor analytically, and then to see what could be said about the structure of the broad planning domain. Our subjects in this study were 120 Grade 5 children from regular classes. Twelve measures were selected, four from each of the domains.

The measures selected from the frontal lobe literature and adapted to suit our subjects were:

(a) *Trail Making*. This task requires subjects to connect dots as quickly as possible within a 3-min period. The correct sequence of dots is indicated by a series of letters (A, B, etc.), numbers (1, 2, etc.), or letters and numbers (A, 1, B, 2, etc.). The score is the number of points correctly connected; this is thought to measure planning in that subjects must search in a planful manner for the next dot.

(b) *Verbal Fluency*. In this task, subjects are required to write as many words beginning with the letter *p* that they can in a 3-min period. Responses are scored for the number of different words written. This task measures planning in that an efficient search must be made of one's long-term memory.

(c) *Matching Familiar Figures (latency)*. In each problem in this test, subjects are shown a standard shape and six variants of it. Their task is to locate as quickly as possible the variant that is exactly the same as the standard. Each subject's score is the number of seconds taken to make the first choice in each problem, totaled over all the problems. In this task, long latencies are usually associated with more systematic and efficient planning, and with better performance (fewer errors).

(d) *Mazes (corrected)*. Subjects are presented with five mazes, ranging from simple to difficult. Their task is to trace the correct path through as many of the mazes as possible in 3 min. Planning is again involved in the systematic exploration of possible routes, given limited time. The score is the number of "choice points" successfully passed, minus the number of careless errors made (crossing lines, cutting corners, etc.).

The reader will have noticed that these "frontal lobe" measures share several features that are not essential to the concept of planning. All four are timed measures, although this was not true for all the original measures (e.g., mazes is often given with unlimited time, subjects being scored for number of errors and unsuccessful attempts). Time pressures are not inimical to the concept of planning, however. A second feature that these measures share is the requirement for a search, either of a visual display or of long-term memory. This again is another legitimate component of planning.

The second set of measures came from the memory and cognition literature, and were derived from two experimental paradigms. In the first of these, subjects were shown a set of eight digits in successive spatial positions across a screen, one at a time. They were then shown a "probe" digit and asked to indicate where in the series it had been (Sternberg's memory-scanning paradigm). Previous research (e.g., Kail, 1979) has argued that good performance on the early items of such a task reflects use of a rehearsal strategy. While such a strategy might be automatic or at least common in older subjects, it is by no means so in subjects of the age used in this study. The two measures derived from this paradigm were:

(e) *Serial Position 1 score*
(f) *Serial Position 2 score*

It should be noted that, while there was no arithmetic dependency between these variables, it is likely that they would be highly correlated (e.g., subjects are very likely to use the rehearsal strategy on item 1 if they use it on item 2).

The second memory and cognition paradigm used was adapted from a study by Moely, Olson, Halwes, and Flavell (1969). Subjects were given 5 min to study 20 cards, on each of which was a printed word. Though the cards were arranged randomly, the words were members of one of four categories (animals, foods, forms of transportation, furniture). Subjects were encouraged to move the cards around or do anything else to help them study them. Following the study period, subjects were asked to recall as many of the words as they could. The two measures derived were:

(g) *Study Clustering.* This was an index of whether subjects moved the cards during the study period and, if they did, what types of clusters they formed. Highest scores were given for exhaustive semantic categorization, but intermediate scores were given for incomplete semantic categorization, incomplete functional combinations ("You could put the *dog* on the *bus*"), or idiosyncratic pairings ("*Dog* and *television* go together").

(h) *Recall Clustering.* Subjects' recall was scored for the degree to which the four semantic categories were used, the clustering index employed being Frender and Doubilet's (1974) statistic (Ratio of Repetition).

Again it is worth noting some of the characteristics of these measures. While all are independent in the strict sense, it would not be surprising to find high correlations within paradigms. It is also clear that the two serial position measures reflect performance as well as planning components. The study clustering measure is probably the purest measure of planning so far, in that it reflects foresight. Both the serial position and clustering measures could be labeled "strategy" rather than "planning" measures; while the strategies themselves have a broad range of application, in the present study they were assessed within rather narrow contexts.

The third set of measures related to metacognition and were adapted from Kreutzer, Leonard, and Flavell (1975). All measures were derived from an interview, in which subjects were presented with four problems and asked to supply as many different solutions as possible. The problems were remembering to bring a bathing suit to school the next day, remembering to go to a birthday party on a certain day, figuring out how old a dog was, and finding a lost sweater. Following Kreutzer *et al.*, responses to each problem were scored on a number of dimensions. We then collapsed scores across problems, forming four scores relating to different types of responses (not all problems were represented in each score). The scores were:

(i) *Metacognition (external aids).* This score was the number of different solutions that relied upon some sort of external aid (writing a note, leaving an object somewhere).

(j) *Metacognition (internal aids).* This score reflected attempts to use internal strategies, including forming mental images, mentally retracing steps, etc.

(k) *Metacognition (other persons).* This score was the number of solutions that relied upon another person ("Get my mother to remind me").

(l) *Metacognition (purposefulness).* This score came only from the first two (memory-oriented) problems and assessed whether or not the subject's solution showed a clear goal orientation (e.g., instead of "I'd write myself a note," "I'd write myself a note and put it in a place where I'd be sure to see it").

The scores for these 12 variables were correlated, and the correlations entered into a principal components analysis. This analysis yielded four factors with eigenvalues greater than 1.0, which were then rotated to a Varimax criterion. The results of this analysis are shown in Table 4.1.

While this type of analysis can not prove that a certain number of dimensions underlies the data, it can be seen that there is little evidence for a unitary planning construct. If a single factor were extracted, it would be based upon the performance tasks rather than the interview responses; on the one hand, this argues against such a factor, but on the other, it questions the validity of the interview items as planning measures. (This latter issue will be addressed later in the "Planning and Achievement" section.) The validity of the four-factor solution was supported by an oblique rotation, which did not change the loadings noticeably, and by a higher order solution, which yielded a second-order factor similar to the first principal component (see Kirby & Ashman, 1981, for details).

The four factors in Table 4.1 are not difficult to identify, because they correspond to the a priori clusters of variables. The first factor is defined by the four measures that require subjects to search arrays (whether visual or mental) for a relevant feature and then make the appropriate response

TABLE 4.1
Four-Factor Solution of Kirby–Ashman Data (Principal Components, Varimax Rotation)[a]

	Factor			
	1	2	3	4
Variable	Search	Rehearsal	Clustering	Metacognition
Trail Making	<u>740</u>	121	193	114
Verbal Fluency	<u>673</u>	107	−008	338
Matching Familiar Figures	<u>−756</u>	154	158	008
Mazes	<u>480</u>	163	175	−215
Serial Position 1	125	<u>796</u>	188	−034
Serial Position 2	−016	<u>846</u>	−001	−059
Study Clustering	009	−034	<u>866</u>	152
Recall Clustering	123	205	<u>854</u>	−017
Metacognition (external)	−035	−230	−156	<u>681</u>
Metacognition (internal)	−012	−107	193	<u>481</u>
Metacognition (other)	193	379	−090	<u>475</u>
Metacognition (purpose)	030	128	123	<u>608</u>
Variance	1.872	1.692	1.691	1.499

[a]Salient loadings have been underlined to emphasize factor structure.

(drawing, writing, pointing). These measures all derive loosely from the literature relating to the functioning of the frontal lobes, and this factor resembles previous Planning factors identified by Ashman (1978) and by Das (Chapter 3, this volume). Rather than use the broad term *planning,* however, it would seem preferable to use a more restrictive term in the present context. *Search* is the obvious candidate, and it is not difficult to see that the organization and coordination of searches is an important aspect of planning. Kirby and Ashman also present an argument that this factor could represent *selective attention,* which is often measured by the Matching Familiar Figures and Mazes tests (cf. Ross, 1976). This is not unreasonable, as selective attention usually implies the choice of an item while excluding other competitors. For clarity's sake, I will refer to Factor 1 as *Search,* but the implication of selective attention should be remembered.

Factor 2 is defined by the two serial position measures, performance on which was argued to be due to the use of a rehearsal strategy. Thus, this factor can be identified as *Rehearsal,* which in the present context appears to be quite narrow in scope.

Factor 3 similarly represents semantic *Clustering.* It is worth noting again that the two clustering measures were quite independent; this factor stresses that study clustering is strongly associated with recall clustering, although again the factor is narrow in scope.

Factor 4 is defined mainly by the *Metacognition* variables, from which it obtains its label. The moderate loading for Verbal Fluency upon this factor is likely due to the requirement in metacognition performance for the searching of long-term memory for possible solutions.

At this point, it can be concluded that the planning domain can be represented by as many as four factors. Each of these taps an aspect of planning that differs from the others in a variety of ways; for instance, the Rehearsal and Clustering factors appear to be relatively specific stretegy factors, whereas the Search and Metacognition factors would seem to have greater generality. The natures of these factors and how they relate to the general concept of planning will be considered later, after their relationship to achievement has been examined in the next section. Let us now turn to a second study of the structural characteristics of the planning domain.

Moore–Kirby Study

Instead of the entire planning domain, Moore and Kirby (1983) selected the metacognition area for investigation and further narrowed the scope to reading-related metacognition. Their study was based upon previous studies by Myers and Paris (1978) and by Moore and Kirby (1981), which had helped develop a questionnaire that examined children's knowledge of various aspects of reading. The subjects for this study were 88 children in Grades 2, 4, and 6. Each child was interviewed individually, as well as being given a number of other group and individual tests.

The questionnaire consisted of 15 questions, which were either selected from those used by Myers and Paris (1978) or designed for this study. The questions are listed in Table 4.2. In all cases, subjects' responses were graded on ordinal sclaes, such that a high score represented "better" performance, in the sense that it represented reliance upon internal as opposed to external resources and in that it was more likely to be successful. This was not always easy to do (e.g., which is a better strategy to discover what a word means: to ask the teacher or to consult a dictionary?), but the scales were intuitively acceptable (see Moore & Kirby, 1983, for further details).

The scores on the 15 items were analyzed by means of a principal components analysis with Varimax rotation. The four factors that emerged are shown in Table 4.3 (items have been reordered according to the factor upon which they mainly load). This analysis is much less clear than the preceding one, which probably reflects less coherence in the metacognition domain or at least less coherence in the questionnaire. It is, however, possible to identify these factors. Again the reader is advised to consult the original source for more complete arguments concerning factor identification.

The items that load highly upon Factor 1 appear to share two broad characteristics. The first of these is the requirement of withholding closure in responding—that is, learning to say "it depends" when asked an essen-

TABLE 4.2
Questions Asked during Moore–Kirby Interview

Code	Question
1. Good reader	What makes someone a really good reader?
2. Math	The other day I talked to a boy/girl who was really good at arithmetic. Do you think that he/she was also a good reader? Why?
3. Home	Suppose there were two boys named John and Alan who came from different homes. John's parents were rich and John had lots of toys and books. Alan's parents were poor and didn't have many books at home. Do you think that one of the boys was a better reader at school? Which one? Why?
4. Remember	The other day I asked a boy named Bill to read a story so that he could remember it. Before he started reading, though, he asked me if I wanted him to remember the story word for word, or just remember the story in his own words. Why do you think he asked me that? Which would be easier for you to do, remember the story word for word or remember it in your own words. Why?
5. Length	I asked a boy named Jim to read a story that was five pages long, and a boy named Tom to read a story that was two pages long. Which boy took longer to read his story? Why?
6. Fast	What do you do differently when you read fast than when you read slow?
7. Sentence order	Is there anything special about the way sentences go into stories?
8. First sentence	What does the first sentence usually do in a story?
9. Last sentence	What does the last sentence usually do?
10. Skim (words)	If I asked you to read a story really fast and you could only read some of the words, which ones would you try to read? This is called skimming. How would you skim?
11. Retell	After reading a story, do you ever tell it to someone else? What do you try to tell them? Why?
12. Image	When you're reading, do you ever make up pictures in your head? Why? What are the pictures like?
13. Word	When you're reading, what do you do if there's a word you don't understand?
14. Sentence	When you're reading a story, what do you do if there's a whole sentence you don't understand?
15. Age	How old are you? Do you think that x-year-olds read as well as adults? Why?

TABLE 4.3
Four-Factor Solution of Metacognition in Reading Questions (Principal Components, Varimax)[a]

	Factor			
Variable	1 Withholding Closure	2 Reading Skill	3 Reading Strategy	4 Use of Context
Math	74	26	08	30
Home	71	03	13	17
Remember	50	22	32	03
Length	59	04	03	31
First Sentence	64	28	38	−15
Good reader	29	68	20	−15
Sentence order	12	60	16	26
Skim (words)	02	66	−09	37
Age	18	64	07	−02
Retell	−13	53	60	11
Fast	16	05	73	29
Last Sentence	34	25	55	−18
Image	30	−05	62	31
Word	21	12	28	70
Sentence	17	06	08	69
Variance	2.51	2.22	2.00	1.65

[a]Salient loadings have been underlined to emphasize factor structure.

tially indeterminate question. The second characteristic is that the items tap knowledge that would be likely to develop in the absence of specific instruction. This factor was labeled *Withholding Closure,* but its general developmental nature should be remembered.

Factor 2, in contrast, was defined by items that require subjects to state specific reading skills, ones that are likely to be the subject of specific instruction. Accordingly, it was labeled *Reading Skill.*

Factor 3 was defined by a group of items that related to more advanced reading strategies (e.g., use of imagery) and was therefore labeled *Reading Strategy.* These strategies, unlike the skills included in Factor 2, are not likely to be included in traditional forms of reading instruction.

Factor 4 was defined by two very specific items, concerning the resolution of comprehension failure at word and sentence levels. Because of the way in which it was scored, it was labeled *Use of Context.* It is also unlikely that this skill, using context to determine probable meaning, is often taught in traditional reading instruction.

It is clear that we are far from the traditional domain of mental abilities when defining these factors. As would be true of most interview-derived metacognition measures, these are more dependent upon specific knowledge (including knowledge of how to do something) than they are upon ability to act upon that knowledge. The factors differ in terms of their dependence upon reading instruction: All except the Reading Skill factor are unlikely to have been taught, and the general developmental factor (Factor 1) would probably be difficult to teach in a meaningful way.

In the following section, these factors will be related to a variety of other performance measures, which will aid in validating the nature of these factors and in describing them in terms of the conceptual framework developed in the initial part of this chapter.

Overview

From the two studies examined here, it is safe to conclude that the planning domain can be analyzed into a number of domains (perhaps metacognition, attention, and various strategies), and each of those further analyzed into problem or content areas (e.g., strategies into rehearsal and clustering; metacognition into metacognition about reading, metacognition about memory, etc.). Individual areas could also be subdivided (e.g., metacognition about reading into Withholding Closure, Reading Skill, Reading Strategy, and Use of Context factors), and no doubt those subdivisions further subdivided. The various domains and areas are by no means cleanly separated—the more one subdivides one, the more one sees connections with other units (e.g., the Reading Skill factor may relate more to knowledge schemes than to metacognition, the Reading Strategy factor similarly to the strategies domain). Furthermore, the utility of a particular level of analysis has to be considered: A level—or for that matter, a factor—is useful only if it correlates with academic performance (see next section) or provides a basis for instruction (see "Improving Planning and Achievement" section).

Planning and Achievement

Kirby–Ashman Study

After identifying the four planning factors (Table 4.1), we used these factors to derive factor scores for each subject, in effect giving each subject a score for how much of each factor he or she could be said to have. These factor scores were then divided at their medians, so that a series of 2 (Search) × 2 (Rehearsal) × 2 (Clustering) × 2 (Metacognition) analyses of variance could be performed, with additional variables as the dependent variables. The more interesting of these analyses will be briefly described here.

Several measures were included to help determine the nature of the factors. Digit Span was one of these; if it were highly related to Rehearsal, the planning or strategic nature of this factor would be cast into doubt. Fortunately for our purposes, Digit Span was not significantly related to any of the planning factors or their interactions.

Several measures were included in ways that, technically speaking, broke statistical rules. For instance, even though the Mazes score (i.e., correct performance minus a carelessness score) was part of one of the factors, the two component scores (correct and carelessness) were entered as dependent variables, with interesting results. As would be expected, the correct score was significantly related to the Search factor. Contrary to expectations, the carelessness score was not related to Search, but was significantly and *positively* related to Metacognition; thus, high Metacognition subjects made more carelessness errors. Our interpretation was that these subjects had engaged in a speed–accuracy trade-off—the task demanded speed, and although the instructions had specifically discouraged "carelessness," no ongoing feedback was provided that carelessness was "wrong." The fact that these subjects would have finished more quickly would have acted as an encouragement to continue this strategy. This finding is important because it relates the somewhat nebulous Metacognition factor to the performance domain, and in a way that confirms its metacognitive nature.

Several interactions were also found, and these help to describe possible functional relationships among the factors. The first of these was for the variable representing the number of words recalled in the clustering task (again this breaks the rules, but not in a way that affects the interesting findings). In addition to Search and Clustering main effects, which were not surprising, there was a Rehearsal × Metacognition interaction, which is graphed in Figure 4.3. We interpreted this effect as indicating that a rehearsal strategy was only helpful in this task in the presence of an awareness of how to use it. In other words, rehearsal blindly applied was not helpful—this is not surprising, as the words were semantically related and so simple rehearsal might even be counterproductive. When applied "intelligently," however, perhaps in conjunction with the clustering strategy or in a way that was at least compatible, performance was aided. This finding is important because it further confirms the nature of the Metacognition factor. It also shows that this factor is functionally related to the Rehearsal factor, with reference to a dependent measure (i.e., a certain level of Metacognition is required for Rehearsal to be effective; an alternative description would be that a certain level of Rehearsal is required for Metacognition to be effective, though this seems less plausible).

The final and most important dependent measure was an achievement test in mathematics, testing subjects' ability to solve arithmetic equations

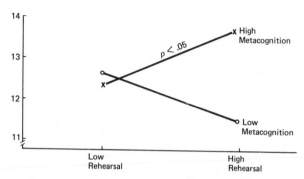

Figure 4.3. Rehearsal × Metacognition interaction for number of words recalled.

(the Operations Test, Australian Council for Educational Research, 1977). This test yielded significant Search, Clustering, and Metacognition main effects, but the most interesting result was a Search × Rehearsal × Metacognition interaction, graphed in Figure 4.4. In general, all the factors contribute positively and independently to performance; the exception to this rule is the Search factor. When it is "high," performance appears to take its "normal" position; when it is "low," however, the effect is disastrous. Our interpretation here was that adequate Search ability acts as a prerequisite for the effective implementation of the other planning skills. Especially

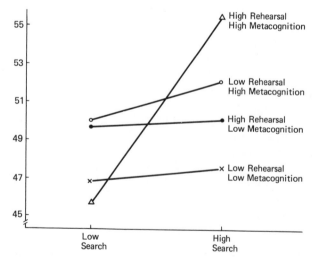

Figure 4.4. Search × Rehearsal × Metacognition interaction for mathematics achievement.

if one recalls the implication of selective attention in Search, this finding makes sense of the often reported finding that learning disabled children are of normal intelligence but have poor selective attention skills (e.g., Ross, 1976). The "intelligence" in which they are normal does not include the attention skills in which they are deficient. In other words, here again is evidence for a functional relationship among the planning factors, but only with respect to other, dependent variables.

These further analyses helped clarify or validate the natures of some of the factors: Rehearsal was shown to be distinct from rote memory, and Metacognition was shown to be involved in a speed–accuracy trade-off concerning Mazes. They also provided the first evidence for a functional structuring of the factors, but only with regard to other performance variables: Metacognition was argued to be a necessary condition for the use of Rehearsal during the clustering task, and Search (selective attention) was a prerequisite for the use of Rehearsal and Metacognition in the mathematics achievement task. For the present purposes, it is important to note that planning factors of reasonable generality were identified and that these were shown to be related in a meaningful way to classroom achievement.

Moore–Kirby Study

The four metacognition in reading factors were also related to a variety of other measures, including grade, sex, metamemory, and reading comprehension. In this study, simple correlations between variables were used because of the smaller sample and the range across three grade levels.

Table 4.4 contains the correlations between the factors and grade, sex, and two metamemory measures. Not surprisingly, the general developmental factor Withholding Closure is strongly related to grade level ($p < .01$); the magnitude of this correlation, given the "sloppiness" of the metacognition factor, supports the description given to this factor. The only other significant correlate of grade is Reading Strategy ($p < .01$), suggesting that

TABLE 4.4
Moore–Kirby Correlations across Grades

	Variable			
Factor	Grade (2, 4, 6)	Sex (M = 1, F = 2)	Metamemory (bathing suit)	Metamemory (sweater)
Withholding Closure	.58	.12	.24	.08
Reading Skill	.13	.04	.22	.15
Reading Strategy	.30	.17	.31	.27
Use of Context	.18	.24	.10	.13

this factor too takes a while to become established. The other two, more reading-specific factors are not significantly related to grade, suggesting that they are not a part of a general increase in mental ability but that they may be more easily manipulable through instruction. Only the fourth, reading-specific factor correlates with sex, and even then weakly ($p < .05$), indicating that girls are more likely to use context in resolving a comprehension problem. This is not surprising, given the usual superiority of girls in reading, but the magnitude of the relationship is not large.

Table 4.4 also contains correlations with two metamemory measures; each of these is the total number of solutions that the child proposed for (a) remembering to bring a bathing suit to school the next day, and (b) finding a lost sweater. The rationale for including these measures was to investigate which metacognition in reading factors were related to the more often studied metamemory skill. At the .01 level, only the Reading Strategy factor is significantly related, and to both metamemory items. At the .05 level, Withholding Closure and Reading Skill are related to question (a); the weakness and unreliability of these effects casts doubt upon them. These results suggest that Reading Strategy is the closest to a reading metacognition factor in the group; Withholding Closure is more broadly developmental in nature, and the other two are quite specific to reading.

Table 4.5 shows the correlations between the metacognition in reading factors and a reading comprehension score (obtained from the Progressive Achievement Test). Because this score is standardized within grades (i.e., stanine scores in each grade range from 1–9), the grades were considered separately, which allowed for the investigation of developmental changes in relationships. (This also increased the size of the correlation needed for significance.)

Withholding Closure is related positively but nonsignificantly at all grade levels. Reading Skill is similarly unrelated to performance. Both of these results are reassuring, as neither factor concerns the processes that are actually involved in performing a reading task. Reading Strategy appears to

TABLE 4.5
Moore–Kirby Correlations within Grades

	Correlation with reading comprehension in grade		
Factor	2	4	6
Withholding Closure	.23	.24	.32
Reading Skill	.26	.24	.16
Reading Strategy	.43	−.09	.32
Use of Context	−.10	−.36	.62

be significantly correlated with comprehension in Grade 2 ($p < .05$), although not thereafter. The grade 2 effect might reflect the value of even a vague orientation toward meaning, which loses its effectiveness as skills become established. It is possible that this relationship might reestablish itself in later school years, as the strategies themselves become more effective.

By far the most interesting effect is for the Use of Context factor. In Grade 2, there is no relationship; in Grade 4, there is a weak *negative* relationship ($p < .05$); and in Grade 6, a strong *positive* relationship ($p < .01$)! This shift in direction need not be as confusing as it appears, especially if one considers that the use of context strategy is a very demanding one, requiring much in the way of cognitive resources. At the very least, it would require sufficient working memory to retain the problem item and the local context while that local context was being searched for relevant cues; it is also likely that the strategy requires a good amount of selective attention for the execution of the context search. Thus, it is possible that Grade 2 students would not use it at all, so it cannot be correlated with performance. By Grade 4, however, some students are using context, but it is beyond their resources. By shifting to a meaning perspective, these students are penalized, at least in terms of the way in which reading achievement is measured. By Grade 6, cognitive resources have caught up with the strategy, so that it can now be implemented effectively. This explanation is admittedly post hoc and based upon few subjects, but it does account for the findings. Moreover, it predicts that instruction in the use of context would be effective in or just before Grade 6, but ineffective or even counterproductive in or before Grade 4. Studies to investigate this are currently under way.

These results have been helpful in a number of ways. In the first place, they have revealed a problem that is commonly suspected—that some of what is often called metacognition is actually a very vague index of general cognitive development and thus very difficult to apply instructionally. Second, they have suggested that children can be asked many apparently reading-relevant questions, whose answers are not particularly related to reading success (the so-called Reading Skill items). Finally, two other clusters of items can be seen—one (Reading Strategy) more general in nature (a macroplan) and less specifically related to achievement; the other (Use of Context) very specific in nature (a microplan) but strongly related to achievement.

Overview

The question for this section was whether or not planning factors of reasonable generality could be identified that were correlated with academic performance. The factors identified in the two studies have been of reasonable generality, at least with regard to the performance measures with which they were correlated; by this I mean that there was no possibility of a necessary relationship, as would be the case if a rote memory factor were correlated with some memory performance, The point is to find planning measures that are separate enough from the academic performance so that a trivial relationship is not found (i.e., one in which the implication of planning is not needed), yet that are related enough to performance so that they can be used instructionally. With these criteria, what can be concluded?

Of the general planning factors, Search and Metacognition would seem to hold the most potential. It is probably true that Rehearsal and Clustering, as measured in this study at least, are more narrow (micro) in nature. In spite of this, it should be noted that Rehearsal, perhaps the most micro of all, entered into interactions related to mathematics achievement. All these factors could be the target of instruction, though different combinations might be effective in different criterion contexts (e.g., Search, Rehearsal, and Metacognition for mathematics, perhaps a different set for reading). Search is probably a broad prerequisite factor, tapping selective attention; as such, it should have broad applicability. Metacognition is similarly broad, but it would seem to have its greatest applicability in more specific situations, such as in the training of the Use of Context. At this point, however, it becomes debatable whether metacognition in the sense of awareness is all that is being trained. Probably not. But then it is difficult to conceive of any awareness coming about that had no impact upon performance. For this reason, it seems preferable to conceptualize the domain as planning in the sense of decision making; awareness itself may be an epiphenomenon.

Improving Planning and Achievement

At the outset of this section, it must be admitted that the studies to be described were conducted prior to much of the theorizing and evidence that have been presented so far. For this reason, they will not seem to tackle as specifically as possible the points that have been raised; other studies are currently being conducted to address these points. The studies to be presented do, however, raise points that are relevant to any study designed to train planning and thus improve achievement.

The most fundamental point concerns the ecological validity of the criterion measure. For example, training digit memory strategies is fine, as long as the training generalizes beyond that training session and to a task that is of some interest. In the context of education, we would hope that training would generalize to achievement tasks. Unfortunately, we are likely to find that the very skills we most want to change are the most difficult to change.

The task-specific skills that are easy to change are at the micro level, while the more generalizable ones that are resistant to change are at the macro level. It would be highly unrealistic to expect that variables that have been demonstrated over many years to have reasonable stability (level of achievement, intelligence) can be changed over a short period of intervention. This is particularly true of achievement levels: The average low-achieving child has usually had several teachers and parents working overtime to help. There is reason to be optimistic about the benefits of a planning-oriented intervention program, but no cause to anticipate miracles.

Even if we accept ecologically valid measures as the ultimate criteria, a dilemma remains. On the one hand, we want to train at a reasonably high level in the hierarchy, so as to have psychologically interesting effects. Similarly from a methodological point of view, we want to avoid "teaching to the test"—ideally, our training should not resemble the criterion test at all. On the other hand, we want to design our training realistically, keeping the locus of intervention close enough to the outcome behaviors so that a beneficial effect is feasible. Especially from an educational point of view, if we want a child to read more proficiently, there is no reason to avoid reading materials in our training and good reason to expect that they should be included.

Many previous intervention attempts have foundered on this dilemma. Studies that have been psychologically and methodologically "pure" have often failed to show generalization, whereas many "practical" educational efforts seem unfortunately trivial. It is probable that the appropriate locus of instruction will vary from problem to problem, such that a relatively specific skill would be the optimal goal in one situation and a more general skill the goal in a different situation. The danger of triviality, of teaching to the test, is always present, but it seems preferable to risk erring in that direction rather than to avoid the most ecologically valid task content. More generally, generalization is only likely to occur when it has been built into the instructional program; thus, a relatively specific skill can be the basis for a broader one if instruction presents sequences of problems that gradually shift content or format, etc.

Lawson–Kirby Studies

The first set of studies that I would like to discuss was done in conjunction with Michael Lawson. They involve identifying strategies children use in solving Raven's Progressive Matrices problems, and also the effects of training them to use those strategies more efficiently. As it is a well-accepted measure of general intelligence, we were not hoping to produce large increases in subjects' Raven's scores; even if large increases were produced, we realized that this could not be taken to mean that "intelligence" had been improved. Our interest was in the strategies that were associated with success, as these would seem likely candidates for the "underlying cognitive processes" indicated in Figure 4.1 as the basis of both intelligence and achievement test performance. Strategy training in this case was very brief, so no carry-over to achievement was expected. However, it should be noted that the analytic strategy described later is relevant to many educational tasks and that the effects of an extended intervention program are worth investigating.

These studies (Lawson & Kirby, 1981; Kirby & Lawson, 1983; Lawson & Kirby, Note 2) concerned two strategies indentified by Hunt (1974) for solving Raven's items. The *gestalt* strategy treats the problems as spatial objects—one fills in the missing piece by extending lines, completing patterns, repeating lines, etc. Hunt hypothesized and our data confirm that this is the strategy spontaneously adopted by most children, at least until early adolescence. Not surprisingly, this strategy alone allows children to score within the normal range until that same point. It also seems that this is more of a spatial than a reasoning strategy, and in fact scores at this age correlate more highly with spatial ability than with reasoning ability (Kirby & Das, 1978). The *analytic* strategy is what one must use to go beyond the early adolescent level: It requires the child to think more abstractly, treating the problem as a set of features, one of which is missing. Features are counted and rules inferred to determine what the missing piece must be. The items that require this strategy are all the "harder"ones for preadolescents, so those children who do use it score very well. Thus, there are two types of strategies (gestalt and analytic) and two types of problems (those requiring the gestalt and those requiring the analytic strategy). A complicating factor is that the gestalt items can all be solved by the analytic strategy.

I will report only some of the results of our most recent study (Kirby & Lawson, 1983). Our subjects were 150 children in Grade 4, 168 in Grade 6, and 252 in Grade 8. Each child was randomly assigned to one of four treatment conditions: weak gestalt, weak analytic, strong gestalt, and strong analytic. In the weak conditions, strategy use was manipulated only by altering the early items that the child performed. Gestalt items were predicted to encourage the gestalt strategy (this situation is comparable to the normal design of the test and can be taken to represent a control condition), and the analytic items were predicted to encourage the analytic strategy. In the strong conditions, explicit verbal instruction was given about how to solve the problems. The strong gestalt subjects were told to imagine the problem as a picture and to attempt to extend lines or balance the pattern, etc., to complete it. The strong analytic subjects were told to discover the rule upon which each problem was constructed and to use that rule to decide which answer was correct (counting of features was stressed). Following training and some sample problems in the strong conditions (all of which lasted no more than 10 min), Set I of the Advanced Progressive Matrices was administered, six items of which were judged to be gestalt and six analytic.

Our basic results are presented in Figure 4.5. Several general trends can be easily seen. The strong analytic subjects do very well, although their advantage disappears by Grade 8. Similarly, the weak gestalt subjects do poorly, and their disadvantage is least at Grade 8, particularly for the gestalt items. With regard to the gestalt items only, strong analytic training is more effective than strong gestalt training, until Grade 8. This is at first surprising, but it should be remembered that both strategies can solve the gestalt items. If subjects are presumed to be somewhat adept with the gestalt strategy before training, analytic training provides them with a second method of solving the problems, whereas subjects receiving strong gestalt training would still only have one such method. The maximum impact of training on the gestalt items is at Grade 4—that is, the spread of the groups is greatest there. With regard to the analytic items, training has its maximum

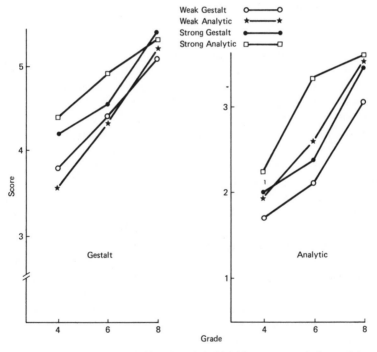

Figure 4.5. Number of gestalt (left) and analytic (right) items correct in four training groups in three grades.

effect at Grade 6, and not surprisingly, the most effective condition is the strong analytic.

The results of this study are interesting in their own light for what they have to say about intelligence and its measurement. For instance, they suggest that the Raven's matrices assess not only how well a particular skill (i.e., reasoning) is used but also how well the subject chooses the appropriate solution strategy. The skill level itself may contribute relatively little to the observed score, at least in comparison to the strategic or planning component involved in approaching the problem. This could be taken to imply either that reasoning should be assessed by "cleaner" measures, uncontaminated by strategies, or that intelligence is more closely related to planning and that planning should be more explicitly addressed. I shall return to this issue in the final section of this chapter.

For the present purposes, we can conclude from this study that strategies are important, that they can be trained, and that training does affect performance. Several cautions must be added to that statement. The first is that the effects are relatively age specific. It appeared as though the Grade 4 children had not yet mastered the gestalt strategy and thus could still benefit from training in it. These children were not much helped by strong analytic training, perhaps because it required more resources than they had at their disposal. Grade 6 children could be argued to have the resources, but to require training to actually use the strategy effectively. These patterns recall Flavell's (1970) description of a *production deficiency,* a transitional state in which subjects have the component skills required for a certain performance, do not spontaneously put them together in the correct manner (i.e., their plan or strategy is suboptimal), but can be trained to do so. In the context of the Raven's matrices, the gestalt strategy would appear to be concrete operational in nature and thus should be approaching its asymptotic level by age 10–12. The Analytic strategy is more formal operational in nature and should still be developing at age 12–14 (cf. Hunt, 1974). Such statements are too gross for instructional purposes (cf. Biggs & Kirby, 1980), but they do describe the general pattern of our results.

The second caution is that the improvements due to training were quite small. Figure 4.5 shows that the greatest effect for gestalt items was less than a full item (comparing strong analytic and weak analytic at Grade 4) and that that for analytic items was about 1¼ items (comparing strong analytic and weak gestalt at Grade 6). Of course, a 2-point increase on a 12-item test is not to be scoffed at, but future research will have to show that this effect is carried over proportionally to a larger test. More to the point, these small increases underline the fact that we are dealing with relatively stable abilities in addition to the more easily modifiable strategies. The Raven's items have ecological validity in the sense that they have been shown to be central to the complex of behaviors that are used to assess intelligence and that are strongly related to school performance. If less ecologically valid items had been used for the criterion measure, for instance trick items in which one strategy would lead you to the right answer and the other to a plausible but incorrect answer (unlike the gestalt items), more dramatic results would have been shown (such an effect was actually found, Kirby & Lawson, 1983). Again it appears that the greater the ecological validity of the measures, the greater the difficulty in changing them.

A final point concerns the length of intervention. In this study, it was short, lasting only several minutes; thus long-lasting effects could hardly have been anticipated. If more durable effects were desired, especially those generalizing to academic tesks, a longer and more comprehensive intervention would be necessary. Such an intervention not only would introduce the student to a strategy, which is only likely to be effective if the student is ready to learn and use it, but would devote time to anchoring that strategy in various content or problem domains through practice. Thus, one deficiency in previous strategy training research may be that strategies were not taught so that meaningful connections between them and other skills and knowledge were established. The following study represents a step in that direction.

Spatial Study

The spatial study reported here derived from a larger developmental study of children's knowledge of spatial skills that are required for some mathematical performances. The major achievement measure in the larger study was the Space Test, developed by the Australian Council for Educational Research (1978) as part of its Mathematics Profile Series; this test consists of word problems that either require spatial skills by themselves (e.g., figure rotations, block counting, paper folding) or spatial skills plus mathematical knowledge (e.g., Cartesian coordinates, angles). The purpose of the small study to be described was to see whether some children's low scores could be improved through training in how to approach spatial tasks (necessitating some teaching of spatial skills as well). The intervention itself was thus relatively "dirty," in that no specific process or strategy was trained exclusively. A variety of problems was deliberately utilized, in which several spatial skills (e.g., rotation, three-dimensional construction, copying, scanning) were involved.

Thirty Grade 5 children who had scored in the bottom half of the Space Test distribution were selected as subjects. Half of these came from an average school, which had only slightly more than its fair share of learning problems among its children. The other half came from a school with a far greater incidence of learning problems; accordingly, achievement levels were lower for these children at the beginning of the study. Within each school, subjects were randomly assigned to one of three conditions: a control condition, in which they remained in their regular class; an arithmetic condition, in which they received instruction and practice in basic operations for 2 hr per week for 6 weeks; and the spatial condition, in which they received practice in spatial problems such as paper folding, figure copying, figure rotation, jigsaw puzzles, and mazes. In this last condition, emphasis was placed upon how to approach the problem: Subjects were required repeatedly to take their time, to predict likely outcomes of actions, and to plan their actions. This condition is the most relevant for the present concerns, as the subjects were being taught to plan their processing, at least within the spatial context. The children were pretested in the middle of their academic year, intervention took place in the latter half of that year, and posttesting was carried out 1 week following the end of the intervention.

The results of interest here are presented in Figure 4.6. Using pretest Space Test scores as a covariate, there was a significant difference among treatment groups, due to the superiority of the spatial group. While the School × Condition interaction only approached significance ($p < .09$), it can be seen that most of the spatial group's advantage is due to those children from the school with the less severe problems. It should be noted that the difference of four scale points between the control and spatial subjects in

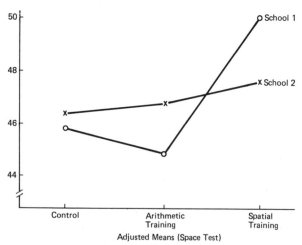

Figure 4.6. Adjusted scaled scores in spatial study. (There was a far greater incidence of severe learning problems in School 2 than in School 1.)

this school is comparable to the increase found in average students between Grades 4 and 6.

This exploratory study demonstrates that meaningful increases in achievement can be obtained through strategy instruction with specific reference to problem content. In a relatively crude form, this study may provide a blueprint for future studies, combining an emphasis upon planning and strategies with practice in the problem domain, all with reference to achievement measures that yield more detailed information about student abilities than usual (e.g., no improvement in "general mathematical ability" would have been likely in the study described). Given that increases are possible from such a nonspecific intervention, it remains to be shown what are the relative contributions of practice with spatial materials, as opposed to instruction in planning. In either case, it would be valuable to determine which precise spatial skills (rotation, etc.) are causing the problems. We are also pursuing the apparent difference between "moderately" and "extremely" poor achievers; one hypothesis at the moment is that the latter children, in addition to lacking spatial problem solving strategies, are low in a more general academic skill, such as control of selective attention. If this were the case, strategy instruction would have to wait upon the remediation of the more fundamental problem. This possibility also recalls our finding (cf. Figure 4.4) that a certain degree of search ability or selective attention is required before other planning skills can become effective.

Overview

These two studies of strategy training have shown that planning skills can be taught. In the case of the Raven's matrices, a reasoning strategy was taught in a narrow context; in the spatial study, a more general planful approach was taught, in a broader context and over a longer period of time. Strategy-oriented instruction would appear to hold a great deal of promise, both for normal and remedial teaching. It must be stressed, however, that strategy instruction is not magic—strategies do not exist in isolation from domain knowledge (e.g., spatial knowledge), from more general planning skills (e.g., selective attention), or perhaps from more general intellective limits (e.g., general intelligence).

CONCEPTUALIZING PLANNING

Having reviewed several studies dealing with planning and its relationship to achievement, the time has now come to assemble as much of this information as possible into a working model and to address some general issues that have been touched on throughout this chapter.

Toward a Model of Planning

These studies have emphasized the multidimensional character of planning and have provided some clues about how various aspects of it fit together. What follows is based upon the results of these studies but also relies heavily upon a more theoretical analysis of what planning should be.

Consider the model outlined in Figure 4.7. The vertical central core of this diagram is derived from the Kirby and Ashman factor analytic study described previously. Three levels of planning are differentiated. The metacognition level is the most advanced, involving conscious awareness of alternative plans and choices of appropriate plans. Planning at this level is of the macro type, although often particular microplans will be indicated by decisions made. The metacognition level is the most appropriate locus for what is normally termed *decision making*.

The second planning level, and the central unit to the model, is selective attention. This system shares many of the characteristics of the "limited capacity short-term store" or "working memory" found in traditional models of information processing: Information derived from the environment or from long-term memory takes up "space" here, as do plans. (The notion of "space" is metaphorical; clearly no physical objects are being moved around. This construct of space is meant to include limitations imposed by efforts required to retrieve an item's code, as well as limitations related to the number of codes that can be accessed or excited at the same time.) Selective attention's contents can be described in terms of both the number of independent units held at one time (i.e., number of chunks) and the complexity of those units (i.e., size or depth of chunks). Selection of information, either from the environment or from long-term memory, is made on the basis of the current plan, which may or may not be operating smoothly. Space is taken up in selective attention both by units of information (knowledge schemes) and by units of plans; space required can be

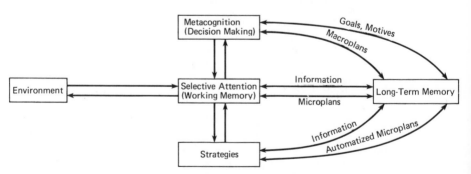

Figure 4.7.   Schematic outline of the planning system.

reduced by assembling schemes into higher order schemes or by automatizing plans.

The third level of planning is where various processing strategies function. In response to the operating plan, particular strategies (or subplans, or microplans) are called upon to process information. Some of these strategies would be quite situation specific, whereas others would be more generalizable. Some would also be able to operate relatively automatically, taking up little selective attention or processing space, whereas others might even have to be constructed during the task.

The horizontal axis of Figure 4.7 concerns information and its storage. The environment is scanned according to the operating plan, information is coded into the processing space, this information is transformed in accordance with knowledge schemes selected from long-term memory (also determined by the operating plan), and some of these new transformed knowledge schemes may be stored in long-term memory.

In addition to knowledge schemes, long-term memory contains macroplans, as well as the goals and motives that will act as broad guides for macroplanning. This is shown in the model by the lines connecting long-term memory and the metacognition unit; by bypassing selective attention, these lines indicate that these aspects do not take up processing space, operating relatively unconsciously. Other aspects would take up selective attention space (see next paragraph), as would the more macro features when operational. In other words, macro aspects take up little space when acting unconsciously or as background, but they require space if they become part of an operational plan. Put more simply still, the metacognition unit takes up space when it acts; this is indicated by the lines connecting it to selective attention.

Other lines connect long-term memory with the selective attention and strategy units: These indicate that information and microplans are being transferred. To the extent that the schemes or microplans are integrated or automatized, selective attention can be largely bypassed; to the extent that they are not, processing space will be required.

How does this model account for the factor analytic findings presented in the preceding sections? With respect to the Kirby–Ashman study, the Metacognition factor assesses the unit of the same name. Both the Rehearsal and Clustering factors would be seen as strategies, thus relating to the third unit. The Search factor would be seen as a major index of selective attention. While each unit has its factor(s), no claim is made that any of the units has been exhaustively assessed by these factors (e.g., working memory aspects of the selective attention unit are not included).

In the factor analytic study of metacognition in reading, the factors are more difficult to assign to units. Even though each factor was assessed by metacognition-type questions, all do not appear to be essentially metacognitive in nature. The developmental Withholding Closure factor is the most likely macroplanning factor of the four, indexing a broad cognitive developmental function. As a macroplan, it would be represented by structural characteristics of long-term memory and would operate through the metacognition system. The Reading Strategy factor is also metacognitive in nature, representing conscious choices among broad approaches to reading: Perhaps a better label for it would have been Reading Plan. The Reading Skill factor may not be a planning factor as such; rather it might be seen as an index of specific knowledge contained in long-term memory (if anything, these specific elements of knowledge might represent microplans or specific strategies). Finally, the Use of Context factor is most easily seen to be a strategy factor, representing a microplan for dealing with relatively specific (though important) problems.

This model also accounts for the evidence presented earlier about the functioning of the planning system. For example, it will be remembered (see Figure 4.4) that the Search factor acted as a prerequisite for the effectiveness of the Rehearsal and Metacognition factors in increasing mathematics achievement. In the model's terms, this shows that a certain level of selective attention (Search) is required before the other planning or strategic factors could be employed. A second example would be the developmental changes in the correlation between the Use of Context strategy and reading comprehension (See Table 4.5). While neither selective attention nor working memory was measured in this study, it is known (e.g., Case, 1980a) that working memory efficiency does increase during the Grade 2 to Grade 6 period. Thus, selective attention may again be acting as a prerequisite, this time for the Use of Context strategy. If children attempt to use that strategy before their resources are adequate (Grade 4), poor performance results; when resources are adequate (Grade 6), use of the strategy improves performance. As a final example, recall the performance of the children from the more disadvantaged school in the spatial study (see Figure 4.6). Their relative lack of response to training may be due to poor selective attention; in order for strategy training to be effective, control over selective attention would have to be increased first.

This model is a first attempt to describe some very complex behaviors and systems. As such, there is no doubt that it is wrong, or at least inaccurate. Hopefully, it will act as a guide for future research, so that features of the model can be challenged, tested, and amended.

Planning and Intelligence

How is planning related to intelligence? This is a major issue, which can not be dealt with completely here. Theoretically, they should be strongly related, in that planning (as described here) controls the functioning of the cognitive system. With regard to measurement, however, planning has not featured prominently in any of the factor theories that have generated tests. The tests used here to assess planning have not been normally employed (at least not in the same way) to assess intelligence. If anything, traditional tests of intelligence appear to minimize the impact of planning, in that they do not assess how the subject solves the task, only how well. Such tests probably do assess planning, though, in that the choice of an inappropriate plan results in poorer performance (cf. the Lawson–Kirby studies of Raven's matrices mentioned earlier). It may also be the case that typical test instructions do not fully explain to children what they have to do; to the extent that children "figure things out for themselves"—that is, select the correct strategy—their scores will improve.

One could conclude, then, that planning adds nothing new, that it is really intelligence under a different label. If all one did was call it planning, this would be a valid criticism. The point, however, is that *planning* is a more precise term concerning some aspects of intelligence (there are other aspects) and should facilitate an information processing analysis of what intelligence is. Thus, intelligence is the phenomenon that is ultimately to be explained, and planning is a feature of the information processing approach that currently offers the greatest chances of progress. (This is not to deny that other approaches are possible and that others may consider them to have more potential.)

The Role of Planning in Instruction

Education has long been plagued by an often tedious debate concerning the relative merits of "basics" (or fundamentals) and "understanding." In information processing terms, these extremes relate to what is input to long-term memory, either discrete and highly specific schemes, or integrated and highly generalizable schemes. From an information processing perspective, either view is absurd by itself. The cognitive system would have trouble learning large numbers of unrelated schemes, and if it appeared to learn them, it would probably be doing so by covert integration and generalization. Similarly, the learning of higher level schemes would be meaningless without more concrete specific schemes as instantiations. The system that appeared to be learning such higher level units either would be treating them as lower level units (e.g., learning by rote, without any ability to generalize) or would in fact be discovering lower level examples.

A similar debate could ensue from attempts to apply planning research to the design of instruction. Should one teach planning and decision making in the broadest sense, emphasizing awareness, or rather teach a variety of more narrow, task-specific strategies? As has been hinted here, neither of these approaches would be very successful in isolation. Broad macroplanning skills are very resistant to change, and in any case, it would be difficult to attack them in the absence of specific task contexts. Narrow microplans, on the other hand, are easy to change, but they are unlikely to generalize.

The solution to the basics versus understanding debate is to combine both within a coherent approach: A few highly specific schemes or skills must be taught first to provide a basis for understanding, but some higher level accomplishments must follow soon to preserve motivation. Basic schemes should be highly practiced, so as to minimize the processing resources they absorb, but drill should not last long at any particular time. It should be alternated with higher level activities, which in turn make use of the lower level schemes just drilled (see Case, 1980b, for a more complete example of such an approach).

The solution to the hypothetical planning debate would be analogous. Both micro- and macroplans must be addressed, changes in the former being the means to changes in the latter. In planning, there is the added complication of selective attention as a prerequisite, but that too is probably susceptible to intervention (e.g., Ross, 1976). Plans, like schemes, will be retained and used to the extent that they form a coherent part of a larger integrated cognitive structure. Thus, they must be taught in carefully chosen, concrete, and specific contexts, but their relevance to other problem contexts must also be indicated, preferably in a practical way.

As was said at the beginning of this chapter, the mere invocation of the concept of planning or even its use in instruction will not be an immediate solution to all educational problems. I see the planning approach as emphasizing an aspect of instruction that has not been well articulated (and has not yet been completely articulated). If teachers can be made more aware of planning and strategies, and if they can be encouraged to teach them to their students, some increases in achievement should follow. Perhaps more important would be the generalization of a planful approach beyond the school to life in general, making students more aware of their options or goals and the means to obtain them.

ACKNOWLEDGMENTS

The assistance of David Porter, Kathy Russell, and Helen Ward in data collection and analysis is greatly appreciated.

REFERENCE NOTES

1. Ekstrom, R. B., French, J. W., Harman, H. H., & Derman, D. *Manual for Kit of Factor-Referenced Cognitive Tests*. Princeton, N.J.: Educational Testing Service, 1976.

2. Lawson, M. J., & Kirby, J. R. An initial investigation of the development of solution strategies for Raven's Progressive Matrices items. Unpublished manuscript, Flinders University, Australia, 1978.

REFERENCES

Ashman, A. F. The relationship between planning and simultaneous and successive synthesis. Unpublished doctoral dissertation, University of Alberta, 1978.

Atkinson, R. C., & Shiffrin, R. M. Human memory: A proposed system and its control processes. In K. W. Spence & J. T. Spence (Eds.), *The psychology of learning and motivation* (Vol. 2). New York: Academic Press, 1968.

Australian Council for Educational Research. Operations Test. Mathematics Profile Series. Hawthorn, Australia, 1977.

Australian Council for Educational Research, Space Test. Mathematics Profile Series, Hawthorn, Australia, 1978.

Biggs, J. B. Developmental processes and learning outcomes. In J. R. Kirby & J. B.Biggs (Eds.), *Cognition, development, and instruction.* New York: Academic Press, 1980.

Biggs, J. B., & Kirby, J. R. Emergent themes and future directions. In J. R. Kirby & J. B. Biggs (Eds.), *Cognition, development, and instruction.* New York: Academic Press, 1980.

Carroll, J. B. Psychometric tests as cognitive tasks: A new "structure of intellect". In L. B. Resnick (Ed.), *The nature of intelligence.* Hillsdale, N.J.: Erlbaum, 1976.

Case, R. The underlying mechanism of intellectual development. In J. R. Kirby & J. B. Biggs (Eds.), *Cognition, development, and instruction.* New York: Academic Press, 1980. (a)

Case, R. Implications of neo-Piagetian theory for improving the design of instruction. In J. R. Kirby & J. B. Biggs (Eds.), *Cognition, development, and instruction.* New York: Academic Press, 1980. (b)

Das, J. P., Kirby, J., & Jarman, R. F. Simultaneous and successive syntheses: An alternative model of cognitive abilities. *Psychological Bulletin, 1975, 82,* 87–103.

Das, J. P., Kirby, J. R., & Jarman, R. F. *Simultaneous and successive cognitive processes.* New York: Academic Press, 1979.

Ferguson, G. A. On learning and human ability. *Candian Journal of Psychology, 1954, 8,* 95–112.

Flavell, J. H. Developmental studies of mediated memory. In H. W. Reese & L. P. Lipsitt (Eds.), *Advances in child development and behavior* (Vol. 5). New York: Academic Press, 1970.

Frender, R., & Doubilet, P. More on measures of category clustering—although probably not the last word. *Psychological Bulletin, 1974, 81,* 64–66.

Hunt, E. Quote the Raven? Nevermore! In L. Gregg, (ED.), *Knowledge and cognition.* Potomac, MD.: Erlbaum, 1974.

Hunt, E. Intelligence as an information processing construct. *British Journal of Psychology, 1980, 71,* 449–474.

Kail, R. Use of strategies and individual differences in children's memory. *Developmental Psychology, 1979, 15,* 251–255.

Kirby, J. R. Individual differences and cognitive processes: Instructional application and methodological difficulties. In J. R. Kirby & J. B. Biggs (Eds.), *Cognition, development, and instruction.* New York: Academic Press, 1980.

Kirby, J. R., & Ashman, A. F. Metacognition and strategic behaviour. Final report, Australian Research Grants Committee. Newcastle, Australia: Univ. of Newcastle, 1981.

Kirby, J. R., & Biggs, J. B. Learning styles, information processing abilities, and academic performance. Final report, Australian Research Grants Committee. Newcastle, Australia: Univ. of Newcastle, 1981.

Kirby, J. R., & Das, J. P. Skills underlying Colored Progressive Matrices. *Alberta Journal of Educational Research*, 1978, *24*, 94–99.

Kirby, J. R., & Lawson, M. J. Effects of strategy training on progressive matrices performance. *Contemporary Educational Psychology*, 1983, *8*, in press.

Kreutzer, A., Leonard, C., & Flavell, J. An interview study of children's knowledge about memory. *Monographs of the Society for Research in Child Development*, 1975, *40* (1, Serial No. 159).

Lawson, M. J., & Kirby, J. R. Training in information processing algorithms. *British Journal of Educational Psychology*, 1981, *51*, 321–335.

Luria, A. R. *Higher cortical functions in man*. New York: Basic, 1966.

Luria, A. R. *The working brain*. Hammondsworth, Great Britain: Penguin, 1973.

Miller, C. A. The magical number seven, plus or minus two: Some limits on our capacity to process information. *Psychological Reveiw*, 1956, *63*, 81–97.

Moely, B. E., Olson, F. A., Halwes, T. G., & Flavell, J. H. Production deficiency in young children's clustered recall. *Developmental Psychology*, 1969, *1*, 26–36.

Moore, P. J., & Kirby, J. R. Metacognition and reading performance: A replication and extension of Myers and Paris in an Australian context. *Educational Enquiry*, 1981, *4*, 18–29.

Moore, P. J., & Kirby, J. R. Metacognition and comprehension in reading. Final Report, Educational Research and Development Committee. Newcastle, Australia: Univ. of Newcastle, 1983, in preparation.

Myers, M., & Paris, S. G. Children's metacognitive knowledge about reading. *Journal of Educational Psychology*, 1978, *70*, 680–690.

Neisser, U. *Cognitive psychology*. New York: Appleton, 1967.

Ross, A. O. *Psychological aspects of learning disabilities and reading disorders*. New York: McGraw-Hill, 1976.

Sternberg, R. J. *Intelligence, information processing, and analogical reasoning: The componential analysis of human abilities*. Hillsdale, N.J.: Erlbaum, 1977.

5

Being Executive about Metacognition

MICHAEL J. LAWSON

Use of the term *metacognition* is now common in the literature of cognitive psychology. Although concern for aspects of metacognition emerged early in this century (e.g., Brown, 1981, quotes the work of Huey, 1968, and Dewey, 1910, although, disappointingly, fails to mention Louis), it was not until the 1970s that widespread use of the term began. Now metacognition is implicated centrally in many areas of study in psychology, language, and education. Metacognition is regarded as important for memory, comprehension, attention, communication, and general problem solving (Flavell, 1978). Models of intelligence (Sternberg, 1980) and individual differences (Snow, 1981) include metacognitive components. Researchers interested in language and reading (see Downing & Leong, 1982) emphasize the importance of metacognitive awareness and argue that this awareness is lacking in some degree in learning disabled readers (Leong, 1981). Cognitive behavior modifiers also regard learning disabled children as having "defective metacognitive processes" (Meichenbaum, 1980, p. 273).

While the reception for this construct has been enthusiastic, there has been relatively little careful analysis of its nature and of its relationship to other aspects of cognition. Consequently, there is now a good deal of

Cognitive Strategies
and Educational Performance

confusion in the literature dealing with metacognition about just which aspects of cognition should be labeled *metacognitive* and how these relate one to the other and to performance. This conceptual confusion has been accompanied by conflicting sets of results and the use of unsuitable research techniques. It is the purpose of this chapter to identify some of the sources of this confusion in order to facilitate more satisfactory study of the construct and of its operation.

WHAT IS METACOGNITION?

The referents of the label *metacognition* have not always been identical in studies within different areas of psychology, nor have they been applied consistently within any one given area of research. In part, this inconsistency has arisen because researchers with different interests have defined the term within their local contexts. Thus, Cazden (1972) wrote about metalinguistic awareness in her study of language learning in terms that were similar in meaning to those used by Flavell (1976) in his discussion of metamemory. Both writers were using the *meta* prefix to refer to a *reflective awareness* of cognitive processes, yet Flavell went further and included *control of cognition* in his definition of metacognition. At about the same time, researchers in the field of mental retardation were proposing that a set of processes responsible for control over cognition should become the subject of study (e.g., Butterfield, Wambold, & Belmont, 1973). These processes were, however, labeled *executive processes* even though their functions were subsumed within Flavell's and Brown's (1978) definitions of metacognition.

This confusion over labels and their referents continues at the present time. Thus, while Baker and Anderson (1982) refer to metacognition as "one's knowledge and control of one's own cognitive processes [p. 282]," Cavanaugh and Perlmutter (1982) argue, "Only the contents of memory knowledge should be termed metamemory. While this knowledge can be derived from the use of executive processes and can contribute to their effectiveness, the processes themselves should be distinguished from metamemory [p. 16]." Cavanaugh and Perlmutter argue that these two aspects of cognition should be seen as distinct for purposes of future research, and this position is supported by Brown (1981) and Belmont, Butterfield, and Perfetti (Note 1). Separation of these knowledge and control dimensions is present in some current research though continued description of both as metacognition makes analysis of research more difficult than it need be. Conflation of these two dimensions in several studies has lead to conflicting patterns of results and inconsistencies in research procedures.

METACOGNITIVE KNOWLEDGE AND
EXECUTIVE PROCESSES

Both the knowledge and control dimensions of cognition have been the concern of psychologists in this century. Vygotsky (1962) identified the importance of reflection upon cognitive activity:

> The activity of consciousness can take different directions; it may illumine only a few aspects of a thought or an act. I have just tied a knot—I have done so consciously, yet I cannot explain how I did it, because my awareness was centered on the knot rather than on my own motions, the *how* of my action. When the latter becomes the object of my awareness, I shall have become fully conscious. We use consciousness to denote awareness of the activity of the mind—the consciousness of being conscious. A pre-school child who, in response to the question, "Do you know your name?" tells his name lacks this self-reflective awareness: He knows his name but is not conscious of knowing it [p. 91].[1]

The "consciousness of being conscious," the awareness of "the how of my action" is the defining feature of meacognitive knowledge. The cognitive activity is the object of a higher (meta-) process, and the result of this reflection becomes part of the individual's knowledge base. A view very close to that of Vygotsky's was put by Cazden (1974) when she described metalinguistic awareness as "the ability to make language forms opaque and attend to them in and for themselves [p. 29]."

The notion of an executive has been central to information-processing models of cognition. Herbert Simon (1979), one of the most influential figures in the development of an information-processing view of cognition, describes the executive process as "The control structure governing the behaviour of thinking man in a given task is a strategy or program that marshals cognitive resources for performance of a task [p. 42]." It is the marshalling, regulating function that is the defining feature of the executive processes. The description obviously is influenced by the functions allocated to the executive components of a computer through it is not to be bound only to these. As utilized in the literature of psychology, the executive processes have been identified as planning, analysis, monitoring, evaluating, and modifying processes (Brown, 1981; Brown & Deloache, 1978; Lawson, 1980). Executive processes are seen to be higher-level processes because of their controlling role in cognition, and it was this higher-level, or

---

[1]Reprinted with permission from L. S. Vygotsky, *Thought and Language,* copyright 1962 by The MIT Press.

meta-, characteristic that led many to extend the label *metacognitive* to these processes.

Following Cavanaugh and Perlmutter it is suggested here that the knowledge and control dimensions of cognition should be seen as logically distinct. This separation is represented visually in Figure 5.1. Individuals do have knowledge of their cognitive activity. They can reflect upon the nature, the operation, and the outcomes of this activity, and it is the result of this reflection that should be termed *metacognitive knowledge*. Executive processes should be seen as logically distinct from this metacognitive knowledge. In being executive the individual is controlling or regulating cognitive processes. As Cavanaugh and Perlmutter (1982) suggest, the nature of the executive operation may well depend upon the individual's metacognitive knowledge, but this knowledge should be seen as one source of influence upon, not synonymous with, executive processes.

If metacognitive knowledge is the result of deliberate reflection upon cognitive activity, then, as the product of a conscious, or controlled, process it should be available for report by the individual. Within psychological literature metacognitive knowledge has been limited to this conscious reportable knowledge—knowledge which Brown (1981) describes as "stable, statable, fallible and late developing [p. 21]." Disregarding for the moment the problems of accessibility as distinct from availability of information, it is clear that not all executive processes will be conscious, controlled processes. In Shiffrin and Dumais's (1981) terms, many executive operations will be automatic and therefore not conscious or reportable. The skilled processor of information may show little evidence of executive processing simply because he or she is an expert at a given task. The novice may, on the other hand, be overtly executive on the same task because the task is new and the novice's processing requires much more careful planning, analysis, and modification than that of the expert. Examination of the problem-solving protocols of experts and novices solving physics problems (Simon & Simon, 1978) reveals just such a pattern. It was the novice who evaluated the greater frequency of checking, modifying, and evaluation behaviors. Fredericksen (1980) made a similar point when he suggested that we may

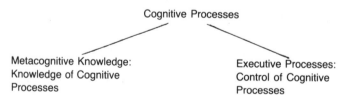

Figure 5.1. Distinguishing between knowledge and control of cognition.

see little sign of executive activity in skilled performers; that is, we expect the skilled reader to be in many ways "executiveless."

Given that they are of a high-level nature, executive processes will be expected to have a general influence across most cognitive domains. Individuals who display consistent use of these processes in one domain should be expected to utilize them in related cognitive activities. This is not to claim that such executive skills are uniformly transferable across all cognitive activities. Nor will the individual who employs efficient executive strategies always succeed, for the outcome of executive activity does depend crucially upon the state of the individual's knowledge base. (The theoretical physicist sometimes fails to consider that the reason for the car's failure to start could be lack of gasoline.) However, given their high-level controlling function, it follows that these skills should not be limited to one area of cognitive activity. In this respect, the executive processes differ from metacognitive knowledge which is domain specific or even task specific. What an individual comes to know of the operation of memory would not be expected to improve her or his knowledge of linguistic processes, except where the latter depended upon memory. Lack of the appreciation of the domain specificity of metacognitive knowledge is apparent in research concerned with child language (e.g., Clark, 1978) and we will see later that this leads to confusing experimental procedures.

Consideration of the nature of metacognitive knowledge and executive processes in this way suggests that we can be more specific about the relationship between these two dimensions. If use of the term *metacognition* is to be limited to metacognitive knowledge, and if metacognitive knowledge is the result of reflection upon cognition, we must consider how to characterize that process of reflection. It is argued here that this reflection upon cognition that results in metacognitive knowledge is best thought of as an executive operation. Seen in this way, the act of reflection involves an examination of the stream of cognition—an examination that includes *analysis, evaluation* of progress in terms of *plans, monitoring,* and *modification* of cognition. To relate this back to an earlier quotation, it is suggested that we become "conscious of our consciousness" and make the cognition the object of our cognition through the operation of executive processes. We can now therefore modify Figure 5.1 and suggest in Figure 5.2 that the source of metacognitive knowledge is executive processing.

In this section, it has been argued that the label *metacognition* should henceforth be applied only to metacognitive knowledge and that this knowledge should be seen as logically distinct from, and as resulting from, the operation of the executive processes that are concerned with the control of cognition. In addition, these two dimensions have been differentiated in terms of the extent to which each:

1. Is conscious and therefore able to be reported by the individual
2. Is specific to a cognitive domain, or is expected to transfer across domains
3. Runs off automatically, or is a controlled, effortful process

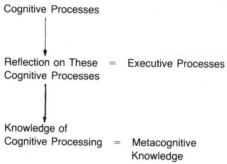

Figure 5.2.   Metacognitive knowledge as the outcome of executive processes.

NOVICES, EXPERTS, AND THE QUALITY OF COGNITIVE PROCESSING

Consideration of the nature of cognitive expertise throws further light on the relationship between metacognitive knowledge, executive processes, and other aspects of cognition. This is particularly relevant because both the knowledge and control of cognition are looked to for providing ways of alleviating a range of developmental disabilities by making novice, or less mature, thinkers more expert.

Relative to the novice, an expert in a given field will be expected to enjoy a number of cognitive advantages. First, the expert will be expected to possess a superior knowledge base. If we consider mathematics performance for the moment, this superiority will be manifested in two areas of knowledge:

1. The expert will have a superior knowledge of mathematical content, both in the extent of his or her conceptual network and in the complexity of that network. For example, if a problem requires knowledge of concepts A, B, C, and D, the expert will know more about each of these concepts, about how they are interrelated, and about how they relate to other concepts. Research in areas of chess (Chi, 1978) and the development of memory (Lindberg, 1980) supports this position.
2. The expert will also have a superior knowledge of task-specific strat-

egies—of ways in which the task can be carried out, of procedures or algorithms that might be used to manipulate the concepts in the problem. The description of digit span performance given by Chase and Ericsson (1981) and the analyses of question asking given by Miyake and Norman (1979) provide good examples of the experts' task-specific strategies.

The expert will also be able to use this superior knowledge base in appropriate ways, and so:

3. The expert will be expected to have welldeveloped general strategies for the storage, organization, and retrieval of information (Chase & Ericsson, 1981; McKeithen, Reitman, Rueter, & Hirtle, 1981).

For the present discussion, it is important to consider whether the expert will also show:

4. More effective executive processes
5. Superior metacognitive knowledge

While the general tendency is to answer "yes" to both 4 and 5, the reasons for doing so need to be considered. It seems that the answer must take into account just who the expert and novice are, and how metacognitive knowledge and executive processes develop in the young child. To consider this further, we will set out two hypothetical cases for consideration, again in the context of mathematical problem solving.

Case I: When the Novice and Expert are Both Adult and Assumed to Be Generally Sophisticated Processors of information (e.g., Two Politicians?)

In this case, the expert and novice will differ markedly in terms of knowledge base and task-specific strategies. While the novice might possess quite sophisticated general strategies for storing, organizing, and retrieving information, it is likely that he or she will be handicapped in employing these because of a lack of knowledge of mathematics. The novice will also be at a disadvantage with regard to metacognitive knowledge, since the expert will have much more extensive experience in manipulating the content in this field and thus will have had more opportunity to reflect upon the cognitive processes involved in the mathematical tasks.

Consideration of the nature of executive processing in this case is more complex. Since both novice and expert are assumed to be sophisticated information processors, both should exhibit a comparable tendency to plan, analyze, monitor, evaluate, etc. However, the incidence and outcome of this executive processing could be quite different for the two individuals.

As suggested previously, an expert is likely to run off the problem solving procedure at a rapid rate, perhaps by employing a well-established algorithm that he or she knows to be applicable for this task. So after an initial analysis of the problem type, the expert will access the appropriate content and algorithm and generate the solution. A minimum degree of executive control is needed if this occurs.

By way of contrast, the novice may exhibit a much greater quantity of planning, analyzing, monitoring, and modifying activities and still not achieve success because he or she lacks a suitable knowledge base. If the expert did strike a problem, the ensuing executive activity would be more effective than that of the novice, simply because the expert has access to a satisfactory base of knowledge, including metacognitive knowledge. So in Case I, the expert will have superior metacognitive knowledge although may show less evidence of executive processing activity if the problem is routine. The superiority of the expert will be largely a function of the state of a knowledge base that allows more complex processing of the stream of cognition.

Case II: When the Adult Is the Novice, a Child the Expert, and Neither Shows any Cognitive Disability

Descriptions of this situation are given by Chi (1978) and by Lindberg (1980). The situation of the novice here is identical to that in Case I, and the expert enjoys the same superiority in knowledge base and task-specific strategies as in the prior case. However, with regard to metacognitive knowledge and executive processes, the level of development of the expert may introduce some complicating factors. While children in the early grades of elementary school are able to reflect successfully upon a wide range of mnemonic activities (Kruetzer, Leonard, & Flavell, 1975), this metacognitive knowledge is held to be "late developing" in such other tasks as text processing (Brown, 1981). Chi (1978), however, worked with 10-year-olds who were relatively expert in chess and found that their metamemory performance was better than that of adults new to that game. The samples used by Chi and Brown are not, therefore, directly comparable. While Chi (1978) studied the performance of young experts who had a great deal of experience with their subject, Brown (1981) did not use children expert in text analysis. Degree of expertize must therefore be taken into account in making assessments of metacognitive knowledge, and it seems unwise to divorce judgments about the developmental path of metacognitive knowledge from assessment of knowledge base. Gelman (1979) has shown that underestimation of children's competence is likely if knowledge base is not considered. Thus, it seems probable that the child expert will have greater metacognitive knowledge of processing related to mathematics than the adult novice, although this superiority would not be expected to hold for the executive processes of these novices and experts.

Information about the executive processes employed across the span of development is meager. Research currently available suggests that degree of executive processing skill depends upon the nature of the task and upon the level of expertise of the individual. Brown (1981), in reviewing a number of her studies of the executive activities related to text processing, found that these skills develop largely in the junior high and high school years. On the other hand, results of studies concerned with children's ability to monitor their comprehension suggest that fourth-grade children who are competent readers can monitor comprehension effectively (Paris & Myers, 1981). Paris and Myers (1981) in fact found that even poor readers showed frequent monitoring behavior, even though this was not particularly effective. So any description of the relationship between age and level of executive functioning must be a complex one. Young experts (and children who are poor performers) do show some signs of effective executive processing but not on all tasks. Young children are clearly less experienced in most situations that have been the subject of research, and thus the efficacy of their attempts to regulate cognition will be reduced because of access to a restricted knowledge base.

If, however, executive skills have some general applicability, we should expect that the adult novice will have access to effective executive processes, since he or she will have had greater experience in a range of problem solving situations and in regulating cognitive activity. Therefore, the adult novice will not be in exactly the same situation as the child novice with respect to executive processing skill. The adult novice will have the benefit of greater experience in executive processing and greater experience as a problemsolver, both of which may compensate to some extent for the poverty of his or her knowledge base on a particular task.

Consideration of Case II suggests that the relationship between metacognitive knowledge and executive activity, and the relative importance of each in performance, depends not only upon the level of expertise but also upon level of development.

We could extend this comparison of novice and expert to consider the case of the developmentally disabled. However, it seems that the line of argument should be quite clear. We would expect the developmentally disabled to show both less effective executive processing and less developed metacognitive knowledge. The reports of research involving mentally retarded children by Borkowski and Cavanaugh (1979) and Brown (1978) support such a conclusion. A similar pattern has been suggested for good and poor performers, both adults and children. Paris and Myers (1981)

noted that poor readers were less aware of effective strategies and of the
counterproductive effects of poor strategies, and were also less effective in
their monitoring activities during reading. Baker and Anderson (1982)
found a comparable pattern of results in their study of the frequency of
comprehension monitoring of college students. For the future instruction
of cognitively disabled performers, the implication seems straightforward
and it is that suggested by the title of Belmont *et al.*'s (Note 1) paper—"to
secure transfer of training instruct self-management skills." Of course, such
a view depends upon how executive processes and metacognitive knowledge are seen to develop with age. The view implicit in Belmont *et al.*'s
argument seems closely tied to a continuity view of the development of
executive skills, yet not all psychologists adhere to that view. In fact, the
literature on the developmental nature of both these dimensions has its own
points of controversy, only some of which are due to the conflation of the
knowledge of cognition and control of cognition dimensions. The major
positions will be considered briefly in the next section.

THE DEVELOPMENT OF METACOGNITIVE
KNOWLEDGE AND EXECUTIVE PROCESSES

Although the problems of how metacognitive knowledge and executive
processes change with age have not been of major concern to developmental psychologists, it is possible to isolate a number of views that reflect the
theoretical controversies of general developmental psychology. These
views range from the discontinuity view of Piaget (1976) to those based
more on continuity models of development. The major complication that
arises in the comparison of these positions is that some deal only with the
metacognitive knowledge and others only with executive processing. There
is at present no one detailed description of the developmental path of both
dimensions.

Piaget's concern was largely with the knowledge of cognition, with *cognizance*. In two of his last works, *The Grasp of Consciousness* (Piaget, 1976)
and *Success and Understanding* (Piaget, 1978), Piaget distinguished between
a practical form of knowledge that arose from successful solution of a
problem and true understanding that involved full awareness, or consciousness, of that action. This true understanding, the "progression from the
practical form of knowledge to thought was effected by cognizance [Piaget,
1976, p. vi]." This cognizance, in Piaget's view, does not emerge fully until
age 11–12 years. Piaget (1976) applied strong criteria to the identification
of a subject's consciousness or cognizance in a problem solving situation: "In
general, when a psychologist speaks of a subject being conscious of a situa-

tion, he means that the subject is fully aware of it [p. 332]." As we have seen, other psychologists have applied less restrictive criteria to the identification of children's ability to reflect consciously on their cognitive activities. For Piaget, the simple act of reflection, divorced from an abstract understanding of the situation, does not imply true understanding. In the terms used here, presumably Piaget would regard metacognitive knowledge prior to the period of formal operations as one aspect of an incomplete conceptualization.

With regard to the executive processes, these late Piagetian works are less explicit. While some part of the role of executive may have been assigned to equilibration mechanisms, the notion of an executive did not form part of the Piagetian model. Yet a reading of most of Piaget's experimental reports shows clearly that his subjects as young as 5 years old were consistently displaying the behaviors included within the definition of executive processes set out in this chapter. In the typical Piagetian report, there is ample evidence of children's analyzing the task environment, monitoring their attempts at solution, modifying their strategies, and evaluating results. Yet for Piaget, these behaviors were subsidiary in importance to the true conceptualization. In other views, such behaviors would be accepted as promising signs of executive processing that was a necessary percursor to successful solution of a problem.

Neopiagetian discussions in the area have included discussions of both metacognitive knowledge and executive processing, although not within the one model. Hakes (1980) completed a series of studies of metalinguistic awareness, which he defined as "conscious awareness of language" or "linguistic intuition." In these studies, data were gathered on children's judgments of the acceptability of utterances according to syntactic and semantic criteria, and judgments of synonymy and of phonemic segmentation. Performance on these tasks was correlated with performance on a range of conservation tasks. For Hakes, the results of his analyses suggested that the metalinguistic ability required in these linguistic tasks "is the same ability as that whose development underlies the emergence of concrete operations [1980, p. 100]." Linguistic awareness, in Hakes's results, emerges at an age considerably earlier than that at which Piaget grants the child "cognizance." The picture of linguistic awareness in young children that emerges from Hakes's work is similar to that suggested by the results of studies of metacognitive knowledge in several other domains (Flavell, 1978).

Two other Neopiagetian theorists, Pascual-Leone and Case, provide explicitly for the development of executive processes within their models of cognitive development. Pascual-Leone (1980) provides for an executive dimension in two distinct ways. The first is in his *metasubject,* a homunculus-type "ideal observer" of the individual's processing. The second regulating component is a series of more specific executives—decentration executive, remembering executive, historical executive—that depend in their operation on the availability of processing space that increases, in a functional sense, across stages of development. Case's (1980) view is similar, although Case does not have any counterpart for Pascual-Leone's metasubject. Instead, control of cognition is carried out in Case's model by executive schemes that have general planning and coordinating functions in the organization of other types of cognitive schemes.

Since Case's is a stage view of development, these executive schemes do change as the child progresses from one stage to the next. But unlike in the Piagetian view, the change in the executive schemes is largely quantitative. There does not appear to be a qualitative change in the nature of the executive schemes but rather an increase or decrease in the demands that the schemes make upon available processing capacity.

While this very cryptic account of these cognitive-developmental models no doubt does not do them justice, it does serve to highlight a number of points. First, there are stage views of the development of both knowledge and control of cognition. However, these accounts differ in the way that they view the nature of the metacognitive knowledge and executive processes. The Piagetian view implies that a distinct process, "cognizance," is implicated in the development of true understanding. Neopiagetian theorists, on the other hand, have incorporated an information processing flavor into their models and relate the operation of the executive to processing capacity and changes in that capacity. Thus, stage theorists neither agree upon the course of development of metacognitive awareness nor provide cohesive accounts of the place of the knowledge and control of cognition dimensions under discussion here. This remains a task for future development of these models.

Non-stage theorists appear to handle this general area in a more satisfactory manner, probably because they are relieved of the task of explaining transitions between stages in cognition and how those transitions occur. The work of Brown (1981) has already been referred to, and she, with Flavell (1981), has reviewed and carried out much of the important research in this area. Brown does distinguish between knowledge of cognition and regulation of cognition and makes different developmental predictions for each dimension. Although Brown acknowledges the incidence of both metacognitive awareness and self-regulating behaviors in quite young children involved in simple tasks, she regards both of these dimensions as late developing. She (1982) supports this view by arguing that children, even child experts, are limited in the degree to which their learning and processing can be extended across domains. In her view, "children are not only hampered by being universal novices, for even when they do gain expertise it tends to be strictly constrained by context [p. 106]." Brown sees the development of self-regulation, and therefore of knowledge of cognition, as a process requiring considerable time. It seems in this work that Brown is placing more stringent criteria on what is to be accepted as both metacognitive and executive. Thus, while her view is essentially a continuity one in which both metacognitive knowledge and a range of executive skills emerge over time, it may be a view that is quite sympathetic to Piaget's definition of *cognizance* as a late-developing "true conceptualization."

In adopting this view, Brown is, however, attracted by somewhat conflicting forces. She does acknowledge, in fact has produced, evidence of both metacognitive knowledge and executive processing in the young child. In this respect she is in accord with the conclusions of Smith and Tager-Flusberg (1982) who argue for quite extensive metalinguistic abilities in 3- and 4-year-old children. Yet because of the child's limited use of these skills, due largely to lack of experience and knowledge, Brown seems to wish to deny the young recognition as self-regulatory individuals. If this latter view was applied universally, it seems that most adults would also be denied that recognition. Expertise, self-regulation, and self-knowledge are all matters of degree, and very few adults are able to be totally unconstrained by context.

A view of the development of executive processing similar to Brown's is that emerging from the work in computer simulation of cognitive processing. This approach is well represented in the work of Klahr (Klahr, 1980; Klahr & Robinson, 1981). Klahr proposes that, beyond age 5, children will not differ in structural features, such as rate and capacity, but will differ from adults in terms of knowledge, strategy, control of attention, and system of information representation. In Klahr's simulation model of cognitive development, the control or executive functions are built into the basic units of action, the productions. One interesting feature of this model is that it provides for self-modification of the production system by these control productions. The implication of this provision for a model of cognitive development is that such executive processes may play a more influential part in all processing beginning at a much earlier age than that suggested by other theorists. In fact, in the study of children's solution protocols on the Tower of Hanoi problem, Klahr and Robinson (1981) showed clear evidence of a significant range of planning, monitoring, and modification skills in children as young as age 6.

There is no one detailed and comprehensive view of the development of metacognitive knowledge and executive processing. The works of Brown and Flavell are those most developed at present, although the recent realization that the two dimensions need to be discussed separately has been cause for reconsideration. In general, the evidence from developmental studies seems to support a view of both these dimensions of cognition as developing quite early in the child and then in a fashion more compatible with a continuity than a discontinuity model of development—the evidence for stages of development in these functions seems just as problematic in these as in all other aspects of cognition (Brainerd, 1978). While the child clearly is a novice in most tasks, it seems unwise at present to deny recognition of both metacognitive and executive behavior in the young just because of this relative lack of expertise. It is important to recognize that lack of application of skills across task domains can arise from at least two sources. The first may be a lack of experience, which is not necessarily a sign either of a lack of metacognitive knowledge and executive processing or of a processing failure in the child. An alternative cause for the child being constrained by context does represent a processing problem—a failure to generalize because of the lack of suitable executive skills. Child experts are likely to be disadvantaged by the first of these (lack of experience), but that should not, of itself, make them less metacognitive or executive. It is suggested, therefore, that the search for evidence of metacognitive and executive activity in the young will be a useful exercise both theoretically and instructionally, since both dimensions have been predicted to have significant influence on task performance. It is this relationship between knowledge and control of cognition, and performance that will be reviewed in the next section.

METACOGNITIVE KNOWLEDGE, EXECUTIVE PROCESSES, AND PERFORMANCE

The study of metacognitive knowledge and executive processes is based firmly on the view that both dimensions are critical factors in affecting performance. As indicated earlier, this is a position adopted within specific congitive domains, such as language and memory, and across domains with regard to intelligence. In the literature of instructional psychology and learning disabilities, work on one or both of these dimensions is expected to provide an important source for the remediation of learning problems. While there is no reason to deviate from this position of belief, research currently available does not overwhelm the reader with findings of a consistent and positive relationship between either of these dimensions and performance. At present, the relationship between poor executive processing and poor performance is more convincingly demonstrated than that between metacognitive knowledge and performance. In fact, in the latter case, the reader is faced with quite significant disparities in research results. Research on executive processes has typically followed a deficiency-training strategy. First, researchers have attempted to show that poor performers on a given task do not exhibit a suitable executive strategy, which is present in the behavior of good performers. Good examples of these studies are available in the fields of mental retardation research (e.g., Brown, 1978; Butterfield & Belmont, 1977) and in studies of comprehension monitoring (Baker & Anderson, 1982; Garner, 1980; Paris & Myers, 1981). In both these cases, it can be shown that poor performers do not monitor their performance or modify their strategies in ways that are appropriate for changing task situations. The second stage of much of this research, particularly in mental retardation, involves training poor performers in the use of the skill that does not appear in their current repertoire. This has involved specific skills, such as monitoring memory capacity (Brown, 1978), and more general, self-instructional skills (Bornstein & Quevillon, 1976). These and other similar studies have produced quite promising results (see Borkowski & Cavanaugh, 1979), suggesting that the influence of executive processes on task performance is both significant and sensitive to instruction.

To date, there has been little effort to trace the course of executive processing in more detail, although verbal protocol studies (e.g., Chase & Ericsson, 1981; Lewis, 1981) show the complexity of the executive processing involved in typical problem solving situations. This remains a task for future studies of the nature of executive processing.

The pattern of results of studies dealing with the metacognitive knowledge–performance relationship is more inconsistent. In part, this is due to confusion about the nature of metacognitive knowledge, but it also arises from differences in research procedure.

Several researchers have examined relationships between metacognitive knowledge and performance across a number of different task domains. In several correlational studies, a weak positive relationship has been found between metamemory (metacognitive knowledge about memory) and memory performance (Cavanaugh & Borkowski, 1980; Yussen, Mathews, Buss, & Kane, 1980). These studies provide good examples of the inconsistency of the patterns of results. Cavanaugh and Borkowski (1980) found that, while this positive relationship between metamemory and memory performance held for their total sample, it disappeared when within-grade correlations were considered. They found no significant relationship between relevant memory knowledge and memory performance and could not show, at the individual level, that good metamemory knowledge was necessary for good memory performance. Yussen and Berman (1981) showed a further puzzling aspect of the metamemory–memory relationship. In their study, a significant relationship between metamemory and memory performance was present for free recall tasks but absent for recognition memory.

Studies in other fields show similarly inconsistent patterns of results. Zutell (1981) assessed the relationship between metalinguistic knowledge and spelling performance. Strong correlations were found between these two sets of measures in his kindergarten sample, but none of the correlations were significant for the Grade 1 sample at the end of the school year. In sharp contrast to Zutell's results, Leong and Haines (1978) reported a high significant canonical correlation between a set of language awareness tasks and reading performance. Smith and Tager-Flusberg (1982) also reported a correlation of $r = .75$ between level of metalinguistic knowledge and sentence comprehension. In a series of studies using a path analysis technique, Leong (1982) again reported a strong positive relationship between language awareness measures and performance on reading tasks. In a wide-ranging study, Kurdek and Burt (1981) examined relationships between the metacommunicative, metamemorial, and metasocial-cognitive skills in children in Grades 1–6. Kurdek and Burt were interested in the relationships across these three metacognitive domains, as well as in the developmental trends. The correlations between tasks within, and across, the three domains, were positive but low, and there was no consistent pattern of relationships across the grade levels. Factor analyses of the scores on these different metacognitive tests also failed to show any evidence for a general metacognition ability, and the factor loading patterns showed no consistency across grade levels.

How can we reconcile such a disparate set of results? We will consider two different arguments here that may elucidate reasons for these different patterns. In the first place, it seems that the search for a general metacognitive ability based upon measures of metacognitive knowledge does not make conceptual sense. Postulation of such an ability fails to take into account the argument made in an earlier section of this chapter that metacognitive knowledge is specific to a domain, and even specific to a given task. Thus, knowledge of linguistic processing would not be expected to generalize to the areas of communication and social cognition. The child's awareness of the nature of a word should not be expected to bear a systematic relationship to his or her understanding of what makes other children cry. So the task or domain specificity of metacognitive knowledge may account for some of the inconsistency of results.

Other inconsistencies are more difficult to explain. In some studies, such as those that have looked at the metamemory–memory relationship, the nature of the metacognitive knowledge assessment does bear a close conceptual relationship to the memory performance; for example, in Yussen and Berman's (1981) study, the predicted level of recall is related to actual recall level. Yussen and Berman did find that this relationship was quite strong, yet they also found only a modest degree of consistency across predictions for individual children. In expecting strong relationships in this type of study, we make the assumption that the possession of the metacognitive knowledge will lead to use of that knowledge. In the face of such evidence as that quoted here, we might regard this assumption as invalid and discard it. Yet to do so at present would involve an unfair trial. Rather we should consider whether the research procedures used do in fact constitute a fair test of the assumption. In essence, we must ensure that there is a high degree of congruence between the topics assessed in the test of metacognitive knowledge and the performance. A discussion of strategies for remembering how to bring skates to school tomorrow involves reflection on a task that is different from the free recall of a list of words. Lack of congruence between sets of measures could lead to unexpected results.

We can also expect that there will be other reasons for the nonuse of a strategy that is known to be appropriate for a given task. The metacognitive assessment and the performance constitute two different task environments in which the nature of the interaction between child and experimenter is different. In one, the child is asked to reflect in an open-ended manner; in the other, the child must perform against a discrete criterion. Furthermore, the task may well be one where more than one strategy can be used. A child or adult may switch rapidly between strategies once the task is encountered simply because the task makes unpredicted demands on his or her processing capacity. The analysis of individual performances in Baker and Anderson's (1982) study led those authors to suggest that subjects were using monitoring strategies that were not predicted by the experimenters, strategies to which the experimental procedures were not sensitive. Until this and the other problems in research procedure are remedied, it seems that the metacognitive knowledge–performance link will remain a hoary problem for researchers.

One final aspect of research procedure that must be considered as a possible source of inconsistency in experimental results is what different researchers accept as measures of metacognitive knowledge. In this chapter, *metacognitive knowledge* has been defined as conscious, reportable knowledge of one's cognitive activity resulting from reflection upon that activity. Tasks that are used to assess this knowledge must therefore require that the subject report knowledge that results from cognitive reflection upon an act of cognition. In the metamemory literature, these criteria have been satisfied in the majority of tasks used as measures of knowledge of mnemonic activity. In other areas, it is not clear that all measures of metacognitive knowledge have used these criteria, and this is particularly true of measures of linguistic awareness. In a frequently used assessment of linguistic awareness, Papandropolou and Sinclair (1974) include four questions that require the child to reflect upon the nature of a word (e.g., what is a word, really?)

and also four tasks that require the child to produce or invent a word (e.g., say a long word). In the first series of tasks, the child must report the results of his or her reflections upon the cognitive activity that leads to a judgment of "wordness." Yet the second set of tasks are performances—they all involve production of words and do not involve conscious reflection upon the cognitive activities used to produce the words. Any inference about awareness of cognitive activity is very indirect. What the tasks tap is the child's knowledge of words.

A similar criticism applies to other measures of linguistic awareness. Leong and Haines (1978) used four tasks, some of which had previously been used by other researchers to assess linguistic awareness. The tasks required the child to indicate the number of phonemic or syllabic segments in words; to discriminate sounds and to perceive the number and order of sources within a spoken pattern; and to recall, verbatim, sentences of different levels of complexity. These measures were combined in the study into an index of linguistic awareness. Yet the tasks differ considerably in the extent to which they satisfy the criteria of metacognitive knowledge. The sentence recall task appears to involve very little reflection on any cognitive activity—it is a performance task. The segmentation tasks tap abilities that are prerequisite for reading, and it could be argued that they are measures of a type of knowledge that need not be the result of reflection upon the process of segmentation. It could be that the child can segment words successfully without being able to reflect upon the nature of the segmentation process. Such variation in definition of measures of metacognitive knowledge must therefore be considered a significant source of variance when results from different studies of metacognitive knowledge are being compared.

CONCLUSION

Metacognitive knowledge and executive processes remain key constructs in the psychology of instruction. There is as yet little reason to deviate from the belief that research into both dimensions will have significant benefit both for our understanding of learning and for the remediation of problems in learning. We need now to reassess our understanding of the nature of both metacognition and executive processes, of the way they are related one to the other, and how they affect performance. We have argued here that knowledge of cognition can be separated logically and empirically from control of cognition, and that both aspects of cognition are causally involved in performance from an early age. Research procedures need to be refined to isolate the nature of that involvement and to trace the ways in which the child comes to know and control his or her cognitive processes.

REFERENCE NOTE

1. Belmont, J., Butterfield, E. C., & Perfetti, C. A. To secure transfer of training instruct self-management skills. Unpublished manuscript, University of Kansas, 1980.

REFERENCES

Baker, L., & Anderson, R. I. Effects of inconsistent information on text processing: Evidence for comprehension monitoring. *Reading Research Quarterly,* 1982, *17,* 281–294.

Borkowski, J. G., & Cavanaugh, J. C. Maintenance and generalization of skills and strategies by the retarded. In N. R. Ellis (Ed.), *Handbook of mental deficiency: Psychological theory and research* (2nd ed.). Hillsdale, N.J.: Erlbaum, 1979.

Bornstein, P. H., & Quevillon, R. P. The effects of a self-instructional package on overactive preschool boys. *Journal of Applied Behavior Analysis,* 1976, *9,* 179–188.

Brainerd, C. J. The stage question in cognitive-developmental theory. *Behavioral and Brain Sciences,* 1978, *1,* 173–215.

Brown, A. L. Knowing when, where, and how to remember: A problem in metacognition. In R. Glaser (Ed.), *Advances in instructional psychology* (Vol. 1). Hillsdale, N.J.: Erlbaum, 1978.

Brown, A. L. Metacognition: The development of selective attention strategies for learning from tests. In M. Kamil (Ed.), *Directions in reading: Research and Instruction.* Thirtieth yearbook of the National Reading Conference. Washington, D.C.: National Reading Conference, 1981.

Brown, A. L. Learning and development: The problems of compatibility, access, and induction. *Human Development,* 1982, *25,* 89–115.

Brown, A. L., & DeLoache, J. S. Skills, plans, and self-regulation. In R. Siegler (Ed.), *Children's thinking: What develops.* Hillsdale, N.J.: Erlbaum, 1978.

Butterfield, E. C., & Belmont, J. M. Assessing and improving the cognitive functions of mentally retarded people. In I. Bailer & M. Sternlicht (Eds.), *The psychology of mental retardation: Issues and approaches.* New York: Psychological Dimensions, 1977.

Butterfield, E. C., Wambold, C., & Belmont, J. M. On the theory and practice of improving short-term memory. *American Journal of Mental Deficiency,* 1973, *77,* 654–669.

Case, R. The underlying mechanism of intellectual development. In J. R. Kirby & J. B. Biggs (Eds.), *Cognition, development, and instruction.* New York: Academic Press, 1980.

Cavanaugh, J. C., & Borkowski, J. G. Searching for metamemory–memory connections: A developmental study. *Developmental Psychology,* 1980, *16,* 441–453.

Cavanaugh, J. C., & Perlmutter, M. Metamemory: A critical examination. *Child Development,* 1982, *53,* 11–28.

Cazden, C. B. *Child language and education.* New York: Holt, 1972.

Cazden, C. B. Metalinguistic awareness: One dimension of language experience. *The Urban Review,* 1974, *7,* 28–39.

Chase, W. G., & Ericsson, K. A. Skilled memory. In J. R. Anderson (Ed.), *Cognitive Skills and their acquisition.* Hillsdale, N.J.: Erlbaum, 1981.

Chi, M. T. H. Knowledge structures and memory development. In R. Seigler (Ed.), *Children's thinking: What develops?* Hillsdale, N.J.: Erlbaum, 1978.

Clark, E. V. Awareness of language: Some evidence from what children say and do. In A. Sinclair, R. Jarvella, & W. Levelt (Eds.), *The child's conception of language.* New York: Springer-Verlag, 1978.

Downing, J., & Leong, C. K. *Psychology of reading.* New York: MacMillan, 1982.

Flavell, J. H. *Cognitive development.* Englewood Cliffs, N.J.: Prentice-Hall, 1976.
Flavell, J. H. Metacognitive development. In J. M. Scandura & C. Brainerd (Eds.), *Structural/Process theories of complex human behavior.* Alphenan der Rijn, Netherlands: Sitjoff & Wordhoff, 1978.
Flavell, J. H. Cognitive monitoring. In P. Dickson (Ed.), *Children's oral communication skills.* New York: Academic Press, 1981.
Fredericksen, J. R. A Thurstonian's reaction to a componential theory of intelligence. *The Behavioral and Brain Sciences,* 1980, *3,* 590–591.
Garner, R. Monitoring of understanding: An investigation of good and poor readers' awareness of induced miscomprehension of text. *Journal of Reading Behavior,* 1980, *12,* 55–63.
Gelman, R. Cognitive development. *Annual Review of Psychology,* 1979, *29,* 297–332.
Hakes, D. T. *The development of metalinguistic abilities.* New York: Springer-Verlag, 1980.
Klahr, D. Information-processing models of intellectual development. In R. Kluwe & H. Spada (Eds.), *Developmental models of Thinking.* New York: Academic Press, 1980.
Klahr, D., & Robinson, M. Formal assessment of problem-solving and planning processes in preschool children. *Cognitive Psychology,* 1981, *13,* 113–148.
Kreutzer, M. A., Leonard, S. C., & Flavell, J. H. An interview study of children's knowledge about memory. *Monographs of the Society for Research in Child Development,* 1975, *40,* (1, Serial No. 159).
Kurdek, L. A., & Burt, C. W. First through sixth grade children's metacognitive skills: Generality and cognitive correlates. *Merrill-Palmer Quarterly,* 1981, *27,* 287–305.
Lawson, M. J. Metamemory: Making decisions about strategies. In J. R. Kirby & J. B. Biggs (Eds.), *Cognition, development, and instruction.* New York: Academic Press, 1980.
Leong, C. K. Cognitive strategies in relation to reading disability. In M. P. Friedman, J. P. Das, & N. O'Connor (Eds.), *Intelligence and Learning.* New York: Plenum, 1981.
Leong, C. K. Promising areas of research into learning disabilities with emphasis on reading disabilities. In J. P. Das, R. Mulcahy, & A. E. Wall. *Theory and research in learning disability.* New York: Plenum, 1982.
Leong, C. K., & Haines, C. F. Beginning readers' analysis of words and sentences. *Journal of Reading Behavior,* 1978, *10,* 393–407.
Lewis, C. Skill in algebra. In J. R. Anderson (Ed.), *Cognitive Skills and their acquisition.* Hillsdale, N.J.: Erlbaum, 1981.
Lindberg, M. A. Is knowledge base development a necessary and sufficient condition for memory development. *Journal of Experimental Child Psychology,* 1980, *30,* 401–410.
McKeithen, K. B., Reitman, J. S., Rueter, H. H., & Hirtle, S. C. Knowledge, organization and skill differences in computer programmers. *Cognitive Psychology,* 1981, *13,* 307–325.
Meichenbaum, D. A cognitive-behavioral perspective on intelligence. *Intelligence,* 1980, *4,* 271–283.
Miyake, N., & Norman, D. A. To ask a question one must know enough to know what is not known. *Journal of Verbal Learning and Verbal Behavior,* 1979, *18,* 357–364.
Papandropolou, I., & Sinclair, H. What is a word? Experimental study of children's ideas on grammar. *Human Development,* 1974, *17,* 241–258.
Paris, S. G., & Myers, M. Comprehension monitoring, memory, and study strategies of good and poor readers. *Journal of Reading Behavior,* 1981, *13,* 5–22.
Pascual-Leone, J. Constructive problems for constructive theories. In R. Kluwe & H. Spada (Eds.), *Developmental models of thinking.* New York: Academic Press, 1980.
Piaget, J. *The grasp of consciousness.* Cambridge, Mass.: Harvard Univ. Press, 1976.
Piaget, J. *Success and understanding.* London: Routledge & Kegan Paul, 1978.
Shiffrin, R. M., & Dumais, S. T. The development of automatism. In J. R. Anderson (Ed.), *Cognitive skills and their acquisition.* Hillsdale, N.J.: Erlbaum, 1981.

Simon, D. P., & Simon, H. A. Individual differences in solving physics problems. In R. Seigler (Ed.), *Children's thinking: What develops?* Hillsdale, N.J.: Erlbaum, 1978.

Simon, H. *Models of thought.* New Haven: Yale Univ. Press, 1979.

Smith, C. L., & Tager-Flusberg, H. Metalinguistic awareness and language development. *Journal of Experimental Child Psychology,* 1982, *34,* 449–468.

Snow, R. Toward a theory of aptitude for learning: I. Fluid and crystalized abilities and their correlates. In M. P. Friedman, J. P. Das, & N. O'Connor (Eds.), *Intelligence and learning.* New York: Plenum, 1981.

Sternberg, R. J. Sketch of a componential subtheory of human intelligence. *Behavioral and Brain Sciences,* 1980, *3,* 573–614.

Vygotsky, L. S. *Thought and language,* Cambridge, Mass.: MIT Press, 1962.

Yussen, S. R., & Berman, L. Memory predictions for recall and recognition in first-, third-, and fifth-grade children. *Developmental Psychology,* 1981, *17,* 224–229.

Yussen, S. R., Mathews, S. R., Buss, R. R., & Kane, P. T. Developmental changes in judging important and critical elements of stories. *Developmental Psychology,* 1980, *16,* 213–219.

Zutell, J. Cognitive development, metalinguistic ability and invented spellings: Comparisons and correlations. In M. Kamil (Ed.), *Directions in reading: Research and instruction.* Thirtieth yearbook of the National Reading Conference. Washington, D.C.: National Reading Conference, 1981.

6

Learning Strategies, Student Motivation Patterns, and Subjectively Perceived Success

Two major approaches to the study of the determinants of academic performance may be distinguished. The first emphasizes personological factors: Some people are better than others at academic tasks because they have the appropriate ability in greater measure, possess more relevant or more extensive background knowledge, and so on. The second emphasizes situational factors: Performance improves when teaching is more efficient, with greater time spent on task, under certain presentation rates and modes, and so forth. The first is the approach of the psychologist interested in individual differences and of the educator who believes that schools perform a selective rather than a formative function. The second is the approach of the experimental psychologist and of the educator who believes that schools preeminently have compensatory and formative functions.

Life is not, however, so dichotomously simple. Cronbach (1975) drew attention to limitations of each such approach and suggested the importance of the mediating and interactive relationship between personological and situational factors in determining performance when he postulated the concept of aptitude–treatment interaction (ATI). The best of both worlds may in this view be obtained if individuals high on a particular aptitude are given Treatment A and those low on that aptitude, Treatment B. Why this may be so invokes the notion of process, which in turn invokes that of strategy

Cognitive Strategies
and Educational Performance

Copyright © 1984 by Academic Press, Inc.
All rights of reproduction in any form reserved.
ISBN   0-12-409580-1

(Kirby, 1980). "Strategy" is a key concept in explicating relationships between person, situation, and performance.

Let us follow Rigney (1978) and define a cognitive strategy in terms of "the operations and procedures that the student may use to acquire, retain and retrieve different kinds of knowledge and performance (p. 165)." This is a broad definition, but it focuses the attention on what happens *between* personological and situational variables on the one hand and performance on the other. If Treatment A is better with a person high on a certain aptitude and Treatment B with a person low on that aptitude, maybe that is because the aptitude refers to particular strategies (operations and procedures) that are selectively called out by the treatments. The concept of strategy, then, appears to have some explanatory power in reconciling the two traditions.

The concept of strategy is, however, still rather broad. Strategies may further be distinguished in terms of their *distance* from the task, their *generality*, and their *teachability*. Rigney (1978), for example, distinguishes "detached" from "embedded" strategies. The former are distant from the task and generally applicable across many tasks, whereas the latter are much more task specific. The most distant and general strategies are generally the least teachable. The most distant refer to metacognitive functioning, such as planning (Ashman, Chapter 11, this volume; Lawson, 1978), and at this level become close to the concept of general intelligence, or g itself.

After abilities, the level next close to performance is that of *process* (Biggs, 1978a; Kirby & Das, 1978). Here there is some concession to the notion of ability—in the sense that some people are better than others in performing a range of tasks of a certain kind—but the major interest is in the way in which a person goes about the task, not essentially in relative mastery of task content.

The distinction between abilities and processes is something of a matter of convenience. If one is more interested in norm-referenced comparisons, *ability* would be the appropriate term; and if one is more interested in the manner of proceeding, the term *process,* which in turn relates to a broad interpretation of *strategy,* would be more appropriate. For example, Guilford's (1967) distinction between convergent and divergent processes refers to strategies in this sense. A convergent strategy requires the assembling of component data and operations to yield the one correct answer; a divergent strategy requires the production of several alternate products. Another conceptualization in the same mold is that of Das, Kirby, and Jarman's (1979) model of simultaneous and successive synthesis, which has been used particularly to derive strategies relevant to academic tasks. For example, different stages in the acquisition of reading skill have been isolated in terms of the relative predominance of simultaneous or successive processing, and intervention strategies may be devised accordingly (Kirby & Das, 1977; Krywaniuk, 1974).

Closer still to the task is the concept of strategy assumed in Biggs's (1978b) model of study processes, which unlike the other models has an idiographic element. Here it is postulated that the strategies students select and use when approaching an academic task will depend upon their perceptions of the task, in terms of what they see as being required of them in the learning situation if they are to meet their goals, as well as upon their basic ability–process profiles.

Finally, strategies may be located very close to the task, yet be general enough to be independent of the content of any particular one. Such strategies are often quite amenable to teaching, as Case (1972) has dramatically demonstrated.

The term *strategy* may therefore be used in rather different ways and at different levels of generality: Three such levels have been distinguished here and may be termed *macrostrategies, mesostrategies,* and *microstrategies,* respectively. These operate within an overall framework, which includes an individual's basic abilities, the situational context, and the performance output. This framework is outlined in the next section.

A GENERAL MODEL OF ACADEMIC PERFORMANCE

In a performance situation, three broad sets of variables can be distinguished: *independent, intervening,* and *dependent.* True independent variables are those that exist prior to and independently of any particular performance, and would include the personological and situational factors mentioned in the previous section. The former would include abilities, processes, cognitive styles, personality factors, and relevant prior knowledge: All these are nomothetic in nature. The latter would include such factors as the nature, content, and difficulty of the task, and the context in which it is presented and evaluated and in which previous related tasks have been taught: All these are instructional in nature.

Intervening variables occur in descending order of generality and would include macro-, meso-, and microstrategies, and such affective components as the student's motivations for performing, or not performing, the task: Here idiographic considerations have an important place.

Finally, performance comprises the dependent variables, which may be evaluated either nomothetically, in terms of how well the performance meets general or *cross-individual* expectations or standards, or idiographically, in terms of how well the performance meets the individual's *own* expectations. These relationships are outlined in Figure 6.1. There are

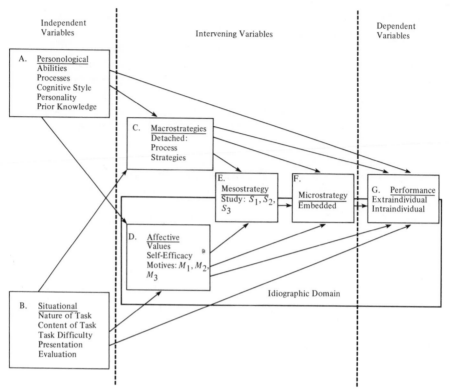

Figure 6.1. Independent, intervening, and dependent variables in academic performance.

many interrelationships depicted in the figure, and it is possible only to trace the major outline here before moving on to the major focus of this chapter.

Independent Variables

A. Personological

The major factors here have been the subject of much psychological research, in the individual differences tradition, relating personological factors directly to performance, along path AG (e.g., Lavin, 1965). Two other paths are of interest here: AC, linking abilities to macrostrategies (e.g., Das *et al.,* 1979), and AD, linking cognitive style and personality factors to values (Hudson, 1968), abilities to beliefs in self-efficacy (Bandura, 1977), and personality to academic motivation (Biggs & Das, 1973).

B. Situational

Situational and instructional factors have an obvious and direct link to performance (BG). In addition, they relate to process (BC) (Das *et al.*, 1979) and to affective factors (BD): A student's beliefs in his or her self-efficacy and motivation will depend in part on how difficult he or she judges the task to be (Bandura, 1977).

Intervening Variables

C. Macrostrategies

Macrostrategies refer to the general way in which a student will order and relate data in the face of particular tasks. Das and his colleagues have found direct relationships with performance (CG). Krywaniuk (1974), for example, gave Canadian Indians training in successive processing and improved their reading achievement. Macrostrategies also determine increasingly specific interactions between student and task. Kirby and Biggs (1981), for example, found relationships between simultaneous and successive processing and students' typical learning (meso-) strategies (such as reproduction by rote and searching for meaning, as discussed later), and Lawson and Kirby (1981) related processes along path CF to task-specific microstrategies for handling Raven's Coloured Progressive Matrices.

D. Affective

Here we are entering the idiographic domain: how the student perceives his or her task. Mischel (1973) refers to this as an individual's "encoding strategy" (which is yet another meaning of *strategy*) as a result of which he or she brings "self-regulatory systems"into play; that is, the student does something about it, at the level of both meso- (DE) and microstrategies (DF). Additionally, direct links between motivation and performance (DG) have long been established (e.g., Lavin, 1965).

This perception by students of a task incorporates a variety of concepts, including the students' values (what importance they accord the task and its context); their beliefs in their self-efficacy (i.e, how well they believe they will be able to handle the task, which is closely related to their intrinsic interest in it [Bandura, 1977]), and their specific motives, which may be extrinsic or instrumental (referred to as M_1), intrinsic(M_2), or achievement related (M_3) (Biggs, 1978b).

E. Mesostrategy

Mesostrategies are middle level—less general than process-related strategies, but not as embedded as task-related microstrategies—and refer to learning styles and study strategies in the context of academic performance. The use here is identical to Rigney's (1978) reference to "detached strategies." Such strategies have been studied in a nomothetic context, as in the usual study skills courses—for example, SQ3R (Robinson, 1961). They have also been studied idiographically—for example, by Marton and Sälsjö (1976a, 1976b), who noted how students adopt "surface level" and "deep level" strategies when faced with particular academic tasks. Biggs (1978b) distinguishes three such mesostrategies: reproducing (S_1), meaning (S_2), and organizing (S_3).

Such strategies may apply across a wide range of tasks, or with differential effectiveness to classes of tasks—for example, science-related tasks as opposed to humanities-related tasks (Biggs, 1976; Kirby & Biggs, 1981). In this last case, mesostrategies may set general constraints within which microstrategies may be appropriately deployed or not, as suggested in path EF.

F. Microstrategies

Strategies at the micro level are closely tied to the nature of the task. They are transferable across different tasks of the same kind, such as writing history essays on different topics, but are not directly transferable across different kinds of tasks. These strategies are the most teachable in context.

This model, then, suggests a complex interaction between independent, intervening, and dependent variables, in which both nomothetic and idiographic approaches are applicable. Thus, some studies relate training in microstrategies to performance in the traditional interventionist framework (e.g., Lawson & Kirby, 1981), whereas others study the mesostrategies that students spontaneously adopt and that make sense to them (e.g., Svensson, 1976).

There are advantages and disadvantages of each methodology. Referring specifically to Marton and Sälsjö (1967a, 1976b) idiographic and phenomenological approach to student learning, Entwistle and Hounsell (1979) say that this work is to some extent "subjective and impressionistic—such methods can also mislead by swamping the researcher in particularities of doubtful general validity [p. 361]." On the other hand, the nomothetic, and particularly psychometric, approach has not been noticeably successful: It is in fact difficult to find general statements of prescriptive and instructional value based on this approach.

The problem is that educational psychology needs to reconcile *generality* with *perspective*. Idiographic research adopts the participant's perspective; nomothetic research that of the "dispassionate observer." Both perspectives are needed, but they have proceeded in separation from each other, having different conceptual backgrounds and methodologies, and this makes them hard to reconcile. Nevertheless, they *are* complementary, and each adds something to our understanding of the determinants of academic performance. Kirby and Biggs (1981), for example, showed that Grade 9 students typically perceived the appropriateness of different mesostrategies to their motivational patterns to vary according to the predominance of simultaneous or successive processing in their abilities profile: High use of a meaning strategy was aligned to achievement motivation in high simultaneous students, and high use of a reproducing strategy to achievement motivation in high successive students.

Given this complexity both within and across nomothetic and idiographic domains, it is small wonder that relatively scant attention has been accorded, until recently, to intervening variables. As noted earlier, performance has usually been predicted by main effects either from the personological domain (e.g., the large but mostly nonexplanatory relationships with such broad factors as *g*) or from the situational domain, which in instructional research has not been markedly successful. Aptitude– treatment interaction (Cronbach & Snow, 1977) was a theoretically helpful reconciliation of the two traditions, but practically speaking it has had minimal impact.

The present study looks at the intervening variables and performance from an idiographic perspective. We shall be concentrating particularly on D, E, and G (i.e., students' motivational patterns, their mesostrategies, and their own perceptions of their success). In concentrating attention in this way, it must not, however, be forgotten that these are just components in a much larger general picture, and by sorting out these relationships, it is to be hoped that the larger picture will itself become clearer.

THE STUDY PROCESS COMPLEX

The intervening variables in Figure 6.1 contain a "study process complex" that consists of the student's motives and mesostrategies for studying (boxes D and E).

In work carried out over several years (Biggs, 1970, 1976), the writer constructed a 10-scale questionnaire covering common study behaviors (such as note taking and scheduling) and affective aspects (such as dogmatism, motivation, and test anxiety) that other writers have associated with academic performance. Each dimension was conceptually distinct, although there were intercorrelations between them in practice. It was found, in fact, that between 62% and 66% of the common variance of these 10 dimensions could be accounted for in a three-factor second-order structure, which recurred over three quite diverse populations in Australia and Canada

(Biggs, 1978b). When the three sets of factor scores were correlated with the original items, it was found that each such dimension consisted of two groups—an affective or motivational group, and a cognitive group—the items of which outlined a clear strategy (see Table 6.1).

This model in fact fits in well with Mischel's (1973) descriptions of how people behave in situations: Students' "encoding strategies" of a learning context, or institution as a whole, are represented by their *motives* (i.e., to gain a qualification, to pursue their academic interests, to gain highest grades, or any one or combination of these), and their "self-regulatory systems" by the *strategies* they adopt (reproducing limited content, etc.). There is, in other words, a "psycho-logic" in how people construe their situations and what they decide to do about them. If a student decides he or she wants only to pass, then it makes sense to the student (if not to the teacher) to rote learn only those facts and details on which the student knows (or guesses) he or she will be tested. If a student is interested in a subject, then it makes sense to the student to find out as much as he or she can about it and work out what it all means, whether or not the student is tested on the content.

Marton and Sälsjö (1976a; 1976b), working from phenomenological psychology, came to a very similar position. They distinguished "surface-level" and "deep-level" processing, which correspond quite closely in practice to the reproducing and meaningful strategies, and showed that students would adopt one or the other means of processing academic tasks according to their intentions in approaching the task in the first place. If they wished merely to learn the words or significates of the task (i.e., to display the symptoms of having learned), they would adopt a surface-level approach; if they wanted to extract maximum meaning by understanding what is sig-

TABLE 6.1
Relationships between Motive and Strategy in Studying

Dimension	Motive	Strategy
D_1: Utilizing	M_1: Instrumental: main purpose is to gain a qualification, with pass-only aspirations and a corresponding fear of failure.	S_1: Reproducing: limit target to bare essentials and reproduce through rote learning.
D_2: Internalizing	M_2: Intrinsic: study to actualize interest and competence in particular academic subjects.	S_2: Meaning: read widely, interrelate with previous relevant knowledge.
D_3: Achieving	M_3: Achievement: obtain highest grades, whether or not material is interesting.	S_3: Organizing: follow up all suggested readings, schedule time, behave as "model student."

nified by the words, they would adopt a deep-level strategy. On reading a short extract from a textbook, for instance, undergraduates with intentions for surface-level learning would report: "Well, I just tried to remember as much as possible" and "sort of memorize as I read." And those using deep-level strategies: "Try to find out what it is all about" and "try to think about how the author built up his argument [from Marton & Sälsjö, 1976a, p. 119]."

The factor analyses, and the idiographic models of Mischel and Marton, thus come up with highly compatible results. The factor analyses provide the basis of the structure of the domain; the idiographic models suggest hypotheses as to how the component motives and strategies relate both to each other and to performance. The following hypotheses may be formulated:

(a) *A formal learning situation generates three common expectations: to obtain a qualification with minimal effort, to actualize one's interests, and to publicly manifest one's excellence.* These expectations correspond to the three motives in Table 6.1. There may well be other motives, such as social ones, but they are not considered here. These three categories of motives correspond well to those nominated in the psychological literature (e.g., Biggs & Telfer, 1981) for motivating academic performance: extrinsic, including both positive reinforcement (task as a means to a desired end) and negative reinforcement (fear of failure); intrinsic; and need achievement. While these motive patterns were derived empirically from tertiary situations, there is no reason why they should not be relevant to high school also.

(b) *Students may endorse any or all of these motives to any extent (the dimensions are independent).* For example, a student may be both intrinsically and achievement motivated (and in fact we shall see that the top-performing students are so motivated).

(c) *It would seem good "psycho-logic" for students to adopt the strategy most appropriate to their own complex of motives.* In other words, instrumental motivation (M_1) is congruent with the reproducing strategy (S_1), intrinsic motivation (M_2) with the meaning strategy (S_2), and achievement motivation (M_3) with the organizing strategy (S_3).

(d) *The motivational mix—and consequent strategy adoption—may vary from subject area to subject area, and from time to time.* For instance, a student who is basically intrinsically interested in one particular subject, and is continuing at school or university in order to pursue it, may nevertheless be instrumentally motivated toward another subject that is needed to make up his or her course pattern; in that case, the student would have pass-only aspirations toward that subject.

(e) *The three strategies are likely to lead to different levels of quality of learn-*

ing. Reproducing is likely to lead to high factual recall, but low meaningfulness; the meaningful strategy is likely to lead to greatest structural complexity; and organizing is likely to lead to whatever goals the student sees as most pertinent to high grades. These predictions were generally confirmed for university students in a study by Biggs (1979) and for Grade 9 students by Kirby and Biggs (1981).

(f) *The effectiveness of strategy deployment is hypothesized to depend upon congruence between strategy and motive.* As just outlined, reproducing is congruent with instrumental motivation (thus forming the utilizing dimension), meaningful learning with intrinsic motivation (internalizing), and organizing with achievement motivation (achieving). Congruence in this case is likely to achieve the result most consistent with the student's goals and hence lead to higher student satisfaction, if not performance (if high performance is not the student's goal).

In general, then, this would suggest that students adopt learning strategies according to the construction they put upon their roles in the learning situation, as indexed by the combinations of motives they bring to the learning task, and that *congruent* motive–strategy combinations would be more effective than *incongruent* ones.

These hypotheses are investigated in the present study in high school and tertiary student populations, where performance is indexed by self-rated ability and by student satisfaction.

A STUDY OF STRATEGY SELECTION AND USE

Learning–Study Process Questionnaire

Motive and strategy preferences are measured by essentially the same instrument in both secondary and tertiary populations. The Learning Process Questionnaire (LPQ) is a 36-item Likert format questionnaire, containing 6 items for each motive and strategy worded to suit the high school context; the Study Process Questionnaire (SPQ) is a 42-item Likert format questionnaire, containing 7 items for each motive and strategy, referring to the same targets as those in the LPQ but worded to suit the college–university context.[1]

---

[1]The data on which the present investigation is based are part of a larger enquiry into the distribution of motives and learning strategies in high school and tertiary populations in Australia. This work will result in national norms available for both questionnaires (Biggs, Note 1).

Subjectively Perceived Success

A General Information Questionnaire was also administered with the LPQ and SPQ. In particular, two items relating to subjectively perceived success were included:

Self-Rated Performance (SR). Students were asked to rate themselves on a five-point scale, ranging from "quite poor" to "excellent," in answer to the question: "In general, compared to others in your year/class, how good at tertiary studies (SPQ)/your schoolwork (LPQ) are you?"

Satisfaction with Performance (SP). Students were asked to rate themselves on a five-point scale, ranging from "not at all satisfied" to "very satisfied indeed" in answer to: "How *satisfied* are you with your current level of performance (whether your performance is actually high or low)?"

Given the idiographic nature of the background theory, the subjective measures are coherent with the motivational measures: That is, students say "I am studying because I want to" and then estimate how successful they are and whether that performance satisfies them or not. It is of course also important to ask whether or not they actually achieve well or poorly, but the constraints under which the tertiary data particularly were gathered included anonymity, thus making it impossible to link students' responses with grade point average or some other performance measure. That question is currently under separate investigation.

Samples

The high school samples[2] involved precise two-stage cluster sampling across Australia: 50 schools were randomly drawn, each school having a probability according to size of being selected, and clusters of 27 students were randomly selected for each school. The target populations were (*a*) all students turning 14 years of age between October 1, 1978 and September 30, 1979 ($N = 1350$); and (*b*) all students in Grade 11 in 1979 ($N = 879$).

The tertiary samples were necessarily voluntary and involved 15 institutions in five Australian states. Questionnaires were administered at the beginning of lectures and were returned by the students (with reminders) in the ensuing week(s): Overall wastage was around 60%, which is unfortunately large but not atypically so for this procedure. The target populations were (*c*) college students with particular reference to arts, education, sci-

[2]The writer is indebted to Dr. J. P. Keeves and Dr. J. Lokan, Australian Council for Educational Research, for invaluable assistance in the collection of these data.

ence, and related faculties or schools (N = 1398); and (d) university students in like faculties (N = 879).

Analyses

The main analyses are as follows:

1. Correlations between all motives (Ms) and all strategies (Ss). According to congruence theory, the r between a motive and its apposite strategy would be higher than that between that motive and other strategies; for example, M_1 would correlate higher with S_1 than with S_2 or S_3.
2. Three-way ANOVAs ($M_1 \times M_2 \times M_3$) on both SR and SP for each of the four samples.
3. Correlations between strategies and subjectively perceived success within each motivational group.

As the three motivational dimensions are orthogonal, there are eight motivationally distinct groups if each dimension is split at the median. The motivational dynamics are postulated to differ between groups; for example, a student fitting the LHL pattern (i.e., low on instrumental [M_1] and high on intrinsic [M_2] and low on achievement [M_3]) may differ quite markedly in his or her motivational dynamics from a student fitting the LHH pattern (i.e., low on the M_1, high on M_2, and high on M_3), although the difference is only in one motive, M_3.

It was decided to use the correlations within each motivational group, rather than a four-way ANOVA ($M_1 \times M_2 \times M_3 \times S_x$) to examine strategy effects, because the interest is on the relative size of the effect a strategy has on performance for a given motivational pattern, not on which use is the "best" overall motivational and strategy combination.

Results

Congruence between Motives and Strategies

The correlations between motives and strategies are reproduced in Table 6.2. As can be seen, the crucial correlations (boxed) are higher for a motive and its congruent strategy than for that motive and any other strategy (circled). The only exception to this is in the college data, where M_3 correlates .31 with S_3 but .32 with S_2. Sometimes motive–motive or strategy–strategy correlations are higher than the congruent motive–strategy correlation (e.g., S_3 correlates with S_2 consistently higher than it does with M_3), but that is irrelevant to considerations of motive–strategy congruence.

Essentially, then, these data confirm the original second-order factor

TABLE 6.2
Congruent (Boxed) and Incongruent (Circled) Motive (M)–Strategy (S) Correlations[a]

	Age 14 (Grade 11)						University					
	M_1	S_1	M_2	S_2	M_3	S_3	M_1	S_1	M_2	S_2	M_3	S_3
M_1	—	[31]	24	(18)	26	(20)	—	[41]	01	(02)	26	(11)
S_1	[31]	—	(−05)	−07	(02)	18	[43]	—	(−11)	−13	(20)	04
M_2	07	−16	—	[60]	47	(41)	−11	(−17)	—	[58]	31	(35)
S_2	(02)	−23	[51]	—	(44)	45	(−10)	−26	[62]	—	32	50
M_3	23	(−02)	29	(32)	—	[45]	26	(22)	25	(24)	—	[31]
S_3	(18)	−28	(38)	50	[44]	—	(10)	01	(31)	48	[31]	—

[a] Decimals omitted.

analyses (Biggs, 1978b) that led to the present formulation. What they do not tell us, however, is whether these congruent pairings are the most *effective,* in terms of subjectively perceived success.

Three-way ANOVAs

The motive main effects and some interactions in the three-way ANOVAs were highly significant (see Table 6.3), following path DG in

TABLE 6.3
Motive Main Effects and Interactions on Subjectively Perceived Success

	Age 14			Grade 11			College			University		
	N	SR	SP	N	SR	SP	N	SR	SP	N	SR	SP
LLL	400	3.16	3.21	205	3.16	2.83	282	3.17	2.97	174	3.18	2.84
LLH	114	3.65	3.67	85	3.52	3.29	115	3.35	3.15	73	3.52	3.05
LHL	126	3.35	3.41	114	3.36	2.87	201	3.25	3.03	127	3.38	2.97
LHH	158	3.75	3.75	108	3.71	3.42	193	3.56	3.19	127	3.72	2.98
HLL	151	3.16	3.14	144	3.09	2.64	182	3.07	2.85	106	3.09	2.80
HLH	118	3.43	3.43	93	3.43	3.04	135	3.22	3.15	109	3.30	2.90
HHL	105	3.27	3.44	93	3.20	2.82	98	3.06	3.06	45	3.11	2.85
HHH	178	3.40	3.51	137	3.45	3.10	192	3.31	3.31	118	3.42	2.95
M_1		000	01		01	01		000	—		000	10
M_2		10	10		01	—		05	—		01	—
M_3		000	000		000	000		000	01		000	—
$M_1 \times M_2$		—	—		—	—		05	—		—	—
$M_1 \times M_3$		01	10		—	—		—	—		—	—
$M_2 \times M_3$		—	—		—	—		—	10		—	—
$M_1 \times M_2 \times M_3$		—	—		—	—		—	—		—	—

Figure 6.1. M_1 and M_3 have consistently strong main effects, M_2 rather weaker ones, and a few interactions are significant.

It can be seen that the means of the eight motivational subgroups, for both SR and SP over all four populations, form a remarkably constant rank ordering within populations, whether in terms of SR or SP, and whether at school or at tertiary level. (Over all such conditions, the consistency of ranking was very highly significant.) The overall rank order is therefore a highly stable index of the relative perceived success of the eight groups.

It is worth noting that achievement motivation (M_3) dominates the rank ordering, all four high M_3 groups leading the low M_3 groups. Differences within M_3 are ordered according to interactions with M_1 and M_2.

Congruence between Motivational Patterns and Strategies, and Perceived Success

Correlations were then calculated with motivational groups between S_{1-3} and SR and SP. The Ns within the motivational groups are given in Table 6.3. There is some variation between group Ns (due to the motive intercorrelations presented in Table 6.2), so that the smallest group is 45, the others ranging from 73–400. These within-group correlations between strategy and perceived success are given in Tables 6.4(a) for self-rated performance (SR) and 6.4(b) for satisfaction with performance (SP). These results are complex and are discussed in the following section.

DISCUSSION

Congruence between Motives and Strategies

In general, the pattern outlined in Table 6.1 is confirmed: Students endorsing a particular motive as predominant tend to choose its congruent strategy rather than another strategy. That is, instrumentally motivated students tend to use the reproducing strategy more than any other; intrinsically motivated, the meaning strategy; and achievement motivated, the organizing strategy. These correlations range from .31 to .62, so that, while the general pattern is as expected, it still remains an open question whether congruent and incongruent motive–strategy mixes correlate with performance in the expected manner.

Effects on Perceived Success of Congruent and Incongruent Motive–Strategy Combinations

We are interested here in the effects congruent and incongruent motive–strategy combinations may have on subjectively perceived perfor-

TABLE 6.4
Within-Group Correlations between Strategies and (a) Self-Rated Performance (SR) and (b) Satisfaction with Performance (SP)

	(a) Self-rated performance				(b) Satisfaction with performance			
	Age 14	Grade 11	College	University	Age 14	Grade 11	College	University
1. S_1								
LHH	-205**	-242**	-117	-027	-276**	-001	030	029
LLH	129	-133	-080	-169	140	-061	-048	-104
HHH	-300**	-323**	-178*	-126	-209**	-159*	050	-118
HLH	-111	-151	061	-160*	033	-096	040	-180*
LHL	-373*	-289**	-213**	-106	-101	-169*	000	004
LLL	-156*	-188**	013	-100	-112*	-137*	030	068
HHL	-145	-170*	-238*	-231*	-170*	-155	-231*	-017
HLL	019	-080	-174*	015	090	-157	000	-036
2. S_2								
LHH	126	192*	083	065	-006	-016	080	-011
LLH	-161*	127	086	-024	106	103	055	021
HHH	012	-154*	091	034	069	029	104	-060
HLH	028	034	-015	059	083	005	133	138
LHL	165*	073	043	080	-006	-016	080	-011
LLL	038	085	173*	-001	126*	070	033	017
HHL	168	095	004	183	-011	-003	116	072
HLL	066	-008	119	-016	-002	-103	-081	080
3. S_3								
LHH	098	-150	039	-047	193*	274**	203**	135
LLH	059	064	174*	-177	261**	023	254**	094
HHH	075	-011	008	-076	056	088	213**	242*
HLH	-015	175*	-026	133	098	213*	105	407**
LHL	213*	044	-022	-090	172*	159*	177*	148*
LLL	163**	137*	112*	022	251**	261**	132*	151*
HHL	244*	008	246**	219	127	169*	265**	241*
HLL	-050	183*	-043	102	128	267**	119	189*

mance. Such an exploration has practical as well as theoretical value, in that the results may suggest suitable strategies for students with particular motivational patterns.

It is evident from Table 6.4 that strategies have different effects across the motivational groups, both within and across samples.

S_1: Reproducing Strategy

The significant effects of S_1 on both SR and SP are uniformly negative, with effects being stronger and more numerous on SR than on SP, and they appear in one sample or another, in all motivational groups except for the LLH group. That is, those students who are *solely* achievement motivated, and who are already high achievers, alone seem able to handle rote reproductive learning in a way that is at least not detrimental to either their self-ratings of performance or to their satisfaction.

In general, however, these results for S_1 offer little support for the congruence hypothesis, which would postulate that highly pragmatic students (HXX) would at least be *satisfied* with a reproductive strategy. One might even expect, particularly at younger levels in high school, that a reproductive strategy may be seen to be advantageous by HXX students.

S_2: Meaningful Strategy

Effects of S_2 are much less numerous and involve two disordinal interactions. S_2 is positively associated with SR in the age 14 LHL group, but negatively with SR in the age 14 LLH group. That is, a meaning strategy is *not* conducive to perceived success with students who are solely achievement motivated, but it *is* with students who are intrinsically motivated, which confirms the congruence hypothesis. The other disordinal interaction in the Grade 11 group only partially confirms that hypothesis: S_2 is positively associated with SR in the LHH group (congruent) but negatively in the HHH group (noncongruent). In high school, the solely intrinsically motivated (LHL) (age 14) and the top-performing intrinsically and achievement motivated (LHH) (Grade 11) see S_2 as improving their performance, which is in keeping with the congruence hypothesis, but so too do unmotivated (LLL) college students, which is not. Only one group (age 14, LLL) shows S_2 related to satisfaction. All correlations are weak, whether with SR or SP.

S_3: Organizing Strategy

Patterns for S_3 are much clearer. With regard to SR, only two samples in the high-achieving groups saw that using S_3 was associated with high performance, whereas all samples in the low-achieving group did. This is, of course, contrary to the congruence hypothesis.

The most striking thing about the SP data is that *all* groups using S_3 felt more satisfied with their performance, whereas only low-achieving students felt it placed them advantageously in terms of performance. Possibly, high-achieving students have their own ways of achieving their good results, and those ways are not necessarily tapped by the strategies sampled here (see results for S_2 and S_1). It is noteworthy that the achieving motive itself had consistently strong main effects on subjectively perceived performance, except for university SP (see Table 6.3). This would at least suggest that achievement motivation makes students feel good about their work, and as a result perceive that they are doing well and generally feel satisfied about it. Whether achievement-motivated students actually perform better is a most important question that cannot unfortunately be answered with these data. If they do, the next question would involve isolating any particular strategies that they use. It is possible that such strategies would be micro-strategies, bound up with the particular tasks attempted, rather than the mesostrategy (S_3) that is congruent with the motive M_3.

Returning to the present data, the most consistent S_3 effects were obtained in the totally unmotivated group, the LLLs. This seems to suggest that organizing and structuring is something that is beneficial, especially to those students who are not achievement or intrinsically motivated. While S_3 is not a strategy that these students tend spontaneously to adopt (see Table 6.2), when they do, they are better off for it, at least phenomenologically. Going through the motions—of submitting assignments on time, scheduling work, etc.—at least makes the student, particularly the underachieving student, feel better about his or her work. To that extent, the usual study habits courses that emphasize organizing (e.g., Robinson's, 1961, SQ3R program) may have a therapeutic effect on the student. The next point, as mentioned, is whether that phenomenological effect is reflected in actual performance, but that cannot be decided with the present data.

Motivational Patterns and Congruence

The findings so far are somewhat paradoxical. On the one hand, it is found that students from middle high school to university tend to adopt learning and study strategies that are congruent with their motives for learning. On the other hand, there is mixed evidence that congruent strategy–motive combinations are beneficial in terms of how students see their overall performance. Thus, while S_2 was often effective with intrinsically motivated students, S_3 was particularly effective with low achievement motivated students.

We are dealing here with overall estimates of performance, not with performance in particular subjects. It is possible that effects might be quite different when actual performance in different content areas is taken into account. Kirby and Biggs (1981), for example, found that particular motive–strategy combinations were differentially effective in English and mathematics in Grade 9.

The motivational groups describe a typology of student motivation. It might help to attempt to capture the flavor of each and note whether strategy effects, if significant, are congruent or incongruent with the motivational pattern. This is summarized in Table 6.5.

The motivational groups are arranged in descending order of perceived effectiveness, with a label attached to give a feeling for the motivational pattern in each. Since the M scales are correlated, the groups are of unequal size: The column "Percentage Total" gives the relative size of each. The next three columns refer to "Congruent," "Nonsignificant," and "Incongruent" strategy effects; the final three give an indication of relative strength and direction of strategy effects ("+" meaning moderate positive effect; "+ +," very strong positive effect; "0," no significant effect; etc.).

The only two groups that have unequivocally congruent effects are the most effective: "ambitious academics" (who were also the most numerous in the sample) and "competitive achievers." The third most effective group, the "hogs" (socalled because they are high on all motives), behave quite contrary to the congruence hypothesis in that all strategy effects should be positive, but S_1 and even S_2 are negative, while S_3 is only minimally effective. They seem to be achieving their relative effectiveness and satisfactions through sheer motivation, using means (strategies) that are not evident here. "Careerists" are motivated to get ahead by minimal effort; strategy effects are generally weak, except in university, where S_3 is strong as far as SP is concerned. As effective performance decreases, so the proportion of noncongruent strategy use increases, there being no effective congruent uses at all in the last two, "defensive achievers" and "underachievers."

We thus have a situation where the two most effective motivational groups have no strategy–performance correlations that involve *incongruent* motive–strategy combinations and the two least effective groups have no *congruent* motive–strategy combinations. Thus, although the size of the effects is weak and the effects themselves are scattered over the four samples, the general pattern is clear.

High-performing groups make effective use of strategies that are congruent with predominant motives; low-performing groups make effective use of strategies that are irrelevant to, or incongruent with, prevailing motives. Those who are inadequately motivated to perform well, in other words, make use of any strategies, whereas those who are adaptively motivated utilize strategies in a way that is consistent with their motivation (and performance, as subjectively estimated).

TABLE 6.5
Summary of Strategy Effects[a]

Rank	Group	Percentage total	Congruent	Nonsignificant	Incongruent	S_1	S_2	S_3
1. LHH	Ambitious academics	23.0	7	17	0	--	+	++
2. LLH	Competitive achievers	9.3	4	20	0	0	-	++
3. HHH	Hogs	11.8	2	16	6	--	-	+
4. HLH	Careerists	13.6	3	9	2	-	0	+
5. LHL	Idealists	10.1	5	14	5	--	+	+
6. LLL	Logs	10.8	4	11	9	--	+	++
7. HHL	Defensive actualizers	7.0	0	15	10	-	0	++
8. HLL	Underachievers	14.4	0	19	5	-	0	+

[a] + Moderate positive effect; ++ strong positive effect; 0 no effect; - moderate negative effect; -- strong positive effect.

Spontaneous versus Instructed Strategy Use

One of the major implications for education practice arising out of the present work would revolve around the question of improving the learning–study strategies of students. This has been an aim of many workers, and it has been achieved with varying success. Mostly such work involves S_3-type strategies—organizing, scheduling, keeping notes, etc.—for students with poor motivation and poor study habits. Although such a strategy is not congruent with low motivation (LLL), the evidence is that S_3 had more positive effects, with respect both to perceived effectiveness and to satisfaction, in the LLL group than in any other. The strategy is not, however, indicated in other groups—for example, the LHH (ambitious academic) group at university.

This evidence of interaction, then, leads to the other major point arising from this study: Strategies are differentially effective according to the student's motivational pattern. In other words, how a student is motivated will determine:

1. *What* strategies the student selects
2. *How effectively* the student wields those strategies

If the world were simple, the two questions would coalesce: That is, the effective student would be the one who selects a strategy cognate to his or her motivation. We see in Table 6.5 that this is partially true. The best performing groups (LHH and LLH) were those who used cognate strategies; thus, LHH should avoid reproducing (S_1) and use meaningful (S_2) and organizing (S_3) strategies, and LLH should avoid the first two and use only organizing. The worst performing groups (HHL and HLL), on the other hand, should, it appears, avoid reproducing (cognate) and use organizing (not cognate) strategies: These uses are incongruent with the motivational pattern. One obviously needs to know more: How did these incongruent strategy uses work in practice? Were actual results poor, despite the subjective impressions of the students concerned? What was their quality of performance like?

There are two, not unrelated, issues here:

1. How do students choose to adopt the strategies they do?
2. At what point should the educator intervene and teach strategies, even if they are incongruent to the student's motivational pattern?

According to the congruence hypothesis, students choose strategies that make sense in their scheme of things. Most students relate S_1 with M_1, S_2 with M_2, and S_3 with M_3, as appeared in the original factor analyses (Biggs, 1978b), in Kirby and Biggs (1981), and in Table 6.2. But what about those who do not, who relate S_2, S_3, or some other strategy to their prevailing M_1? Obviously, such strategy selection is naturalistic, it makes some sense to the student, no matter how inconsistent it is with the selection patterns of the majority of students or how incongruent with the "psycho-logic" imposed by Mischel, Biggs, or anyone else. In an idiographic theory, it is the student's *own* "psycho-logic" that is important. That students might make odd choices of strategy, whether viewed against what the majority do or against theory, is interesting in itself. It is even more interesting when it is discovered that those strategy choices do lead to *worse* self-perception of performance and to considerable dissatisfaction (see Table 6.4). Further, as Table 6.5 indicates, it is the low-achieving students who make these incongruent strategy choices and who use those strategies in ways that would seem to be inappropriate.

Another way of putting this is that high-achieving students choose and use strategies that are appropriate. This observation fits a finding by Kirby and Biggs (1981) that Grade 9 students who were high on either simultaneous ability, successive ability, or both made appropriate choices as to strategy. Those high on both abilities discriminated all three strategy options (S_1, S_2, and S_3) and related them appropriately to motivational patterns. Those high on simultaneous ability alone perceived S_2 and S_3 as the most appropriate strategies, with S_1 as irrelevant, whereas those high on successive ability discriminated S_1 and S_3, with S_2 as irrelevant. Students low on both abilities fused S_1, S_2, and S_3 into an overall unarticulated approach. Paradoxically, however, correlations between strategy use and test performance in mathematics and English were higher in this last group than in the others. It is as if these students have few resources (motivational or cognitive), and as long as they do something—anything—they are relatively better off than those of similar ability who do nothing metacognitive about learning. Those students who are well motivated, or who have cognitive resources of some other kind, use those resources, and hence, compared to the students without those resources, strategy effects are relatively smaller.

This provides support in a roundabout way for an observation by Rigney (1978) that bright students select and use their own appropriate macrostrategies (detached), whereas dull students would perhaps be better off by being taught strategies, especially microstrategies (embedded) that are close to each task. The present discussion, then, would answer the first question by suggesting that high-achieving students spontaneously select and use appropriate strategies mostly according to the congruence hypothesis. Low-achieving students, on the other hand, do not select or use strategies in this way: Rather it is any port in a storm.

To answer the second question, then, intervention is indicated in the lower performing, maladaptively motivated groups, since it appears at this level that congruence of strategy to motive is irrelevant. Even when S_3 is inappropriate, it leads the low-achieving users to *perceive* that they are doing relatively well compared to their peers. If we compare the top four motivational groups in terms of self-rated performance with the bottom four, there are two significant uses of S_3 (both congruent) in groups LHH to HLH, and seven significant uses (all incongruent) in groups LHL to HLL: This difference in *number* of effects is significant ($\chi^2 = 5.56$ for 1 *df*), and that for their *congruence* is highly significant ($\chi^2 = 10.07$ for 1 *df*). In other words, high-performing students are less likely than low-performing students to need the organizing strategy, and when they do use it, it works only when associated with its cognate motive (M_3).Low-performing students, on the other hand, can make use of organizing whether or not it is congruent with their motivation (and it is unlikely to be congruent, as none of the low-performing groups were high in achievement motivation).

SUMMARY AND CONCLUSIONS

The present research has addressed boxes D, E, and G in Figure 6.1 and shown that students' perspectives (as categorized according to their declared motives) may influence the strategies that they habitually adopt and the effectiveness with which they deploy them. Perhaps not very surprisingly, students who are academically motivated and who are high achieving tend to make "good" selections of strategies—ones that tend to be congruent with their motivational patterns and relate to performance accordingly. Poorly motivated and low-achieving students, on the other hand, do not appear to deploy their strategies "sensibly." In fact, there was inferential evidence, in this and other research, that such students should be taught the basics of organizing their work, scheduling time, note taking, etc. The evidence is that, whether or not they are appropriately motivated, they will likely end up achieving better and being more satisfied with their performance.

There are other lacunae in the scheme represented in Figure 6.1. Research summarized or referred to in this chapter has related at various points, singly or in combination, A, B, C, D, E, and G. F (micro- or embedded strategies) has been the subject of rather specialized research, linking with C on the one hand and with G on the other (Lawson & Kirby, 1981). It seems particularly desirable that certain kinds of underachieving students should be taught fairly task-specific strategies independently of their motivations, and conceivably of their processing biases. At this level of specificity, content questions are inevitable, and the analysis of tasks into content components overlaps learning processes. Biggs and Collis (1982), for example, propose a taxonomy for ordering academic tasks in terms of structural complexity. In most tasks, there is a "learning cycle" involving the simplest grasp of a relevant component when the learner first engages the task, and the progressive addition and integration of components as the task is engaged at increasingly higher levels. The point is that the transition from one level of learning to the next can be mapped in terms both of the content component needed and of the psychological process required to integrate that component. Kirby and Biggs (1981) report such an analysis (including macrostrategies and mesostrategies) in the progressive growth of two tasks, writing an essay and appreciating a poem, and suggest (although this has yet to be done experimentally) that task-appropriate microstrategies could easily be devised on the basis of such information and taught to students. Empirical work on this is currently under way.

The overall task is large and complex, and approaches from many directions, and using different methodologies, can all add their contributions to our understanding of student performance. If nothing else, it is hoped that the present contribution emphasizes the need for all kinds of research and for the progressive testing of hypotheses to be carried out within the reality of the perspective, not only of the dispassionate observer or the managerial teacher, but also of the participating student.

REFERENCE NOTE

1. Biggs, J. B. *Student motivation and strategies of learning and studying: Handbook for teachers and school counsellors.* Manuscript in preparation, Australian Council for Educational Research, Hawthorn, Victoria.

REFERENCES

Bandura, A. Self-efficacy: Toward a unifying theory of behavioral change. *Psychological Review,* 1977, *84,* 191–215.

Biggs, J. B. Faculty patterns in study behavior. *Australian Journal of Psychology,* 1970, *22,* 161–174.

Biggs, J. B. Dimensions of study behavior: Another look at ATI. *British Journal of Educational Psychology,* 1976, *46,* 68–80.

Biggs, J. B. Genetics and education: An alternative to Jensenism. *Educational Researcher,* 1978, *7,*(4), 11–17. (a)

Biggs, J. B. Individual and group differences in study processes. *British Journal of Educational Psychology,* 1978, *48,* 266–279. (b)

Biggs, J. B. Individual differences in study processes and the quality of learning outcomes. *Higher Education,* 1979, 8, 381–394.

Biggs, J. B., & Collis, K. F. *Evaluating the quality of learning: The SOLO Taxonomy.* New York: Academic Press, 1982.

Biggs, J. B., & Das, J. P. Extreme response style, internality–externality and academic performance. *British Journal of Social and Clinical Psychology,* 1973, *12,* 199–210.

Biggs, J. B., & Telfer, R. A. *The process of learning.* Sydney: Prentice-Hall (Australia), 1981.

Case, R. Validation of a neo-Piagetian mental capacity construct. *Journal of Experimental Child Psychology,* 1972, *14,* 287–302.

Cronbach, L. J. Beyond the two disciplines of scientific psychology. *American Psychologist,* 1975, *30,* 116–127.

Cronbach, L. J., & Snow, R. E. *Aptitudes and instructional methods.* New York: Irvington (Wiley), 1977.

Das, J., Kirby, J., & Jarman, R. *Simultaneous and successive cognitive processes.* New York: Academic Press, 1979.

Entwistle, N., & Hounsell, D. Editorial: Student learning in its natural setting. *Higher Education,* 1979, *8,* 359–364.

Guilford, J. P. *The nature of human intelligence.* New York: McGraw-Hill, 1967.

Hudson, L. *Frames of mind.* London: Methuen, 1968.

Kirby, J. R. Individual differences and cognitive processes. In J. R. Kirby & J. B. Biggs (Eds.), *Cognition, development, and instruction.* New York: Academic Press, 1980.

Kirby, J. R., & Biggs, J. B. Learning styles, information processing abilities and academic achievement. Final Report, Australian Research Grants Committee, Belconnen, Australian Capital Territory, 1981.

Kirby, J. R., & Das, J. P. Reading achievements, IQ, and simultaneous–successive processing. *Journal of Educational Psychology,* 1977, *69,* 564–570.

Kirby, J. R., & Das, J. P. Information processing and human abilities. *Journal of Educational Psychology,* 1978, *70,* 58–66.

Krywaniuk, L. Patterns of cognitive abilities of high and low achieving school children. Unpublished doctoral dissertation, University of Alberta, 1974.

Lavin, D. E. *The prediction of academic performance.* New York: Russell Sage Foundation, 1965.

Lawson, M. J. Metamemory: Making decisions about strategies. In J. R. Kirby & J. B. Biggs (Eds.), *Cognition, development, and instruction.* New York: Academic Press, 1978.

Lawson, M. J., & Kirby, J. R. Training in information processing algorithms. *British Journal of Educational Psychology,* 1981, *51,* 321–335.

Marton, F., & Sälsjö, R. On qualitative differences in learning: I. Outcome and process. *British Journal of Educational Psychology,* 1976, *46,* 4–11. (a)

Marton, F., & Sälsjö, R. On qualitative differences in learning—II. Outcome as a function of the learner's conception of the task. *British Journal of Educational Psychology,* 1976, *46,* 115–127. (b)

Mischel, W. Toward a cognitive social learning reconceptualization of personality. *Psychological Review,* 1973, *80,* 252–283.

Robinson, F. P. *Effective study* (Rev. ed.). New York: Harper, 1961.

Rigney, J. W. Learning strategies: A theoretical perspective. In H. F. O'Neil (Ed.), *Learning strategies.* New York: Academic Press, 1978.

Svensson, L. *Study skill and learning.* Göteborg Studies in Educational Sciences. 19. Göteborg: Acta Universitatis Gothoburgensis, 1976.

PART III

CROSS-CULTURAL STUDIES

7

Ethnography, Cognitive Processes, and Instructional Procedures

GRAHAM R. DAVIDSON
L. Z. KLICH

A number of writers have commented on the changing face of cross-cultural cognitive psychology. That change can generally be traced to a reemergence within the research tradition of studies of contextual factors surrounding behavior that have focused on a variety of environmental and sociocultural features that affect everyday life activities. These features include the ecology (Berry, 1980), cultural values (e.g., Fry and Ghosh, 1980; Gill & Keats, 1980; Wober, 1974), and linguistic contexts (Bilmes & Boggs, 1979; Labov, 1975). They also include the laboratory experiment, as part of which the language and content of psychological tasks, conditions surrounding testing, and the cultural affiliation of the tester have been studied (Ciborowski, 1980). At all these levels, it is assumed that we cannot really understand behavior until we have gained at least some understanding of the contextual factors surrounding it, including broader socioecological systems and conditions of immediate individual relevance.

The study of context is not new, but it represents a reemphasis of environmentally based understandings of people's behavior. Bartlett (1937), for example, advocated that psychology become more anthropological by broadening the focus of its data base and by studying behavior from the point of view of widely different cultures. Rivers (cited in Campbell, 1964) also emphasized the importance of understanding the social setting of behavior and the way that behavior depends on socially condoned ideas and values: "How can you explain the workings of the human mind without a knowledge of the social setting which must play so great a part in determining the sentiments and opinions of mankind [pp. 10–11]." These principles, however, seem to have been compromised by psychologists' attempts to derive a theory of intelligence that was independent of cultural and situational influences on behavior. Consequently, their persistence with laboratory-type experimental investigations of behavior (Cole, 1975a, 1975b; Price-Williams, 1975) has produced confusion between competence and performance theories of experimental results and, in practical terms, educational intervention programs designed to compensate for areas where incompetencies are thought to exist. The renewed emphasis on the study of contextual variables has been a necessary balance for these culturally myopic experimental procedures and programs.

ETHNOGRAPHY AND THE STUDY OF COGNITIVE PROCESSES

The reemergence of contextual variables in cross-cultural cognitive psychology, including conditions surrounding behavior and their effects on cognitive performance, is due mainly to the development of the method of enquiry called "ethnographic psychology." Such enquiry is based on a view of ethnography as an analysis of elements of a single culture, such as beliefs and customs, with a view to understanding thinking and behavior, as it occurs in the culture and in relation to indigenous understanding of the meaning of the behavior (Hansen, 1979). Using a range of ethnographic techniques, such as those described by Hansen, attempts have been made to clarify the naturalistic context and meaning of behavior and to identify incongruities between these and experimental contexts, as a means of explaining cognitive performance. Wilson (1977) points out that ethnography is useful in this regard in that it eliminates the need to generalize from measures and descriptions of experimentally evoked behavior to statements about behavior in natural settings. Ethnographic psychology, therefore, by definition, is a reaction to laboratory research on cognition, which has attempted to characterize and label individuals, not on the basis of their everyday competencies and skills, but on the basis of their psychological test results.

Secondly, Wilson (1977) and also Duignan (1981) have pointed out that we have a better chance of understanding behavior or test performance if, by using ethnographic analysis, we come to terms with the meaning systems that people use to describe their own behavior. These meaning systems influence performance just as much in the laboratory as they influence behavior in real life. Thus, an ethnographic psychology of cognition attempts to describe the type of behavior that occurs in a variety of social and cultural contexts, and to decipher how behavior is construed by participants and constrained by those contexts. It is based on "the view that observations of intelligent behavior in everyday life are an important source of information about culture and cognitive processes [Cole & Scribner, 1977, p. 366]."

A number of approaches have been devised to study the context of cognitive processing skills. These have been described by the Laboratory of Comparative Human Cognition (1979) and Ciborowski (1980). Such approaches rely heavily on observation and analysis of situations in which cognition is dependent on everyday knowledge or specific cultural knowledge systems. Some of these approaches involve the study of specific cultural institutions, such as exchange, food gathering and production, ceremonies and rituals, and spatial mapping. Other psychological paradigms study cognitive processes as they operate in experimental contexts, which are manipulated systematically and gradually to reflect tasks and materials that are culturally familiar. This technique has been referred to as "situating" or "locating" the experiment (Scribner, 1976) and as "experimenting with the experiment" (Cibrowski, 1980). A more recent approach has attempted to map those naturally occuring contexts in which experimental-type cognitive processing skills are observed or may be operating. In all these approaches, there is the assumption that behavior observed in real-life contexts and tasks is a more efficacious measure of cognitive performance than is behavior in experimental contexts. This is borne out by those studies that reveal a high level of cognitive competence in dealing with culturally familiar tasks (e.g., Gladwin, 1970; Hage, 1978; Hutchins, 1979) and those that demonstrate a shift in cognitive processing skills if familiar tasks and materials are used in cognitive experimentation (e.g., Cole & Scribner, 1974).

ETHNOGRAPHY AND INSTRUCTIONAL PROCEDURES

Educational interest in this type of research focuses on the possibility of indigenizing instructional procedures. The process of indigenization may include:

1. Identification of indigenous cultural activities that can be used in classrooms in order to improve the quality of instruction for culturally different children
2. Transfer of children's perceived cognitive competencies in out-of-school contexts to formal instructional contexts

These instructional aims imply the use of (*a*) indigenous activities and materials, selected from an ethnographic analysis of the indigenous culture; and (*b*) indigenous cognitive strategies as the bases of classroom learning.

So far, ethnographic psychology has been a "methodological reminder" and "needed corrective" (Brislin, 1983) in an area of reasearch where the tendency has been toward the study of *in situ* behavior in culture. It has also provided compelling evidence that non-Westerners' performance on experimental tasks improves if contexts and tasks are altered in accordance with knowledge about indigenous cognitive systems. Moreover, researchers *have* attempted to translate their ethnographic findings into a form that could be useful in designing educational procedures. For example, Ciborowski (1980) mentions an ongoing program involving the study of Hawaiian children's seafaring and food-gathering skills.[1] However, according to Ciborowski, "at present it is perplexing and frustrating to realize that the children possess specific cognitive skills such as inferential ability, yet fail to display this ability in the classroom [p. 292]."

Overall, the approach has provided relatively few positive guidelines for educational instruction in non-Western settings. The reason for this appears to be the difficulty in achieving skills transfer, and this will be discussed in the second part of this chapter. It should be mentioned here, however, that one of the recognized limitations of ethnographic (otherwise referred to as *emic*) research is that it provides few concepts and performance indices, except at the most abstract level, that allow comparison of performance in a variety of cultural situations (see Cole, Gay, & Glick, 1968). In addition, problems have arisen with replication of findings in cultures other than those hosting the original research (Brislin, 1983). This is not surprising, given the variety of dimensions along which the cultural context may vary. Applications of research on contextual variables are generally limited, by definition, to those contexts (see Le Compte & Goetz, 1982, on setting effects).

Before we consider difficulties associated with the transfer of strategies from indigenous to classroom contexts, it is useful to identify the levels at which transfer can take place. The most overt level of strategy analysis suggests the adoption in classrooms of learning-related values, such as group achievement or self–peer management schemes, and of learning styles, such as peer modeling and other observational learning experiences. Some success has been achieved in schools where classroom contexts have been reoriented to reflect characteristic learning patterns of non-Western or nonmajority children (e.g., Gallimore, Boggs, & Jordan, 1974; Ramirez & Castaneda, 1974). It is not specifically with these affective and stylistic

---

[1]We prefer to refer to the transfer of cognitive strategies.

elements of instruction that the present discussion is concerned. At more complex levels, there is the use of indigenous tasks and materials to teach cognitive processing strategies that are prerequisite to, or part of, formal instruction in literacy, numeracy, logical reasoning, and so on, with children using indigenous knowledge systems and cognitive strategies in place of the strategies encouraged by formal schooling. These are the sorts of approaches advocated by some researchers. For example, Ciborowski (1980, p. 292) has proposed that, "after isolating and analysing specific cognitive skills . . . . ways to transfer or translate these skills are sought so that they may be tapped or elicited in the classroom setting." Bruner (1968, p. 53) also has suggested that, "if information is to be used effectively, it must be translated into the learner's way of attempting to solve a problem." However, our thesis in this chapter is that the incorporation of indigenous tasks and strategies into classroom contexts has not provided an assured method of teaching formal educational skills to culturally different children and that there are at present no guaranteed ways of achieving transfer. One of the reasons for this lack of progress is related to specific features of ethnographic analysis and a theory of cognitive processes that is based on the study of contextual variables, as we have suggested. There are other problems associated with skills transfer that will now be addressed, with reference to recent research in ethnographic psychology, anthropology, and linguistics.

LIMITATIONS OF AN ETHNOGRAPHIC PSYCHOLOGY OF INSTRUCTION

There is a tendency in the practitioner literature to suggest that instructional problems that occur with ethnic minority and non-Western children may be alleviated either by altering classroom activities so that they contain tasks that are a familiar part of children's lives at home or at play or by encouraging children to use indigenous knowledge to solve school-type problems (see Graham, 1982, and Brandl, Note 1, on Aboriginal education). However, such alterations to formal classroom procedures are often unsuccessful. In this section, we are not concerned with the possibility, nor do we deny, that indigenous skills and knowledge can be taught in school as part of indigenous culture and language programs. Instead, our focus is on the failure to transfer strategies from indigenous to formal school contexts.

Conceptual Nonequivalence as a Barrier to Transfer

In their discussion of the "situation" or "location" approach to experimentation with non-Western and nonschooled groups, the Laboratory of

Comparative Human Cognition (1979) has pointed out that it is often difficult to "locate" the experiment within a context that is part of the indigenous culture, "because the structure of such tasks is so closely tied to schooling that it may prove difficult or impossible to find extra-curricular contexts in which conditions modeled in the experiment occur [p. 831]." This is a comment on the cognitive limitations of these particular contexts and not on their familiarity per se. These limitations become clearer if we examine some suggestions for the use of ethnographic materials as the basis for instructional tasks. For example, concepts of size, spatial location, weight, similarity, and equality in indigenous systems are known to differ from Western mathematical terminologies (Gay & Cole, 1967). It would be reasonable to expect, if children have learned indigenous concepts before formal schooling begins, that early mathematics education could incorporate those concepts and classification systems, so that children commence their education by learning to classify, measure, and estimate using the systems with which they are familiar, before they are required to use Western systems. In theory, and in practice at the simplest level of operations, this transfer is possible, with similarities and differences between the indigenous and the Western systems eventually being examined and discussed. However, the barriers of which Cole and colleagues speak limit the extent to which these contexts provide a base for further instruction. A number of such examples are available, some involving taxonomic differences between terminological systems and some involving strategy differences in home and school learning.

At the terminological level, Rudder (Note 2) has described two Australian aboriginal number systems from Arnhem Land that have resulted, in part, from attempts to derive an indigenous number system that could be used in school mathematics. These systems are based on indigenous number concepts. The first system he describes contains number terms from 0 to 20 and has a base of 5, being called *goŋ* ("hand"). Thus, *goŋ waŋgany* ("hand solitary") is the term for 5. Primary terms include *duo* (2), *trio* (3), and *duo duo* (4), with other number terms being combinations of these primary terms. For example, 10, 15, and 20 are described respectively as duo hand, trio hand, and duo duo hand; 7 is hand solitary and duo left over; and 14 is hand duo and duo duo left over. A second system, using clusterings of turtle eggs also has a base of 5 (*rulu,* or head-possessing set) and contains secondary terms based on the system of head set and an amount left over. Rudder maintains that "while [these], to the non-Aboriginal appear to be . . . system(s) of counting, [they are] for the Yolnu [or aboriginal] the perception of a qualitative assessment of precise classifiable quantities which are not necessarily in serial order [p. 26]." His analysis of the aboriginal terminology revealed that every primary and secondary term represents a "precise set, each with its own quality." Thus, although each term has its exact English equivalent, it is "a precise description of quantities which require only a cardinal perception of number. There is no necessity for any ordinal perception to precede its establishment, nor has its establishment generated such a perception [p. 27]." Such a system, therefore, unless changed to reflect the ordinality of the English system, would permit simple counting (1–20 only), but not logical addition and subtraction of "sets," or other more complex operations.

We might pinpoint other instances where taxonomies and taxonomic partitionings, especially in relation to counting and measurement, have different bases in indigenous and Western culture. For example, in Gilbertese culture, Arthur Grimble noted that measurements in canoe building were made using parts of the human body. Measurement terms described those parts of the body, with the smallest by Western standards being "the quick of the nail" (the breadth of the half-moon on the digital nail) and the largest being "the fathom" or the "full stretch with arms extended." For purposes of standardization, all measurements were taken from the body of a single man or *te tia-baire* (the measurer). There appeared to be no facility for adding or subtracting these primary terms to produce secondary measurement terms (Grimble, 1972, p. 160).

Hansen (1979) has commented on a similar nonadditivity in Trobriand Islanders' conceptions of time. Within the life cycle of plants and animals, stages in growth and development are not connected into a series of temporal events but are treated as separate states in the life of things until the next state is evident. Thus, "whereas Westerners are prone to see lineal relationships . . . Trobrianders prefer to see the pattern and noncomparative wholeness of things. . . . The satisfaction we take in lineal connection is taken by a Trobriander in this patterned unity [p. 15]."

In relation to cognitive processing strategies, Davidson (1979) has suggested that equating contexts on the basis of similar content or activity should not be taken to mean that those contexts involve the operationalization of similar strategies. This nonequivalence is illustrated by Davidson's study of Australian aboriginal card playing behavior (described by Klich and Davidson, Chapter 8, this volume). Prior to that particular study, this card game had been taken as an indication that Australian aborigines are capable of demonstrating a "quickness of perception and mathematical calculation [Holm & Japanangka, 1976, p. 265]," employing number recognition and arithmetic addition skills of which they otherwise appeared incapable. It was also suggested that the game may be used to advantage in teaching numeracy to aboriginal children in school. However, Davidson's investigations showed that aboriginal styles of play involved neither the use of numbers on the cards in order to identify them nor addition to calculate the score, in the fashion that Westerners would play the game. Instead, complex systems of pattern recognition and grouping were used, in which all combinations of cards for all possible scores were already known before the game commenced. Thus, if used as a school task to teach basic arithmetic procedures, in the community in which Davidson's ethnographic analysis was undertaken the game may elicit cognitive processing strategies that do not accord with Western mathematical interpretations of the game. Thus, despite the game's interest value, the style of play would have to be changed if it were to be a suitable instructional aid in mathematics.

Again, in relation to indigenous games we have found that cognitive processing strategies in indigenous contexts are not always commensurate with those strategies suggested by a Western interpretation of the games. Davidson and Kishor (Chapter 9, this volume) attempted to locate, using available ethnographies, Fijian games that appeared differentially to emphasize the spatial positioning and identity of objects. However, they found that strategies adopted by children in these games often were not commensurate with those suggested by the ethnographic analysis. For example, a game apparently involving memory for the spatial positioning of large seeds on a mat elicited from almost all players a verbal labeling strategy where seeds were associated with the names of players who threw them. Their names were rehearsed in the order in which the seeds were thrown. This strategy for remembering the ownership and positioning of seeds was used instead of a spatial imagery strategy. A second game that, in theory, required verbal naming of objects and rehearsal of those names was found to elicit a combination of imagery and verbal rehearsal strategies. Consequently, training on the indigenous games resulted unexpectedly in better transfer from the second game than from the first to a test of visual spatial memory. When the games materials were retained but the tasks were altered to encourage subjects to perceive them either as spatial imagery or as verbal rehearsal, the initial results were reversed, with greater transfer to the visual memory test occuring for those who played the spatial location game, not the naming game, and for those given the spatial imagery instructions.

It appears, therefore, that "the problem of transferring skills applied on the streets to the classrooms is not solved by demonstrating the existence of the skill on the streets [Cole, Gay, Glick, & Sharp, 1971, p. 234]. Using Cole *et al.*'s terminology, ethnography operates at the "street" level, and aims to analyze "street" skills. These often may be different from skills required in formal instructional situations, and they may be contextually inappropriate.

Functional Equivalence as a Barrier to Transfer

The notion of functional equivalence has previously been used in conjunction with the distinction between *emic* (or culture specific) and *etic* (pancultural) concepts in cross-cultural psychology (Berry, 1969). The analysis of etics requires identification in the cultures to be studied of situations, activities, or specific behaviors that are said to be functionally equivalent. This means that the "behaviours thus serve to help obtain the same goals . . . in different cultures [Brislin, Lonner, & Thorndike, 1973, p. 24; see also, Brislin, 1983]." Activities that have been considered to be equivalent cross-culturally include, for example, child-care practices, food preparation, and marriage. *Functionality* has also been a term applied to everyday usage of materials that might become part of experimentation (Cole & Scribner, 1974).

We use the term in a somewhat different sense to refer to the degree of purposive involvement in a context or with an activity rather than to the outcome of behavior as such. Thus, in relation to child-care practices, the social and personal implications of providing such care might be distinguished from the act of care giving and the outcome in terms of the welfare of the child. Gay and Cole (1967), for example, have alluded to social and occupational aspects of Kpelle tailors' skill at measurement. The inference here is that the development of "street" skills depends on the value attributed to those skills, which is often context specific.

The distinction made between the functionality of objects or actions and the meaning attributed to them is similar to the view of culture as operating at pragmatic, or practical, and symbolic levels, respectively (Firth, 1975). Firth also likens symbolic systems to the Marxist notion of actions and behaviors being representative of, and inextricably tied to, their social context. In that sense, behavior out of context has no social meaning. Such tasks as tailoring, or fishing tasks mentioned by Ciborowski (1980), or card playing may therefore have value only if their outcomes are considered important by the person or the society. Activities may not be considered important if they become primarily teaching–learning tasks, as when indigenous contexts or tasks are used in conjunction with formal instruction in order to "situate" the latter skills. In general, non-Westerners may lack commitment to the process of formal education, which is inimical to life-based learning and irrelevant to the problems of preindustrial and transitional societies.

A pragmatic view of cultural systems also sees cognitive performance as being based on the concept of behavior in context. According to this view, occupational activity may primarily "determine chief modes of satisfaction, . . . furnish working classifications and definitions of value, . . . afford the scheme or pattern of the structural organization of mental traits and . . . integrate special elements into a functioning whole [Dewey, 1902, p. 219–220]."

Individual Differences and Instructional Design

Wilson (1977) has pointed out that a good ethnographer carefully selects and refines the aims of the enquiry, the form the data will take, and the points of field contact and data collection. Thus, ethnographic analysis involves procedures whereby the researcher may check data obtained during particular observational contacts. Such procedures involve identifying categories of persons or situations that offer a different perspective on research questions. There is, therefore, as with quantitative analysis, an attempt to ensure that the sample of individuals contacted or situations observed is representative of the total data base and that the data are a reliable measure of possible future observations of the particular sample (Bruyn, 1966; also see the discussion of reliability and validity by Le Compte & Goetz, 1982). In addition, following the theoretical analysis of initial data, selective sampling of similar events, situations, or persons' views allows for theory testing in the form of confirmatory analysis and replication (Wilson, 1977).

Nevertheless, the final result is a general statement of similarities and variations within the group or culture under investigation, and not a precise description of the individual persons and events that contribute data to the analysis. Individual differences in behavior within events or situations, therefore, are not reported if they are not considered to represent important situational or group differences within the analysis. Observations also are typically representative of behavior that can easily be observed, and is public, because intimate and private exchanges are often inaccessible to the researcher (Barry, 1981). Consequently, it is not unusual to find that, for a given customary event or activity, individuals may participate in different fashions and to differing degrees. Individuals' comprehensions and task-handling tactics may also be considerably different, although not in relation to expected situational and role variations within the group at large. It is unlikely in any particular cultural context or task where a range of cognitive processing strategies are identifiable that all individuals will adopt the same strategy or be equally proficient in applying it. Instead, a task or context will more likely than not elicit a variety of coding and planning strategies within and between individuals, some of which may transfer from one task to another, with others remaining task specific.

Individual differences data available from cross-cultural visual memory research (Knapp & Seagrim, 1981; Davidson & Kishor, Chapter 9, this volume) provide some support for this point of view. Instructional procedures that rely on the existence of culturally determined cognitive strategies, therefore, may not be appropriate for all individuals in the culture. Ethnographic analysis dispenses with this type of information on individual differences and preferences in learning. Brislin (1983), in his discussion of the Knapp and Seagrim (1981) study, also infers that there may be individual differences in the degree to which people are able to transfer specific strategies they use in familiar contexts to new contexts. Such differences in transfer are demonstrated by a study of memory skills among the Kpelle of Africa (Lancy, 1977). Lancy's study was conducted in response to the generally accepted view that members of that society in culturally familiar contexts are capable of remembering a considerable body of verbal information, and to attempts to improve Kpelle verbal memory performance in laboratory-type free recall experiments using a variety of mnemonic strategies. He attempted to investigate the following:

1. The variety of tasks in the culture that required the use of verbal memory
2. The degree to which persons varied in their participation in those tasks
3. The range of specific task–strategy relationships
4. The extent to which Kpelle informants could remember novel verbal information presented in familiar task formats

The study revealed a number of culturally important activities involving the exercise of verbal memory. These included story telling, singing, verbal games, and leaf naming. His analysis of the tasks revealed that they were associated differentially with a range of mnemonic strategies. Large individual differences were evident in amount and accuracy of material remembered, as were broader sex and age differences in memory performance on some of the tasks. Finally, individuals differed in their ability to remember new information presented in those same task formats. Thus, the use of any of these tasks and associated mnemonic strategies as procedures for formal instruction of Kpelle children and youth may be unsuccessful with many of the children because of their differential involvement in the original contexts. This problem will arise with all instruction based on the transfer method.

CONTEXT SWITCHING AS AN ALTERNATIVE INSTRUCTIONAL PROCEDURE

One issue that has been neglected by the research on context and transfer is whether lack of transfer is a result either of the greatly different demands of indigenous and formal educational contexts and the subsequent inability of culturally different children to make the transition, or of the inability of those children to distinguish between the different contexts and to adjust their cognitive strategies accordingly. There is some indication that the latter occurs in relation to experimental performance on certain logical reasoning and memory tasks. For example, African subjects refused to consider experimental tasks as being separate from everyday life situations with which they were familiar and that involved familiar cultural and personal information (e.g., Cole *et al.*, 1971; Scribner, cited in Cole & Scribner, 1974; Luria, 1976). Those subjects' performance was also improved significantly on problem solving and verbal recall tasks by the use of appropriate cognitive strategies that were provided by the experimenters. Children tested by Klich and Davidson (1983) and Davidson and Kishor (Chapter 9, this volume) showed similar increases in visual memory performance when appropriate imagery strategies were used.

Cole and Scribner (1977) have described task performance shortfalls as production (application) deficiencies rather than as mediation (acquisition) deficiencies (see Flavell, 1970). This distinction emphasizes the role that temporary personal variables play in cognitive performance, but it also focuses attention on subjects' awareness of the strategies they can use or are supposed to use in completing these cognitive tasks. Flavell and Wellman (1977) have described a production deficiency as "a child's failure to use any particular memorization strategy *spontaneously* when the situation called for it, even though he could and would use that strategy effectively if directed to do so by someone else [p. 10, italics added]." Thus described, this type of response deficit is indicative of a breakdown in planning or monitoring response systems rather than of processing systems. Take the situation where a non-Westerner apparently refuses, or is unable, to respond to a verbal reasoning activity unless he or she places it within the context of everyday life experiences, and compare that with the situation described by Bransford, McCarrell, and Nitsch (1976), where university colleagues were confronted in a social context, in their offices, with extraneous information (*Bill has a red car*) and their immediate behavior and later thoughts recorded. The immediate response was to evaluate the information as part of the social context in which it was provided and in relation to the testee's knowledge about *Bills, red cars,* and the *tester's knowledge about Bills.* Testees then expressed their confusion about the information and, in doing so, demonstrated their lack of test-wiseness.

Bransford (1979) subsequently has discussed the differing demands of social and experimental contexts and how they might influence the level of processing and prior knowledge that is deemed to be sufficient for understanding the task. However, he does not discuss possible variation in the degree of test-wiseness that might be shown in these contexts. For example, while subjects found the sentence *Bill has a red car* perfectly understandable as part of an experiment, other subjects in their offices responded in a socially appropriate and not an experimentally appropriate fashion. Although the tendency in the latter context was to seek extra meaning in order to comprehend the information, a test-wise response would be, "Just what are you up to?" Alternatively, non-test-wise subjects may have imbued the tester with other motives, such as attempting to embarrass them or to sell them a car.

In the studies of memory by Cole and Scribner, although subjects were questioned about their understanding and recall of the actual problem, it appears that they were never asked directly if they realized that they were involved in an experiment or if they understood the differences between the logical reasoning demand of an experiment and the reality of familiar social situations. Nor does it appear that they were expressly told, "This is a game (or a test). You must not be influenced by what you know happens around you when you are trying to solve this problem." Consequently, in the experiments reported by Cole and Scribner, we do not know whether "the subject possesses the relational information but chooses to ignore it when it conflicts with his personal experience [Cole & Scribner, 1974, p. 164]" or whether subjects possess the relational information but fail to recognize the need to apply it. Whatever is the case, the problem, as in the study by Bransford *et al.*, seems to be one of lack of planning at the metacognitive level rather than one of a cognitive processing deficiency. However, planning at the cognitive processing level may also contribute to an explanation of cultural differences in cognitive performance (see Krywaniuk & Das, 1976).

We can apply a notion of context switching, which Bransford infers in distinguishing situations as social or experimental, to performance in contexts involving indigenous and formal school learning (see Scribner & Cole, 1973). In the first place, performance requirements of the two systems are likely to be different. Goodnow (1976) has outlined some of those differences pertaining to how and when one should respond to the task at hand and to the teacher. In the second instance, contextual changes are likely to involve the need to switch terminological systems and cognitive processing strategies, such as were described earlier. Our limited knowledge of minority ethnic and non-Western children's responses to school, at the moment, does not include information on whether children do not really understand these cognitive tasks in formal instructional (school) contexts, or whether they have cognizance of the tasks and strategies but are unaware of the contextual changes and the need to switch systems and strategies.

Four possible types of metacognitive strategies may be applicable to the study of context switching and to the design of instructional programs.

1. How does the child know when the cultural context of the task changes? This is not simply an issue of deciding when one is in or out

of school, because, within the classroom, familiar as well as novel tasks, experiences, and materials are often employed in order to "situate" the learning activity or "motivate" the student.

2. When the specific context of thinking is recognized, how does one differentiate between appropriate and inappropriate terminological systems, knowledge schemata, and problem solving strategies?

3. How does one know when tasks involving unfamiliar contexts are not properly understood? This has been called *metacomprehension* (Brown, 1978; Flavell, 1979).

4. How does one identify performance criterion levels in unfamiliar contexts, and how does one select strategies that are in keeping with performance expectations? Part of metacomprehension is being able to decide "that one has the optimal information for attacking a particular task [Brown, 1978]."

Instruction based on context switching is reliant on instructors' and pupils' comprehensions of the cultural contexts of instruction. Its emphasis on contextual discontinuities, as well as continuities, probably means that mastery of learning contexts and concepts in school may only occur after there is comprehension of basic indigenous *and* formal instructional concepts. Thus, advanced formal instruction will be more effective if indigenous and school contexts and tasks are equally a part of formal educational instruction, especially during the early years of schooling. Early education of culturally different children, therefore, should include instruction in indigenous and Western conceptual systems, with the emphasis being on the development of metastrategies that enable children to identify contexts in which each of these knowledge systems may be used appropriately (Davidson, 1981). Thus, there is as much need for an ethnographic study of context and skills, along the lines that were mentioned earlier, as there is when instruction is based on transfer.

Possible Direction for Research on Context Switching

There are particular problems arising from our discussion of the strengths and limitations of instructional procedures based on transfer and on context switching that deserve attention. In the first place, our discussions of conceptual equivalence, individual differences factors in performance, and then cognitive monitoring involved the use of examples of contextual and task differences at the levels of taxonomies of knowledge, cognitive processing strategies, and metastrategies. It might be argued, for example, that indigenous counting is quite different from number recognition and classification in playing cards, or that the "red car" and African problem solving situations are not comparable. We acknowledge the unevenness of our examples in that regard, but we have tried to identify each of them as studies of conceptual, strategic, or metastrategic systems, and tried not to make comparison between indigenous and Western knowledge systems across these levels of processing. More detailed studies of the parameters of learning and thinking contexts are necessary if we are to be able to understand what context switching entails and how metastrategies may work.

Second, context switching does not rely on there being conceptual equivalence of tasks, as transfer does. Instruction based on the development of metastrategies also makes allowance for individual differences in quality and level of prior contextual involvements. However, the issue of *cultural relevance* of formal Western schooling still remains, with these schools being an anathema to some minority and non-Western groups. Context switching in these cases may be considered as an unnecessary and unpalatable compromise of separatist values held by members of the indigenous culture. It is not known, therefore, whether one's motivation to context switch is governed by group values or by individual values associated with proficiency within particular contexts. School and "street" skills might well be used in a complementary fashion in instruction, but this requires an appreciation not only of "street" skills by the educational practitioner but also of school skills by the learner.

REFERENCE NOTES

1. Brandl, M. We are going to teach Aboriginal children: The cultural isolation of non-aboriginal education in Australia. Centre for Resource and Environmental Studies, Australian National University, Working Paper C/WP2, 1981.
2. Rudder, J. Concepts associated with the identification of numerical quantity. Unpublished manuscript, Department of Prehistory and Anthropology, Australian National University, Canberra, 1981.

REFERENCES

Barry, H., III. Uses and limitations of ethnographic descriptions. In R. H. Monroe, R. L. Monroe, & B. B. Whiting (Eds.), *Handbook of cross-cultural human development*. New York: Garland Press, 1981.
Bartlett, F. C. Psychological methods and anthropological problems. *Africa*, 1937, *10*, 421–435.
Berry, J. W. On cross-cultural comparability. *International Journal of Psychology*, 1969, *4*, 119–128.
Berry, J. Ecological analyses for cross-cultural psychology. In N. Warren (Ed.), *Studies in cross-cultural psychology* (Vol. 2). London: Academic Press, 1980.
Bilmes, J., & Boggs, S. Language and communication: The foundations of culture. In A.

Marsella, R. Tharp, & T. Ciborowski (Eds.), *Perspectives in cross-cultural psychology.* New York: Academic Press, 1979.

Bransford, J. D. *Human cognition: Learning, understanding and remembering.* Belmont, California: Wadsworth, 1979.

Bransford, J. D., McCarrell, N. S., & Nitsch, K. E. Contexte, compréhension et flexibilité sémantique: Quelques implications théoriques et méthodologiques. In S. Ehrlich & E. Tulving (Eds.), *La memoire sémantique.* Paris: Bulletin de Psychologie, 1976.

Brislin, R. W. Cross-cultural research in psychology. *Annual review of psychology,* 1983, *34,* 363–400.

Brislin, R. W., Lonner, W. J., & Thorndike, R. M. *Cross-cultural research methods.* New York: Wiley, 1973.

Brown, A. L. Knowing when, where, and how to remember: A problem of metacognition. In R. Glaser (Ed.), *Advances in instructional psychology.* New York: Halsted Press, 1978.

Bruner, J. S. *Toward a theory of instruction.* New York: Norton, 1968.

Bruyn, S. *Human perspectives in sociology.* Englewood Cliffs, N.J.: Prentice-Hall, 1966.

Campbell, D. T. Distinguishing differences of perception from failures of communication in cross-cultural studies. In F. Northrop & H. Livingstone (Eds.), *Cross-cultural understanding: Epistemology in anthropology.* New York: Harper, 1964.

Ciborowski, T. The role of context, skill, and transfer in cross-cultural experimentation. In H. Triandis & J. Berry (Eds.), *Handbook of cross-cultural psychology* (Vol. 2) Boston: Allyn & Bacon, 1980.

Cole, M. An ethnographic psychology of cognition. In R. Brislin, S. Bochner, & W. Lonner (Eds.), *Cross-cultural perspectives on learning.* New York: Halsted Press, 1975. (a)

Cole, M. Foreword. In D. Price-Williams, *Explorations in cross-cultural psychology.* San Francisco: Chandler & Sharp, 1975. (b)

Cole, M., Gay, J., & Glick, J. Some experimental studies of Kpelle quantitative behaviour. *Psychometric Monographs Supplement,* 1968, *2* (10, Whole No. 26), 173–190.

Cole, M., Gay, J., Glick, J., & Sharp, D. *The cultural context of learning and thinking.* New York: Basic Books, 1971.

Cole, M., & Scribner, S. *Culture and thought.* New York: Wiley, 1974.

Cole, M., & Scribner, S. Cross-cultural studies of memory and cognition. In R. V. Kail & J. W. Hagen (Eds.), *Perspectives on the development of memory and cognition.* New York: Wiley, 1977.

Davidson, G.R. An ethnographic psychology of Aboriginal cognitive ability. *Oceania,* 1979, *49,* 270–294.

Davidson, G. R. Classroom applications of indigenous culture: A cross-cultural viewpoint. *Fiji Education and Education Gazette,* 1981, *3* (3), 42–45.

Dewey, J. Interpretation of savage mind. *Psychological Review,* 1902, *9,* 217–230.

Duignan, P. A. Ethnography: An adventure in interpretive research. *Alberta Journal of Educational Research,* 1981, *27,* 285–297.

Firth, R. Development and the cultural heritage. In S. Tupouniua, R. Crocombe, & C. Slatter (Eds.), *The Pacific way: Social issues in national development.* Suva: Institute of Pacific Studies Press, 1975.

Flavell, J. H. Developmental studies of mediated memory. In H. W. Reese & L. P. Lipsitt (Eds.), *Advances in child development and behaviour* (Vol. 5). New York: Academic Press, 1970.

Flavell, J. H. Metacognition and cognitive monitoring: A new area of cognitive–developmental enquiry. *American Psychologist,* 1979, *34,* 906–911.

Flavell, J. H., & Wellman, H. M. Metamemory. In R. V. Kail & J. W. Hagen (Eds.), *Perspectives on the development of memory and cognition.* New York: Wiley, 1977.

Fry, P., & Ghosh, R. Attributions of success and failure: Comparison of cultural differences between Asian and Caucasian children. *Journal of Cross-Cultural Psychology*, 1980, *11*, 343–363.

Gallimore, R., Boggs, J. W., & Jordan, C. *Culture, behaviour and education: A study of Hawaiian-Americans.* Beverly Hills: Sage, 1974.

Gay, J., & Cole, M. *The new math and an old culture.* New York: Holt, 1967.

Gill, R., & Keats, D. Elements of intellectual competence: Judgements by Australian and Malay university students. *Journal of Cross-Cultural Psychology*, 1980, *11*, 233–243.

Gladwin, T. *East is a big bird: Navigation and logic on Puluwat atol.* Cambridge, Mass.: Harvard Univ. Press, 1970.

Goodnow, J. J. Some sources of cultural difference in performance. In G. E. Kearney & D. W. McElwain (Eds.), *Aboriginal cognition: Retrospect and prospect.* Atlantic Highlands, N.J.: Humanities Press, 1976.

Graham, B. Can we count on maths? *The Aboriginal Child at School*, 1982, *10*(2), 4–10.

Grimble, R. *Migration, myth and magic from the Gilbert Islands: Early writings of Sir Arthur Grimble.* London: Routledge & Kegan Paul, 1972.

Hage, P. Speculations on Puluwatese mnemonic structure. *Oceania*, 1978, *49*, 81–95.

Hansen, J. F. *Socio-cultural perspectives on human learning: An introduction to educational anthropology.* Englewood Cliffs, N.J.: Prentice-Hall, 1979.

Holm, N., & Japanangka, L. The mathematics of card playing in an Aboriginal community. *The Aboriginal Child at School*, 1976, *4*, 19–22.

Hutchins, E. Reasoning in Trobriand discourse. *Quarterly Newsletter of the Laboratory of Comparative Human Cognition*, 1979, *1*, 13–17.

Klich, L. Z., & Davidson, G. R. A cultural difference in visual memory: On le voit, on ne le voit plus. *International Journal of Psychology*, 1983, *18*(2).

Knapp, P., & Seagrim, G. N. Visual memory in Australian Aboriginal children and children of European descent. *International Journal of Psychology*, 1981, *16*, 213–231.

Krywaniuk, L. W., & Das, J. P. Cognitive strategies in native children: Analysis and intervention. *Alberta Journal of Educational Research*, 1976, *22*, 271–280.

Laboratory of Comparative Human Cognition. Cross-cultural psychology's challenges to our ideas of children and development. *American Psychologist*, 1979, *34*, 827–833.

Labov, W. Academic ignorance and Black intelligence. In M. L. Maehr & W. M. Stallings (Eds.), *Culture, child and school.* Monterey: Brooks Cole, 1975.

Lancy, D. F. Studies of memory in culture. In L. L. Adler (Ed.), *Issues in cross-cultural research.* New York: New York Academy of Sciences, 1977.

Le Compte, M. D., & Goetz, J. P. Problems of reliability and validity in ethnographic research. *Review of Educational Research*, 1982, *52*, 31–60.

Luria, A. R. *Cognitive development: Its cultural and social foundations.* Cambridge, Mass.: Harvard Univ. Press, 1976.

Price-Williams, D. *Explorations in cross-cultural psychology.* San Francisco: Chandler & Sharp, 1975.

Ramirez, M., III, & Castaneda, A. *Cultural democracy, bicognitive development, and education.* New York: Academic Press, 1974.

Scribner, S. Situating the experiment in cross-cultural research. In K. F. Riegel & J. A. Meacham (Eds.), *The developing individual in a changing world.* Chicago: Aldine, 1976.

Scribner, S., & Cole, M. Cognitive consequences of formal and informal education. *Science*, 1973, *182*, 553–559.

Wilson, S. The use of ethnographic techniques in educational research. *Review of Educational Research*, 1977, *47*, 245–265.

Wober, M. Towards an understanding of the Uganda concept of intelligence. In J. Berry & P. Dasen (Eds.), *Culture and cognition: Readings in cross-cultural psychology.* London: Methuen, 1974.

8

Toward a Recognition of
Australian Aboriginal Competence
in Cognitive Functions

L. Z. KLICH
GRAHAM R. DAVIDSON

Far too much of human psychology is based on studies of White, Male, Middle-Class, Anglo-Saxon, Protestant, Undergraduates for us to attach much confidence to the claim that the models it generates describe general characteristics of human beings [Serpell, 1976, p. 10].

Differences in performance between aboriginal Australians and white Australians on measures of cognitive functioning have a long history. For many years nonaboriginal researchers and educators viewed such differences from a perspective based largely on a selective interpretation of accumulated evidence that aboriginal people, confronted with tests of mental "capacities" valued in white culture did not handle the demands of such tasks as well as their white counterparts. This supposedly demonstrated a lack of basic intellectual abilities and the underdevelopment of learning attributes considered desirable in the context of formal education. Those views about aborigines showed little sympathy for, nor sensitivity to the ways in which they interpreted their environment or the cognitive functions they may have utilized in responding to its demands.

More recently, research concerned with examining operational skills exercised in the context of aboriginal culture has highlighted the cognitive proficiency of aboriginal people and outlined a complex array of culture-

Cognitive Strategies
and Educational Performance

relevant learning strategies used in that society. However, as yet there is no clear theoretical framework that provides an explanation of the differences and similarities in patterns of cognitive functioning between aboriginal and white Australians, and which at the same time takes account of the wide range of individual differences found within each cultural group. Watts (1982) has pointed out that research in this area has generally paid "little heed" to the notion of individual differences within groups, and this has reduced the potential usefulness of such research for educationists.

The intent of this chapter is to draw attention to aboriginal cognitive skills in a way that may assist educators and psychologists. Initially, research studies of aboriginal cognition will be reviewed. While much of that research encouraged belief in aboriginal cognitive deficit, a detailed examination suggests aboriginal cognitive strengths that have been given little recognition.

A handful of research studies have aimed specifically to identify and analyze cognitive skills valued within aboriginal culture, and these more emic findings will then be considered. The term *emic* (Berry, 1969; Brislin, Lonner, & Thorndike, 1973) is applied in cross-cultural psychology to research concerned with the observation and recording of behavioral characteristics from within a cultural system, necessarily involving a consideration of what is valued by the group members themselves. In contrast, the *etic* approach attempts to expand or modify psychological theory by studying behavior across cultures. Other terms, such as *intracultural* and *intercultural* (Poortinga, 1971) or *culture specific* and *culture common* (Triandis, Vassiliou, & Nassiakou, 1968), have also been used to describe this conceptual distinction between the two methodologies and their different research goals.

In the final section of this chapter, an etic model of individual differences in cognitive processing based on Luria's neuropsychological theory of brain functions will be examined, in order to analyze performance of aboriginal and nonaboriginal Australian children on a variety of cognitive tasks. Luria's theory of cognitive functions appears to provide a coherent framework for interpreting aboriginal cognitive emics as well as evidence from cross-cultural comparisons.

THE FIRST AUSTRALIANS

The first Australians were aborigines, as indeed the name proclaims. Having mastered the complex skills needed to cope with the vicissitudes of extreme environmental conditions, and having survived even harsher treatments meted out in the process of subsequent European colonization, their descendants today number about 180,000, or a little over 1% of the total Australian population.

They may be living in modern housing estates and metropolitan suburbs, under deplorable conditions in groups of shanties on the fringe of small country towns, or in northern islands and coastal communities set among the lush vegetation of a tropical climate; or they may still be traveling between remote settlements across the wilderness of central Australia, perpetuating ceremonial rituals steeped in mythical significance and linked to the visual features of an immense, arid habitat. In an unbroken and timeless lineage, innumerable generations of nomadic desert dwellers have similarly shaped and passed on an intricate set of beliefs and practices in response to environmental demand, considering themselves the embodiment of those mythical ancestors who through their actions had given form and meaning to the land around them.

Whatever their present situation, the cultural heritage of aboriginal people is unique, extensive, and diverse (Berndt & Berndt, 1981; Elkin, 1974). Scientifically dated archaeological finds provide evidence that aborigines have occupied the Australian continent for at least 30,000 years and probably longer, coming originally from Asia via the areas now known as Indonesia and New Guinea. It is not known for certain if there was one rather than a series of migrations, but once in Australia, there is little evidence of any protracted contact between them and other cultural groups prior to the arrival of Europeans. Investigations of blood group patterns and distribution clearly differentiate between aboriginal and other populations and indicate prolonged genetic isolation.

DEFICIENCY THEORIES OF ABORIGINAL COGNITION

The earliest recorded assessments by Europeans of aborigines and their way of life were couched in harsh and derogatory terms (Kearney, 1966). Disparaging commentaries by early Dutch and English navigators, with the notable exception of Captain Cook (Franklin, 1976), began a fairly consistent pattern of negative value judgments by the new arrivals.

The advent of further exploration and colonization after Cook's visit brought in its wake anthropologists and historians as well as convicts, soldiers, and administrators, but increased contact and more detailed observation produced little if any amelioration of earlier reactions to aborigines. Their comparative lack of material possessions, instead of being viewed as the purposeful and successful product of efficient adaptation by hunter—gatherers, was rather interpreted as a sign of cultural impoverishment, with its inevitable concomitant of intellectual inferiority.

Anthropological work in Australia concentrated initially on physical characteristics and was gradually extended to encompass social anthropology, as it became clear that aboriginal social organization was more complex than had at first been realized—so much more complex in fact that a noted anthropologist, writing much closer to our own day, considered that, where the organization of the family was concerned, aborigines "are so far ahead of the rest of mankind that, to understand the careful and deliberate systems of rules they have elaborated, we have to use all the refinements of modern mathematics [Levi Strauss, cited in Franklin, 1976, p. 9]."

However, the notion of a general evolutionary scale in the biological domain and its extension into Spencer's doctrine of social evolution had become a central focus of scientific thinking and appraisal through the nineteenth century (Cole & Scribner, 1974). Examination of mental capacity or intellectual functioning within the constraints of social evolutionary theory characterized the aboriginal as representing "one of the lowest rungs on the ladder of intellectual development [Chase & von Sturmer, 1973, p. 6]," if indeed not the lowest.

Occasionally, almost gratuitous observational concessions were made to aboriginal cognitive competence, usually referring to displays of visual skills apparent in hunting or tracking. For example, it was thought that all "blacks" could find their way through scrub or bush as if by instinct, and that the senses of the Australians, especially sight, were decidedly keener than those of Europeans. Chase and von Sturmer (1973) have pointed out that where such seemingly positive comments did occur they were nevertheless interpreted within an evolutionary perspective as evidence for linkage with lower animal forms, since fauna also relied more heavily than human beings for everyday survival on such keenly developed senses as sight and smell.

Kearney (1973) lists the Baudin expedition of 1801–1804 (commissioned by Napolean to "convey the blessings of civilisation") as the earliest record of testing conducted with Australian aborigines, but it was not until the end of the century in what was probably the first major cross-cultural research endeavor that any attempt was made systematically to investigate selected aspects of the cognitive skills of the first Australians.

The Cambridge Expedition

In April 1898, members of the Cambridge Anthropological Expedition to the Torres Straits organized by A. C. Haddon arrived at Thursday Island and continued for nearly 7 months to gather ethnographic, linguistic, physiological, and psychological data on the inhabitants of surrounding islands and of the New Guinea mainland. Although deriving their approach from the laboratory-based anthropometric methods of experimental psychology initiated by Galton (1883), in which mental attributes were examined through sensory and psychomotor behavior, the expedition constituted "the first occasion on which trained psychologists provided with what apparatus they needed had worked among a primitive people in their natural surroundings [Haddon, 1935, p. xii]."

Six visiting Australian aborigines were tested for visual acuity on Mabuiag Island, and their mean result was higher than that of the local islanders. Suggesting that this was probably due to the comparative youth and health of the aborigines, Rivers (1901) further observed that "the ease with which most of them acquired the method and their general behaviour in connection with the testing gave me the impression that . . . they are far from being so low in the scale of intelligence as has sometimes been supposed [p. 41]."

Rivers concluded that, on the basis of their findings, the visual acuity of the average islander was marginally superior to that of a normal European, but not such as to be considered extraordinary. Their powers of observation to detail, on the other hand, were "equal to any of those which have excited the admiration and wonder of travellers elsewhere [Rivers, 1901, p. 42]." This was attributed to specialized knowledge acquired through exclusive and practiced attention to minute details of objects in familiar surroundings. However, the same emphasis on "the sensory side of mental life," itself a conjectural explanation, was then interpreted as precluding access to other cognitive functions, such that "the predominant attention of the savage to concrete things around him may act as an obstacle to higher mental development [Rivers, 1901, p. 45]."

This post hoc rationalization (that the very exercise of those cognitive skills required for efficient survival within a particular environment prevents the development of "higher" mental functions as defined by European culture) is hardly surprising when one considers that among the tenets of then current scientific thinking was T. H. Huxley's notion that aborigines were the missing links in the evolution of human beings (Kearney, 1966), presumably somewhat closer to the apes than to an English don. Further, Kearins (1977) has drawn attention to the fact that Rivers himself, faced with data suggesting few major differences and some confusing inconsistencies on the performance measures between aborigines, islanders, and whites, later came to see the limitations of the evolutionary approach to understanding cultural differences.

Unfortunately, the legacy of social evolutionary theory is still manifest today through such terms as *primitive people, Stone Age culture,* or *stages of civilization,* which have persistently remained entrenched in everyday language and, by implication, thought.

Porteus Maze Test

S. D. Porteus was asked in about 1913 to supervise the education of "mental defectives" in Melbourne. Trying to devise an effective procedure

for selecting those students who might best profit from specialized schooling, he concluded that the Binet tests, which were then exclusively used to
assess educationally retarded children, did not thoroughly examine "foresight, prudence and sustained attention," which he considered essential
components of intelligence. A series of maze tests were the result, and
nearly 40 years later, Porteus still claimed "no other performance test or
battery of tests has as close a relation to planning capacity as the Maze
possesses [Porteus, 1950, p. 18]."

In 1915 Porteus was invited to South Australia as adviser on training
facilities for the mentally handicapped and, having expressed an interest in
aboriginal culture, was taken to a mission station, where he took the opportunity to test 28 aboriginal children. The mean chronological age of the
children, gleaned from mission records, was 10 years 2 months and their
mental age scores on the Porteus Maze Test averaged 9 years 9 months.
Porteus (1950) evaluated the results as unusually good in a racial group that,
in his opinion, was almost universally considered among the least intelligent
of mankind.

A more extensive testing program was undertaken in 1929 with aboriginal groups in the Kimberley district of the northwest regions and also with
desert-dwelling Arunta aborigines of central Australia. While still predominantly concerned with assessing mental age through the use of the Porteus
Maze Test and the measurement of cranial capacity, Porteus's interests had
expanded to include a range of cognitive functions represented in different
but contextually relevant intellectual skills.

> A very interesting question which arises with regard to the memory of the aborigine has
> to do with the matter of relative efficiency in auditory and visual memory. Here is a race
> whose survival has depended very greatly on visual alertness and observation rather
> than on auditory acuity. . . . There may be a cumulative effect of this kind of experience
> in the race . . . through the selective effect of environment in the struggle for exis-
> tence. . . . . It is reasonable then to suppose that in a race such as the Australian, which
> is dependent largely for existence on keenness of visual observation, visual memory will
> be disproportionately developed [Porteus, 1931, p. 390].

A tapping arrangement in which order of execution had to be recalled
was used to test for visual rote memory, and the auditory version required
the repetition of digits. Results indicated that by comparison with their own
age scores on the Porteus Maze test aborigines were generally "deficient in
memory for unrelated material," allowing Porteus to state that "Australians
in respect to rote memory provide an unmistakable example of divergent
mental evolution [1931, p. 388]."

A comparison of their performances on the two measures, however,
showed that mean mental age scores on the visual task were over 2 years
ahead of auditory memory scores, a difference sufficient in Porteus's judg-

ment to "bear out the view that the dominant use of the visual sense does eventually, in racial experience, bring about an innate superiority of visual memory [1931, p. 395]." Auditory rote memory scores did not improve when syllables derived from aboriginal place names were substituted for digits.

In a further effort to assess visual capacity more in line with aboriginal experiences, Porteus had developed a Footprint Test, in which duplicate photographs of footprints had to be matched with a series of eight original photographs. Test norms had been established with a white high school sample from Hawaii, and although aborigines tended on average to take a few seconds longer to complete the task, their mean performance score equalled that of the whites. Allowing for aboriginal unfamiliarity with photographs, this was certainly no mean achievement and, in describing it as "exceptional," Porteus added that "with test material with which they are familiar the aborigines' ability to discriminate form and spatial relationships is at least equal to that of whites of high-school standards of education and of better than average social standing [1931, p. 401]."

Some of his other results though were not so favorable. The Porteus Maze Test gave aborigines a mean IQ of 82; cranial capacity was judged as being smaller than in Europeans; the mean mental age of male adults was 10.48 years, that of female adults 8.22 years. Porteus (1933b) later claimed reliability for these results by analyzing supporting data from maze tests administered by Piddington and Piddington (1932) and Fry and Pulleine (1931).

One of Porteus's general conclusions, that the central Australian aborigines were slightly but consistently superior in intelligence to those from the northwest, was seriously questioned by Elkin (1932) who, on the basis of considerable anthropological experience, considered that greater familiarity with the language used in testing among the central Australian sample was an alternative explanation. Elkin was also careful to point out that the large range of individual differences in cognitive performance among aborigines cast doubt on the predictive finality of the summary statement in Porteus's report that "they are not unintelligent—but are certainly inadaptable to a civilised environment [1931, p. 420]."

Porteus's reply (1933a) to Elkin placed emphasis on the "social intelligence" displayed by aborigines in their own surroundings but nevertheless reaffirmed his expectations of aboriginal inadaptability to white culture. In a subsequent discussion, he elaborated that aborigines probably suffered from an earlier cessation of brain growth than occurred in Europeans and that their considerably inferior auditory rote memory indicated a "deficient capacity" within the race to benefit from school instruction, so that continued poor scholastic achievement seemed inevitable (Porteus, 1933b).

The results of many further years of research on "australid mentality" using the Porteus Maze Test, together with similar studies from around the world are summarized in Porteus (1965). The culmination is a tabular ranking of "comparative mentalities" as represented by mean maze age scores, such that the gradation of 25 culturally different groups of "illiterate adults" ranges from the rural Bhil of India at one extreme, with a mental age of 7.44 years, to the Tamil immigrants in Malaya at the other, with a mental age of 13.18 years. Three separate Australian aboriginal samples appear in positions 16, 18, and 19, with mean mental ages of 10.4, 10.48, and 10.52 years, respectively. An intellectual "ladder" of this kind graphically illustrates the pervasive influence of social evolutionary thinking.

Kearney (1973) has pointed out that, although Porteus repeatedly asserted that degree of contact with European culture had little if any effect on maze test results, this could be challenged on the grounds that higher scores among aborigines were either associated with more recent testing or else were achieved by aboriginal samples from settlements with a long history of contact, such as Hermannsberg, established in 1877.

It is intriguing, therefore, to note that, while Porteus consistently advocated a high opinion of aboriginal "social intelligence" as expressed in creative and living skills within their own environment, when it came to cognitive skills, he adamantly denied the effect of environmental influence through prolonged European contact, preferring instead to promulgate belief in "biologically determined inferiority [1965, p. 164]."

The Queensland Test

An important contribution to the study of aboriginal cognition has been the work of McElwain and his associates at the University of Queensland. Originally McElwain had accompanied Fowler, who tested 31 aboriginal people of the Gascoyne River area of western Australia in 1940 on a number of performance measures, including the Ferguson Form Board and the Alexander Passalong Test. They reported encouraging results overall, emphasizing (a) the very wide range of individual results obtained (adult male mental age scores ranged from 7.5 to 17 years, adult females from 9 to 17 years); (b) the large variation in scores between different tribal groups; and (c) the considerably smaller difference between the male and female scores than had been reported in previous studies (e.g., on the Alexander Passalong Test, median scores were 12.3 years for men and 12.6 years for women). The conclusion was "if we can rely on our results, some natives have intelligence of a high degree [Fowler, 1940, p. 127]."

A substantial number of established measures of cognitive ability validated in European contexts were in subsequent years carefully examined for validity with indigenous groups in Australia and New Guinea (Kearney,

1966), eventually resulting in the development of the Queensland Test (McElwain & Kearney, 1970), which aimed to reduce the effects of cultural and educational influences on performance.

The Queensland Test is described as an individually administered performance test of general cognitive ability, particularly designed for use under conditions of reduced communication. The subtests are nonverbal in administration and response, with the tester inviting the subject to reproduce arranged materials or to imitate manipulative procedures. The materials are nonrepresentational, the test goals are unambiguous, and all items gradually increase in difficulty.

There are five subtests in all:

1. Knox Cubes: The tester taps out a sequence among four black cubes and the subject's task is to repeat it.
2. Beads: The subject is required to copy a prearranged mixed chain of spherical, cylindrical, or cuboid beads.
3. Passalong: Blue and red tiles of different sizes are arranged in a fixed starting position, and the subject attempts to slide them around within a frame into a mirror-image reversal of the starting position, with the desired end point pictured on an adjacent card.
4. Form Assembly: The subject indicates which of a number of set shapes (separately or in combination as the items become more difficult) will fill a vacant shape displayed by the tester.
5. Pattern Matching: The subject's task is to reconstruct a more complex white and red pattern shown on a card by grouping together individual red, white, or mixed tiles.

Over 1000 aboriginal children and adults were tested from communities and settlements widely differing in degree of European contact, and their performance compared with children of European descent. The overall results indicated that "aboriginal groups are inferior to Europeans, and in approximately the same degree as they have lacked contact (McElwain & Kearney, 1973, p. 47)." Three sets of test norms corresponding to three degrees of estimated contact with white majority culture (high, medium, and low contact) were established, thus allowing greater confidence that the test was in all cases with aborigines a measure of "cognitive ability" rather than an acculturation index.

The reasons for the lower aboriginal scores on the Queensland Test nevertheless remain problematic, given that language and experience with formal education are presumed to have been minimized as intervening variables. McElwain and Kearney (1973) suggest several possible contributing factors, in particular that aboriginal language systems do not appear to have many quantitative components, that aboriginal children do not use symmetry as freely as European children in solving problems, and that they tend to have difficulty in handling flat surface representations.

McElwain (1976) further reasoned that, although the goal of the test may be clear, competent strategies for solution involve appropriate selective attention. The aboriginal child may have in fact preferred learning or processing strategies that are contextually inefficient or may lack the necessary experience with these particular problem solving situations to appropriately deploy his or her attentiveness and thus, in paying attention to all the features of a given task, may well be dealing with some that are irrelevant.

McElwain (1976) also indicated that alternative interpretations might be made as to what it is that the Queensland Test actually measures—for example, instead of general cognitive ability, it could be argued that the first two subtests involve rote memory or encoding of sequential information, and the last three are measures of spatial ability. Horan (1966), for example, provides evidence that the Passalong, Form Assembly, and Pattern Matching subtest scores are especially likely to be negatively affected by lesions of the right cerebral hemisphere among European adults.

In stark contrast to Porteus, McElwain and Kearney asserted that "there are no inborn or genetic limitations on the basic intelligence of Aborigines [1973, p. 50]" and instead viewed environmental experience as the major variable influencing performance on measures of cognitive ability.

Recent Research

A proliferation of psychological interest in aboriginal people has occurred since the mid-1960s. A bibliography of psychological research with aborigines compiled by Kearney and McElwain (1975) listed 280 studies and revealed that the total body of work, with a few exceptions, was "grossly inadequate [p. 2]." Davidson (1980) has computed that some 70% of those studies were commenced or published after 1970.

Watts (1982), in the most recent and comprehensive summary available, has tabulated research studies of aboriginal cognitive ability from 1967 onward. Only a handful of studies have been concerned with examining aboriginal cognitive strengths. In the majority of cases, the remainder have overwhelmingly contributed to "the emphases of the last decade on deficit [Watts, 1982, p. 304]."

Three broad categories of research may be identified based on the use of similar instruments: those studies that have used supposed measures of general intelligence; those that have examined psycholinguistic abilities; and those concerned with Piaget's theory of intellectual development.

General Intelligence Measures

Probably the most widely used measure of general intelligence among aboriginal children (apart from the Queensland Test) has been the Peabody

Picture Vocabulary Test (PPVT: Dunn, 1965). Watts (1982) lists 15 studies that have produced consistent findings of inferior performance on the PPVT by aboriginal children.

Such results have in some cases been used to bolster argument in favor of the "cultural deprivation" hypothesis and in others have been seen as direct confirmation of it. The following account of home circumstances facing the fringe-dwelling aboriginal child, for example, forms part of an elaborate preamble describing the introduction of an intervention program (de Lacey & Nurcombe, 1977; Nurcombe, 1976) where the PPVT was used for assessment:

> There is little privacy, little concept of personal property and small chance to develop those habitual modes of behaviour that develop into foresight, anticipation, the capacity to plan ahead and the desire for achievement. The individual . . . reaches his limit of educability in a conventional setting by about the fourth year of primary school, around the time when hypothetical arithmetical concepts are introduced. The deficits are cumulative . . . the basic deprivation is of certain *patterns* of experience that are of major importance in later educational achievement. The fringe-dweller's home contains no books, magazines or pictures. There are few of those toys and objects that provide the child with the early sensorimotor experiences underlying concepts of number, symmetry, equivalence and class. Adults speak or read to him infrequently . . . . His parents, moreover, are poor language models. Not only is his vocabulary limited, but his syntax is impoverished. He lacks efficient schemata of transformation by which word combinations can be manipulated in the service of rational thought. His communication skills are therefore limited and predominantly concrete and descriptive in nature. . . . The total picture is of a series of interlocking and self-perpetuating vicious circles: malnutrition, infection, infestation, low achievement aims, language and concept impoverishment and social disintegration. The question arises: what are the most critical times and places to intervene and reverse the process [Nurcombe & Moffitt, 1970, p. 253].[1]

Brislin (1976) addressed problems in the methodology of cognitive studies, especially with aboriginal Australians. Commenting specifically on the use of the PPVT, he suggested that performance on it by aborigines could be due to a number of factors, such as unfamiliarity with test materials, nervousness in the sole presence of the test administrator, indifference at working on an apparently irrelevant task, total boredom, efforts to end the procedure as soon as possible, and ingratiation tendencies. Any one or combination of these, in addition to the "real competence" that the test was designed to measure, might explain depressed scores by non-test-sophisticated aboriginal children.

Watts (1982) considers that the PPVT, developed and normed in the United States, has questionable value for assessing aboriginal cognition

---

[1]Quoted with permission of the author and by courtesy of the Australian Psychological Society.

since the language used is standard English and some of the content is clearly inappropriate. She suggests accordingly that it might better be seen as a measure of "receptive language" rather than as a test of general intelligence.

Studies by Money and Nurcombe (1974) and McIntyre (1976) represent efforts to assess aspects of aboriginal cognition using tests and procedures more attuned to content and process within aboriginal culture. Money and Nurcombe (1974) used the nonverbal Draw-a-Person Test (Harris, 1963) and the Bender Visual-Motor Gestalt Test (Koppitz, 1964) with a sample of 76 Yolngu children from Galiwinku in eastern Arnhem Land, operating on the assumption that graphic tasks were appropriate for use in a culture with a long and revered tradition of art expressed in carving, painting, totemic design, and ceremonial decoration. Their results showed that aboriginal male mean scores were consistently above the expected norm, but aboriginal female scores were slightly below, and they interpreted this as the result of a cultural heritage where the arts belong to the predominantly male preserve of sacred and ceremonial knowledge.

McIntyre (1976) investigated dimensions of cognitive style among urban and rural aboriginal and nonaboriginal children, and used the Queensland Test as one measure of general cognitive ability. She found no significant difference on the Queensland Test score between cultural groups in the urban location, but in the more remote rural environment, white children performed significantly better, thus confirming McElwain and Kearney's (1973) rationale that Queensland Test performance for aboriginal children was dependent on degree of contact with European culture, or on some variable related to contact.

The cognitive style variables in her study were standard and modified tests of field independence, reflectivity, and conceptual style, and measures of school achievement were also included. Using discriminant function analysis to explore the nature of the differences between the four samples of 7–12-year-old children, McIntyre found that no discriminant function differentiated between the groups on the basis of culture. The first function produced an urban–rural distinction, and the second involved a set of variables with educational content. The third was described as possibly involving sequential versus wholistic processing, with the Beads and Knox Cubes subtests of the Queensland Test as indicators of sequential processing. This appears to lend further credence to the notion of spatial-sequential dimensions underlying the Queensland Test.

Psycholinguistic Testing

The Illinois Test of Psycholinguistic Abilities (ITPA: Kirk, McCarthy, & Kirk, 1968) has been extensively used with aborigines, and studies have typically reported inferior performance by aboriginal children on many of the ITPA scales. Kearney and McElwain summarized the overall findings as clearly indicating "a significant deficit in psycho-linguistic abilities in English over all categories for Aboriginal children [1976, p. 400]."

A closer scrutiny suggests that some of the tasks involving visual processing produced relatively more positive results for aborigines. Bruce, Hengeveld, and Radford (1971) found that, among 5–12-year-old children from metropolitan and country regions of Vicgoria, aboriginal children performed better than nonaboriginal children on the visual closure scale, and Nurcombe and Moffit (1970) found no significant difference on the same scale among 3–4-year-old aboriginal and white children at Bourke in New South Wales. Aboriginal children of preschool age from the midnorth coast of New South Wales were "within the normal range" of scores on the Visual decoding and Visual-motor sequential subtests, although "retarded" on all others by up to 2.5 years (Harries, 1967). Teasdale and Katz (1968) reported no differences on Visual decoding and Visual-motor association scales among 5-year-old aboriginal and white schoolchildren in New South Wales.

ITPA is administered in standard English, and it is therefore not surprising to find depressed scores among aborigines on subtests predominantly involving verbal processing. Although none of the ITPA studies tested children from traditional backgrounds, the expectation of equivalent familiarity with standard English among rural aborigines and whites is nevertheless unrealistic, given widely varying degrees of fluency between and within aboriginal groups (Watts, 1982). Smith (1966) has argued that an inverse relationship exists between the amount of English verbal content in psychological tests and aboriginal children's scores on them.

A useful critique of the ITPA and guarded recommendations for its use with aboriginal children appear in Teasdale and de Vries (1976), who concluded that it may legitimately be employed, preferably in a diagnostic capacity, only when certain lingustic prerequisites have been met.

Piagetian Research

Piaget's ideas on the progression of intellectual functioning from a sensorimotor stage in infancy through to the stage of formal operations in adolescence have stimulated a series of investigations among aborigines. de Lemos (1969) argued that according to Piaget's theory the stages of development and their order should be invariant since they are biologically determined, but that their rate of development is a result of environmental interaction, and thus children exposed to different social and cultural influences could be expected to achieve the same order of stages, but not necessarily at similar ages.

Her own research (de Lemos, 1969) examined the development of the concept of conservation and found that it developed much later in aboriginal than in European children, with a number of cases where it did not develop at all. Whereas European children invariably acquired the conservation of quantity, weight, and volume in that order, aboriginal children in samples from Galiwinku and Hermannsberg appeared to develop the concept of conservation of weight earlier than that of quantity. Finally, a statistically significant difference between the performance of part-aboriginal and full-blooded aboriginal children living in identical conditions at Hermannsberg favored the former, suggesting that "genetic factors affecting the average intellectual potential of these children may therefore have contributed to the retardation in the development of conservation concepts [de Lemos, 1969, p. 268]." This finding was later cited by Jensen (1973) as strong support for the idea that Piagetian tests were highly sensitive indicators of genetic factors in mental development.

Several studies (de Lacey, 1970, 1971a, 1971b, Taylor, Nurcombe, & de Lacey, 1973) have tested classificatory ability, and results in general favour nonaborigines, although degree of European contact is again clearly implicated in performance.

The study by de Lacey (1970) drew four samples designated as "relatively advantaged" and "relatively disadvantaged" from both European and full-blooded aboriginal populations. The two European samples were described as of high or low socioeconomic status (SES), and the two aboriginal samples as high and low contact. On all four tests that were employed, the order of classificatory performance was high-SES Europeans, followed by low-SES Europeans, then high-contact aborigines, with low-contact aborigines last. However, after an extension of the study with very high-contact full-blooded aboriginal children, a reanalysis of the data showed that the combined scores of the high-contact and very high-contact aboriginal children were not significantly different from those of the white low-SES children. de Lacey's conclusions emphasized that the critical element in the development of classificatory ability was the degree of enrichment in children's environments (degree of enrichment appears in his argument to be equated with degree of European contact), and he extended this to encompass potential welfare action:

> That the relationship between milieu and classificatory ability was found to obtain so unequivocally throughout the test battery points to possible important implications for Aboriginal welfare policy [so that] it could be argued that the interests of the optimal cognitive development of Aboriginal children would best be served by ensuring that they should in the future be reared near or even integrated with substantial European settlements [de Lacey, 1970, p. 303].[2]

[2]Reprinted by permission of Sage Publications, Inc.

Dasen (1973) carried out a replication and extension of de Lemos's study with low-contact aboriginal children from Areyonga settlement, a higher contact aboriginal group from Hermannsberg, and European children from Canberra. An additional goal of the research was to assess the relative development of logicomathematical operations (related to concepts of number and measurement) and of spatial operations. He found that the stages described by Piaget occurred in the same order in both European and aboriginal children, although the rate of concept development in aboriginal children was "very slow," which meant in effect that a reasonably large proportion of aborigines did not develop some of the concrete operational concepts at all, even in maturity.

In contrast to the results of de Lemos, there was no difference in the performance of part-Aboriginal and full-blooded aboriginal children, and of particular interest to Dasen was that, while the Canberra European sample acquired logicomathematical operations earlier than spatial operations, this sequence was reversed for both aboriginal samples—that is, the aboriginal children from central Australia developed spatial concepts earlier than logicomathematical concepts.

Dasen (1975) went on to apply an ecocultural model of behavior (Berry, 1976) to the Piagetian cognitive domain and predicted that, on the basis of ecological adjustment, spatial concrete operational concepts would of necessity develop earlier and faster among low food-accumulating groups, such as the Eskimos, characterized by small group numbers and nomadic hunter–gatherer survival mechanisms, than among high food-accumulating cultures, such as the West African Ebrié, in which larger groups remained as sedentary agriculturalists, with Australian aborigines showing an intermediate rate of development. Results fully supported the hypothesis. The additional prediction that conservation of quantity, weight, and volume would develop among the groups in the reverse order to spatial concepts received some support, but only in the 12–14-year-old groups, where the African sample showed the fastest rate of development, followed by aborigines and then Eskimos.

A number of procedural and methodological criticisms may be leveled at the Piagetian approach in general to the cross-cultural study of cognition and in particular to the research so far carried out with Australian aborigines. Kamara and Easley (1977) and Watts (1982) have raised the issue of likely language barriers between the subjects and the interviewer in cross-cultural Piagetian research, such that, where there is a lack of fluency in English, it is difficult to be certain that adequate comprehension exists of what the task entails. All Piagetian testing with aboriginal children discussed here appears to have been conducted in standard English.

This is a particularly trenchant criticism when considered in conjunction with a further problem highlighted by Dasen and Heron (1981) and Kamara and Easley (1977)—namely, that in cross-cultural Piagetian studies the tendency has been to collect data through performance tests rather than through Piaget's original "method of critical exploration,"which utilizes clinical interviews. The task, or experimental situation, is merely the starting point for an extensive dialogue between interviewer and child in which the child's responses are clarified and probed with follow-up questions. Thus, in any interviewing situation other than one where quality of communication is assured through shared ease in language and culture between interviewer and child, doubts must be raised as to whether performance is an unambiguous measure of competence.

> When the task is presented by an interviewer of a Western culture in his own language, *he* may be at ease, but the subject may be unable to understand and to express himself fully. When the task is presented by a Western interviewer in the child's native language, the subject may be at ease but the interviewer is handicapped in his ability to follow the child's explanations or to follow up on clues spontaneously. When interpreters are used, or no language at all is used, both parties are handicapped in their ability to communicate the subtleties of thought involved in these tasks [Kamara & Easley, 1977, p. 34].

However, given that the use of decontextualized, impersonal, or hypothetical questions within a question-and-answer routine has now come to be recognized as a predominantly Western verbal learning–teaching ritual (Cole, Gay, Glick, & Sharp, 1971; Luria, 1976) and inappropriate in traditional aboriginal culture (Harris, 1977), it seems unlikely that the Piagetian clinical interview technique of probing the reasoning behind task performance will be productive with aboriginal children from remote areas.

The appropriateness of responses by subjects in one culture to the stimuli and procedures devised in another has been the concern of other criticisms examining such cultural (as opposed to linguistic) barriers to adequate communication and performance.

Goodnow (1980) has described Piagetian tasks as usually containing a "perceptual trap," with subjects being tempted to follow a misleading visual cue. The assumption underlying such procedures appears to be that the best way to measure intelligence is to face people with an unfamiliar task that cannot be solved by drawing on past experience. While appropriate in those sections of Western culture where psychological testing is reasonably commonplace, with a different cultural population (e.g., Australian aborigines), such tasks may simply be measuring the degree to which individuals in that culture are familiar with the rules and assumptions of test procedures.

Buck-Morss (1975) has challenged the universality of the Piagetian ideal of reasoning divorced from practical content and context (and therefore experience) as being derived from a culture where schooling and learning are themselves generally far removed from real-life settings or from questions of relevant application.

In support of this view, the work of Harris (1977) suggests that it is difficult to locate the relevance of the Piagetian intellectual ideal within the context of formal and informal learning among Australian aborigines. Harris examined the learning styles of tradition-oriented aborigines at Milingimbi and described five major learning strategies: learning through real-life performance rather than through practice in contrived settings; the mastering of context-specific skills rather than abstract, generalizable principles; learning through observation and imitation rather than through oral or written verbal instruction; learning through personal trial-and-error as opposed to observing demonstrations accompanied by verbal instructions; and an orientation to people rather than to tasks, information, or systems.

Results of Piagetian tests, like those from measures of general intelligence and psycholinguistic ability, have typically been interpreted as demonstrating that environmental factors have retarded the development of cognitive functions and that this "cognitive deficit" can be remedied or forestalled by compensatory education, often in the form of early intervention programs.

Seagrim has reached a very different conclusion (Seagrim, 1977; Seagrim & Lendon, 1976, 1980). Faced with the now predictable pattern of aboriginal inferiority on Piagetian tasks from a large-scale project in central Australia, he acknowledged that the logical conclusion of the interventionist approach was that "Aboriginal children, if they are to become intellectually competent in a Western sense, should be removed from their natural families as early as possible and for as long as possible [Seagrim & Lendon, 1976, p. 225]." This was manifestly unacceptable as an educational goal. Having reviewed the long-term and sometimes unforeseen effects of well-intentioned intervention programs, he specifically issued the warning *caveat interventor* (Seagrim, 1977).

An alternative approach was to question the assumption that cognitive competence in white culture necessarily precluded cognitive competence in aboriginal culture, or vice versa. Certainly evidence from bilingual education programs overseas suggested that competence in dual language systems could be achieved, and through that competence, members of a minority culture could access the process of "learning how to learn" (Davidson, 1976) in the majority culture. Why not then promote dual learning systems where neither one emphasized the exclusion of those situations allowing for development in the other—that is, bicultural cognitive competence achieved through bicultural learning or education.

Adequate cognitive development for the handling of the demands of white culture by Aboriginal children may equally well be achieved by the persistence (or recovery) of Aboriginal culture in its richest and most fully integrated forms as by its complete destruction [Seagrim & Lendon, 1976, p. 230].

One of the prerequisites for the fulfillment of such a bicultural goal is the recognition within white culture of aboriginal cognitive strengths and an understanding of the underlying cognitive processes.

COMPETENCE THEORIES OF ABORIGINAL COGNITION

Route Finding

Exceptional Australian aboriginal skills in tracking and geographic orientation have long been the subject of admiration, analysis, and debate (Lahiri, 1965; Strehlow, 1943; Wallace, Note 1). Spencer and Gillen's early comment, cited by Porteus (1931, p. 214), that "in many respects their memory is phenomenal" has been strongly reiterated in the work of Lewis (1976a), who was primarily concerned with how desert aborigines find their way across the vast and, to Western eyes, apparently featureless terrain of central Australia.

> All the Aborigines with whom I travelled demonstrated extraordinary acuity of perception of natural signs and ability to interpret them, and almost total recall of every topographical feature of any country they had *ever* crossed. A single visit forty years ago would be sufficient to make an indelible imprint [Lewis, 1976a, p. 32].

Trying to find an answer to the critical question of how aborigines are able unerringly to cover such enormous distances, Lewis started off with a number of plausible hypotheses derived from navigational procedures in other cultures—for example, use of the sun during the day, or orientation by star positions at night. In unusual circumstances, such as when lost or traveling in "strange" country (i.e., country that was unfamiliar because the stories associated with it were not known or accessible to those individuals), aborigines did use such information as the placing of the sun or the quality and direction of the wind for assistance in traveling, but such times were very rare. Instead, what became evident to Lewis was that under normal conditions aborigines utilized a complex "topographical schema" (Gibson, 1950) relying primarily on (a) knowledge of important landmarks; (b) familiarity with the body of mythical stories associated with those landmarks; and (c) the use of dynamic mental maps.

On a number of occasions, aborigines were asked to point out the direction of distant places, and in 33 such instances, accuracy varied from absolutely correct to 67° error, with an average error of 13.7°. However, the larger errors always occurred when indicating nonsacred places or cardinal compass points. The highest degree of accuracy related to the positions of mythically important places. For six sacred sites, each of which was at least 200 km away, the largest error was 10° and the average was 2.8°.

Verbal directions were also often given by the aborigines visualizing themselves at some distant point of significance, assumed to be known to the listener, from which a course would subsequently be stated. The direction of the common reference point was frequently indicated by gesture when first mentioned.

Spiritually significant landmarks, then, seemed to be particularly relevant to the aborigines' geographic orientation, but landmarks are simply focal points within a broader and coherently integrated body of mythical knowledge, in which "the whole Western Desert is criss-crossed with the meandering tracks of ancestral beings, mostly though not invariably following the known permanent and impermanent waterhole routes [Berndt, 1959, p. 97]." Familiarity with the mythical stories and the lore associated with the wide-ranging and visibly marked actions of dreamtime beings also therefore provides access to invaluable route-finding information.

In addition, Lewis described a number of hunting incidents where spatially oriented behavior was impressively accurate yet appeared not to have utilized any distant external reference points. From his own observations, and from explanatory comments made by his aboriginal guides, he deduced that constant cognitive synthesis of perceptual and spatial information seemed to be the process by which precise orientation was maintained.

> It would appear then, that the essential psychophysical mechanism was some kind of *dynamic image* or *mental 'map'*, which was *continually updated* in terms of time, distance and bearing, and more radically *realigned at each change of direction*, so that the hunters remained *at all times* aware of the precise direction of their *base and/or objective* [Lewis, 1976b, p. 262].

A detailed examination of traditional art designs among the same Walbiri aborigines suggested that some of the designs were stylized depictions of such mental maps, and similar abstracted designs were in fact produced by the guides when drawing or painting details of the stories associated with visits to particular locations.

In summary, Lewis considered that the highly developed visual–spatial orientation skills of desert aborigines could be attributed to the use of complex mental mapping processes, following "terrestrial conditioning" through emotional and spiritual links with a land patterned by networks of mythical events.

Visual Memory

The original research of Kearins (1976, 1977, 1978, 1981) is based on the assumption that selection not only of the more obvious physical characteristics but also of sensory and cognitive adaptations may result from environmental demand. For reasons of extended isolation, as evidenced by blood group distribution, aborigines of the Western Desert regions of Australia were considered by Kearins to be "obviously very interesting subjects for an investigation of the genetic outcome of environmental pressures [1976, p. 200]," and she hypothesized that, for such hunter–gatherer groups living in a harsh environment, visual memory for patterns of diverse features and the spatial relationships among them constitutes a significant survival requirement.

The task designed by Kearins to measure these memory skills was a spatial modification of Kim's game (Kipling, 1908) in which the child was first asked to view a grid-marked array of objects for 30 sec, after which the array was disarranged, and the child was then asked to replace the items in their original locations.

Four arrays were used: 20 manufactured objects all different by name from each other; 20 assorted objects found in nature, with different names; 12 natural but same-name objects, specifically small rocks varying in size, shape, and color; and 12 manufactured but same-name objects, a collection of small bottles. The natural–manufactured object distinction recognized experiential differences between aborigines and Europeans, and the same-name categorization was intended to control verbal labeling.

Aboriginal children of desert origins aged 12–16 years who comprised an entire school population were tested, and 44 white children from a suburban Perth school were chosen to match the aboriginal group for age and sex. Scoring was in two forms: the total number of items correctly replaced in each array (Kearins, 1977), and an error extent score, which consisted of summing the number of squares by which objects were misplaced (Kearins, 1976).

On all four memory tasks, the performance of the desert aboriginal adolescents was superior to that of the European descent group, and while aborigines performed equally well on all arrays, white children were significantly less successful with the same-name arrays than with arrays of different objects. There were no sex differences.

Kearins (1976, 1978) considered that these results provided strong support for the environmental pressures hypothesis. In some instances, observations made of the children's behavior during testing (e.g., incidence of lip movements) implied the use of visual strategies by the aborigines and verbal strategies by the whites, but the superiority of aboriginal children's performance on all tasks, and its extent, made it more likely that they "possessed a superior mechanism (cognitive-sensory?) for the processing of the type of information contained in the arrays" while "the European descent children would presumably have employed verbal strategies because of the absence or imperfection of a better mechanism [Kearins, 1976, p. 211]."

In a series of minor studies designed to examine more closely possible processing differences (Kearins, 1977), it appeared that eidetic imagery was not contributing to the superior performance of aborigines, that strategies adopted by the aboriginal children were "exclusively" visual as opposed to the predominant verbal coding behavior of whites, and that among European descent children there was no correlation between verbal ability and visual-spatial memory ability. Further research (Kearins 1977, 1978) showed that nontraditionally reared aboriginal children of desert origin aged 6–12 years also demonstrated superiority to whites of similar age and that nontraditionally reared aboriginal children performed at about the same level as traditionally reared children of equivalent ages. Kearins concluded that "the simplest and most likely explanation for the high level of Aboriginal skill appears therefore to be the genetic one [1977, p. 154]."

The notion of "visualizers" and "verbalizers" in memory strategy is of course not new. Bartlett (1932) referred to "those who in remembering relied mainly upon visual images, and those who were predominantly determined by the use of language cues [p. 59]." Imagery techniques as an aid to memory themselves go back at least some 2000 years (Yates, 1966). Cicero in *De Oratore,* for example, cited the case of Simonides, who while presenting a paper in the form of a lyric poem at a symposium was called outside for a message. In his fortuitous absence, the roof fell in, and Simonides was eventually called back in to what remained of the banquet in order to try and identify the unrecognizable bodies. He did so by recalling the places where individuals had been sitting during his lyric delivery, a memory task not dissimilar to, if somewhat more gruesome than, Kim's game.

Bruner, Olver, and Greenfield (1966) have examined verbal and nonverbal representations developmentally, and extensive reviews of nonverbal imagery and verbal symbolic processes appear in Richardson (1969), Paivio (1971), and Sheehan (1972). Bower (1970) has suggested that, of these "two major components of thinking [p. 507]," the verbal system appears better suited for handling abstract and sequential information, whereas the imagery system is more attuned to concrete and spatial tasks. Paivio (1971) points out that the systems do not operate independently, but in their continual interaction, the nature and demands of a given situation are likely to determine which mode may be *functionally* dominant: "Visual imagery, when readily generated, may be more effective than verbal mediation because the information in the image is spatially organised, permitting a rapid readout of the relevant components [p. 391]."

Memory strategies relying predominantly on visual–spatial information processing therefore appear to be particularly suited to the task demands of Kearins's Kim's game. That their use by desert aborigines is supposedly the result of genetic endowment has generated considerable discussion.

Drinkwater (1976) stated that if Kearins' evolutionary–ecological hypothesis were to be accepted one would predict a similar pattern of performance elsewhere in Australia. Using a variation of Kearins' tasks in which only two arrays were presented—one a mixture of 10 natural and 10 manufactured objects, and the other an assortment of 20 plastic letters—Drinkwater found no significant differences in recall for either objects or letters between 22 aboriginal children aged 11–14 years from a nontraditional island community in Queensland and 22 European-descent children of comparable age and sex from a city suburb. For both groups, more manufactured objects than natural objects were replaced, and letters were significantly more difficult to replace. Although there were no sex differences on correct replacement scores, analysis of error scores showed that error extent for girls was smaller than for boys. Drinkwater concluded that her results provided no evidence of cognitive processing differences between aborigines and whites, and offered no support for an evolutionary as distinct from a nongenetic ecological explanation of Kearins's results.

Kearins (1978) reply was unequivocal. No generalizations had been made to any but desert people, and since Drinkwater's sample was not of desert origin, then the habitat-specific hypothesis of Kearins's research had no relevance for Drinkwater's study. While the mixed objects array was "clearly related" to the Kearins tasks, the letters array had no place in work examining an ecological rationale aimed toward "a preliterate people."

The response from Drinkwater (1978) was equally direct: The specific "desert" skills referred to by Kearins were surely required by ecological pressures acting on all hunter–gatherer groups, and if such skills were attributed to genetic advantage as opposed to cultural experience and lifetime environmental pressure, then they would be more widely evident in the descendants of Australian aborigines. Other attempts at replication by Harris (1977), Knapp and Seagrim (1981), Lendon and Seagrim (cited in Knapp & Seagrim, 1981), and Meredith (1978) have produced mixed results, and the debate has been more extensively reviewed in Klich and Davidson (in press).

Two questions were originally raised by Kearins: Given that visual memory is likely to be a valuable aid in survival within a desert environment, will *desert* aboriginal children excel on a task designed to measure it? If indeed they do, then the next question is whether those skills are the result of genetic advantage or cultural practices.

A third question, and one that may help to unravel the complexities of the second, has been raised in the work of Davidson (1979, Note 2): What are the cognitive processes that underlie the range of aboriginal and European strategies for handling the demands of such tasks?

Card Playing

A number of researchers have described a card game often played in aboriginal communities and commonly called *bayb kad* (Berndt & Berndt,

1947; Holm & Japanangka, 1976; Robinson & Yu, 1975). Davidson (1979, Note 2) not only has provided a detailed description of the game as played at Bamyili, in the Northern Territory, but also has analyzed the specific cognitive skills developed among the aborigines who play it.

The game itself is straightforward. Court cards and jokers are removed leaving ace to 10 in each of the four suits. Players receive five cards and must then attempt to combine any three of the cards so that their total will be either 10, 20, or 30. If a player has this requisite combination of three "keycards," the score is the sum of the remaining two cards, ignoring multiples of 10 (i.e., take the unit value of the sum, so that the highest possible score is 10). A player registers no score if he or she cannot produce the keycards combination.

Davidson discovered that, while Europeans simply use recognition of the numerical symbol in the corner of each card to identify cards initially and then mathematical counting skills to calculate combinations and scores, aborigines instead often utilized the large amount of visual information on the rest of the card for pattern recognition and identification, and then maintained such visual information about their cards in a spatial memory array to be retrieved as the task demanded in either keycard combinations or "scores."

Three distinct pattern recognition procedures were identified. In the procedure called *rib,* the card to be classified is partially covered in a systematic way from the side by another card (see Figure 8.1), and the pattern of suit motifs exposed to the left is surveyed (the procedure may also be carried out equally effectively from the right side). Four possibilities exist. The first, called *binisrib,* reveals no visible suit symbol to the left. The second arrangement, *broknrib,* reveals the edges of two suit motifs; *trilayn* reveals three; and *bolayn* shows four symbols uncovered. With this initial step completed, a further partial exposure of suit symbols is made, either toward the center (in *binisrib* and *broknrib*) or at the top or bottom of the card (in *trilayn* and *bolayn*). Thus, either two moves (*binisrib, broknrib,* or *bolayn*) or three (*trilayn*) are sufficient to classify any card accurately. Davidson considers *rib* to be the most common of the pattern recognition procedures employed, and it is often used in conjunction with the two others.

The procedure called *hed* involves visual scrutiny of the numerical symbol shape when it has been partially covered by another card (see Figure 8.2). A flat top indicates what Europeans would recognize as a 3, 5, or 7 card; a round top could be 2, 6, 8, or 9; a sharp point indicates an ace or a 4; and a double point is clearly a 10. Thus, an initial categorization of a card by *rib* into *binisrib, broknrib, trilayn,* or *bolayn* may be made and followed by *hed* scrutiny, or vice versa, and is sufficient for accurate identity to be established in all cases except the 6 and 8.

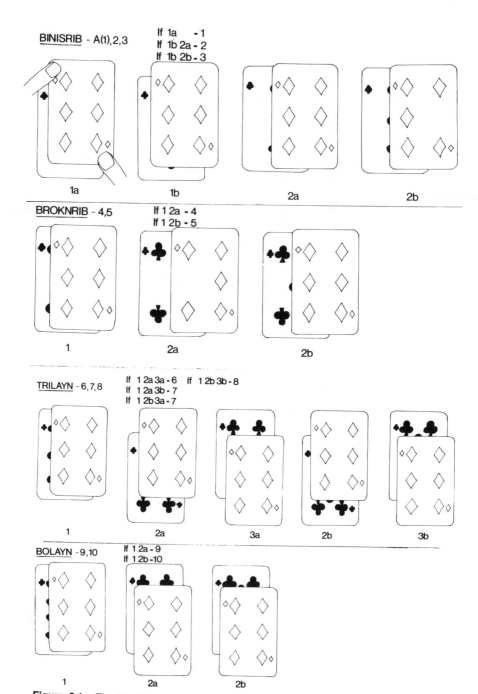

Figure 8.1. The identification of cards by *rib*. (From Davidson, 1979, by permission of *Oceania*.)

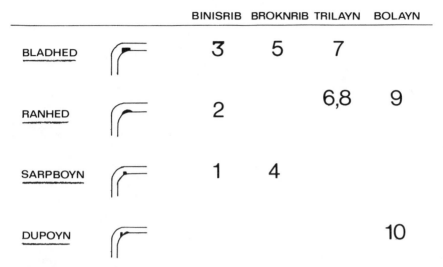

Figure 8.2.   The identification of cards by *hed*. (From Davidson, 1979, by permission of *Oceania*.)

The third procedure, called *badn,* relies on the process of visually detecting slight differences among the individual suit symbols that are placed just below the number in the opposite corners of each card (see Figure 8.3). It is a somewhat restricted procedure, since it can be used only with the Queen's Slipper brand-name cards, and occasionally minor differences exist between the suit motifs in the corners of the same card, but in such cases *rib* may still be used to verify *badn* judgments.

A fourth classifactory procedure does not use pattern recognition but stores information about the actual numerical symbol, so that an appropriate spatial image or verbal label may be assigned to the visible number. Davidson, however, emphasizes that such recognition does not then lead to logical addition, as in the European procedure, but is rather encoded spatially, as with the pattern sorting; for example, players describing the use of such a procedure referred to visualizing how the cards "fitted together" to produce keycard combinations.

Essentially, then, what involves in the European case a serial process of logically ordered number recognition and addition, entails for the aborigines the storage and recall of spatial information. Thus, aborigines using the *rib* or *badn* pattern recognition strategies can and do competently play the game using cards on which the numerical symbols in the corners have been rubbed off through prolonged handling, a task of considerable if not insurmountable difficulty for most Europeans.

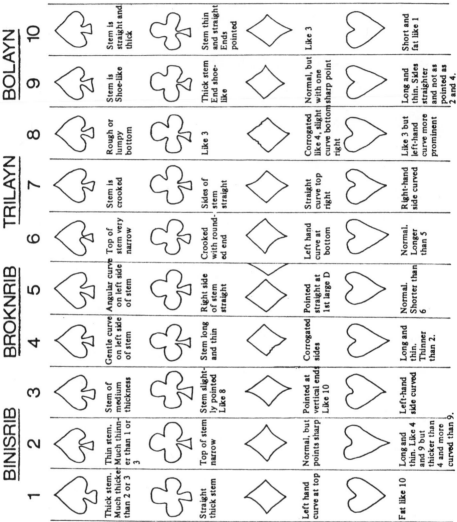

Figure 8.3. The identification of cards by *Badn*. (From Davidson, 1979, by permission of *Oceania*.)

Temporal and Spatial Ordering

Attempts to investigate temporal and spatial ordering with children have tended to focus on observed preferences for one type of contextual association over the other in free recall, generally with emphasis on processing in the visual mode, and have overwhelmingly involved research with children of urban European origins.

Three main issues have arisen: (*a*) whether children have a preference for one order of recall over the other; (*b*) whether they alter their preference from spatial to temporal ordering as they get older; and (*c*) whether accuracy of recalling information temporally and spatially increases with age.

Freeman (1975) found a significant and linear age progression from recall of visual information by spatial position to recall by temporal position among white urban 5–8-year-olds and concluded that as normal children got older they responded consistently to temporal patterning of stimuli, but not to spatial patterning. Freeman (1975) also suggested that exceptions to this trend—for example, deaf and mentally retarded children who had shown a greater recall preference for spatial rather than temporal order (O'Connor & Hermelin, 1973)—were probably due to a slower rate of acquisition of the encoding skills associated with temporal ordering.

Davidson and Klich (1980) used two free recall tasks, one involving pictures and the other natural objects, to examine temporal and spatial ordering among aborigines. The sample consisted of 30 male and 35 female aboriginal children aged 9–16 years living in a central Australian desert community, and comprised the entire school population from Grades 4 to Grade 7.

Results showed that a majority of the desert aboriginal children preferred spatial over temporal order in the free recall of visual information, and this did not significantly decrease with age. In addition, the use of natural objects instead of picture stimuli elicited significantly more changes in the direction of spatial than temporal recall order.

In contrast therefore to Freeman's suggestion that continued preference for spatial order with increasing age was probably due to the prolongation of an earlier developmental stage, Davidson and Klich (1980) argued that it might equally well be interpreted as a deliberate adaptive response to cultural influence and ecological demand.

Summary

Much of the earlier research on aboriginal cognition, while framed within a deficit model of performance, nevertheless suggested relative aboriginal cognitive strengths in visual and spatial information processing. Lewis has emphasized exceptional aboriginal skills in geographic orientation through the use of dynamic mental maps relying on the complex manipulation of spatial information. Kearins has argued for superior visual–spatial memory skills among desert aborigines, and Davidson and Klich have indicated an aboriginal preference for spatial ordering. Davidson's research has demonstrated that aboriginal cognitive strategies within the context of card-playing involved the storage and retrieval of spatial information in such a way that any part of the information was constantly surveyable, as opposed to the Western strategy of serially processing numerical data so that encoded information is not totally accessible at any one point in a continuous procedure.

A STUDY OF COGNITIVE PROCESSES

In attempting to analyze the cognitive functions behind such contrasting preferred modes of organizing information, Davidson (1979) suggested that the neuropsychological work of Luria might provide a coherent theoretical framework for interpreting these apparent cultural differences.

The Luria Model

The cerebral bases of psychological processes, or how intellectual functions relate to cortical and subcortical structures, were the research concern of A. R. Luria. He stated that higher mental functions are complex, organized *functional systems* that operate as the result of interactions between differentiated brain structures. This dynamic localization of functional systems relies on components represented in different areas of the brain that may be integrated according to the demands of a processing task. Luria stresses that such functional systems of conjointly working cortical zones are not independent structures but are formed during the course of each individual's development in response to social influences (Luria, 1966a).

The functional organization of the brain, according to Luria (1970, 1973) can be understood in terms of three basic units, or blocks. The first unit is responsible for regulating the energy level and tone of the cortex (i.e., for arousal) and is located in the brain stem and reticular formation. The second unit is highly specialized for the analysis, coding, and storage of information, and Luria (1966b) considered that it operated through two forms of integrative activity: *simultaneous synthesis,* or the integration of stimuli into maintained spatial groupings, and *successive or sequential synthesis,* where serial perceived stimuli are temporally ordered such that each element exists only as part of a retraceable sequence. The occipitoparietal zones are responsible for simultaneous synthesis, and the frontotemporal regions for successive synthesis. The third unit of the brain, comprising the frontal lobes, is involved in the organization of conscious activity through the programming, regulation, and verification of behavior (Luria, 1973). A detailed consideration of Luria's theory of brain functions appears in Das, Kirby, and Jarman (1979).

Using Luria's neuropsychological approach, Davidson (1979) surmised that "where the task permits, Aborigines may be more likely to employ a simultaneous or synchronous than a successive or serial method of synthesis of perceptual information [p. 288]," and certainly that assumption appears warranted from the research reviewed earlier.

Davidson (1979) then proceeded to reanalyze correlational data from the Queensland Test (McElwain & Kearney, 1970), suggesting that, if the five subtests were designated as requiring either simultaneous or successive synthesis of information, or both, depending on the nature of the task, then using factor analytic procedures two factors identifiable as simultaneous and successive would be evident, but differences could be expected between aboriginal and white samples on the patterns of variable loadings. This did indeed turn out to be the case (see Table 8.1), although while general support for the overall interpretation is provided, several aspects are clearly ambiguous.

For example, Factor 1 for the high-contact aboriginal sample could be interpreted as a general ability or intelligence factor, since loadings on Factor 2 for that group are negligible. However, if so, one would therefore expect age to load on the general ability factor, but that is clearly not the case. Factor 1 for the nonaboriginal sample might be similarly construed, since only one variable (Beads) loads extensively on the second factor. The clearest support for the two-process coding model appears in the pattern of

TABLE 8.1
Varimax Factor Loadings for Five Subtests of the Queensland Test and Age[a,b]

Subtest	Nonaboriginal		High-contact aboriginal		Low-contact aboriginal	
	1	2	1	2	1	2
Knox Cubes	30	25	24	04	54	22
Beads	35	82	43	12	42	14
Passalong	45	28	63	01	54	33
Form Assembly	42	26	70	−13	12	99
Pattern Matching	88	31	86	05	49	55
Age	46	40	03	98	45	01

[a]From Davidson, 1979, by permission of *Oceania*.
[b]Decimal points omitted. Factor 1 = Successive; Factor 2 = Simultaneous.

loadings for the low-contact aboriginal group. Factors 1 and 2 for the non-aboriginal sample would in fact provide a greater similarity to the pattern of loadings for the low-contact aboriginal group if they were labeled in reversed order (i.e., Factor 1 for the white sample called simultaneous and Factor 2 successive). The relative major loadings for the Pattern Matching, Form Assembly, and Beads subtests would then be comparable to those for the low-contact aboriginal group, while Passalong and Knox Cubes remain with rather split loadings for both samples.

Nevertheless, given that this was a reanalysis of data from research designed for a different purpose and using tasks not specifically selected to access simultaneous and successive cognitive syntheses, two important points clearly emerge from Davidson's admittedly post hoc explanations:

1. A model of cognitive processes based on Luria's neuropsychological theory of brain functions may provide a parsimonious framework for interpreting available research evidence concerning aboriginal cognitive skills.

2. A study specifically designed to examine the Luria model of simultaneous and successive cognitive processes with aboriginal and nonaboriginal samples would provide not only a critical validation of Davidson's interpretations but also a cross-cultural evaluation of the Luria model.

A factor analytic study was therefore designed to address the following questions:

1. Is it possible to identify the two coding processes of simultaneous and successive synthesis in samples of aboriginal and nonaboriginal children? In order to minimize the kinds of interpretive problems of cross-cultural factor analyses outlined by Irvine and Carroll (1980), and to try and maximize confidence that the same kinds of processes were being sampled in both groups, previously validated measures of simultaneous and successive processing were used as marker tests. Four measures of simultaneous synthesis and two of successive syntehsis were considered more suitable for cross-cultural use by the criteria of minimal language content and ease of communication over the test instructions.

2. If identified, is the coding process model of any interpretive value in relation to previous research on aboriginal cognition? Two subtests of the Queensland Test, Form Assembly and Beads, were included in order to examine Davidson's explanations, and Drinkwater's version of Kim's game was added as the relevant measure from the visual memory debate.

3. Is it possible to incorporate planned modifications to specific tasks in order to access a particular coding process? If the coding model adequately represents the Unit 2 brain functions, then one ought to be able to predictively validate the processes by making coding more or less successive or simultaneous as a result of task presentation.

A revised version of the Beads subtest was prepared so that presentation was assumed to encourage successive processing, and a second presentation of the Kim's game task was included where the task itself was preceded by a procedure designed to orient individuals toward a more visual processing strategy (see Klich & Davidson, in press).

The Samples

The aboriginal Australian sample consisted of 76 children from two communities in the remote northwest desert area of South Australia and within the region known as the Western Desert. These two communities together with several others in that vast area share a common religious, ceremonial, and linguistic tradition. There is considerable movement between them, and populations fluctuate widely as a result. The schools there are described within the state education system as "tribally oriented."

The community that formed the major research site was selected because it appeared to represent the best available exemplar of the bicultural learning system outlined earlier in relation to the work of Seagrim. The idea of teaching in the vernacular of the people was originated there when the school was started 40 years previously. It was some 30 years later that the importance of the vernacular approach to teaching came to be recognized in other Australian aboriginal community schools. The school has always used local language materials in its teaching programs, and literacy texts and general reading series for adults have also been produced. English is taught as well as the local language.

There is much direct aboriginal involvement in the school, with traditional aboriginal activities incorporated into the school program when the people so desire. An aboriginal teacher aide shares the instructional activities alongside a white teacher in every classroom except one, which is under the control of a fully qualified aboriginal teacher who is also a fully initiated member of the local tribal group. Children are taken on trips into their own tribal country by aboriginal elders as well as on organized excursions to major European centers with their teachers and parents. A preschool was set up several years ago and is now run completely by aboriginal people.

Sixty-three of the children were the entire attending school population aged about 9 years and above at this community, but as only a few children aged 12–13 years were present, a further 13 children comprising one class of approximately that age attending at the second community were added to the sample. Ages of the total sample ranged from 107 to 207 months (mean = 154.4, SD = 26.2), and there were 36 males and 40 females.

Matching has long been criticized by methodological specialists (Campbell & Stanley, 1966; Brislin et al., 1973), and therefore no attempt was made in this study to match exactly for age. Instead, the use of reasonably intact groups having approximately the same age range was preferred.

The white Australian comparison group comprised 91 children from the rural area of northern New South Wales. Forty-three of them (20 male and 23 female) were the entire school population aged 8.5–12 years at a small primary school. The remaining 48 children (28 male, 20 female) were aged 12–17 years, attended a high school in a larger town about 30 km away from the primary school, and were those members of the school population who came from country areas outside the town. Ages of the total sample ranged from 102 to 207 months (mean = 152.4, *SD* = 31.1).

The Tasks

The following tasks were administered to all children:

Matrix Test. This was originally developed by Fitzgerald (Note 3) as a measure of simultaneous processing based on the work of Luria (1966b) and consists of 40 shapes each drawn on a 3 × 3 dot matrix. In the first part of the test (Matrix A), each of the first 20 shapes is shown for 5 secs, and the child is required to draw the shape on a supplied empty dot matrix after each presentation. The second part of the test (Matrix B) uses the remaining 20 shapes in exactly the same way, but the child is required to draw the shape after it has been mentally inverted. The score for both tasks is the number correctly drawn.

Figure Copying Test. The task requires the child to copy geometric forms that increase in difficulty and are visible to the child at all times. Given the large age range of both samples, an additional 3 forms used by Ashman (1978) were added to the original 10 (Das *et al.*, 1979) to avoid possible ceiling effects in performance, making a total of 13 items. Each drawing is scored as 0, 1, or 2 according to the degree of correctness of reproduction. Scoring criteria emphasize the maintenance of geometric relations and proportions, rather than exact reproduction, and are available in Ashman (1978).

CF3. This is a flexibility of closure task from the Ekstrom, French, and Harman (Note 4) Kit of Factor-Referenced Cognitive Tests, and has been used as a measure of simultaneous processing by Hunt (1980). The child is presented with a shape and is asked to superimpose it onto a supplied matrix that constitutes a strong visual field. The original pattern is in view the whole time, and the score is the number correctly transposed.

Number Span. The child listens to an oral presentation of a series of numbers and is then required to write them down when the series is finished. The size of the series varies randomly over the 20 items, and there is a 1-sec interval between each number. The items are the first 20 from the

Auditory Number Span Test (MS1) of the Ekstrom *et al.* (Note 4) kit, and this has been used as a measure of successive processing in studies by Green (1977), Hunt (1980), and Randhawa and Hunt (1979). A similar form of Digit Span has been extensively used in the Das *et al.* (1979) studies.

Letter Span. Series of letters are visually presented, and the child is asked to write them down at the end of each series. As in the Number Span measure, the size of the series varies randomly over the 20 presentations, and scoring for both tests is the number of letters or digits given in the correct sequential order irrespective of intrusions. The task is assumed to involve successive processing and has been so used by Green (1977) and Randhawa and Hunt (1979).

Form Assembly and *Beads.* These subtests of the Queensland Test were described earlier. Administration and scoring of the tests followed the instructions in the Queensland Test Handbook (McElwain & Kearney, 1970). Form Assembly has 13 items scored correct or incorrect, and 4 practice items. Beads has 10 items similarly scored, and 2 items for practice.

Kim. The task is the same as Drinkwater's (1976) Tray One: A grid-marked array of 20 different-name items—10 of them natural, 10 of them manufactured, and all of them similar to those used by Kearins (e.g., button, leaf, nail, feather). Testing procedures closely followed those of Kearins, and instructions and explanation provided were identical to those of Drinkwater (1976). The score was the number of items replaced correctly.

Revised Beads. The presentation of the Beads subtest was modified so that a sliding wooden cover over the chain of beads allows only one bead to be seen at any given time, and the beads are exposed in sequential order. It was intended that such a procedure maximize successive processing strategies. Scoring was the same as for Beads.

Kim with Imagery Orientation (KIO). The visual strategy or imagery orientation procedure adopted was derived from Kearins's same-name object arrays and is described in detail in Klich and Davidson (in press). Visual imagery instructions were used in conjunction with the imagery orientation procedures. The final presentation was the same 20-object array that had been used originally for Kim's game, except that the individual objects were randomly allocated to new positions in the array. Performance on this KIO task was then recorded as for Kim, and scoring was the same.

The first six tasks described (i.e., the simultaneous and successive marker variables), were administered to small groups of about 5–10 aboriginal children and to normal school classes of nonaboriginal children. Care was taken to adhere to the cross-cultural data collection procedures advised by Irvine (1973) and Irvine and Carroll (1980). For example, as well as written

instructions in English that were also read out by the researcher, oral instructions in the local vernacular were prepared in conjunction with the
aboriginal teaching staff and delivered by the aboriginal teacher aide who
normally worked with that particular group of children. The Figure Copying test was given first since it involved the simplest response procedure,
and practice items for each task were supervised by both researcher and
aboriginal teaching staff to ensure that test instructions had been understood.

The other five tasks were individually administered. With aboriginal
children, this was in the presence of an aboriginal teacher aide, usually in
areas adjacent to normal schoolrooms and within sight and hearing of other
aboriginal children and adults. With nonaboriginal children, a vacated store-
room and an unused office area next to classrooms were utilized. The
Revised Beads and KIO were on average administered some 2 weeks after
the other individual tasks. Children who had just completed a task were
asked if they wished to nominate who was to have the next turn, and they
generally appeared to be friendly, cooperative, and keen to participate.

Evidence for the Model

The methodological constraints advocated by Irvine and Carroll (1980,
p. 2) in the analysis of cross-cultural data were followed in order to maximize confidence that tasks and individuals had in general interacted in the
same fashion. Item statistics and reliability checks on each measure for
aboriginal and nonaboriginal samples appeared satisfactory. Raw scores on
the 11 tasks were intercorrelated for each sample separately, and then
partial correlations were obtained, removing the influence of chronological
age. The resulting partial correlation matrices for both groups appear in
Table 8.2.

Given the questions addressed by this study, exploratory and confirmatory factor analysis (Gorsuch, 1974; Mulaik, 1975) were considered the
methodologically appropriate procedures to investigate the latent structure
underlying the 11 variables for both samples. One advantage of using these
maximum likelihood methods is that a statistical test of significance for the
number of factors can be derived, giving a chi-square statistic for "goodness
of fit" to test the hypothesis that the population variance has been extracted
by a specified number of factors. If the chi-square is significant at the
designated probability level, then the residual matrix still contains significant variance.

The aboriginal data were examined using exploratory or unrestricted
common factor analysis (McDonald, 1974). A one-factor solution was clearly unacceptable; ($\chi^2 = 141.93$, $df = 44$, $p < .0001$). On the other hand, the

TABLE 8.2
Correlations among Eleven Tasks for Two Cultures with Age Partialled Out[a]

Task	1	2	3	4	5	6	7	8	9	10	11
1. Matrix A		595	707	535	088	065	552	294	396	148	385
2. Matrix B	729		637	602	089	032	523	258	439	-002	494
3. Figure Copying	629	569		649	211	174	538	272	271	138	454
4. CF3	675	704	697		107	089	496	223	225	130	333
5. Number Span	212	077	221	081		658	-097	360	179	490	011
6. Letter Span	168	053	139	024	456		-023	505	091	583	-036
7. Form Assembly	518	566	511	555	186	102		107	364	055	374
8. Beads	239	185	245	206	304	411	186		239	423	035
9. Kim	425	396	324	319	289	269	383	245		-003	498
10. Revised Beads	082	032	082	-056	511	588	074	607	220		-127
11. KIO	642	618	458	505	182	200	469	237	479	074	

[a]Aborigines: above diagonal; nonaborigines: below diagonal; decimal points omitted.

hypothesis that two factors fitted the data could not be statistically rejected. The two-factor Varimax rotated solution is presented in Table 8.3. A Promax oblique solution produced only a marginally better simple structure for the two-factor solution of aboriginal data, and the correlation between oblique factors was .17.

The four marker variables hypothesized to require simultaneous processing had loadings of .71–.82 on Factor 1 and failed to load above .21 on Factor 2. Similarly the two successive marker variables had inconsequential loadings on Factor 1, but loaded .74 and .89 on Factor 2. It seems reasonable to infer, therefore, that Factor 1 reflects simultaneous processing and Factor 2 successive processing.

Mulaik (1975) has reviewed the limitations of exploratory factor analysis, suggesting that it be used to obtain estimates of a model with an initial sample. The model should then be tested on data from another sample using confirmatory factor analysis, which allows the formulation of a specific analytic model of how certain factor variables determine the common variance of the observed variables. This analysis provides a chi-square "goodness of fit" test of the model to the data. Parameters of the model may be constrained in advance, and others can be left free to be estimated from the data, conditional on the fixed parameters. This allows the confirmation of factor patterns found in one sample on data from another and "for the first time makes it possible to cross-validate factors directly rather than by judgment [Brislin *et al.*, 1973]."

TABLE 8.3
Rotated Factor Matrix for Aboriginal Data[a]

	Varimax		
Task	1[b]	2[c]	Uniqueness (U^2)
1. Matrix A	78	11	13
2. Matrix B	79	05	14
3. Figure Copying	82	21	08
4. CF3	71	12	22
5. Number Span	04	74	20
6. Letter Span	−01	89	04
7. Form Assembly	68	−04	28
8. Beads	24	56	38
9. Kim	46	10	59
10. Revised Beads	02	67	30
11. KIO	57	−06	45

[a]Decimal points omitted. Goodness of fit: $\chi^2 = 44.59$, $df = 34$, $p = .106$.
[b]Simultaneous.
[c]Successive.

Based on the two-factor solution of the aboriginal data, a two-factor confirmatory, or restricted, factor analysis (McDonald & Leong, 1976) was carried out on the nonaboriginal data. Following the aboriginal pattern of loadings, each variable was constrained to be estimated on only one factor, thus creating a set of specific hypotheses as to which coding process, simultaneous or successive, was primarily involved in each task. The two factors were also orthogonally yoked, and the resulting factor matrix is displayed in Table 8.4.

It can be seen from the table that the hypothesized two factors and factor pattern of the model provided a good fit to the nonaboriginal data. It would seem reasonable to conclude, therefore, that no apparent difference in the underlying *pattern* of cognitive processing functions between these samples of aboriginal and nonaboriginal children could be statistically established on these 11 tasks.

The answers to all three questions posed earlier in this study appear to be in the affirmative. Simultaneous and successive processing factors were identified in both samples. Simultaneous synthesis of information appears to be implicated in performance on the Form Assembly and Kim's game tasks, and successive synthesis seems to be the dominant processing mode on the Beads subtest. The two tasks that were presented specifically to access a designated coding process appear to have done so, if the factor pattern is any indication.

TABLE 8.4
Confirmatory Factor Analysis for Nonaboriginal Data[a]

Task	Factor matrix 1[b]	2[c]	Estimated uniqueness (U^2)
1. Matrix A	85	00*	08
2. Matrix B	84	00*	08
3. Figure Copying	73	00*	21
4. CF3	81	00*	11
5. Number Span	00*	56	46
6. Letter Span	00*	65	32
7. Form Assembly	66	00*	31
8. Beads	00*	65	34
9. Kim	48	00*	58
10. Revised Beads	00*	91	03
11. KIO	70	00*	25

[a]Decimal points omitted; asterisks denote parameters constrained a priori to be zero. Factors constrained orthogonally. Goodness of fit: $\chi^2 = 55.49$, $df = 44$, $p = .115$.
[b]Simultaneous.
[c]Successive.

Differences in Performance

Irvine and Carroll (1980) have suggested that analysis of variance of group differences in mean levels of achievement on tasks is only feasible when such factor analytic equivalence has been ascertained. They warn, though, that any comparisons are equivocal, for although factor analytic checks may support the assumption of similar interaction between stimuli and subjects, they do not prove it.

For purposes of analysis by age, the children were placed into five age groups, each of which spanned 2 years, so that Group 1 consisted of 8–9-year-old children ($N = 25$); Group 2, 10–11 years ($N = 44$); Group 3, 12–13 years ($N = 40$); Group 4, 14–15 years ($N = 40$); and Group 5, 16–17 years ($N = 18$). A multivariate analysis of variance was then performed using the *Multivariance* program version VI (Finn, Note 5), in order to assess the effects of Culture (2) and Age (5) on performance differences across the 11 tasks.

Given a nonorthogonal design the Culture × Age interaction was tested first (Appelbaum & Cramer, 1974), and the multivariate F ratio was significant ($F(44,564) = 1.85$, $p < .005$). The univariate F ratios for all 11 tasks (see Table 8.5) showed that primarily Number Span and Letter Span were contributing to this effect.

Means for Number Span and Letter Span by Culture and Age appear in Table 8.6, and it is reasonably clear that, not only have all nonaboriginal age

TABLE 8.5
Univariate F Ratios for Eleven Tasks Analyzed by Culture and Interaction with Age

	Culture × Age	Culture
Task	F (4,157)	F (1,157)
1. Matrix A	1.11	3.77
2. Matrix B	2.24	1.87
3. Figure Copying	1.56	0.25
4. CF3	1.59	59.98***
5. Number Span	3.66*	244.26***
6. Letter Span	4.22**	146.34***
7. Form Assembly	0.65	1.09
8. Beads	1.98	62.36***
9. Kim	0.32	10.86***
10. Revised Beads	1.44	112.18***
11. KIO	1.25	0.63

* = $p < .01$.
** = $p < .005$.
*** = $p < .001$.

TABLE 8.6
Means on Two Tasks by Culture and Age

	Number Span		Letter Span	
Age group	Aboriginal	Nonaboriginal	Aboriginal	Nonaboriginal
8–9	27.1	52.9	29.5	48.5
10–11	34.0	57.1	34.8	60.4
12–13	40.8	68.0	42.0	59.0
14–15	36.4	74.5	35.3	74.4
16–17	35.7	80.1	42.2	81.6

groups performed better than all aboriginal age groups (i.e., even the youngest whites have done better than the oldest aborigines on these two tasks), but the rate of improved performance on these tasks among white age groups was significantly greater than the age-related rate of improvement for aborigines.

The multivariate F ratio for Age was also significant ($F(44,564) = 3.08, p < .0001$), and the univariate F ratios for all 11 variables showed that, as expected, older children had performed significantly better than younger ones.

Of particular interest here, though, were the results for the effect of Culture. The multivariate F ratio ($F(11,147) = 43.8, p < .0001$) indicated a significant overall difference, but a scrutiny of the univariate F ratios (see Table 8.5) suggested that differences in performance between aborigines and nonaborigines had occurred on 6 tasks. The means and standard deviations for the two groups on all 11 tasks appear in Table 8.7. The means show that aborigines have performed significantly better than non-aborigines on the Kim's game task. On all the other five tasks where a significant difference occurred, performance favored nonaborigines.

If these differences are related to the factor matrices in Tables 8.3 and 8.4, an interesting pattern emerges. There were no significant differences in performance between aborigines and nonaborigines on five of the seven simultaneous processing tasks. Of the two where differences did occur, aborigines had superior performance on one (Kim), and inferior performance on the other (CF3). However, on all four of the successive processing tasks, nonaborigines performed significantly better than aborigines. In summary, the aboriginal children, relative to the nonaboriginal children, performed better on measures of simultaneous processing than on measures of successive processing (significantly better in the case of Kim's game).

TABLE 8.7
Means and Standard Deviations on Eleven Tasks for Two Cultures[a]

	Aboriginal		Nonaboriginal	
Task	Mean	SD	Mean	SD
1. Matrix A	13.49	4.1	12.29	4.8
2. Matrix B	9.17	3.8	10.09	5.8
3. Figure Copying	16.18	3.8	16.43	4.0
4. CF3+	19.00	9.6	30.09	11.7
5. Number Span+	35.82	11.0	65.56	16.4
6. Letter Span+	36.86	13.2	63.74	18.6
7. Form Assembly	8.30	2.1	8.60	1.8
8. Beads+	3.01	1.7	5.30	2.1
9. Kim+	14.72	3.3	13.11	3.2
10. Revised Beads+	2.51	1.3	4.79	1.6
11. KIO	14.28	3.6	13.87	3.2

[a] + Denotes a significant difference (see Table 8.5).

Differences in Strategies

Can we therefore argue on the basis of these findings that aborigines are likely to be more competent in situations involving simultaneous processing than in those that require successive synthesis?

A theory of abilities might postulate that inferior performance indicates an inherent deficit. Alternatively, an interpretation framed within a processing theory raises a number of issues pertaining to the use of contextually inappropriate strategies.

One important methodological concern relates to the question: What exactly does functional invariance mean? Snart, O'Grady, and Das (1982) have pointed out that similar factor loadings between groups do not necessarily indicate that similar processing strategies have been utilized. In other words, aborigines may be using similar strategies to handle the demands of Number Span and Letter Span, which are different from those used by them on the simultaneous tasks. However, their strategies need not be identical to those used by nonaboriginal children on Number Span and Letter Span, which may also be similar to each other, but different from those used by them on simultaneous measures. For example, to memorize number or letter series, nonaboriginal children may be using efficient chunking and rehearsal strategies that are perhaps not readily available to many of the aboriginal children.

Take the Beads subtest of the Queensland Test as a case in point. After testing was completed, children were asked about the strategies they had used to remember bead sequences. Some children, presented with Item 5 of the Beads subtest (see Figure 8.4, a full illustration also appears on p. 23 of the Queensland Test Handbook), simply rehearsed names, such as "square," "cylinder," and "circle," in sequential order. Others devised shorter labels for rehearsal purposes (e.g., 1–2–3–2–1–2). One child used the labels "box-equals-zero-equals-box-equals," unaware that the test handbook instructs the researcher in almost identical fashion to use a coding sequence of + = 0 = + = to record responses for this item.

Other strategies used by children involved chunking, visual reconstruction, and verbal coding in the one response. For example, one child "saw" that the square (more correctly cuboid) bead followed by the cylindrical one looks like a three-dimensional letter *T* lying on its side; the round one followed by the cylinder looks like the letter *i* in the same position; and the last two are therefore also a letter *T*. A chain of beads consisting of six separate units has thus been reduced to three letters or, in this case, just one word.

Some visualizing strategies may be more individually unique. Another child faced with this particular item "saw" it in terms of familiar toys at home: The first three beads were seen as a wooden tower that had fallen on its side, and the last three (a square in the middle with a cylinder on each side) as the handlebars of a wooden push-along toy.

Observations of the behavior of aboriginal children on the same task also suggested that very specific strategies were being employed by individuals. Sometimes the three cylinders were put into their respective positions first, then the two square beads, and then the round one. Another child replaced the two outermost beads and gradually worked inward. Yet another, when confronted with the Revised Beads task where only one bead at a time was visible, looked back to the loose beads each time another bead was exposed, as if visually "marking" the beads to be then picked up and replaced.

In another context, Bennett and Chandra (1974) reported that children of the southern Gilbert Islands in the Central Pacific during testing with the Beads subtest used an imagery strategy "in which they were able to hold the outline of the beads, and then reproduce them from the image they were holding. This seems consistent with the kind of skill required in fixing positions in an atoll environment where there are very few physical cues [p.

Figure 8.4.   Item 5 of the Beads Subtest.

188]." This appears to be an example where transfer of habitual preferred processing strategies has been effected, presumably as the result of functional equivalence between tasks (Berry, 1969; Brislin *et al.,* 1973).

Cole and Scribner (1974) have argued that a major implication of Luria's functional systems approach to cognition is that "we are unlikely to find cultural differences in basic component processes [p. 193]." The findings of this study, and the interpretations placed upon them, provide support for that prediction. In addition, observations of children's behavior have reflected individual and cultural differences in coding and rehearsal strategies used in conjunction with the different tasks.

An educationally relevant implication of the processing framework is that inferior or superior performance may be analyzed not in relation to supposed qualities inherent in the learner but rather in terms of the ways in which solutions were attempted, thus examining the contextual viability of alternative procedures. As a result, two educational responses have gradually emerged. The first, that of providing training or experience in the use of nonpreferred but situationally more effective strategies, such as chunking and rehearsal, has been successfully demonstrated in the work of Kaufman and Kaufman (1979) and Krywaniuk and Das (1976). The second, that of attempting to match instructional procedures to the assumed preferred processing style or strategies of the learner, is perhaps best exemplified in the work on holist and serialist styles by Gordon Pask (Daniel, 1975; Pask & Scott, 1972). However, caution needs to be exercised in transposing knowledge of processing skills or strategies evidenced by an individual in one situational context to expectations of his or her performance in another. In the first place, processing strategies may be task specific. Thus, while aboriginal children may have been utilizing contextually inefficient coding strategies on the successive processing measures used in this study, other contexts may well evoke aboriginal proficiency in successive processing. Second, tasks must be considered conceptually and functionally equivalent (see Davidson & Klich, Chapter 7, this volume) before familiar aboriginal strategies may be operationalized in educational contexts. The latter issue has arisen, for example, when attempts have been made to transfer aboriginal strategic skills in visualization or tracking to such educational tasks as reading (Seagrim & Lendon, 1980).

The concept of strategy itself has been an important addition within the processing framework (Kirby, 1980). No single task is likely to be a pure measure of one coding process or the other, and even within modes of encoding, as our own observations show, there may be variations in the strategies employed.

Strategies can be *applied* (if already available); they can be *selected* (from a range of alternatives); or they can be *devised* (generated in response to the demands of a particular task). In terms of Luria's model of the functional organization of the brain, this represents an interdependence of the executive or planning functions of Unit 3, located in the frontal lobes, and the coding and integration functions of Unit 2. A study of the relationship between planning and simultaneous and successive synthesis is reported in Ashman (1978), and further research in that area is presented elsewhere in this volume.

Kirby (1980) has addressed the range of educational problems associated with the three units of brain function and has examined relevant instructional approaches within the processing framework. That research suggests that children can be taught to apply particular strategies and that they can learn to select from available strategies. However, the monitoring of strategy use, the modification of ongoing strategies, appropriate use of strategy switching, and the generation of alternative, relevant strategies remain largely uncharted research areas in metacognitive functions (Lawson, 1980). Research at this level of cognitive activity is likely to make a useful contribution to the development of a theory that encompasses aboriginal cognitive competence.

REFERENCE NOTES

1. Wallace, P. Tracking ability—Aboriginal women and children. *Report to the Australian Institute for Aboriginal Studies,* Canberra, 1968.
2. Davidson, G. R. Simultaneous and successive synthesis as an alternative model of Aboriginal cognition. Paper presented at the tenth meeting of the Australian Conference on Cognitive Development, Canberra, 1978.
3. Fitzgerald, D. A matrix test for measuring simultaneous processing. Unpublished report, Division of Educational Research Services, University of Alberta, 1971.
4. Ekstrom, R. B., French, J. W., & Harman, H. H. *Manual for kit of factor-referenced cognitive tests.* Princeton: Educational Testing Service, 1976.
5. Finn, J. D. *Multivariance: Univariate and multivariate analysis of variance, covariance, regression, and repeated measures.* Chicago, Ill.: International Educational Services, 1977.

REFERENCES

Appelbaum, M. I., & Cramer, E. M. Some problems in the nonorthogonal analysis of variance. *Psychological Bulletin,* 1974, *81,* 335–343.
Ashman, A. The relationship between planning and simultaneous and successive synthesis. Unpublished doctoral dissertation, University of Alberta, 1978.
Bartlett, F. C. *Remembering.* London: Cambridge Univ. Press, 1932.
Bennett, M., & Chandra, S. Some ecological factors in individual test performance. In J. L. M. Dawson & W. J. Lonner, (Eds.), *Readings in cross-cultural psychology.* Hong Kong: International Association for Cross-Cultural Psychology, 1974.

Berndt, R. M. The Concept of the Tribe in the Western Desert of Australia. *Oceania, 30,* (2), 1959, 81–107.

Berndt, R. M., & Berndt, C. H. Card games amongst Aborigines in the Northern Territory. *Oceania,* 1947, *17,* 248–269.

Berndt, R. M., & Berndt, C. H. *The world of the first Australians* (2nd ed.). Sydney: Landsdowne Press, 1981.

Berry, J. W. On cross-cultural comparability. *International Journal of Psychology,* 1969, *4,* 119–128.

Berry, J. W. *Human ecology and cognitive style.* New York: Sage, 1976.

Bower, G. H. Analysis of a mnemonic device. *American Scientist,* 1970, *58,* 496–510.

Brislin, R. Methodology of cognitive studies. In G. E. Kearney & D. W. McElwain, *Aboriginal cognition.* Canberra: Australian Institute for Aboriginal Studies, 1976.

Brislin, R., Lonner, W., & Thorndike, R. *Cross-cultural research methods.* New York: Wiley, 1973.

Bruce, D. W., Hengeveld, M., & Radford, W. C. *Some cognitive skills in Aboriginal children in Victorian Primary Schools: Progress Report No. 2.* Melbourne: Australian Council for Educational Research, 1971.

Bruner, J. S., Olver, R., & Greenfield, P. *Studies in cognitive growth.* New York: Wiley, 1966.

Buck-Morss, S. Socio-economic bias in Piaget's theory and its implications for cross-cultural studies. *Human Development,* 1975, *18,* 35–49.

Campbell, D. T., & Stanley, J. *Experimental and quasi-experimental design for research.* Chicago: Rand McNally, 1966.

Chase, A., & von Sturmer, J. Mental man and social evolutionary theory. In G. E. Kearney, P. R. deLacey & G. R. Davidson, (Eds)., *The psychology of Aboriginal Australians.* Sydney: Wiley, 1973.

Cole, M., Gay, J., Glick, J., & Sharp, D. *The cultural context of learning and thinking.* London: Methuen, 1971.

Cole, M., & Scribner, S. *Culture and thought.* New York: Wiley, 1974.

Curr, E. M. *The Australian Race: Vol. I. Melbourne: Government Printer,* 1886.

Daniel, J. S. Learning styles and strategies: The work of Gordon Pask. In N. Entwistle & D. Hounsell, (Eds.), *How students learn.* Lancaster: Institute for Research and Development in Post-Compulsory Education, 1975.

Das, J., Kirby, J., & Jarman, R. *Simultaneous and successive cognitive processes.* New York: Academic Press, 1979.

Dasen, P. R. Piagetian research in Central Australia. In G. E. Kearney, P. R. de Lacey & G. R. Davidson, (Eds.), *The psychology of Aboriginal Australians.* Sydney: Wiley, 1973.

Dasen, P. R. Concrete operational development in three cultures. *Journal of Cross-cultural Psychology,* 1975, *6*(2), 156–172.

Dasen, P. R., & Heron, A. Cross-cultural tests of Piaget's theory. In H. C. Triandis & A. Heron, *Handbook of cross-cultural psychology* (Vol. 4). *Developmental Psychology.* Boston: Allyn & Bacon, 1981.

Davidson, G. R. Learning to learn. In G. E. Kearney & D. W. McElwain, (Eds.), *Aboriginal cognition.* Canberra: Australian Institute for Aboriginal Studies, 1976.

Davidson, G. R. An ethnographic psychology of Aboriginal cognitive ability. *Oceania,* 1979, *49*(4), 270–294.

Davidson, G. R. Psychology and Aborigines: The place of research. *Australian Psychologist,* 1980, *15,* 111–121.

Davidson, G. R., & Klich, L. Z. Cultural factors in the development of temporal and spatial ordering. *Child Development,* 1980, *51,* 569–571.

de Lacey, P. R. A cross-cultural study of classificatory ability in Australia. *Journal of Cross-Cultural Psychology,* 1970, *1,* 293–304.

de Lacey, P. R. Classificatory ability and verbal intelligence among high-contact Aboriginal and low socio-economic white Australian children. *Journal of Cross-cultural Psychology,* 1971, *2*(4), 393–396. (a)

de Lacey, P. R. Verbal intelligence, operational thinking, and environment in part-Aboriginal children. *Australian Journal of Psychology,* 1971, *23*(2), 145–150. (b)

de Lacey, P. R., & Nurcombe, B. Effects of enrichment preschooling at Bourke: A further follow-up study. *Australian Journal of Education,* 1977, *21*(1), 80–90.

de Lemos, M. M. The development of conservation in Aboriginal children. *International Journal of Psychology,* 1969, *4,* 255–269.

Drinkwater, B. A. Visual memory skills of medium contact Aboriginal children. *Australian Journal of Psychology,* 1976, *28,* 37–44.

Drinkwater, B. A. A reply to Kearins. *Australian Journal of Psychology,* 1978, *30,* 33–56.

Dunn, L. M. *The Peabody Picture Vocabulary Test.* Circle Pines, Minn.: American Guidance Service, 1965.

Elkin, A. P. The social life and intelligence of the Australian Aborigine. *Oceania,* 1932, *3,* 101–113.

Elkin, A. P. *The Australian Aborigines* (Rev. ed.), Sydney: Angus & Robertson, 1974.

Fowler, H. L. Report on psychological tests on natives in the north of Western Australia. *Australian Journal of Science,* 1940, *2,* 124–127.

Franklin, M. A. *Black and white Australians.* Australia: Heinemann, 1976.

Freeman, N. H. Temporal and spatial ordering in recall by five-to-eight year old children. *Child Development,* 1975, *46,* 237–239.

Fry, H. K., & Pulleine, R. H. The mentality of the Australian Aborigine. *Australian Journal of Experimental, Biological and Medical Science,* 1931, *8*(3), 153–167.

Galton, F. *Inquiries into human faculty and its development.* London: Macmillan, 1883.

Gibson, J. *The perception of the visual world.* Cambridge, Mass.: Riverside Press, 1950.

Goodnow, J. J. Everyday concepts of intelligence and its development. In N. Warren, (Ed.), *Studies in cross-cultural psychology* (Vol. 2). London: Academic Press, 1980.

Gorsuch, R. L. *Factor analysis.* London: Saunders, 1974.

Green, K. N. An examination of a model of individual differences in sequential and simultaneous processing for the study of aptitude-treatment interaction Unpublished doctoral dissertation, University of New England, Armidale, 1977.

Haddon, A. C. *Reports on the Cambridge Anthropological Expedition to Torres Strait* (Vol. I: General Ethnography). London: Cambridge Univ. Press, 1935.

Harries, W. T. The effect of attendance at a pre-school kindergarten on the level of intellectual functioning of mixed-blood Aboriginal children on the mid-north coast of New South Wales. Unpublished Litt.B. thesis, University of New England, Armidale, 1967.

Harris, D. B. *Children's drawings as measures of intellectual maturity.* New York: Harcourt, 1963.

Harris, S. A. Milingimbi Aboriginal learning contexts. Unpublished doctoral dissertation, University of New Mexico, 1977.

Holm, N., & Japanangka, L. The mathematics of card playing in an Aboriginal community. *The Aboriginal child at school,* 1976, *4,* 19–22.

Horan, M. C. The differential effects of lesions in the right cerebral hemisphere. Unpublished Master's dissertation, University of Queensland, Brisbane, 1966.

Hunt, D. Intentional-incidental learning and simultaneous–successive processing. *Canadian Journal of Behavioural Science,* 1980, *12*(4), 373–383.

Irvine, S. H. Tests as inadvertent sources of discrimination in personnel decisions. In P. Watson (Ed.), *Psychology and race*. London: Penguin Books, 1973.

Irvine, S., & Carroll, W. Testing and assessment across cultures: Issues in methodology and theory. In H. C. Triandis, & J. W. Berry, *Handbook of cross-cultural psychology: Vol. 2*. Boston: Allyn & Bacon, 1980.

Jensen, A. *Educability and group differences*. London: Methuen, 1973.

Kamara, A. I., & Easley, J. A. Is the rate of cognitive development uniform across cultures? In Dasen, P. R. (Ed.), *Piagetian psychology*. New York: Gardner Press, 1977.

Kaufman, D., & Kaufman, P. Strategy training and remedial techniques.*Journal of Learning Disabilities*, 1979, *12*(6), 416–419.

Kearins, J. Skills of desert Aboriginal children. In G. E. Kearney & D. W. McElwain, (Eds.), *Aboriginal cognition*. Canberra: Australian Institute for Aboriginal Studies, 1976.

Kearins, J. Visual spatial memory in Australian Aboriginal children of desert regions. Unpublished doctoral dissertation, University of Western Australia, 1977.

Kearins, J. Visual memory skills of Western Desert and Queensland children of Australian Aboriginal descent: A reply to Drinkwater. *Australian Journal of Psychology*, 1978, *30*, 1–5.

Kearins, J. M. Visual spatial memory in Australian Aboriginal children of desert regions. *Cognitive Psychology*, 1981, *13*, 434–460.

Kearney, G. E. Some aspects of the general cognitive ability of various groups of Aboriginal Australians as assessed by the Queensland Test. Unpublished doctoral dissertation, University of Queensland, Brisbane, 1966.

Kearney, G. E. Early psychological studies. In G. E. Kearney, P. R. de Lacey & G. R. Davidson, (Eds.), *The psychology of Aboriginal Australians*. Sydney: Wiley, 1973.

Kearney, G. E., & McElwain, D. W. Psychological research in Aboriginal Australia. *A.I.A.S. Newsletter*, 1975 (New Series, No. 4).

Kearney, G. E., & McElwain, D. W. Prospect. In G. E. Kearney & D. W. McElwain, (Eds.), *Aboriginal cognition*. Canberra: Australian Institute for Aboriginal Studies, 1976.

Kipling, R. *Kim*. London: Macmillan, 1908.

Kirby, J. R. Individual differences and cognitive processes: Instructional application and methodological difficulties. In J. R. Kirby & J. B. Biggs, (Eds.). *Cognition, development,and instruction*. New York: Academic Press, 1980.

Kirk, S. A., McCarthy, J. J., & Kirk, W. D. *Examiners manual: Illinois Test of Psycholinguistic Abilities*. Urbana: Univ. of Illinois Press, 1968.

Klich, L. Z., & Davidson, G. R. A cultural difference in visual memory: On le voit, on ne le voit plus. *International Journal of Psychology*, in press.

Knapp, P. A. Visual memory in Australian Aboriginal children and children of European descent. Unpublished B. A. (Hons) thesis, Australian National University, 1979.

Knapp, P. A., & Seagrim, G. N. Visual memory in Australian Aboriginal children and children of European descent. *International Journal of Psychology*, 1981, *16*, 213–231.

Koppitz, E. M. *The Bender Gestalt Test for young children*. New York: Grune & Stratton, 1964.

Krywaniuk, L., & Das, J. Cognitive strategies in native children: Analysis and intervention. *Alberta Journal of Educational Research*, 1976, *22*(4), 271–280.

Lahiri, T. K. Tracking as a fine art. *Citation*, 1965, (December) 6–9.

Lawson, M. J. Metamemory: Making decisions about strategies. In J. R. Kirby & J. B. Biggs, *Cognition, development,and instruction*. New York: Academic Press, 1980.

Lewis, D. Route finding by desert Aborigines in Australia. *Journal of Navigation*, 1976, *29*, 21–38. (a)

Lewis, D. Observations on route-finding and spatial orientation among the Aboriginal peoples of the Western Desert region of Central Australia. *Oceania*, 1976, *46*, 249–282. (b)

Luria, A. R. *Higher cortical functions in man.* New York: Basic Books, 1966. (a)

Luria, A. R. *Human brain and psychological processes.* New York: Harper, 1966. (b)

Luria, A. R. The functional organization of the brain. *Scientific American,* 1970, *222*(3), 66–78.

Luria, A. R. *The working brain.* London: Penguin, 1973.

Luria, A. R. *Cognitive development: Its cultural and social foundations.* Cambridge, Mass.: Harvard Univ. Press, 1976.

McDonald, R. P., & Leong, K. S. *COFA: A FORTRAN IV programme for common factor analysis.* Toronto: Ontario Institute for Studies in Education, 1974.

McDonald, R. P. *COSA: A FORTRAN IV programme for analysis of covariance structures.* Toronto: Ontario Institute for Studies in Education, 1976.

McElwain, D. W. Problems of problem solving. In G. E. Kearney & D. W. McElwain, (Eds.), *Aboriginal cognition.* Canberra: Australian Institute for Aboriginal Studies, 1976.

McElwain, D. W., & Kearney, G. E. *Queensland Test Handbook.* Australian Council for Educational Research, Hawthorn, Victoria, 1970.

McElwain, D. W., & Kearney, G. E. Intellectual development. In G. E. Kearney, P. R. de Lacey & G. R. Davidson, (Eds.), *The Psychology of Aboriginal Australians.* Sydney: Wiley, 1973.

McIntyre, L. A. An investigation of the effect of culture and urbanization on three cognitive styles and their relationship to school performance. In G. E. Kearney & D. W. McElwain, (Eds.), *Aboriginal cognition.* Canberra: Australian Institute of Aboriginal Studies, 1976.

Meredith, J. Visual spatial memory of Australian Aboriginal children at the Cherbourg settlement. Unpublished B. A.(Hons) thesis, University of Queensland, 1978.

Money, J., & Nurcombe, B. Ability tests and cultural heritage: The Bender and Draw-a-Person Tests in Aboriginal Australia. *Journal of Learning Disabilities,* 1974, *7*(5), 297–303.

Mulaik, S. A. Confirmatory factor analysis. In D. J. Amick & H. J. Walberg, *Introductory multivariate analysis.* Berkeley: McCutchan, 1975.

Nurcombe, B. *Children of the dispossessed.* Honolulu: Univ. Press of Hawaii, 1976.

Nurcombe, B., & Moffitt, P. Cultural deprivation and language deficit. *Australian Psychologist,* 1970, *5*(3), 249–259.

O'Connor, N., & Hermelin, B. Short term memory for the order of pictures and syllables by deaf and hearing children. *Neuropsychologia,* 1973, *11,* 437–442.

Paivio, A. *Imagery and verbal processes.* New York: Holt, 1971.

Palmer, E. Notes on some Australian tribes. *Journal of the Anthropological Institute,* 1884, *13,* 276–334.

Pask, G., & Scott, B. Learning strategies and individual competence. *International Journal of Man–Machine Studies,* 1972, *4,* 217–253.

Piddington, M., & Piddington, R. Report of fieldwork in north-Western Australia. *Oceania,* 1932, *2,* 342–358.

Poortinga, Y. H. Cross-cultural comparison of maximum performance tests. *Psychologia Africana,* 1971 (Monograph Suppl. No. 6).

Porteus, S. D. *The psychology of a primitive people.* London: Arnold, 1931.

Porteus, S. D. Correspondence—The psychology of a primitive people. *Oceania,* 1933, *4,* 107–109. (a)

Porteus, S. D. Mentality of Australian Aborigines. *Oceania,* 1933, *4,* 30–36. (b)

Porteus, S. D. *The Porteus Maze test and intelligence.* Palo Alto: Pacific Books, 1950.

Porteus, S. D. *Porteus Maze tests: Fifty years of application.* Palo Alto: Pacific Books, 1965.

Randhawa, B. S., & Hunt, D. Some further evidence on successive and simultaneous integration and individual differences. *Canadian Journal of Behavioural Science,* 1979, *11*(4), 340–355.

Richardson, A. *Mental imagery.* London: Routledge & Kegan Paul, 1969.

Rivers, W. H. R. *Reports of the Cambridge Anthropological Expedition to the Torres Strait* (Vol. 2). Physiology and Psychology. London: Cambridge Univ. Press, 1901.

Robinson, M. W., & Yu, P. A note on Kuns: An Aboriginal card game from the north-west of Western Australia. *Dept. of Aboriginal Affairs Newsletter,* 1975, *11,* 41–39.

Seagrim, G. N. Caveat interventor. In P. R. Dasen, (Ed.), *Piagetian psychology: Cross-cultural contributions.* New York: Gardner Press, 1977.

Seagrim, G. N. & Lendon, R. The settlement child and school. In G. E. Kearney, & D. W. McElwain, (Eds.), *Aboriginal cognition.* Canberra: A.I.A.S., 1976.

Seagrim, G. N., & Lendon, R. *Furnishing the mind.* Sydney: Academic Press, 1980.

Serpell, R. *Culture's influence on behaviour.* London: Methuen, 1976.

Sheehan, P. W. *The function and nature of imagery.* New York: Academic Press, 1972.

Smith, K. K. *A validation of the Queensland Test.* Unpublished B. A. (Hons) dissertation, University of Queensland, 1966.

Snart, F., O'Grady, M., & Das, J. P. Cognitive processing by subgroups of moderately mentally-retarded children. *American Journal of Mental Deficiency,* 1982, *86*(5), 465–472.

Strehlow, T. G. H. Black tracker. *SALT, Army Education Journal,* 1943, *6,* 6.

Taylor, L. J., Nurcombe, B., & de Lacey, P. R. Classification ability in Aboriginal children: A re-evaluation. *Australian Psychologist,* 1973, *8,* 246–249.

Teasdale, G. R., & de Vries, T. The use of the Illinois Test of Psycholinguistic Abilities with Australian Aboriginal children. In G. E. Kearney & D. W. McElwain, (Eds.), *Aboriginal cognition.* Canberra: A.I.A.S., 1976.

Teasdale, G. R., & Katz, R. M. Psycho-linguistic abilities of children from different ethnic and socio-economic backgrounds. *Australian Journal of Psychology,* 1968, *20*(3), 115–160.

Triandis, H. C., Vassiliou, V., & Nassiakou, M. Three cross-cultural studies of subjective culture. *Journal of Personality and Social Psychology,* 1968, *8* (4, Pt. 3, Monograph Suppl.).

Watts, B. H. *Aboriginal futures: Review of research and developments and related policies in the education of Aborigines.* Report No. 33, Education Research and Development Committee, Canberra, 1982.

Yates, F. A. *The art of memory.* London: Routledge & Kegan Paul, 1966.

9

Indigenous Games and
the Development of Memory Strategies
in Children[1]

GRAHAM R. DAVIDSON
NAND KISHOR

Psychological research that has used culture as a medium for studying memory strategies and their development has been constrained by, and thus has highlighted, several key issues in the study of thinking generally. In the first place, there is the problem of establishing experimentally the existence of actual individual or cultural differences in memory when intuitively, or according to observation, these differences should exist. Where the researcher believes that there are individual or cultural differences, theoretically they may be a result of either selective hereditary, or sociopsychological responses to demands that culture and ecology place on individuals by way of physical survival, geographic, or social needs. If, subsequently, the nature–nurture dichotomy is dismissed, and psychological outcomes of ecocultural demands on memory and thinking are considered, the researcher must then choose either to treat culture and physical environment as having broad, pervasive influences on thinking, where overall patterns of child rearing and broader ecological demands are responsible for memory development, or to consider, separately, particular activities,

[1]The research was supported by an Internal Research Grant from the University of New England, Australia, and was carried out while the senior author was visiting senior lecturer at the University of the South Pacific. This chapter is based on a paper presented at the University of the South Pacific International Conference on Thinking, Suva, Fiji, January 1982.

experiences, and training during childhood and adulthood that are designed consciously or unconsciously to develop memory strategies. Thus, in order to study exhaustively the relationship between culture and memory, as our research here demonstrates, it is important to consider at some stage or another the development of memory strategies in relation to specific cultural activities and the skills that those activities require. If research is designed to look only for superior memory in a particular cultural group or cultural type, the researcher may be forced into giving ad hoc, usually untestable, explanations about the cultural and ecological origins of those processes.

STUDIES OF MEMORY AND CULTURE

Cross-cultural studies of memory have already been reviewed by Cole and Gay (1972), Cole and Scribner (1977), and Klich and Davidson (1983). These reviews have suggested that there are impressive differences between anthropological accounts and experimental studies of memory performance in non-Western cultures. There is, for example, evidence in anthropological accounts from New Guinea (Bateson, 1958), the Pacific (Gladwin, 1970; Hage, 1978), and Africa (Evans-Pritchard, 1963) that non-Westerners are capable of astounding memory feats. In these examples, memory appears to be aided by culturally prescribed mnemonic systems and retrieval of relevant and important cultural knowledge. However, Bartlett (1932) and later Cole and Gay (1972) have pointed out that these feats in themselves are insubstantial evidence that there are significant and irreversible cross-cultural differences in memory, as they may reflect situational and cultural variations in the importance of the material to be remembered and the style of recall. Thus, differences may be more related to the situational aspects of the memory activity than to actual, fixed memory capacities of individuals. There is now considerable evidence, for example, to suggest that performance on experimental memory tasks, especially those involving verbal recall, is greater as amount of Western-type education increases (Cole & Scribner, 1974, 1977). However, this trend disappears if appropriate commencement and encoding strategies are provided, along with the task, as aids to memory. Consequently, Cole and Scribner (1977) have placed considerable emphasis on the work of early Russian psychologists, such as Vygotsky and Leontiev, that attempted to distinguish between basic memory processes and learned memory skills that are part of functional thinking systems developed within a culture to meet specific social and ecological demands. Cross-cultural research by Wagner (1978) has provided evidence that it is possible to distinguish between basic processes and learned memory strategies in single thinking activities involving memory and that, while the former processes are relatively unchanging across cultures and groups, the strategies are affected by social and cultural factors, such as rural–urban residence and schooling.

CROSS-CULTURAL STUDIES OF VISUAL MEMORY

Research studies of verbal memory have generally failed to reveal a superiority on the part of nonliterate, non-Western people as suggested by anthropological research. In contrast, studies of visual memory strategies have provided an important stimulus to the study of memory and culture because some non-Western groups have been found to be superior to their Western counterparts on visual memory tasks and because that superiority appears to coincide with certain ecological and sociocultural conditions. In addition, it has been suggested that this superiority may possibly be the result of selective genetic differences due to continual social and physical isolation under those conditions. For example, Kearins (1976), who worked with Australian aboriginal children from the Western Desert region, found that they performed significantly better than European Australian children on various tests of visual recall and recognition. Similar results were obtained by Kleinfeld (1971) for Eskimo and European Canadians. In both these cases, ecocultural and hereditary influences were considered as possible reasons for the differences.

Klich and Davidson (1983), after reviewing the two studies and subsequent attempts at replication with aboriginal children, have suggested, however, that such performance is the result of survival demands placed on such peoples as aborigines by their environment and can be trained. In their study of Central Desert Aborigines and rural white Australians, the difference between the two groups was reduced so as to be statistically nonsignificant when white Australians were trained to use a memory imagery strategy. Klich and Davidson pointed out that not all studies have found significant differences between the two groups in favor of aborigines. For example, Drinkwater (1976) with rural aborigines living in coastal north Australia, Harris (1977) with tribal aborigines in Arnhem Land, North Australia, and Knapp and Seagrim (1981) with semitribalized aborigines in a central Australian town have found either no difference or a white Australian superiority on visual memory tests. However, given the wide range of cultural, ecological, and child-rearing backgrounds of the children tested in these studies and the demonstrated effects of training children to remember visual information using a specific strategy (see Klich & Davidson, 1983), these discrepant findings are neither surprising nor in conflict with the theory that culture and ecology contribute significantly to the development of functional thinking systems, including functional memory strategies. What is needed, therefore, is attention to specific aspects of culture and to specific experiences and training that may contribute to differences between some groups but not others. It is in this way that indigenous games are said to play an important part in training memory strategies in children.

INDIGENOUS GAMES AND
VISUAL MEMORY PERFORMANCE

Drinkwater (1978) has cited an aboriginal game found in central Australia that may have been familiar to Kearins's desert sample but not to her own coastal sample as an example of specific cultural training and activities that contribute to the development of visual memory strategies. The game requires that children remember a series of objects placed in a line on the ground. Some children were reported to have remembered in correct sequence as many as 40 objects displayed in this fashion. The game is not dissimilar to the visual memory task known as Kim's game, after that of the same name coined by Rudyard Kipling, which has been used in these cross-cultural studies. Knapp and Seagrim (1981) have suggested also, but this time in relation to the superiority of their white Australian sample, that differences in performance may have been due to white Australian children's familiarity with common memory games using playing cards. These interpretations, though post hoc, deserve consideration, as there is other evidence that indigenous games may provide the opportunity for developing useful thinking strategies and for remembering information that is essential to survival, to knowing about self and others, or to passing on myths and traditions. However, these games and activities mainly involve the rehearsal of verbal knowledge by means of various concrete cuing devices (see Hage, 1978). One example is the game of cat's cradle, where individual steps in the building of the cradle or string figure represent discrete elements of a particular myth or story of cultural significance (see, for example, Andersen, 1969, pp. 288–230; Firth & Maude, 1970; Maude & Maude, 1958, for descriptions and interpretations of string figures from Oceania). The game requires that a player remember the sequence of steps involved in the construction of the cradle and, in addition, the particular part of the story that each step represents. Action songs and games that include social and technical information lend themselves to a similar interpretation (e.g., see Kaeppler, 1967; Thompson, 1966–67; Tippett, 1980).

Despite these observations, there is no clear evidence to suggest that indigenous games contribute in a significant way to the development of visual memory. If they do, then the degree to which strategies learned in the context of games transfer to other games and memory tasks and the amount of games training required to have a significant effect on memory strategies may also vary. We will now summarize briefly some current research in Fiji into the effects on visual memory performance of learning and playing indigenous games.

A STUDY OF INDIGENOUS GAMES IN FIJI

The first part of the research included identification in Fijian culture ethnographies of two games that could be said to promote visual memory performance. The games we located appear to have the advantage of directing attention separately at different attributes of visual material. Second, these games, although apparently widely known in Fijian culture in the earlier part of this century, seem now to have disappeared from the games repertoire of younger Fijians. Hence, outcomes of training on the games and comparison of trained and nontrained (control) children would not be differentially influenced by prior knowledge of the games. Finally, people of the coastal cultures from which children were drawn have a considerable degree of contact with the physical environment in the form of boating and fishing, although they are not widely acclaimed as navigators or hunters. Therefore, the research was not concerned with tapping into existing exceptional visual memory performance but with assessing the effect of games training using culturally familiar objects and concepts on the visual memory performance of children known to have a reasonable amount of rapport with their physical environment.

The indigenous games used in the research were *veilavo* and *veisole gone* (Thompson, 1940; Verebalavu, 1979) and were chosen to reflect a difference in emphasis respectively on location of objects and identity of objects. Thus, training on *veilavo* (location training) was seen as training children to remember the positioning in a two-dimensional space of objects that are all similar to one another. The game traditionally was played by two opposing teams with flat beans known as *lavo* (*toto* or *giri*) on a long grass mat. The aim of the game was for players to flick their beans as close as possible to the end of the mat, if necessary dislodging an opponent's bean from the mat. A large number of beans may be on the mat at any time, thus requiring teams to distinguish between their own and their opponents' beans, which are similar in size, shape, and color, but which are lying in different positions on the mat. The second game, *veisole gone* (identity training) was used to train children to remember the identity of objects not related topographically. It was a guessing game played by teams when traditionally one member of a team or one of a number of objects was hidden under a grass mat, with the other team having to guess the identity of the hidden person or object. Two experiments have so far been completed, involving respectively 60 and 55 Fijian children from Forms 1 and 2 of rural junior secondary schools in coastal Viti Levu.

Experiment 1

In the first experiment, the traditional styles and purposes of the games were adhered to as closely as possible. Six children were involved in any one training sessions. Those playing *veilavo* ($N = 24$) were divided into two teams of three and flicked their beans on the mat in the appropriate style. They were required individually twice in each session as part of the training to remember to which team the beans belonged. Those playing *veisole gone* ($N = 24$) were divided into two teams of three and allowed as a team to view objects presented in a small grass basket. Teams took alternate turns at hiding objects under a grass mat while a member of the other team had to deduce, with the aid of the remaining objects in the basket, which one had been hidden. The training sessions for both games each lasted about 30 min. The children were told to adopt the same way of remembering that they had used during the game to help them on the visual memory test. Half of the children in each game received the game training on three successive days (full training) and were tested after each training session on a 24-item version of Kim's game (see Klich & Davidson, 1983). The other half received training only on the first day (partial training) but were tested on all 3 days. This division was designed to assess the effects of amount of training on visual memory performance. A control group who received no training was tested on 3 successive days. Thus, children were allocated randomly but equally by sex and grade to five groups: full location training, partial location training, full identity training, partial identity training, and control. Mean correct replacement scores on Kim's game for each of these five groups are plotted in Figure 9.1. Absolute differences between the games, between the amounts of training, and between performances over the 3 days were not statistically significant. However, the interaction between type and amount of training was reliable ($p < .05$). A further comparison of the means plotted in Figure 9.1, using appropriate protections (Winer, 1962), showed that the full identity training group performed significantly better ($p < .05$) on the visual memory task than the partial identity training and full location training groups, and the control group.

The results of this experiment indicate that visual memory performance did not improve on the average, despite 3 days of testing and training. In addition, only the full location training group performed significantly better than the control group. These results are not inimical with those obtained by Klich and Davidson (1983). In that study, the performance of both

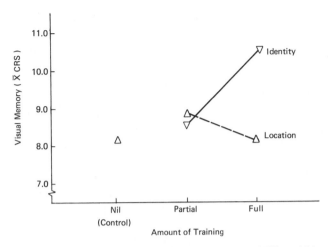

Figure 9.1. Experiment 1: Mean correct replacement scores of Fijian children on Kim's game.

Australian aboriginal and white children under imagery instructions (training) did not differ significantly from their performance when no instruction was given (control), despite the fact that the difference between aborigines and whites was reduced significantly by imagery instruction. However, it is incongruous that full identity training involving predominantly naming was more beneficial than full location training apparently involving spatial decisions. The latter training, instead, appeared to adversely affect visual memory performance. The reason for this lies possibly in the way children approached the games.

When children were questioned after the training sessions about the location game, a large number of them said that they remembered the location of their team's and the other team's beans by associating each bean with its owner. Thus, the game in its traditional format may have demanded the verbal labeling, or naming, of beans rather than the spatial location of them, as was expected. In contrast, a number of children who received identity training reported the combined use of verbal labeling and picture imagery (i.e., forming memory images of the objects). According to these reports, neither game appeared to provide a clean strategy that aided visual memory. Either combined strategies or a labeling strategy that might be said to limit performance were adopted (see Klich & Davidson, 1983).

Experiment 2

Thus, in Experiment 1 there appeared to be a difference between the strategies that children used in the games and the strategies that we expected them to use. This difference may have influenced visual memory test scores. The second experiment was designed, therefore, to provide children with explicit mnemonic strategies within the context of the two games. Whereas children in the first experiment played the games in teams, children here played individually because of the nature of the instruction. Twenty-two children were trained on each game, and 11 children acted as controls. Half the children who received location training were given specific instructions to make a memory photograph of the beans on the mat. As part of their training, the beans were removed at the end of each game, and the children were required to replace them in their positions on the mat. The other half were instructed to verbally rehearse the ownership of the beans (i.e., trainer's or child's), and they were asked to identify them at the end of each game. Half of the children who received identity training were told to make mental photographs of the objects in the basket and were then asked to describe a number of them. The other half were instructed to repeat the names of objects a number of times and were then asked to recall as many as possible. All children were trained on 3 consecutive days and then tested using Kim's games on the third day, immediately after the final training session. The children were told when they took the visual memory test to use the strategy they had been given in training. A control group met as a group with the experimenter on 3 consecutive days and were tested individually on Kim's game after the final meeting. Thus, children were allocated to five groups: location training—imagery, location training—verbal, identity training—imagery, identity training—verbal, and control. Mean correct replacement scores on Kim's game for these five groups are plotted in Figure 9.2.

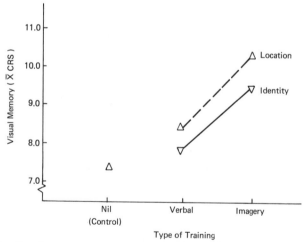

Figure 9.2. Experiment 2: Mean correct replacement scores of Fijian children on Kim's game.

Analysis of the data collected under these conditions revealed that children given imagery training on the average performed significantly better than the controls ($p < .05$) and marginally better than those given the verbal training ($p < .10$). The difference between the imagery and control groups was due mainly to the significantly better visual memory performance of children who had received location training—imagery, not identity training, as was the case in the first experiment.

In this experiment, the performance of the imagery training group was not exceptionally accurate when compared, say, with the Australian groups tested by Klich and Davidson (1983). This is despite the significant improvement that they showed over the control group. While we do not wish to make cross-cultural comparisons between the Fijian and Australian groups, it should be mentioned that the size of the visual array in this experiment was larger than that used in the Australian research. An important variable in this type of research may be the amount of visual information, including the number of objects to be remembered and their spread. It is also possible that the relationship between the size of the array and recall may be different for different strategies. For example, people who are able to use eidetic strategies efficiently often demonstrate exceptionally accurate recall of *large* amounts of visual information, in spite of the difficulty they have in recalling it in forms other than that in which it is presented.

GAMES AS TEACHING DEVICES

Our experiments so far have provided some useful information on the prior roles and possible future uses of indigenous games as aids to memory. In the first place, it cannot be assumed that the games that were used here or similar sorts of games that appear to require memory for objects or locations will automatically enhance visual memory performance. On the contrary, memory games may involve the use of mnemonic strategies that are inimical to the development of those skills. Thus, it is impossible to say, in relation to the differences between aboriginal and white Australians mentioned earlier, that they are the result of children having played certain memory games, without first analyzing the strategies that children use in those games. Mnemonic strategies uncovered by that analysis then need to be considered in relation to the actual memory tasks. Games training may differentially affect visual memory performance if the aim of the game is changed slightly or if a different mnemonic strategy is suggested. Therefore, the focus of research that attempts to foster cognitive or memory development through indigenous games—or, for that matter, games generally—should not be the game per se but rather the strategy or thinking style that the game requires. Further, the strategy imparted in the game must be evaluated according to its appropriateness for the particular aspect of thinking to be fostered. In our research, for example, a game based on verbal rehearsal did not improve visual spatial memory but, in other circumstances, may have provided a useful mnemonic strategy for serial verbal memory activity. As games become more complex, like chess or *Master Mind,* and as attention is given to the development of complex problem solving strategies, instead of simple cognitive and mnemonic strategies, then there is increased difficulty in isolating particular strategies that the games impart and of matching these strategies to new problem situations. However, the emphasis should still be on possible strategies to be employed in the games rather than on the games themselves.

Indigenous games, even in relatively homogeneous cultural settings, may be played in a variety of ways, may draw on different mnemonic strategies, and do not ensure conformity between participants where these strategies are concerned. It is important, therefore, in addition to analyzing the strategies of these games, to investigate their cultural background and importance before we afford them a major role in the development of children's memory.

Educationally, it is often tempting to look around for activities and games that can be used as instructional tasks in classrooms. The aim of doing so is to find familiar activities that provide an incentive for children, particularly from non-Western cultures, to be interested in learning at school. Although the interest value of these games is often high, before adopting them teachers should attempt to analyze strategies that children are using spontaneously when they play the games. This can be done by asking them in specific terms to describe their thoughts as they play and by carefully observing what they do in the course of the game. As Davidson and Klich have pointed out in Chapter 7, the study of children's strategies often shows that indigenous and Western versions of games differ enormously. The educational value of these games and other activities should, in the final analysis, be measured in terms of the degree to which they promote *desired* mnemonic and reasoning strategies.

ACKNOWLEDGMENTS

We wish to express our thanks to the administrators, principals, teachers and pupils of Natovi and Lomery Communities for their interest in the project and for allowing us to carry out the research in their junior Secondary Schools.

REFERENCES

Andersen, J. C. *Myth and legends of the Polynesians.* Rutland, Vt.: Charles E. Tuttle, 1969.
Bartlett, F. C. *Remembering.* London: Cambridge Univ. Press, 1932.

Bateson, G. *Naven* (2nd ed.). Stanford: Stanford Univ. Press, 1958.

Cole, M., & Gay, J. Culture and memory. *American Anthropologist,* 1972, *73,* 1066–1084.

Cole, M., & Scribner, S. *Culture and thought.* New York: Wiley, 1974.

Cole, M., & Scribner, S. Cross-cultural studies of memory and cognition. In R. V. Kail & J. W. Hagen (Eds.), *Perspectives on the development of memory and cognition.* New York: Wiley, 1977.

Drinkwater, B. A. Visual memory skills of medium contact Aboriginal children. *Australian Journal of Psychology,* 1976, *28,* 37–44.

Drinkwater, B. A. A reply to Kearins. *Australian Journal of Psychology,* 1978, *30,* 33–36.

Evans-Pritchard, E. E. Sanza, a characteristic feature of Zande language and thought. In E. E. Evans-Pritchard (Ed.), *Essays in Social Anthropology.* New York: Free Press, 1963.

Firth, R., & Maude, H. D. *Tikopia string figures.* London: Royal Anthropological Institute of Great Britain and Ireland, 1970.

Gladwin, T. *East is a big bird.* Cambridge, Mass.: Harvard Univ. Press, 1970.

Hage, P. Speculations on Puluwates mnemonic structure. *Oceania,* 1978, *49,* 81–95.

Harris, S. A. *Milingimbi Aboriginal learning contexts.* Unpublished doctoral dissertation, University of New Mexico, 1977.

Kaeppler, A. L. Folklore as expressed in the dance in Tonga. *Journal of American Folklore,* 1967, *80,* 160–168.

Kearins, J. Skills of Desert Children. In G. E. Kearney & D. W. McElwain (Ed.), *Aboriginal cognition: Retrospect and prospect.* Atlantic Highlands, N.J.: Humanities Press, 1976.

Kleinfeld, J. Visual memory in village Eskimo and urban Caucasian children. *Arctic,* 1971, *24,* 132–137.

Klich, L. Z. & Davidson, G. R. A cultural difference on visual memory: On le voit, on ne le voit plus. *International Journal of Psychology,* 1983, *18*(2).

Knapp, P. A., & Seagrim, G. N. Visual memory in Australian Aboriginal children and children of European descent. *International Journal of Psychology,* 1981, *15,* 213–231.

Maude, H. C., & Maude, H. E. *String figures from the Gilbert Islands.* Polynesian Society Memoir No. 13. New Plymouth: Avery Press, 1958.

Thompson, L. *Southern Lau, Fiji: An ethnography.* Bernice P. Bishop Museum Bulletin No. 162, 1940.

Thompson, L. Fijian music and dance. *Transactions of the Fiji Society,* 1966–1967, *11,* 14–21.

Tippett, A. R. *The transmission of information and social values in Early Christian Fiji,* 1835–1905. Canberra: Council of St. Mark's Library, 1980.

Verebalavu, S. Some traditional Fijian games. *Fiji Heritage,* October 1, 1979, pp. 5–10.

Wagner, D. Memories of Morocco: The influence of age, schooling and environment on memory. *Cognitive Psychology,* 1978, *10,* 1–28.

Winer, B. J. *Statistical principles in experimental design.* New York: McGraw-Hill, 1962.

PART IV

STUDIES OF
THE COGNITIVELY DISABLED

10

Some Thoughts on Research in Learning Disabilities and Attention

JUDY LUPART
ROBERT MULCAHY

Anyone who has attempted to conduct his or her own research with learning disability groups has no doubt been challenged by the diversity of the literature to be found in this area. In our own work, we have also been frustrated by the multitude of problems associated with research with these exceptional learners. In this chapter, we will describe our way of working through these various aspects related to research with learning disability samples and, as a result, hopefully provide other researchers with an alternate and perhaps more valid approach to research with such groups.

SOME CONCEPTUAL ISSUES IN LEARNING DISABILITY RESEARCH

In comparison to any other area of exceptionality, learning disabilities is unique for its characteristic diversity of disciplines and theories relative to definition, identification, and instruction. Lerner (1976), in a discussion of this cross-disciplinary approach, pointed to the direct involvement of the medical, language, education, and psychology professions in working with learning disabilities, as well as to the less direct involvement of a number of other professions, such as optometry, audiology, social service, physical

*Cognitive Strategies
and Educational Performance*

therapy, genetics, biochemistry, guidance and counseling, systems analysis, and clinical administration.

While some might suggest that such a situation has yielded a greater understanding of the nature and remediation of learning disabilities, others would argue that the interdisciplinary approach has resulted in a state of chaos due to the confusion of terminology and a seeming conflict of ideas of the diverse professions.

Irrespective of which argument is more accurate, a large majority of present-day researchers have become increasingly sensitive to the need to sort out those factors that might be primary to the condition of learning disability and how the problem can be remediated (Cruickshank & Hallahan, 1975; Lerner, 1976; Myklebust, 1971). A classic effort in this regard is Torgesen's (1975) review of the problems entailed in the study of learning disabilities. He suggested that "the problems of defining the subject of study, establishing proper goals for research, and understanding the concept of ability deficit [p. 387]" were the major factors that needed clarification to bring order to the chaotic state of research at that time. However, in the early 1980s, the field remains in a state of confusion.

It would be wrong to suggest that the efforts of Torgesen (1975) and others were of no value. It might, however, be argued that the approach that was taken to resolve the problem was too generalized to be of value for any one particular discipline. In other words, the three areas that Torgesen (1975) outlined would differ substantially for the medical doctor, the educator, and the psychologist; yet all three disciplines would agree to the apparent need for a clarification of such issues. Therefore, it seems logical to suggest that researchers examine their specific disciplines to determine the issues most relevant to clarification of existing research, as well as to provide a framework for choosing essential factors to consider in the planning of future investigations.

There appear to be three major issues that are central to research on learning disabilities from an educational perspective. These are definition, structural versus control processes, and ecological validity.

Definition

The problems surrounding the formulation of an acceptable definition of learning disability have been recognized in the past (McCarthy & McCarthy, 1969) and continue to defy ready resolution in the present-day literature (Artley, 1980; Lerner, 1975; Ohlson, 1978). According to McCarthy and McCarthy (1969), the definition selected will determine the terminology to be used, the number of persons who may be so categorized, the criteria for selection, the characteristics of the population, as well as the type of intervention and subsequent remediation that will be chosen. Johnson and Morasky (1980) suggest that the cross-disciplinary approach, central to the learning disability area, makes it even more difficult for the representative disciplines to reach a consensus with respect to an appropriate definition, and as a result "overlap and interdisciplinary ignorance cause expensive, wasteful and inefficient duplication [p. 55]."

Another dimension that has only recently been alluded to in the literature is the need not only to specify the characteristics of the sample investigated but to specify the task variables that are also operating (Krupski, 1980). For example, Vernon (1979) has argued that a great deal of our confusion with regard to the reading disabled is due to the fact that we treat our samples as though they form a qualitatively homogeneous group and compound this error by treating reading as a unitary process. He suggests that it is far more conceivable that different readers may encounter difficulty at different stages of reading skills acquisition and that such difficulties may be causally related to distinct deficiencies in conceptual thinking.

Although only a few of the definition problems concerning learning disabilities have been briefly outlined here, it is clear that the issue should be carefully considered by all researchers in this area. Probably the most direct manner in which some of the confusion can be resolved is by providing detailed accounts of sample characteristics, a rationale for selection, and a careful analysis of what processes and subskills are involved in the experimental task.

Structural versus Control

The distinction between structural features and control processes was first introduced in the memory study literature (Atkinson & Shiffrin, 1968) but has subsequently gained notable prominence in the developmental literature (Brown, 1975) and particularly in the literature pertaining to the handicapped (Brown, 1974; Butterfield & Belmont, 1975; Torgesen, 1978). According to Torgesen (1978), "the structural features have to do with basic capacities of the system and perhaps how rapidly the processes are executed, while the control processes describe activities which the organism engages in to maximize the performance of a limited capacity system [p. 61]." When the distinction is applied to handicapped groups, the structural features can be considered as those that are more or less permanent (i.e., disability or deficit) or those that are developmentally determined. Control processes refer to any processes, strategies, or metacognitive abilities within the child's repertoire of resources that he or she can rely upon in a learning or problem solving situation. The utility of the distinction is advanced by Brown (1974), who points out that structural features are of interest to those who are concerned with the labeling (causal) or identification of specific groups, whereas the control processes are of interest to those who are more practically concerned with how to improve or remediate the problem. The latter concept entails a variety of metacognitive dimensions (Brown, 1978), such as metamemory and meta-attention, and all of the strategic interventions that can be imposed on a task or problem solving situation that will optimize the performance of the individual.

Although the area is still in its infancy, the results of memory investigations and various training studies (Belmont & Butterfield, 1971; Bray, Justice, Ferguson, & Simon, 1977; Brown & Barclay, 1976; Brown, Campione, & Murphy, 1974, 1977; Moely & Jeffrey, 1974) present exciting possibilities in the sense that we can carry out investigations to specify those processes that work optimally for specific tasks for normal and handicapped children, and ultimately can lead to the provision of relevant training for the handicapped youngster to improve his or her performance.

Soviet studies have traditionally combined both the structural and control concepts. Vygotsky's (1963, 1978) theory of the zone of potential development involves the determination of at least two levels of a child's development that define the "correct relation between the course of development and potentiality for learning in each specific case [1963, p. 28]." At the first level, the zone of actual development represents those mental functions that have been attained as a result of a specific or already accomplished course of development (i.e., structural). The second level, the zone of potential development, represents a learning potentiality that may become actualized under the direction of adult guidance, demonstration, or questioning (i.e., process). A major assumption of this theory is that the interaction of the individual with his or her older peers or adults constitutes the initial stage of learning. As children gain more experience and practice, they begin to specify their own plans for carrying out a task, assuming increasing self-control and relying less on others to provide assistance. Thus, learning precedes development, and "it presupposes that the one is converted into the other [Vygotsky, 1978, p. 91]." The importance of Vygotsky's theory for educators has been acknowledged in American literature (Brown, Campione, & Day, 1981; Brown & French, 1979; Lupart, 1978; Wertsch, 1979), and the possibility of direct application and utility for the study of learning disabilities has already been identified (Brown & French, 1979). We will come back to this concept later when we present work completed in our laboratory.

Ecological Validity

There is a growing concern regarding the apparent division between research and the contexts and real-life needs of the people whom we are studying (Brown & French, 1979), and the problem is probably most obvious when handicapped populations are considered (Brooks & Baumeister, 1977; Gaylord-Ross, 1979). Within the realm of cognitive science, Brown and French (1979) sagaciously point out that efforts have mainly been directed toward the understanding of problems of academic intelligence. For example, other than being able to predict fairly accurately the school failure of the slow learning and learning disabled, there is little else that our IQ tests and achievement tests offer. This negative orientation has undoubtedly biased both our research as well as our attitudes and treatment of the learning disabled. In contrast to the overwhelming evidence concerning what the learning disabled child cannot do or is deficient in, we know very little about what the child can do, under what learning conditions he or she can work best, and on what tasks this occurs. The latter concerns, it will be noted, are, of course, of much greater concern from an educational perspective.

In summary, it seems apparent that investigative efforts concerning the learning disabled could be of much greater utility from an educational perspective if the three conceptual issues (definition, structural versus control processes, and ecological validity) were consistently accounted for in the initial planning stages of one's research. Although a majority of educators would agree that these issues are indeed very central to learning disabilities, there has been relatively little concentrated effort on the part of educational researchers to resolve such issues. One important way, as we see it, would be to examine directly the key areas that the literature has consistently demonstrated to be problematic for the learning disabled.

For example, we know that a major proportion of learning disabled sutdents have difficulty in the reading and reading-related subject areas in school. One of the major factors hypothesized as the cause of this difficulty is attention deficit. However, despite the considerable amount of investigative effort that has been undertaken to identify the nature and extent of the relationship and, indeed, how to remediate the problem, there is considerable controversy and contradiction even on what appear to be major issues. For example, it is unclear whether the learning disabled have a general disposition for attention deficit (Dkyman, Ackerman, Clements, & Peters, 1971), whether this is true only for a distinct subgroup of learning disability (Douglas & Peters, 1979), or whether it is a specific aspect of attention that creates the predominant impediment to the learning disabled child's learning (A. O. Ross, 1976).

Our task, then, as it will be described in this chapter, was to examine the areas of attention and reading with respect to learning disabilities by providing a directive research framework to resolve the conceptual issues of definition, structural versus control processes, and ecological validity. Our initial efforts were necessarily directed at examining traditional theories, approaches, and frameworks for the study of attention and reading. A brief discussion of the literature in these two areas will follow.

SOME BRIEF HISTORICAL ASPECTS OF ATTENTION

During the early study of psychology, attention was generally considered to be a significant variable for experimentation (e.g., James, 1890; Titchener, 1908). Attention during this period was a highly emphasized construct for learning (e.g., Huey, 1908/1968). For the most part, the examination of attention was generally carried out through introspection and led to such statements as:

> Everyone knows what attention is. It is the taking possession by the mind, in clear and vivid form, of one of what seem several simultaneously possible objects or trains of thought. Focalization, concentration of consciousness, are of its essence. It implies withdrawal from some things in order to deal effectively with others [James, 1890, pp. 403–404].

In the early twentieth century, however, the study of attention was essentially halted because of emergence of the behaviorist movement. The examination of internal organismic variables was thought to be impossible and would only lead to vague inferences. The study of the directly observable (i.e., inputs and outputs) was held to be the key to the understanding of all human behavior. To a great extent, this emphasis on the impact of external variables (inputs) on overt behavior is still very much in evidence.

It is our belief that this is precisely where many of the existing attention models are of limited value in much of the current thinking in psychology, education, and other related disciplines.

TRADITIONAL THEORIES AND MODELS OF ATTENTION

Two of the most widely accepted models of attention, following the banishment of James's introspective techniques by the behaviorists and associationists, are the filter and capacity models. Virtually all research on attention during the past two or more decades has revolved around these two basic ideas.

The filter model was first introduced by Broadbent (1958). The model assumes that only one stimulus can be perceived at a time and that, in the case of two competing bits of sensory information, one item is immediately perceived while the other is held momentarily as an unanalyzed echo or image. Only after the perceptual analysis of the first item is completed can such echoes or images undergo perceptual analysis. The model then suggests a blocking of irrelevant perceptual information by means of selective filtering, in order that physical properties of high information concerning the event are attended to.

Subsequent to the introduction of the filter model, various theorists and researchers have presented experimental results to refute the original model (Triesman, 1964), and elaborations and modifications of the model have been advanced (Deutsch & Deutsch, 1963). The major adjustments concern whether information gets selected early or later on in perceptual analysis and whether the selection is based on physical or meaningful information about the event (Norman, 1976).

Douglas and Peters (1979) have outlined a poignant attack against all filter theory models on both empirical and theoretical grounds. They point out that over the last two decades there has been considerable investigative effort given to distractibility studies and incidental learning studies with hyperactive and learning disabled children. Following a filter theory of explanation, the accepted belief is that these special populations have an attentional deficit that limits their ability to block off irrelevant information. After a review of several such distractibility studies, Douglas and Peters (1979) conclude that there is no conclusive evidence to support a distractibility hypothesis, particularly for hyperactive samples.

As an alternative to structural filter models, capacity models, which are couched within a general information-processing theory, are based on the assumption that, although there is an upper limit in the perceiver's capacity to process information, this limited capacity can be rather flexibly allocated among a number of concurrent activities (Moray, 1969). Information that is essentially sensory or well recognized will be quite readily attended to, whereas semantic or unfamiliar inputs will require more effort or capacity allocation (Kahneman, 1973). Information processing failures or slowdowns, then, occur when task demands exceed the limits of capacity, when insufficient capacity remains for task performance because of allocation of some capacity to less relevant inputs (Maccoby & Hagen, 1965), or as a result of insufficient input of relevant information (Posner & Snyder, 1975).

Capacity models have achieved considerable status in contemporary investigations of attentional phenomena, and the popularity can be attributed mainly to their accountability of a wide range of experimental results, from reaction time performance to selective attention studies. Indeed, these models are also intuitively useful in accounting for the now all too familiar results that show significant learning and memory differences between children and adults (as well as between exceptional and nonexceptional groups). In essence, the model simply suggests that younger children have less overall capacity to attend, to remember, or to learn than adults do. Although the above description drastically oversimplifies what are often comprehensive and elaborate models of developmental differences, the core assumption that capacity increases with age (i.e., structural changes) is central to most.

It should be pointed out, however, that several sources in the memory literature point to serious theoretical limitations of a capacity model of memory. Beginning with the attack by Craik and Lockhart (1972) on the inflexibility of a capacity model to explain major areas of data inconsistencies, others have criticized the undue emphasis upon structural as opposed to control features of a memory system (Brown, 1975) or have noted how a capacity model biases the interpretation of experimental results to provide quantitative as opposed to qualitative explanations about memory performance (Lupart & Mulcahy, Note 1).

Chi (1976, 1978) also presents a very convincing case against the fixed capacity notion. Her studies, involving chess playing, with children and adults demonstrate quite clearly that developmental differences attributed to a fixed capacity (particularly a fixed memory capacity) are misleading. The difference may be due instead to differences in background knowledge and strategy knowledge. Dempster (1981) also supports a view of differences in knowledge rather than fixed capacity or span differences per se. Given the strong objections to capacity theory on the basis of developmental memory studies, one is led to speculate as to whether similar shortcomings would not be attributable to the related attention studies. Not surprisingly, similar criticisms have appeared in the literature concerning the attentional development of children. Gibson and Rader (1979), for example, "argue that attention is not a capacity that increases with development but, rather, that our perception changes with increasing knowledge of oneself and the world, allowing us to pick up the information more and more economically to perform a specified task. [p. 6]."

In the same way that we denounce filter models as failing to account adequately for behavior, so it is for capacity models (Neisser, 1976). As Neisser (1976) writes, "In my opinion the notion of a single central information limit is equally [as filter theories] misguided [p. 98]." He goes on to suggest that the concept itself connotes a passive vessel into which things are placed rather than an active and developing structure. Rather than attributing the limiting factors in performance to some fixed capacity structure, Neisser (1976) suggests the possibility that the limiting factors are concerned with the interaction of individual activities and skills involved.

While both the filter and capacity theories have served to generate a considerable amount of research, the failure to specify how attention is associated with learning and cognition appears to be a major shortcoming of both models. The preceding comments by Gibson and Rader (1979) and Neisser (1976) allude to what might be termed a *cognitive view of attention.* This presently emerging view of attention will be briefly described in the next section.

A COGNITIVE VIEW OF ATTENTION

In the previous section of this chapter, the notion of a cognitive view or component of attention was introduced. Even though the approach can hardly be described as a generative theory at this point, there appears to be a growing number of similarly based approaches being described in the literature by several prominent researchers (Douglas & Peters, 1979; Gibson & Rader, 1979; Hochberg, 1978). The major strength of this approach is that, unlike the filter and capacity models of attention, the primary emphasis is upon how attentional processes relate to cognition and cognitive development. Krupski (1980) has suggested that the approach be considered an interactionist view of attention, since it deals with both task variables and child characteristics.

Presented as an alternative to filter theory, Hochberg (1978) views attention as "plan-matching and schema-testing." He argues for the advantage of such a cognitive approach in that:

It brings us a view of perception that builds intention and attention right into the heart of the perceptual process: Perception is the active prediction and sensory testing of expected objects and events, so that by its very nature perception is selective—by electing to test one possible expectation, it rules out many others. No additional mechanism is needed to explain how we fail to hear what we do not attend to [pp. 182–183].[1]

In a similar vein, Gibson and Rader (1979) suggest that "attending refers to perceiving in relation to a task or goal internally or externally motivated [p. 2]." Within a developmental context, Gibson and Rader (1979) argue that:

The child gains progressively in the specificity of correspondence between what information his perceptual processes are engaged with (what he is attending to) and its utility for performance in the service of his needs. He gains in flexibility because more alternatives become open to him. He gains in preparedness for events in readiness for performance. And he gains in how much he can do because of the increasing economy of his pickup of information [p. 14].

[1]This and subsequent quotes cited to Hochberg, 1978 are from Julian E. Hochberg, *Perception,* 2nd ed., © 1978. Adapted by permission of Prentice-Hall, Inc., Englewood Cliffs, N.J.

The important points concerning a cognitive or interactionist view of attention as we see it are (*a*) attention is inextricably tied to cognitive development; and (*b*) changes in attention (which traditional models of attention have insufficiently characterized as quantitative) are really very basic qualitative differences that maximize and optimize the attention of the growing child or adult. In other words, attention begins to take on a strategic role in the child's learning processes, and the child becomes increasingly adept at managing his or her own attentional processes. Douglas and Peters (1979) advance the concept one logical step further by suggesting that normal attentional functioning can be attributed to an individual's ability to utilize prior knowledge to guide the perception and cognition of present events, as well as to an ability to impose voluntary (i.e., conscious, intentional, deliberate) control over current perceptions and cognitions. Both of these considerations are integral to Brown's investigations and discussions of metacognition (Brown, 1978) and self-regulation (Brown & Deloache, 1978).

According to Brown (1978), metacognitive skills are those that characterize and define efficient thought and include a wide variety of potential attentional organizers, such as predicting, checking, monitoring, and reality testing. Whether these are collectively or only partially applied, they are some of the skills that typify and dominate any person's learning and problem solving.

The self-regulation concept can be quite flexibly applied to both young children or novices (and it might be added, to students with learning problems). In an attempt to describe the typical pattern of the process from novice to expert, Brown (1978) contends that:

> First the absolute novice would show little or no intelligent self-regulation due to complete unfamiliarity with the task. This would be followed by an increasingly active period of deliberate self-regulation as the problem solver becomes familiar with the necessary rules and subprocesses, and attempts to orchestrate these activities which are deliberate and demand effort. Finally, the performance of the expert would run off smoothly as the necessary subprocesses and their coordination have all been overlearned to the point where they can be coordinated relatively automatically [p. 20].

Just as Douglas and Peters (1979) have moved the concept of attention, to the crucial interrelationship with metacognition and self-regulatory abilities, we would additionally propose that there is a natural compatability of those ideas to the zone of potential development framework. As Douglas and Peters (1979) describe it:

> The distinction that Brown (1975) and Vygotsky (1963) make between knowledge that can be acquired in a relatively automatic, unconscious way and knowledge that must be self-consciously and deliberately sought may be very relevant for an understanding of these children's cognitive strengths and weaknesses [p. 231].

Given this perspective, it is then possible to view the attentional problems of the learning disabled as an inability to spontaneously impose self-regulatory attentional strategies on school-related tasks in particular. According to Brown (1975), the problems become most notable when a child is faced with school tasks in which no obvious purpose is clear to the child. In other words, even though two young students may have the same IQ and mental age, the child who has an attention deficit fails to adopt effort-maximizing attentional strategies to cope with school tasks, and that child's academic achievement suffers as a result. From a zone of potential development perspective, special training or adult tutoring should enable the learning disabled child to reach his or her zone of maximal development.

Referring to the three conceptual issues for learning disability research discussed earlier, it would seem apparent that the cognitive view of attention holds considerable promise for the resolution of the structural versus control process issue. Unlike the capacity or filter models, which would tend to bias researchers toward a structural or deficit orientation to learning disabilities, the cognitive model of attention can simultaneously account for developmental or structural issues as well as for the basic qualitative factors that maximize or optimize the attention of the growing child or the adult. Although no specific model or experimental paradigm has yet been proposed for the study of cognitive attention, it would appear that the recent writing and research in the areas of metacognition, self-regulation, and zone of potential development are a logical basis from which to start. Before a brief description of such a framework, the next key area of learning disability research, reading, as it is related to attention, will be presented.

ATTENTION AND PROFICIENT READING

With respect to the process of reading, the close interrelationship between perception and attention processes has been acknowledged as early as the turn of this century. Huey (1908/1968) wrote:

> Perceiving being an act, it is performed more easily with each repetition . . . to perceive an entirely new word . . . requires time and close attention . . . repetition progressively frees the mind from attention to details, makes facile the total act, shortens the time and reduces the extent to which consciousness must concern itself with the process [p. 104].

However, there is considerable disagreement as to how this relationship is defined.

Gibson and Levin (1975) surmise that the crucial attentional processes with respect to reading include the abilities to ignore irrelevant information and to utilize effectively the peripheral mechanisms of attention. The former process implies that one must be able to visually discriminate between stimuli. Allington (1975) proposes that the development of such differential responding involves first learning to attend to the distinguishing feature(s) of a stimulus, and second, learning to quickly identify and remember the feature(s). Even though LaBerge and Samuels (1974) would agree with Allington's (1975) delineation of the two stages, their notion of the role of attention in the reading process implies a quite different perspective. LaBerge and Samuels (1975) suggest that there are both an accuracy level of performance and an automatic level of performance that affect the reading process. Attention is presumed necessary only for the accuracy level of performance. The rationale for this point of view is elaborated by Samuels (1976). Here, Samuels suggests that with repetition and increasing experience, a behavior that formerly required effort and attention would eventually become more or less automatic and could be executed without attention. Therefore, if we were to conceptualize the reading process as a combination of decoding and processing meaning, Samuels suggests that the immature learning disabled reader must devote most of his or her attention to the decoding aspects, which thereby greatly limits comprehension. Alternatively, the mature or skilled reader, for whom decoding skills have become automatized, can devote the time to processing meaning.

Wright and Vlietsra (1975), however, in contrast to Samuels (1976), assert that attention is a necessary component of all information processing, although qualitative differences are apparent. By this, it is postulated that attention is controlled initially by salient features of stimuli and later by logical features of the task. This shift, then, proceeds from passively tracked to actively sequenced attending.

Along with the discrimination of relevant versus irrelevant stimuli, Gibson and Levin (1975) suggest that the more proficient reader must effectively utilize the peripheral mechanisms of attention. The visual peripheral mechanisms of attention can be considered to be exploratory in function and are primarily associated with visual scanning or looking behavior. As Gibson and Levin (1975) describe it, the peripheral mechanisms of attention are responsible for exposing the receptors to selected aspects of potential stimulation, and they propose that the process is highly susceptible to learning and development.

In support of this view, Day (1975) in a major review of the literature has identified six developmental trends in visual scanning. Although the list is not specifically referenced to reading, the overall significance such development imparts to the reading process will become apparent to the reader and thus justifies inclusion here:

With increasing age, children:

1. Demonstrate more systematic, task-appropriate strategies for acquiring visual information

2. Show an increasing ability to maintain optimal performance across variation in the content and arrangement of stimuli
3. Exhibit visual scanning that becomes more exhaustive and more efficient
4. Show an increasing focus on the portions of visual stimuli that are most informative for the specific task
5. Show an increase in the speed of completion of visual search and comparison tasks
6. Show an increase in the size of the useful "field of view" (Day, 1975, pp. 186–187)

In summary, it would appear that there are both structural (i.e., developmentally determined or constrained) as well as process (i.e., visual scanning and selective attention) limitations related to attention that would negatively affect the young child's (or it could be argued, the learning disabled child's) reading acquisition. In addition, attentional processes that are available are of limited utility until they can be performed automatically in the context of the reading process. The trend toward reading proficiency, with respect to attentional processes, is referred to by Gibson and Levin (1975) as the *optimization of attention*.

The Optimization of Attention in Reading

In the field at present, there is considerable controversy as to how the optimization of attention becomes actualized in the reading process. The distinction, it might be suggested, is generally parallel to that which comprises the bottom-up versus top-down theories of reading (Calfee & Drum, 1978). Norman (1976) describes a bottom-up or data-driven view as "any sequence of operations that proceeds from the incoming data, through increasingly sophisticated analyses [p. 41]." As a leading proponent of the bottom-up view of reading, Gough (1972) maintains that the reading process is a combination of several subskills that are initially awkwardly performed but that through practice become seemingly automatic and integrated, as in the case of the proficient reader. Thus, Gough (1972) imparts that all readers must rely on the same skills in reading, and differences in ability to read arise on the basis of the facility with which the reader is able to apply these skills to the visual information provided by the text. With respect to the role of attention in the perception of visual stimuli, Gough (1972) fails to make allowances for individuals other than for rate of reading. However, in view of the earlier discussion concerning the interrelationship of reading, perception, and attention, it would indeed appear that any number of individual differences (i.e., attention to high information distinctive features, inability to ignore irrelevant information) might also account for differences in reading performance.

Norman (1976) refers to a top-down or "conceptually driven" system in which "visual signals might start with the highest level expectations of an object that is further refined by analyses of the context to yield expectations of particular lines in particular locations [p. 41]."

Goodman (1973, 1976), who is widely held to represent a top-down approach to reading, emphasizes the reader's active involvement in the reading process as he or she utilizes psycholinguistic knowledge to make predictions about the author's message. The implication with respect to visual perception is that, for the reader to become more proficient, he or she must become increasingly discriminating in regard to the graphic information, and search out or attend to only those stimuli that will facilitate the hypothesis testing or extraction of meaning. For Goodman (1969, 1973), it would seem, then, that the search aspects of attention, as opposed to the exploratory aspects, are the most important in the process of reading.

Several suggestions would appear plausible with respect to bottom-up versus top-down attentional processing in this reading controversy. It would seem that Gough's (1972) views have greater relevance when we consider the allocation of attention for the beginning reader. On the other hand, Goodman's (1969, 1973) description of the reading process might be more aptly applied to the analysis of the attentional process of the proficient reader. Or it could be alternatively suggested that the controversy will never be satisfactorily resolved for one side or the other, and it is very likely that both systems simultaneously play an integral role with respect to the optimization of attention as other researchers have already suggested (McConkie & Rayner, 1976; Norman, 1976). The point that is, however, most crucial to the present discussion is that, even though there appears to be wide acknowledgment of the importance of attention for both bottom-up and top-down processing in reading, the majority of reading studies concerning attention have primarily been based upon a bottom-up perspective. This may not be all that surprising considering the pressure from psychology during the last five decades to focus on measurable behavioral responses (i.e., visual scanning, eye movement, reaction times) and a traditional view of perception that emphasized stimulus reception (i.e., symbol recognition, orthography, or tachistoscopic perception), as opposed to how children "learn to predict and anticipate what is coming next in reading" and "what the goals and the appropriate units are for the different intentions that initiate and maintain reading behavior [Hochberg & Brooks, 1970, pp. 249–250]." In other words, we know a great deal about what a reader does attend to, but we do not know how or what determines how the reader guides his or her attention. In the following segment of this chapter, a summary of some of the work of the few reading researchers who are beginning to explore this potentially fruitful top-down perspective of attention in the reading process will be given. In addition, it should become quite apparent that the top-down approach to attention, as it is developing in the reading literature, is very similar and quite consistent with the interactive approach or the cognitive approach that was alluded to in the earlier discussion of general psychological models of attention.

Reading as an Intentional Behavior

The logic for stressing a top-down approach to attention in reading is outlined by Hochberg and Brooks (1970):

> The reader does not merely regard a block of text and immediately realize its message. He must "intend" to read the display, must "pay attention" to its meaning if he is able to respond to its contents. What a phrase like "pay attention to" might mean in this context has not received much thought or experimental research, but it would seem to be a fundamental importance to any understanding of what the reading process is all about [p. 242].

The importance of an intentional or planning component to attentional processing in reading has been gaining increased recognition (Hochberg, 1976, 1978; Hochberg & Brooks, 1970; Mackworth, 1977; Stauffer, 1977). Hochberg (1978) proposes that there are two interacting systems that affect our reading behavior: parafoveal or peripheral search guidance and cognitive search guidance. The former system (formulated on the basis of mainly eye-movement studies) must make optimal use of the information being picked up by the successive extrapolations of the fovea, whereas the latter guides the eye movement on the basis of anticipating what comes next. According to Hochberg (1978):

> The skilled reader is set for most of his glances before he perceives them so that his long-term memory is primed; and within each speech plan, he is testing a chunk that is already in short-term memory. He does not combine successive samples by adding each to the preceding one. Instead, he moves his eyes to test and fill out his expectations and formulate new ones [p. 177].

In an attempt to explain just how the planning function relates to reading, as well as to other such skilled actions as typing, Hochberg (1978) refers to the Miller, Galanter, and Pribram (1960) Test-Operate-Test-Exit (TOTE) model, the unit of purposive, planned, sequential behavior. There are three key features to the TOTE model that Hochberg (1978) outlines and that are important to the discussion here. The first point is that there is a hierarchical progression in that:

> A part or detail at one level of analysis becomes a unit with its own parts at the next. . . .
> The second point is that perception, expectation (or "internal representation" or "im-

age" or the desired state), intention and action are all intertwined in this analysis. The tests consist of comparison of the existing state of affairs (roughly, perceptions) with the desired state of affairs—i.e., with a particular representation of the world that is selected by the organism's goal or intentions. . . . The third point is that there are limits to how far down the analysis can go [p. 181].

To the present line of discussion, the TOTE model as it is outlined here would appear to be quite consistent with both a top-down and a bottom-up attentional view of the reading process. What is unacceptable, however, is the way that Hochberg (1976, 1978) applies this model to a "speech-plan eye-movement model of reading." In his discussion of Types 1, 2, 3, and 4 reading, Hochberg (1976), despite his intuitive acknowledgment of the importance of top-down attentional processing, relies on bottom-up experiments (i.e., eye movements or adjustments to the visual information) to back his statements. In fairness to Hochberg (1976), he acknowledges the limitations of his approach in stating: "Perhaps the large regressive movement back to a word that the reader makes when he discovers later on that he must have misread the word (Geyer, 1966) is the closest we have come to a direct record of cognitive guidance in the course of reading [p. 405]."

Also, by making reference to a speech-plan view of reading, one might misinterpret Hochberg's (1976, 1978) notion of cognitive search guidance as one that is dominated by linguistic parameters rather than cognitive plans. The former linguistic perspective would be typified by the work of, for example, Vellutino (1977), who hypothesizes "that poor readers may have difficulty both in linguistic coding of incoming information and in the retrieval of linguistic referents associated with given stimuli [p. 348]." This view would, therefore, confine the cognitive search guidance attentional processing to the semantic, syntactic, or phonological components of the written text. In contrast, top-down attentional processing, as we view it, includes any of the executive, planning, or self-regulative attentional strategies that the reader can impose on the reading situation to increase the proficiency of the performance.

In a more philosophical discussion of the role of intention in reading and thinking, Stauffer (1977) makes the notion of attention as cognitive search guidance quite clear:

In brief, then, it appears that reading is a mental process akin to thinking or to state it differently, critical reading is akin to reflective or productive thinking. One must also allow for the fact that reading can be done for vague, unclear affective reasons and/or for unregulated thinking. Thus, reading can be done at various degrees of sophistication both for entertainment and learning. Likewise, thinking can be either regulated or largely unregulated. When reading to learn is required, the reading–thinking process must be productive. When reading for entertainment, the reading–thinking process can be largely unregulated, varying with the amount of involvement desired [p. 52]."

In corroboration with this view, Mackworth (1977) makes the important distinction between the stimulus-bound versus self-ruled tasks in reading. In a stimulus-bound task, such as monitoring another's reading, the person must simply match the spoken and printed patterns.

The self-ruled task (being what most reading situations for the proficient reader are) is quite the opposite. The self-ruled reading situation is one in which the good reader is more actively involved and establishes his or her own control over the stimuli. Mackworth (1977) suggests that in poor readers "the short-term memory cannot provide the proper context or subroutines to use in the searching of long-term memory [p. 21]." By this he makes the implication that the short-term memory capacity limitations of the poor and younger reader cause the difficulty. On the basis of the previous discussion concerning capacity models, however, it is argued that a more plausible explanation would be that the poor or disabled reader fails to impose his or her own self-regulation on the reading task, thereby making it an activity that is more stimulus bound than self-ruled. In other words, the older poor or disabled reader fails to set his or her own purposes for reading and most likely views the major reading task as essentially a decoding activity. A further argument against Mackworth's (1977) hypothesis of short-term memory capacity limitations in older poor or disabled readers is that the problem is most often manifested only in the reading situation and does not generalize to other subject areas or learning tasks. In any case, it would appear that the counterargument of the poor reader's failure to impose his or her own self-regulation can be fairly straightforwardly examined by having the poor reader attend to self-regulatory or planning strategies on a reading task, and observing performance differences when no self-regulation is encouraged.

In an attempt to clarify the interrelationships between regulation or metacognition and cognition in the reading process, Forrest and Waller (Note 2) suggest that:

> Cognition refers to the actual processes and strategies that are used by a reader. On the other hand, *meta*-cognition is a construct which refers first to what a person *knows* about his/her cognitions (in the sense of being consciously aware of the processes and of being able to tell you about them in some way), and second, to the ability to *control* these cognitions (in the sense of planning cognitive activities, choosing among alternative activities, monitoring the performance of activities, and changing activities) [p. 2].

This view appears to be consistent with the notion of top-down attentional processing as it has been developed here.

In summary, the preceding review of the literature in the area of reading suggests that the proficient reader is one who can flexibly apply his or her attention to the visual information on the page, to the interpretation of the author's meaning, to the reader's own reflective or background knowledge, or to an overriding macrogoal that can be self-regulated or other imposed. Where the attention gets allocated is both self- and situationally determined. The decision for attentional allocation is dictated by the reader's self-defined, self-regulated, or interpretive view of the task purpose. It seems likely that different attentional allocation strategies are more efficient for different tasks, and the proficient reader will rely on those most expedient to her or his goal.

Although this review of the literature on attention and reading has been selective and brief, it appears quite obvious that when we want to examine the optimization of attention we must necessarily consider both the top-down and bottom-up perspectives. Before presentation of a brief discussion of learning disability and attention deficit, two points by way of summary of this segment of the chapter are necessary.

1. Researchers in the area of reading have begun to explore attention as a top-down process, and there appears to be considerable agreement to the notion that optimal attention involves intentional planning and self-regulation. This position is very similar to the interactive or cognitive approach that is similarly beginning to appear in the general literature on attention.
2. So far, the investigations concerning attention as a top-down process in reading have been based on bottom-up investigations (Hochberg, 1978; Mackworth, 1977).

In concluding this segment, it is suggested that there is a conspicuous need for an investigation of top-down attentional processing using a top-down investigative approach. In the following segment concerning learning disability and attention deficit, we argue that this particular sample group (i.e., learning disabled) would be a logical choice for an initial exploration of top-down attentional processing using a top-down investigation approach.

LEARNING DISABILITY AND ATTENTION DEFICIT

The literature pertaining to learning disabled samples has consistently attributed the characteristic learning problems of this group to problems in attending (Clements, 1966; Ross, 1976; Tarver & Hallahan, 1974). The research in this area to date has focused on very specific factors that have been proposed as subcomponents of the general construct of attention. For example, numerous studies in the last 10 years have examined the problems children with learning disabilities have in selective attention (Anderson, Halcomn, & Doyle, 1973; Keogh & Margolis, 1976; Kirchner & Knopf, 1974; Noland & Schuldt, 1971).

In general, the orientation with respect to the literature on attention and learning disability has consistently viewed attention from a bottom-up perspective only (cf. Samuels & Edwall, 1981). The search has been to identify some specific aspect of attention (arousal, selectivity, capacity, etc.) that would account for the child's learning difficulty. This, as it was noted in the previous section on attention, can lead one only to a structural or deficit orientation. As such, the approach is of limited utility for educators who are more interested in the factors that improve or optimize the students' learning potentials.

It should also be pointed out that the experimental paradigms that have been used to assess attention in the learning disabled are typically simple discrimination tasks, time tasks, etc. Such tasks, it is argued, would have little relationship to the complex processes that are involved, for example, in reading (i.e., ecological invalidity). Yet the results of such studies are consistently used as evidence for attention deficit, which is purported to be the major cause of reading problems in learning disabled youngsters. Our own assessment is that such studies should be seriously reconsidered if not totally abandoned.

Instead we propose that the emerging views of attention and reading as an interactive process, involving both top-down and bottom-up aspects, should be alternatively considered as an investigation framework for the examination of the notion of "attention deficit" in disabled readers. Since it is apparent that the majority of the existing studies have been bottom-up in orientation, our arguments will be addressed to our belief that a top-down approach in reading offers a number of advantages to the study of attention and reading disability. To begin with, it provides a necessary completion to an investigation framework that is decidedly bottom-up oriented, from both the reading and the learning disability perspective. Since learning disabled students are of comparable intelligence with respect to their normal peers, it is possible that many of the metacognitive routines are already developed and utilized in learning tasks other than reading. If so, one could expect that for the older learning disabled students who have outgrown or overcome any possible perceptual problems, prompting them to rely on or attend to such metacognitive abilities during a reading task should markedly improve their performance. In addition, the ecological validity of the experimental task is established by the fact that it is the actual reading task that is used in the investigation and as such the specific task variables versus child characteristics can be clearly examined (Krupski, 1980).

Referring now to the initial discussion on conceptual issues and learning disability research, we can clearly see that the issues of structural versus control processes and of ecological validity can readily be accounted for by using this approach. The remaining issue, definition, is at this point quite straightforward and in fact has already been alluded to in the preceding paragraph. If, as we propose, proficient reading is comprised of both bottom-up and top-down attentional processes, then the logical group of disabled readers to examine for our purposes would be those having adequately developed bottom-up reading skills. The assumption here is that, if the student has developed adequate word identification abilities (i.e., bottom-up attention) and yet is still assessed as reading disabled, then it must be the top-down attentional abilities that are inadequate. If we can then identify such subjects, we can begin to explore the notion of top-down attentional processing in reading.

With that, it is determined that the basic conceptual issues for our study have been adequately resolved, and the next stage of the process is to devise the appropriate experimental paradigm in which to examine the direct issues of top-down attention and reading disability. The following section will briefly review some of the literature related to this aspect of our task.

AN EXPERIMENTAL PARADIGM TO EXAMINE TOP-DOWN ATTENTION PROCESSES

No studies could be found in the literature that specifically have dealt with a model of attention incorporating both bottom-up and top-down processing. As previously mentioned, even the reading researchers who advocate a top-down view of attention and the reading process (Hochberg, 1976, 1978; Mackworth, 1977) appear to rely on bottom-up type investigations (i.e., text manipulation, tachistoscope studies). However, the work in the area of metacognition that has been burgeoning in the developmental literature (Brown, 1978; Flavell, 1978) would appear to be a logical starting point for an analysis of attention in the reading process from a top-down perspective. Although there appear to be any number of metas (i.e., metamemory, metacomprehension, metalearning) that fall under the rubric of *metacognition,* the collective term, as defined by Flavell (1976):

> refers to one's knowledge concerning one's own cognitive processes and products or anything related to them, e.g., the learning-relevant properties of information or data. . . . Metacognition refers, among other things, to the active monitoring and consequent regulation and orchestration of these processes in relation to the cognitive objects or data on which they bear, usually in the service of some concrete goal or objective [p. 232].

It is of considerable interest to note that the preceding description of *metacognition* captures many of the features that researchers in the areas of attention (i.e., Douglas & Peters, 1979; Gibson & Rader, 1979) and of reading and attention (i.e., Hochberg, 1978; Mackworth, 1977) have begun to explore. In fact, we are beginning to see an increasing number of investigations in the literature dealing with the metacognitive and metacomprehension aspects of reading (Brown, Campione, & Barclay, 1979; DiVesta, Hayward, & Orlando, 1979; Myers & Paris, 1978; Forrest & Waller, Note 3). Myers and Paris (1978), for example, conducted an interview study with 8- and 12-year-old children in an effort to determine metacognitive awareness of personal abilities, task parameters, and cognitive strategies. On the basis of the findings that the younger children were less sensitive to the semantic structure of paragraphs, goals of reading, and strategies for resolving comprehension failures, the authors concluded that metacognitive knowledge indeed appears to be a major factor in the acquisition of proficient reading skills.

Of even greater significance to the present discussion are the ever increasing number of studies that suggest that both other-regulated and self-regulated top-down strategies have a significant effect on learning and performance. Lichtenstein and Brewer (1980) were able to demonstrate that a plan schema of underlying events was the most important factor in both behavioral and narrative prose recall. Similarly, Ross, Rakow, and Bush (1980) have shown that helping the student to improve his or her strategies for self-managed learning systems results in significantly better retention and learning efficiency, over both traditional instructional aid to the student (i.e., the teacher giving the response as opposed to the student solving the problem) as well as incentive effects. Utilizing a somewhat unusual approach, Denney (1975) and Denney, Jones, and Krigel (1979) have utilized a number of cognitive strategy modeling and training techniques that have been successfully adopted and applied by children and elderly adults to improve their performance on a Twenty Questions task.

The preceding studies suggest a number of ways in which a top-down approach might be operationalized, as well as the kinds of concerns that can be effectively examined in this way. With respect to the role of attention and its significance as a top-down process, there are a number of areas that need to be explored. For example, we need to know how the hierarchy of self-regulation is sequenced (i.e., metacognitive level, to metacomprehension, etc.) and if the upper-level processes are available to the child. If they are available, does the child use them? And in which particular reading situations? How can we train the child to give attention to higher level cognitive strategies during the reading task? And what are the instructional conditions that facilitate this?

There are already some good examples in the reading literature of how one could begin to investigate these kinds of problems (Dee-Lucas & DiVesta, 1980; DiVesta et al., 1979; Forrest & Waller, Note 2, Note 3). Forrest and Waller (Note 2), for example, examined the ability of young children to make appropriate verbalizations about the decoding, comprehension, and strategic aspects of reading, and used stepwise multiple regressions to predict reading ability. They found that:

> At the grade 3 level, the multiple regression equation accounted for 46.82% of the variance with decoding being the best predictor from the set of reading skills. At the grade 6 level, the multiple regression equation accounted for 62.73% of the variance with strategies being the best predictor from the set [p. 7].

Techniques such as those used in this study are still at a pioneering level in this kind of research, but the findings do appear to provide substantial support for continued investigations of this sort.

In another study, Owings, Petersen, Bransford, Morris, and Stein (1980) gave the least and most successful boys from a regular Grade 5 class study stories to read that varied in the degree to which they made sense relative to participants' prior knowledge. The difference is exemplified by the sensibility of the following two sentences: *The tall boy played basketball* versus *The hungry boy took a nap*. Their findings are of interest on several accounts. The Owings *et al.* (1980) compendium of the results is as follows:

> For both groups, cued recall test scores (e.g., "What did the hungry boy do?") were substantially higher for stories that made sense than for stories that did not. Successful students spontaneously monitored as they read and studied; they were aware of having difficulty learning the less sensible stories, and they could explain why they were having trouble. Less successful students did not rate difficulty accurately and seemed unaware of the manipulation. When allowed unlimited study time, successful students spontaneously regulated learning, that is, they chose to study difficult stories more than easy stories. Less successful students studied equally for both. When prompted, less successful students were able to distinguish between stories, but they did not do so spontaneously. The results suggest that many students perform below their potential, in part because they do not spontaneously monitor and regulate their learning [p. 250].

The preceding study, it might be pointed out, also exemplifies the utility of observing samples of more and less reading proficiency using this top-down approach.

Brown (1980) as well has been engaged in continuing research on metacognition and reading in her laboratory over the past few years. Her studies have been directed toward what she terms "selective attention" strategies for understanding prose. Among the types of strategies she has been studying are underlining, taking notes on main ideas, self-questioning, concentrating on missed or difficult segments of text, as well as the purposive act of attention-directing. Her work suggests that some of the important meta skills relative to reading are (*a*) the subjects' knowledge of what strategies may be available for directing attention; (*b*) knowledge of their own characteristics as learners; (*c*) knowledge of the text characteristics; and (*d*) the nature of the criterial task. These, however, all have to be coordinated in an effective manner in order to produce skilled reading. This aspect of attention, however, is not captured in current conceptualizations of attention and reading.

From the preceding literature review, it seems apparent that one can quite readily integrate the current metacognitive literature to the notion of top-down attentional processing in reading. One plausible way in which this could be systematically examined would be to present subjects with a reading task, under differential instructional conditions that vary according to the amount of other direction for the promotion of attentional self-regulation (i.e., top-down attentional processing). The conditions would range from incidental (no knowledge of posttask recall or comprehension question answering requirement) to trained intentional in which subjects would be specifically trained to adopt and apply systematic top-down attentional processing to a reading task. By examining normal and disabled readers on a silent reading task under different instructional conditions, one could answer several questions.

First, it might be determined whether attentional self-regulation in reading is apparent in normal reading development. Next, by comparing performance across experimental conditions, information can be derived with respect to improvement in performance resulting from attentional self-regulation. This approach may also provide data that are relevant for classroom utilization, since the instructional approach yielding maximal performance for each group may be ascertained. If significant discrepancies in top-down attentional self-regulation between normal and reading disabled students can be eliminated through instructional conditions, the results would be of interest to those with theoretical, experimental, or remedial concerns in the areas of attention, reading, and learning disability.

In our laboratory during the past few years we have utliized a particular research paradigm to examine gradations of self-regulated attentional behavior in normal and special groups. The paradigm is based upon the voluntary–involuntary learning concept (Meacham, 1977), and we have used experimental conditions that impose increasing degrees of other-directed control on the subjects' attentional behaviors. The general paradigm involves increasing levels of direct intervention, proceeding from a condition of basically none (incidental) through to an explicit solution (strategy conditions). Through this paradigm, one is able to determine the degree of self-regulation of attention that exists as well as the amount of other direction necessary to improve the performance of certain subgroups of exceptional learners (Brown *et al.*, 1981; Vygotsky, 1978).

We have conducted a number of studies with variations in conditions

(Lupart & Mulcahy, Note 1, Note 4); however, one study carried out with reading disabled children has particular relevance here and will be described in some detail. Complete description and results are given elsewhere (Lupart, Note 5).

This study involved an examination of the attentional self-regulation abilities of reading disabled and average-achieving youngsters. What we hoped to achieve in this study was to determine if within an older reading disabled group it would be possible to increase recall and comprehension performance through increasing other direction for attentional regulation. The majority of research in attention and reading has been decidedly one-sided toward a view of attention as a unidirectional process. We thought it conceivable that attention to top-down strategies or metacomprehension plans during the reading process might distinguish somewhat older (14-year-old) reading disabled youngsters from their younger (11–12-year-old) skilled reading peers. Sixty Grade 5 skilled readers (mean grade level 5.04 on the Schonell Graded Word Reading Test) and 60 Grade 7 disabled readers (mean grade level 5.6 on the Schonell) were involved in the study. Subjects from each sample were then randomly assigned to one of four possible experimental conditions.

Incidental. The instructions to each subject here were, "I would like you to read this story. Let me know when you have finished reading."

Intentional. The instructions to each subject here were, "I would like you to read this story and then tell me as much as you can remember of it. Let me know when you are ready to recall the story."

Planned intentional. Subjects were preinterviewed, utilizing questions devised to encourage the subjects to think about and adopt a self-selected metacognitive plan to utilize on the task. The instructions then were, "I would now like you to read the story and then tell me as much as you can remember of it. Let me know when you are ready to recall the story."

Trained intentional. Subjects in this condition were given four 45-min training sessions in which a specific metacognitive reading strategy was taught, with practice given in self-regulating attention to the overall strategy during the silent reading of short passages. This SQ3R approach (Sargent, Huus, & Andersen, 1970) simply consists of five steps that readers can apply to their reading. These include the initial surveying of the text, questioning while reading, reading, reciting, and finally reviewing. Prior to experimental task performance, the following instructions were given, "I would like you to read this story and then tell me as much as you can remember of it. Use the SQ3R approach for this. Let me know when you are ready to recall the story."

The story utilized for all conditions was the Japanese folktale "The Dragon's Tears," used in several previous studies (Brown & Smiley, 1977;

Brown, Smiley, & Lawton, 1978; Smiley, Oakley, Worthen, Campione, & Brown, 1977). The story is broken down into idea units relative to the degree of importance to the theme.

The results, in brief, were very interesting, since differential instructional conditions were found to be beneficial for the reading disabled youngsters' recall. The reading disabled subjects under the incidental conditions evidenced significantly poorer recall as compared to their younger skilled reader peers; however, under the intentional and planned intentional conditions, the youngsters with reading problems performed as well as or better than the skilled readers in recall and comprehension. This to us provides some evidence to support the idea that older disabled readers here do in fact have access to top-down attention organizing strategies but they do not tend to rely on these in a general reading situation where no particular goal has been specified. Of greatest import, is the finding that under the trained intentional condition the reading disabled youngsters obtained significantly better comprehension and recall performances than the skilled reading groups. We propose to follow up this study with youngsters who are proficient readers of the same age as the reading disabled of this study.

CONCLUSION

It is evident from the literature and the data from our laboratory that we need a somewhat different conceptualization of what attention is and how it functions. We agree with many of the researchers (e.g., Douglas & Peters, 1979; Gibson & Rader, 1979; Hochberg, 1978) that current models of attention (particularly with respect to reading) are no longer appropriate. Krupski (1980), as was mentioned earlier, has suggested that an interactionist position is needed and has put forth the idea of looking at attention from a two-way interaction (i.e., task characteristics, child characteristics). This is a step in the right direction; however, we believe that there is the need for a model that includes more than just these two aspects.

What is needed now is a model of the attentional process that includes both a bottom-up and top-down perspective. It is clear that this interactive approach to attention may more readily capture the current directions needed in research and the attentional process.

In our laboratory, we are currently engaged in developing and refining a comprehensive model of attention (Lupart, Note 5) that will guide our continuing research over the next few years. The model at this stage is a fuzzy concept; however, we envisage it incorporating a number of key aspects among which are the following.

1. *Learner characteristics.* Included here would be the individual's knowledge base: intellectual, motivational, memorial, personal, social, etc. The

affective aspects are included here, as major variables to be examined in interaction with context and internal–external attention. We have chosen to include affective aspects because of the inseparable, interactive relationship with what is termed *cognition* (Meichenbaum, 1980). This variable has been too long neglected in models of information processing and attention.

2. *Task characteristics.* Included here are task demands, situations, goals, etc. This component considers all aspects of the total context in which performance is observed.

3. *Bottom-up predominant attention.* Included here are attention to color, shape, form, etc. It involves those aspects external to the individual.

4. *Top-down predominant attention.* Here would be what is termed both conscious and subconscious aspects. Attending to one's own thought processes is the essence of this component. We would include here such things as comprehension monitoring and memory monitoring.

As this model depicts it, the acquisition of knowledge is an active–interactive process, not a static instantaneous, discrete point in time. The majority of information processing systems are depicted as data-driven systems beginning with the analysis of stimulus information and then proceeding to higher levels of processing. Hoyer (1980) makes the suggestion that it may be useful to consider conceptually driven systems that permit higher mental processes to influence component sensory and perceptual processes. Neisser (1976), Gibson and Rader (1979), and Hochberg (1978) also have suggested this. The model we are suggesting as being a more adequate depiction of attentional processes places emphasis on the influence of context, experience, and expectation in the processing of information and thus is not unidirectional in moving from data to conceptual but is, in fact, interactive in nature.

The model currently being developed is a broad-based model of attention and learning that we believe will capture those aspects most critical to learning performance.

We are beginning with a breakdown first of the internal–external attentional strategies young children and adults use in different reading contexts (utilizing a task analytic approach). It is because reading is one of the most important tasks children are faced with during their school years and because a significant number of children demonstrate problems in reading that we have decided initially to focus on the reading task. The paradigm presented earlier with respect to varying degrees of other-directed attentional allocation will again be refined and utilized to assist in delineating degrees of internal attentional self-regulation. This will be accomplished through a sequential series of experiments involving an examination of the interaction of the previously described four key aspects of attention. It is further anticipated that through this systematic sequential approach we will be able to explore Vygotsky's (1963, 1978) theory of the zone of potential development and be able more precisely to determine within groups of exceptional children their zone of actual and potential development. This, we hope, will provide data more relevant to the educational aspects of our work.

REFERENCE NOTES

1. Lupart, J. L., & Mulcahy, R. F. A look at the memory performance of retarded and normal children utilizing the levels of processing framework. Paper presented at the meeting of the American Educational Research Association, San Francisco, 1979.
2. Forrest, D. L., & Waller, T. G. What do children know about their reading and study skills? Paper presented at the meeting of the American Educational Research Association, Boston, April 1980.
3. Forrest, D. L., & Waller, T. G. Cognitive and metacognitive aspects of reading. Paper presented at the biennial meeting of the Society for Research in Child Development, San Francisco, March 1979.
4. Lupart, J. L., & Mulcahy, R. F. Attention and disabled readers: A top-down perspective. Paper presented at the meeting of the Canadian Psychological Association, Montreal, 1982.
5. Lupart, J. L. Toward a functional model of attention. *Canadian Journal of Exceptionality.* in press.

REFERENCES

Allington, R. Attention and application: The oft forgotten steps in teaching reading. *Journal of Learning Disabilities,* 1975, *8,* 22–25.
Anderson, R. R., Halcomn, C. C., & Doyle, R. D. Measurement of attentional deficits. *Exceptional Children,* 1973, *39,* 534–539.
Artley, A. S. Learning disabilities versus reading disabilities: A vexing problem. In C. M. McCullough (Ed.), *Inchworm, inchworm: Persistent problems in reading education.* Newark, Del.: International Reading Association, 1980.
Atkinson, R. C., & Shiffrin, R. M. Human memory: A proposed system and its control processes. In K. W. Spence & J. T. Spence (Eds.), *The psychology of learning and motivation: Advances in research and theory* (Vol. 2). New York: Academic Press, 1968.
Belmont, J. M., & Butterfiled, E. C. Learning strategies as determinants of memory deficiencies. *Cognitive Psychology,* 1971, *2,* 411–420.
Bray, N. W., Justice, E. M., Ferguson, R. P., & Simon, D. L. Developmental changes in the effects of instructions on production-deficient children. *Child Development,* 1977, *48,* 1019–1026.
Broadbent, D. E. *Perception and communication.* London: Pergamon, 1958.
Brooks, P. H., & Baumeister, A. A. A plea for consideration of ecological validity in the experimental psychology of mental retardation: A guest editorial. *American Journal of Mental Deficiency,* 1977, *81,* 407–416.
Brown, A. L. The role of strategic behavior in retardate memory. In N. R. Ellis (Ed.), *International review of research in mental retardation* (Vol. 7). New York: Academic Press, 1974.
Brown, A. L. The development of memory: Knowing, knowing about knowing, and knowing how to know. In H. W. Reese (Ed.), *Advances in child development and behavior* (Vol. 10). New York: Academic Press, 1975.

Brown, A. L. Knowing when, where and how to remember: A problem of metacognition. In R. Glaser (Ed.), *Advances in instructional psychology*. Hillsdale, N.J.: Erlbaum, 1978.

Brown, A. L. Metacognitive development and reading. In R. J. Spiro, B. C. Bruce, & W. F. Brewer (Eds.), *Theoretical issues in reading comprehension*. Hillsdale, N.J.: Erlbaum, 1980.

Brown, A. L., & Barclay, C. R. The effects of training specific mnemonics on the metamnemonic efficiency of retarded children. *Child Development*, 1976, *47*, 71–80.

Brown, A. L., Campione, J. C., & Barclay, C. R. Training self-checking routines for estimating test readiness: Generalizations from list learning to prose recall. *Child Development*, 1979, *50*, 501–512.

Brown, A. L., Campione, J. C., & Day, J. D. Learning to learn: On training students to learn from texts. *Educational Researcher*, 1981, *10*, 14–21.

Brown, A. L., Campione, J. C., & Murphy, M. D. Keeping track of changing variables: Long-term retention of a trained rehearsal strategy by retarded adolescents. *American Journal of Mental Deficiency*, 1974, *78*, 446–453.

Brown, A. L., Campione, J. C., & Murphy, M. D. Maintenance and generalization of trained metamnemonic awareness by educable retarded children. *Journal of Experimental Child Psychology*, 1977, *24*, 191–211.

Brown, A. L., & Deloache, J. S. Skills, plans, and self-regulation. In R. S. Siegler (Ed.), *Children's thinking: What develops?* Hillsdale, N.J.: Erlbaum, 1978.

Brown, A. L., & French, L. A. The zone of potential development: Implications for intelligence testing in the year 2000. *Intelligence*, 1979, *3*, 255–273.

Brown, A. L., & Smiley, S. S. Rating the importance of structural units of prose passages: A problem of metacognitive development. *Child Development*, 1977, *48*, 1–8.

Brown, A. L., Smiley, S. S. & Lawton, S. C. The effects of experience on the selection of suitable retrieval cues for studying texts. *Child Development*, 1978, *49*, 829–855.

Butterfield, E. C., & Belmont, J. M. Assessing and improving the executive cognitive functions of mentally retarded people. In I. Bialer & M. Sternlicht (Eds.), *Psychological issues in mental retardation*. Chicago: Aldine-Atherton, 1975.

Calfee, R. C., & Drum, P. A. Learning to read: Theory, research, and practice. *Curriculum Inquiry*, 1978, *8*, 3–40.

Chi, M. T. H. Short-term memory limitations in children: Capacity or processing deficits? *Memory and Cognition*, 1976, *4*, 559–572.

Chi, M. T. H. Knowledge structures and development. In R. S. Siegler (Ed.), *Children's thinking: What develops?* Hillsdale, N.J.: Erlbaum, 1978.

Clements, S. *Minimal brain dysfunction in children: Terminology and identification*. U.S. Public Health Service, Pub. No. 1415. Washington, D.C.: U.S. Government Printing Office, 1966.

Craik, F. I. M., & Lockhart, R. S. Levels of processing: A framework for memory research. *Journal of Verbal Learning and Verbal Behavior*, 1972, *11*, 671–684.

Cruickshank, W. M., & Hallahan, D. P. *Perceptual and learning disabilities in children* (Vol. 2); *Research and theory*. Syracuse, N.Y.: Syracuse Univ. Press, 1975.

Day, M. C. Developmental trends in visual scanning. In H. W. Reese (Ed.), *Advances in child development and behavior* (Vol. 10). New York: Academic Press, 1975.

Dee-Lucas, D., & DiVesta, F. J. Learner-generated organizational aids: Effects of learning from text. *Journal of Educational Psychology*, 1980, *72*, 304–311.

Dempster, F. N. Memory span: Sources of individual and developmental differences. *Psychological Bulletin*, 1981, *89*, 63–100.

Denney, D. R. The effects of exemplary and cognitive models and self-rehearsal on children's interrogative strategies. *Journal of Experimental Child Psychology*, 1975, *9*, 476–488.

Denney, N. W., Jones, F. W., & Krigel, S. H. Modifying the questioning strategies of young children and elderly adults with strategy-modeling techniques. *Human Development,* 1979, *22,* 23–36.

Deutsch, J. A., & Deutsch, D. Attention: Some theoretical considerations. *Psychological Review,* 1963, *70,* 80–90.

DiVesta, F. J., Hayward, K., & Orlando, V. P. Developmental trends in monitoring text for comprehension. *Child Development,* 1979, *50,* 97–105.

Douglas, V. I., & Peters, K. G. Toward a clearer definition of the attentional deficit of hyperactive children. In G. A. Hale & M. Lewis (Eds.), *Attention and cognitive development.* New York: Plenum, 1979.

Dykman, R. A., Ackerman, P. T., Clements, S. D., & Peters, J. E. Specific learning disabilities. An attentional deficit syndrome. In H. R. Myklebust (Ed.), *Progress in learning disabilities* (Vol. 2). New York: Grune & Stratton, 1971.

Flavell, J. H. Metacognitive aspects of problem solving. IN L. B. Resnick (Ed.), *The nature of intelligence.* Hillsdale, N.J.: Erlbaum, 1976.

Flavell, J. H. Metacognitive development. In J. M. Scandura & C. J. Brainerd (Eds.), *Structural process theories of complex human behavior.* Leyden: Sijthoff and Noordhoff, 1978.

Gaylord-Ross, R. J. Mental retardation research, ecological validity, and the delivery of longitudinal education programs. *Journal of Special Education,* 1979, *13,* 69–80.

Gibson, E. J., & Levin, H. *The psychology of reading.* Cambridge, Mass.: MIT Press, 1975.

Gibson, E., & Rader, N. The perceiver as performer. In G. A. Hale & M. Lewis (Eds.), *Attention and cognitive development.* New York: Plenum, 1979.

Goodman, K. S. Analysis of oral reading miscues: Applies psycholinguistics. *Reading Research Quarterly,* 1969, *5,* 9–30.

Goodman, K. S. Strategies for increasing comprehension in reading. In H. M. Robinson (Ed.), *Improving reading in the intermediate years.* Glenview, Ill.: Scott, Foresman, 1973.

Goodman, K. S. Reading: A psycholinguistic guessing game. In H. Singer & R. B. Ruddell (Eds.), *Theoretical models and processes of reading* (2nd ed.). Newark, Del.: International Reading Association, 1976.

Gough, P. B. One second of reading. In J. F. Kavanagh & I. G. Mettingly (Ed.), *Language by ear and by eye.* Cambridge, Mass.: MIT Press, 1972.

Hochberg, J. Toward a speech-plan eye-movement model of reading. In R. A. Monty & J. W. Senders (Eds.), *Eye movements and psychological processes.* Hillsdale, N.J.: Erlbaum, 1976.

Hochberg, J. E. *Perception* (2nd ed.). Englewood Cliffs, N.J.: Prentice-Hall, 1978.

Hochberg, J., & Brooks, V. Reading as intentional behavior. In H. Singer (Ed.), *Theoretical models and processes of reading.* Newark, Del.: International Reading Association, 1970.

Hoyer, W. J. Conceptions of learning and the study of life span development: A symposium. *Human Development,* 1980, *23,* 361–399.

Huey, E. B. *The psychology and pedagogy of reading.* Cambridge, Mass.: MIT Press, 1968. (Originally published, 1908.)

James, W. *The principles of psychology* (Vol. 1). New York: Henry Holt and Company, 1890. (Republished by Dover, 1950.)

Johnson, S. W., & Morasky, R. L. *Learning disabilities* (2nd ed.). Boston: Allyn & Bacon, 1980.

Kahneman, D. *Attention and effort.* Englewood Cliffs, N.J.: Prentice-Hall, 1973.

Keogh, B. K., & Margolis, J. Learn to labor and to wait: Attentional problems of children with learning disorders. *Journal of Learning Disabilities,* 1976, *9,* 18–28.

Kirchner, G. L., & Knopf, I. J. Difference in the vigilance performance of secondary grade children as related to sex and achievement. *Child Development,* 1974, *45,* 490–495.

Krupski, A. Attention processes: Research, theory, and implications for special education. In B. K. Keogh (Ed.), *Advances in special education* (Vol. 1). Greenwich, Conn.: JAI Press, 1980.

LaBerge, D., & Samuels, S. J. *Toward a theory of automatic information processing in reading. Cognitive Psychology,* 1974, *6,* 293–323.

Lerner, J. W. Remedial reading and learning disabilities: Are they the same or different? *Journal of Special Education,* 1975, *9,* 119–131.

Lerner, J. W. *Children with learning disabilities* (2nd ed.). Boston: Houghton, 1976.

Lichtenstein, E. H., & Brewer, W. F. Memory for goal-directed events. *Cognitive Psychology,* 1980, *12,* 412–445.

Lupart, J. *Levels of processing in EMR and normal children.* Unpublished master's thesis, University of Alberta, 1978.

Maccoby, E., & Hagen, J. Effect of distraction upon central versus incidental recall: Developmental trends. *Journal of Experimental Child Psychology,* 1965, *2,* 280–289.

Mackworth, N. H. The line of sight approach. In S. Wanat (Ed.), *Language and reading comprehension.* Arlington, Va.: Centre for Applied Linguistics, 1977.

McCarthy, J. J., & McCarthy, J. F. *Learning disabilities.* Boston: Allyn & Bacon, 1969.

McConkie, G. W., & Rayner, K. An on-line computer technique for studying reading: Identifying the perceptual span. In H. Singer & R. B. Ruddell (Eds.), *Theoretical models and processing of reading.* Newark, Del.: International Reading Association, 1976.

Meacham, J. A. Soviet investigations of memory development. In R. V. Kail & J. W. Hagen (Eds.), *Perspectives on the development of memory and cognition.* New York: Wiley, 1977.

Meichenbaum, D. A cognitive-behavioral perspective on intelligence. *Intelligence,* 1980, *4,* 271–283.

Miller, G. A., Galanter, E., & Pribram, K. *Plans and the structure of behavior.* New York: Holt, 1960.

Moely, B. E., & Jeffrey, W. E. The effect of organization training on children's free recall of category items. *Child Development,* 1974, *45,* 135–143.

Moray, N. *Attention: Selective processes in vision and hearing.* London: Hutchison Educational, 1969.

Myers, M., & Paris, S. G. Children's metacognitive knowledge about reading. *Journal of Educational Psychology,* 1978, *70,* 680–690.

Myklebust, H. R. *Progress in learning disabilities* (Vol. 2). New York: Grune & Stratton, 1971.

Neisser, U. *Cognition and reality.* San Francisco: Freeman, 1976.

Noland, E. C., & Schuldt, W. J. Sustained attention and reading retardation. *Journal of Experimental Education,* 1971, *40,* 73–76.

Norman, D. A. *Memory and attention: An introduction to human information processing.* New York: Wiley, 1976.

Ohlson, E. L. *Identification of specific learning disabilities.* Champaign, Ill.: Research Press, 1978.

Owings, R. A., Petersen, G. A., Bransford, J. P., Morris, C. D., & Stein, B. J. Spontaneous monitoring and regulation of learning: A comparison of successful and less successful fifth graders. *Journal of Educational Psychology,* 1980, *72,* 250–256.

Posner, A. I., & Snyder, C. R. R. Attention and cognitive control. In R. L. Solso (Ed.), *Information processing and cognition: The Loyola Symposium.* Hillsdale, N.J.: Erlbaum, 1975.

Ross, A. O. *Psychological aspects of learning disabilities and reading disorders.* New York: McGraw-Hill, 1976.

Ross, S. M., Rakow, E. A., & Bush, A. J. Instructional adaptation for self-managed learning systems. *Journal of Educational Psychology,* 1980, *72,* 312–320.

Samuels, S. J. Automatic decoding and reading comprehension. *Language Arts,* 1976, *53,* 323–325.

Samuels, S. J., & Edwall, G. The role of attention in reading with implications for the learning disabled student. *Journal of Learning Disabilities,* 1981, *14,* 353–361.

Sargent, E. E., Huus, H., & Andresen, O. How to read a book. In C. T. Mangrum (Ed.), *Reading aid series.* Newark, Del.: International Reading Association, 1970.

Smiley, S. S., Oakley, D. D., Worthen, D., Campione, J. C., & Brown, A. L. Recall of thematically relevant material by adolescent good and poor readers as a function of written versus oral presentation. *Journal of Educational Psychology,* 1977, *69,* 381–387.

Stauffer, R. G. The role of intention in reading and thinking. In R. W. Shuy (Ed.), *Language and reading comprehension.* Arlington, Va.: Centre for Applied Linguistics, 1977.

Tarver, S. G., & Hallahan, D. P. Attention deficits in children with learning disabilities: A review. *Journal of Learning Disabilities,* 1974, *7,* 560–569.

Titchener, E. B. *Lectures on the psychology of feeling and attention.* New York: Macmillan, 1908.

Torgesen, J. Problems and prospects in the study of learning disabilities. In E. M. Hetherington (Ed.), *Review of child development research* (Vol. 5). Chicago: Univ. of Chicago Press, 1975.

Torgesen, J. K. Performance of reading disabled children on serial memory tasks: A selective review of recent research. *Reading Research Quarterly,* 1978, *14,* 57–87.

Triesman, A. Monitoring and storage of irrelevant messages in selective attention. *Journal of Verbal Learning and Verbal Behavior,* 1964, *3,* 449–459.

Vellutino, F. R. Alternative conceptualizations of dyslexia: Evidence in support of a verbal-deficit hypothesis. *Harvard Educational Review,* 1977, *47,* 334–354.

Vernon, M. D. Variability in reading retardation. *British Journal of Psychology,* 1979, *70,* 7–16.

Vygotsky, L. S. Learning and mental development at school age. In J. Simon & B. Simon (Eds.), *Educational psychology in the U.S.S.R.* Stanford, Cal.: Stanford Univ. Press, 1963.

Vygostky, L. S. *Mind in society: The development of higher psychological processes* (M. Cole, V. John-Steiner, S. Scribner, & E. Souberman, Eds.). Cambridge, Mass.: Harvard Univ. Press, 1978.

Wertsch, J. V. From social interaction to higher psychological processes: A clarification and application of Vygotsky's theory. *Human Development,* 1979, *22,* 1–22.

Wright, J. C., & Vlietstra, A. G. The development of selective attention: From perceptual exploration to logical speech. In H. W. Reese (Ed.), *Advances in child development and behavior* (Vol. 10). New York: Academic Press, 1975.

11

The Cognitive Abilities
of the Moderately and Severely Retarded

A. F. ASHMAN

Over the past 100 years, we have seen many changes in attitudes and approaches toward the retarded people in our society. While it is easily conceded that the present orientation of normalization has led to many positive developments, there is still much to be achieved, notably in a reorientation in views toward the management of community-based resources and in the development of vocational, self-help, and academic training programs for those not yet independent. A review of the literature on mental retardation reveals apparent mild interest in research on the institutionalized and on severely and profoundly mentally retarded groups, although it is notable that a shift is apparent in the focus of more recent literature (Haywood, 1979).

Regardless of the reasons for the increasing interest in the less able, much of the research has a behavioral orientation (see for example Haring & Brown, 1976; Payne, Polloway, Smith, & Payne, 1977). While there is little justification for denegrating behavioristic approaches, greater attention needs to be given to the cognitive aspects of learning. This may be achieved through an examination of the ways in which retarded individuals process information and through the study of the effects of limitations imposed by such factors as distractability, poor memory, and poor selection of problem solving strategies. Research has shown that moderately and

Cognitive Strategies
and Educational Performance

severely retarded children have limitations in such areas as receptive and expressive language skills, gross and fine motor coordination, discrimination learning, short- and long-term memory, and the integration of new information with material already stored in the brain.

This chapter is divided into two general segments. The first three sections provide a review of several areas of research, each of which has provided the professional community with useful insights into the cognition of retarded persons. What seems to be missing, however, is a synthesis of the literature into a coherent and comprehensive approach toward educational programming based upon cognitive competencies. The last two sections report on the application of a model of information integration designed to encourage the development of processing abilities in a group of institutionalized retarded persons.

ATTENTION, MEMORY, AND THE USE OF AVAILABLE STRATEGIES

It is well accepted that retarded and nonretarded children differ in the rate at which they learn. Many factors appear to play important roles, but at the most basic level of cognition, vigilance and attention may be regarded as necessary prerequisites for learning. Early research focused on the attentional deficits of retarded subjects within the context of discrimination learning and short-term memory paradigms (Ellis, 1970; Heal & Johnson, 1970; Zeaman & House, 1963). It was claimed that the root of the deficits was to be found through the study of stimulus inhibition—that is, in the retarded person's inability to suppress unnecessary stimulus input when inhibition was adaptive. Further evidence could be derived from the retarded person's inability to efficiently cue select. Bryant (1967), for example, showed that the performance of retarded subjects became more disrupted when novel cues were embedded in the target task, and Bray and Ferguson (1976) found that neither retarded nor mental age-matched children use effective strategies to eliminate interference from irrelevant information.

While later literature has added to our knowledge of the retarded person's behavior under a variety of experimental conditions (Fisher & Zeaman, 1973), the focus of such work remains narrow and situation specific. Certainly the use of strategies for maintaining attention are important for the reception of stimuli, discrimination learning, and selection of cues relevant to task demands. However, a reinterpretation of attention deficits may be made in the light of the contemporary neuropsychological literature. Specifically, a link exists between the arousal center of the brain (midbrain and reticular formation), which would mediate attention, and the organizational center located in the prefrontal region of the neocortex (Luria, 1973). It may be argued that the retarded person's distractability and failure to accrue sufficient salient information is related to poor maintenance of goal-directed activity and poor judgments regarding the regulation of behavior. Such a proposal emphasizes the role of the process that maintains cortical tone and of those strategies that focus and alter attention and aid in the filtering process during which meaningful and nonmeaningful dimensions may be identified. When meaning is lost, attention and task commitment become less important, and these in turn affect the encoding and retrieval of information.

Differences between the strategic behavior of retarded and nonretarded subjects have been widely documented since the early 1970s, notably in memory research. Ellis (1970), for example, reported that retardates experience difficulty with rehearsal, and Cohen and Nealon (1979) supported Ellis and others in demonstrating that retarded subjects neither rehearse as proficiently as nonretarded subjects, nor do they show evidence of changing strategies during probed versus nonprobed conditions.

The rehearsal deficit hypothesis gains support from research into serial position effect, pause patterns in serial learning, and increases in performance following training. Since the use of rehearsal strategies is a control process, retardates can be trained to use them. The extent to which training in rehearsal strategies improves performance, however, depends on the retarded person's rehearsal capacity, which is a structural feature of memory.

The rehearsal capacity of institutionalized, mildly (mean IQ = 74) and moderately (mean IQ = 50) retarded residents was examined by McBane (1976). She claimed that, when general instructions and feedback were given, the children needed no specific prompting on how, or if, to rehearse. Feedback effectively told children that a device for recollection was needed. Although no systematic examination of subjects' modes of coding was made, McBane stated that the children reported that they used various mnemonic aids, such as verbal repetition and visual imagery. The results of her experiments, however, demonstrated that the memory capacity of subjects reflected the degree to which rehearsal could be employed and this varied according to level of intelligence.

Differences between ability groups are evident also in the use of other memory strategies.For example, retarded children show limited tendencies to cluster during free recall, and there appears to be both quantitative and qualitative differences between the recall organization of retarded and nonretarded subjects. Nonretarded children tend to cluster by superordinate categories, whereas retardates show groupings by pairs based on complementary relationships (Jensen, 1970). In addition, retarded persons generally fail to spontaneously produce elaborative contexts, although when these are produced, they are of a low level.

Differences are also found in other organizational strategies. Normal children learn the digit series 6–8–5–6–8–5 easily because they recognize the obvious structure of the stimulus input, 685–685 (Spitz, 1973). Retardates experience little difficulty learning number sets if the level of redundancy is high and outstanding, as may be the case in the digit series just mentioned. However, in more complex tasks, they fail to make use of stimulus redundancy to reduce the information load on their memory system (Baumeister & Kellas, 1971). The inadequate use of coding strategies such as the preceding may lead to confusion during input and subsequent chaotic retrieval (Spitz, 1973).

In summary, the use of appropriate strategies in maintaining attention and vigilance in learning situations appears to be one major factor accounting for performance differences between retarded and nonretarded persons. Ineffective maintenance of attention may influence the retarded individual's ability to discern important features of the stimuli, thereby impairing the coding process. In addition, attention deficits may affect the capacity to engage and alter organizational strategies, although two other factors may also limit recall:

1. Interference from previously learned or rehearsed information
2. Rapid decay of material held in memory

The use of various attention and memory strategies in simple tasks or familiar circumstances may be unconscious. However, other factors that affect learning and performance are considered to be under conscious control—for example, the selection of coding strategies and the verification and evaluation of strategy effectiveness. These aspects comprise a group of organizational skills that are discussed in the following section.

STRATEGIES, PLANNING, AND ORGANIZATION

Three limitations on learning performance have been raised in the literature in regard to the efficiency of problem solving by retarded people—namely, their inability to (a) spontaneously generate problem solving strategies; (b) generalize learning from one situation to another; and (c) evaluate the success of strategies in use. Many studies have shown that the memory deficits of the retarded stem not from their access to strategies but from their inability to engage and manage the processes to assist in information recall. For example, Butterfield, Wambold, and Belmont (1973), in a series of three experiments, encouraged mildly retarded adolescents (aged 13–21) to rehearse actively the early items in a letter series and receive passively the last items. Although the subjects achieved some success, Butterfield *et al.* considered the improved performance to be of a short-term and situation-specific nature. They concluded that the retarded young adults possessed the necessary coding processes, but they lacked both spontaneous access to them and the ability to coordinate the processes to achieve consistently excellent performance. Other writers have reported similar findings (see for example Brown, 1974; Brown, Campione, Bray, & Wilcox, 1973; Brown & Lawton, 1977; Hagen, Streeter, & Raker, 1974; Luszcz & Bacharach, 1975; Turnbull, 1974), although several projects have demonstrated improvement in performance and transfer of learning through the use of a variety of mediational strategies.

Mildly retarded children and adolescents may be taught to use verbal or kinesthetic strategies for picture recall to elicit improved performance in the training tasks and facilitated recall in follow-up tests (Conroy, 1978). It was found that enhanced recall could be directly attributed to subject-monitored rehearsal. Similarly, a paired-associate-learning paradigm was used to train retardates in the use of imagery and meaningful word associations. Use and generation of subject's own mediators improved performance significantly and facilitated transfer to new learning situations (Burger & Blackman, 1976). Later research suggested that retarded persons perform poorly on memory tasks because they do not use all the information available to them (Campione & Brown, 1978). Training children to "stop, check, and study" produced generalization from a item recall task to others requiring the recall of passages (Brown & Barclay, 1976; Brown, Campione, & Barclay, Note 1).

Exploring transfer and mediation further, some research indicates that subjects may be trained in the use of active sorting and retrieving strategies to facilitate recall, clustering, and sorting. Their performance is improved by the use of materials that are interesting and meaningful, and by the opportunity to manipulate them. This appears to provide the necessary time for evaluation and organization (Burger, Blackman, Holmes, & Zetlin, 1979). Providing the time, or an appropriate evaluating strategy, has been successful in aiding retarded persons to improve their performance in both training and transfer situations. Similarly, acquisition and transfer of strategies is facilitated if training is logically sound, thorough, and of interest to the subjects (Kendall, Borkowski, & Cavanagh, 1980). These findings suggest that the problem of transfer of learning by retarded subjects may not be their inability to use strategies, but to decide when to use them. This raises the issue of the subjects' awareness of their capabilities, a metacognitive characteristic that constitutes one aspect of planning and organization

(Burger & Blackman, 1979). Consider for example, the seven-digit set of numbers 6–3–5–8–2–4–1. Asking the person to repeat a seven-digit series will evidence the ability to process an unfamilar sequence, and in this task, rehearsal and chunking might be two useful strategies to be employed. Asking for an explanation of how the digits were remembered may elicit: "Easy, I said them over and over again while you were calling them out," exemplifying what Brown (1975) calls "knowing how to know."

In practical circumstances, nonretarded children quickly gain an understanding of regularities and relationships between objects and events. The repetition of events or successful manipulations of their environment become coded as information, strategies for dealing with a specific problem, or plans that might operate within a certain set of environmental conditions.

Mentally retarded children and adults also develop an awareness of their environment. Although it may be far less complex than that of an age peer, the retarded person's conceptualization does reveal decision-making and organizational aspects, especially in situations that are relevant to their day-to-day living (see Mulchahy, 1979). While it may be possible to argue for the use of esoteric tasks, there is evidence that meaningful contexts (Smirnov & Zinchenko, 1969) and content (Burger & Erber, 1976) provide more facilitative learning and testing environments. For example, Freidman, Krupski, Dawson, and Rosenberg (Note 2) used actual school and home environments to observe the memory and problem solving behavior of moderately retarded adolescents. They asked the youngsters to solve real-life problems in terms of the strategies they would use to remember where they had left some article or to recall some activity to be performed the next day. The retarded adolescents demonstrated metacognitive awareness and strategic behavior to much the same degree as did nonretarded youngsters.

Within the area of metacognition, it is possible to distinguish between strategies for future retrieval and strategies that facilitate present retrieval. In a digit span task, for example, the mature information processor is likely to use an approach suitable for immediate recall, permitting the series to be "dumped" from the short-term store if there is no reason for retention. If a more complex task is introduced and recall is demanded over a long period of time, other strategies may be involved. These might include making written notes, using nonverbal prompts, or assimilating the information into several semantic networks in the hope of increasing retrievability. Deliberately preparing for future retrieval is what some have considered as one form of planning (Flavell, 1970; Flavell & Wellman, 1977) and what others have labeled *control* or *executive* processes (Butterfield & Belmont, 1975). The development of the metacognitive skills (the "knowing how to know" aspects) seems to be an important factor in successful day-to-day problem solving.

While studies of metacognition may have been based upon a disillusionment with training memory strategies, there is little conclusive evidence to support the emphasis placed upon increasing children's awareness of their memory system. By itself, a knowledge of one's memory functions may have little effect on memory performance. In both retarded and nonretarded samples, it has been shown that metamemory was not a necessary prerequisite for good memory and, conversely, that the lack of strategy-relevant knowledge cannot account for the failure of some individuals to use the knowledge they possess (e.g., see Cavanaugh & Borkowski, 1979, 1980). In a study of the relationship between metamemory and memory performance using the Kreutzer, Leonard, and Flavell (1975) interview technique, Eyde and Altman (1978) concluded that retarded children recognize a variety of mnemonically relevant variables but "they do not automatically use the knowledge in a task appropriate manner [p. 132]."

Metamemory—or in more general terms, metacognition—has important implications for the mentally retarded. First, it could be argued that the retarded perform poorly in metamemory tasks because they do not construct a conceptual understanding of cognition (a theory of mind in Wellman's, 1980, terms); and second, an awareness of one's thinking processes may be a prerequisite for planning in problem solving situations, which would include the ability to organize, initiate, and evaluate strategies for successful task completion (cf. Flavell & Wellman, 1977; Guilford, Berger, & Christensen, 1955; Kessel, Note 3; Lawson, 1980; Miller, Galanter, & Pribram, 1960; Simon, 1979).

While problem solving has been examined within several memory contexts (e.g., see Bilsky & Evans, 1970; Jensen, 1971; Neimark, Slotnick, & Ulrich, 1971; Riegel, Danner, Johnson, & Kjerland, 1973; Riegel & Taylor, 1974: Rossi, 1964), more direct evidence of organizational skills may be gathered using information-seeking tasks, such as the Twenty Questions game. Early studies supported the notion that the interrogative strategies of retarded subjects were characterized by few constraint-seeking questions and less recognition, formulation, and integration that was found with the nonretarded groups (Denney, 1974; Mosher & Hornsby, 1966). Later, Blackman, Whittesmore, Zetlin, and McNamara (1977) found that institutionalized retarded adolescents used inefficient questions and strategies and were not aware of the relative complexity of the operations to be performed.

It could be argued that many studies on interrogative strategies used material that overwhelmed the retarded subjects, causing them to resort to less efficient strategies. Borys (1979) reduced the task complexity to three- and four-bit problems and found that 20-year-old retarded subjects (IQ = 62.2) performed comparably to nonretarded first-grade children. The primary problem appeared to be the retarded subjects' nonpreference for negative information and their tendency to ask redundant and one-dimensional questions.

The studies reported here show that retarded subjects experience difficulty in understanding the parameters of a relatively simple problem and in the selection of a strategy appropriate for the task demands. Indirectly, these studies (and others not mentioned here) also draw attention to the failure of subjects to monitor and regulate their behavior if the initial approach is unsuccessful. Spitz and his colleagues (Spitz & Nadler, 1974; Spitz & Winters, 1977) used a variety of logical problems, including tic-tac-toe, and indicated that their retarded subjects consistently showed a lack of foresight and an inability to make "if–then" connections. Byrnes and Spitz (1977), using a simple version of the Tower of Hanoi problem, confirmed the previous findings. Unsuccessful institutionalized subjects on a two-disk task perseverated on specific errors and appeared surprised that the outcome of their moves had not led to the solution. Instead of profiting from mistakes, they maintained them or adapted in a nonfunctional way by violating the game rules. In one sense, the retarded subjects regulated their behavior according to experience (by breaking the rules). However, Byrnes and Spitz reported that subjects rarely chose to solve a problem if excessive moves were required, opting to end an unpromising trial rather than to persevere and discover the solution—apparently choosing some idiosyncratic standard of performance.

The research cited draws attention to factors that effect the information processing performance of mentally retarded persons through deficits in strategy selection and verification. Findings may be summarized as follows:

First, several studies have demonstrated that retarded persons are able to use coding strategies, even though:

1. They may not necessarily have sufficient information for successful task completion.
2. They may not be able to access the appropriate strategies spontaneously if they have not done so before.

Second, training studies have shown that retarded persons can learn to select strategies in accordance with the task demands and may in certain circumstances transfer the use of such strategies to other tasks.

Third, retarded persons demonstrate limited awareness of their information processing capabilities. They lack an efficient hypothesis testing approach to problems and in general fail to monitor their performance and verify success.

To a large extent, these conclusions draw attention to the interrelationship between attention variables, coding and strategic behavior, and an integrative component of cognition that might be labeled planning and decision making.

CLARIFYING COGNITIVE PERFORMANCE

The use of appropriate strategies has been shown to facilitate attention and memory functions, and to be primary to coding and integrating information in problem solving situations. While many of the studies reported have far-ranging consequences in terms of training and remediating deficiencies, few writers have adopted a comprehensive theoretical viewpoint. Additionally, few research projects have dealt with the cognitive functioning of more severely retarded persons, and clarification of the information processing capabilities of this group is long overdue.

One approach based on neurological processes that has provided a useful framework for considering interrelationship was elaborated in Das, Kirby, and Jarman (1975). Much of their work on the information-integration model has focused on the description of the coding processes (simultaneous and successive coding), largely in nonretarded groups. More recent studies, however, have examined the role of the organizational aspects of cognition (Ashman, 1979). Planning in this context is defined primarily by specified tests, which when factor analyzed with coding tasks, load uniquely on an independent factor. The independence of the planning factor is predicted by the Das et al. model, although it is understood that the relationship between coding and planning is interdependent: Plans or strategies operate on coded information and conversely are necessary for solving tasks that require simultaneous or successive processing (Ashman & Das, 1980).

The planning process may be conceptualized in terms of temporally related features that include the consolidation of an intention; discernment of task-relevant cues and information; the development or selection of a strategy capable of solving a problem at hand; the monitoring and regulation of behavior consistent with the implementation of a chosen strategy; and the selection of an alternative strategy if others prove unsuccessful. Planning may then be viewed as a process that allows us to problem solve with intent—that is, by means other than random activity—and hence, planning draws not only on our experience (or encoded knowledge about our world) but also on a repertoire of spontaneously generated or learned strategies of which we may or may not be aware. It appears that, in each of these areas, retarded people experience difficulties.

The cognitive functioning of retarded persons has been examined in the context of the information-integration model and reviewed by Ashman, Molloy, and Das (1981). While there are considerable quantitative differences between retarded and nonretarded subjects on coding and planning tasks, the factor structure appears stable across ability groups. This finding suggests that the cognitive processes used by nonretarded children are the same as those available to and identifiable in mentally retarded adults and children with IQs as low as 50 (see Das, 1980). Up to the present time, no research has examined simultaneous–successive and planning processes in retarded people with IQs in the 20–50 range.

While process differences are apparent between and within ability levels, of primary importance is the development of a remedial approach to strengthen processing deficits (see Kirby, 1980, Note 4). Such a strategy may include several steps. For example:

1. Delineating the problem in terms of basic processes
2. Developing an intervention based upon coding and planning processes utilizing task-appropriate strategies
3. Evaluating the training program using relevant measures of performance
4. Designing follow-up interventions to develop and strengthen the processes underlying performance

Such an approach has been adopted by the author and has been applied in a residential institution for the moderately to profoundly retarded.

The information-integration model provided a useful approach for studying coding and organizational processes of moderately and severely retarded persons and for devising programs based upon identified deficits. It must be emphasized that the model is simply one way of conceptualizing phenomena; it is neither the only way nor necessarily the best, although it does satisfy important requirements:

1. It allows for comparison between retarded and nonretarded samples (see Das, 1972; Jarman, Note 5).
2. It places emphasis upon the interdependence of coding (simultaneous and successive synthesis) and integration of information (planning and decision making) (see Ashman & Das, 1980).
3. It deals with basic cognitive processes, thereby cutting across the traditional sensory modalities and polarities, such as visual–perceptual, auditory–sequential, verbal–nonverbal, reasoning–memory (see Das & Jarman, 1980).
4. It provides a basis for remediation of processing deficiencies (see Kaufman & Kaufman, 1979; Krywaniuk & Das, 1976).

The use of the Das *et al.* model necessitated consideration of several characteristics of institutionalized retarded adolescents and young adults, namely:

1. Impairments in sight and hearing
2. A high level of resident distractability associated with academic tasks
3. Variations in performance as a result of age, etiology, and personality
4. Low levels of performance in fine motor skills and even gross motor skills
5. Poor and idiosyncratic language skills of the residents

With these points in mind, it was necessary first to reevaluate the coding and planning measures previously administered and the subsequent down-grading for use with moderately and severely retarded residents. Below is a brief description of the original simultaneous, successive, and planning tests reported in Ashman and Das (1980), and the changes that were made to them.

Raven's Coloured Progressive Matrices (RPM). This is a well-known test of general, nonverbal reasoning (Raven, 1965) that is used widely with non-retarded children. Cattell (1971) argued that the test measured fluid intelligence, and Jensen (1969) proposed that the RPM was a measure of Level II ability. Das (1972) broke away from earlier tradition, arguing that the matrices test simultaneous processing, and, together with colleagues, has administered the RPM to a wide variety of subjects, including the mentally retarded. Pilot testing indicated that moderately and severely retarded persons could satisfy the task demands using the standard book form; however, directions for the standard presentation were simplified and additional instructions were given when it was apparent that subjects were making careless, perseverative, or implusive choices.

Memory-for-Designs (MFD). Graham and Kendall (1960) devised this task using visually presented designs as a screening test for minimal brain damage. It has been used to detect mental retardation (Richie & Butler, 1964) and, additionally, to discriminate between slow and average readers (Lyle, 1969). The MFD has been administered as a simultaneous marker to large groups, with the figures being presented using a slide projector. Since a floor effect occurred when the MFD was administered in the original form to low-ability adults, three changes were made. First, three of the more difficult designs were deleted, and three simple drawings were substituted. Second, card presentation was used to eliminate distraction. And third, presentation time was revised. The revised procedure used a general rule allowing a total of 5 sec for viewing. If the individual began drawing before the end of the 5 sec, the card was left in place so that the person could glance back to view the design once more. When this occurred, the card was removed either at the end of the 5-sec period or when the subject recommenced drawing.

Figure Copying (FC). This task originally devised by Ilg and Ames (1964) was used first as a simultaneous marker by Das (1973). Subjects were required to copy each of 10 geometric figures while each was in view. The copies were scored according to the correctness of the reproduction. Scoring criteria devised by Leong (1974) placed emphasis on maintenance of geometric relations and proportions rather than on exact reproduction. Moderately retarded subjects understand the task demands but perform very poorly because of the relative complexity of even the early items. Another test with similar task demands was introduced into the test battery.

Beery Test of Visual Motor Integration (VMI). This test was developed as a means of establishing children's readiness to perform academic tasks (Beery, 1967). Beery claimed that the integration of motor abilities and the development of visual perception are important prerequisites to successful information processing. The VMI is a series of 24 geometric forms that are copied in much the same way as in the Figure Copying test, and the items are arranged in order of increasing difficulty. Scoring criteria and examples of "pass" and "fail" reproductions are provided in the manual. This test correlated 0.70+ with other simultaneous tasks using a nonretarded, Grade 5 sample.

Auditory Serial Recall (ASR). Originally reported by Das (1972) as a measure of successive processing, this test was revised to start with two-word lists progressing to seven-word lists (there being three lists in each set). One point was given for each word recalled in the correct serial position.

Digit Span (DS). This test was originally taken from Wechsler (1974), being the Digit Span Forward component of the Wechsler Intelligence Scale for Children. Numerous studies have demonstrated high correlation between DS and Auditory Serial Recall, and it is considered a marker test for successive processing (see early reports by Molloy, 1973; Cummins, Note 6). Subjects are generally given two opportunities to recall successfully the lists of digits of increasing length, in the correct order.

Because many moderately and severely retarded persons have very poor verbal skills, the DS was revised so that at the lowest level only one digit was to be recalled, while at the top level, a series of eight digits was presented. In addition, subjects were given three trials rather than two at each level.

Visual Serial Recall (VSR). Tests of visual sequential memory, such as recall of geometric shapes (Kirk, McCarthy, & Kirk, 1969) or bead threading (Hiskey Nebraska Test of Learning Aptitudes, 1966) have been used in various diagnostic batteries. Jarman (1978) and Klish (Note 7) used bead patterns tests that have loaded on a successive processing factor. Bead stringing is a reasonably common activity in which retarded children and adults are engaged. However, since manual dexterity is often poor in retarded people, it could be expected that they would become fixated on simple manipulation to the detriment of serial recall, and this was confirmed during a pilot testing session.

The VSR involved the serial presentation of geometric designs, beginning with one shape and progressing up to a six-shape series. Each sequence was presented one card at a time, so that the whole series was never visible at any one time. At the end of each presentation, the subjects were shown a card containing two to five options and were required to select the series that had been shown immediately before. It was expected that the test would correlate significantly with both Auditory Serial Recall and Digit Span.

Several of the planning tasks described by Ashman and Das (1980) had instructions that were too complex for subjects of low ability. As a result, only three tests were administered: Two were adaptations of original planning tests, and one was developed for the study.

Visual Search (VS). This was a revised version of the test first pre-prepared by Ashman (1978). Although Das (1980) reported the use of the original Visual Search task with trainable mentally retarded subjects, a pilot study showed that moderately retarded subjects had considerable difficulty in locating the target shape among 48 other geometric, letter, or numerical shapes. Search times for the pilot group often exceeded 5 min for one trial, and constant urging was necessary to keep the subjects on task. The downgraded revision used seven search cards, each having a different number of shapes in the search field, from 4 to 38 shapes, plus the target. When instructed, subjects were required to locate the target by pointing.

Trail Making (TM). As Ashman and Das (1980) suggested, the planning and coding processes are in some ways both independent and interdependent. In the original Trail Making test some competency is required in successive and simultaneous coding. If this is unavailable to the individual, then the Trail Making test may become a measure of coding rather than of planning. It could be assumed that the moderately retarded persons would not have an adequate code by which alphabetical sequences from *A* to *Z* could be accessed easily. Thus, the original Trail Making task would be beyond comprehension of the current sample.

To overcome the problem of inadequate coding abilities, a less complex Trail Making test used a picture rather than a letter or number format. Pilot testing confirmed that the subjects recognized each of the line drawings that were presented to them. Similar to the Trail Making test in which numbers were joined in the correct order, the less complex Trail Making task demanded the joining of like objects. For example, on the first trial subjects were instructed to draw a line (or lines) that would join all the balls on the page; this served as a practice trial so that the tester could illustrate the directions. On the six subsequent trials, subjects were instructed to join selected like objects. A correlation of 0.70 was obtained between the original and present versions of the Trail Making test using a sample of nonretarded Grade 6 children.

Alternative Routes (AR). Ashman (1978) found that the Porteus Maze Test (PMT) did not correlate significantly with other planning tests, yet more recently, Kirby and Ashman (1981) used a revised scoring procedure and found significant correlations between the PMT and other search tasks. Many moderately retarded residents did not have adequate fine motor skills to make the PMT a reliable test, although the notion of including a test in which planning one's way through a maze was still attractive. Using the Porteus scoring procedure (Porteus, 1965), there is only one successful solution; a subject who strays into incorrect pathways must attempt another trial at the same level. A task with greater flexibility, permitting a subject to choose the best possible alternative from several options, seemed more consistent with the notion of planning, and the AR task was designed with this objective in mind.

Alternative Routes is a series of mazes in which a line is drawn from a starting base ("School") to an end (the "Home" position) by the most direct route. Subjects choose the best possible alternative from several options. Four trials are instructional, requiring subjects to draw a straight line within the guidelines; later trials involved a decision between two alternatives, and the more complex trials introduce intermediate ("Shop") positions. Subjects can use any means available to draw the most direct route ("fastest" or "shortest" could describe this concept) between the start and the finish, "visiting" all intermediate points.

The second concern, having identified a suitable test battery, was to establish the relationship between the coding and planning processes for a group of lower ability than those tested previously. For example, early work by Ashman (1978) showed quantitative differences between mildly retarded and nonretarded adults on the coding and planning tests, although qualitative differences did not appear. Specifically, the structure produced by factor analyzing the test battery was comparable for the retarded and nonretarded groups. Later, Das (1980) reported a similar three-factor solution using a sample with a mean IQ of 50. It was hypothesized that data obtained from subjects with lower levels of ability would not show independent planning and coding factors. To assess this proposition, 100 volunteers

(54 females and 46 males) from a large hospital for the mentally retarded were administered the test battery described here. Residents attended either the special school, a workshop, or senior activities areas within the hospital. The mean age of the subjects was 19.9 years ($SD = 5.28$) and mean IQ (generally Stanford–Binet or Wechsler Adult Intelligence Scale) was 36.5 ($SD = 11.9$). The language skills of subjects varied greatly, although it was possible to communicate with all through sign language or gestures in combination with words.

Intercorrelations were computed between the coding and planning variables. Overall, correlations were quite high, although the highest correlations were found between associated successive (ASR and DS) and simultaneous (RPM, FC, MFD) variables.

Coding and planning scores were submitted to principal components analysis, and two factors whose eigenvalues were greater than 1 were rotated according to a Varimax criterion (Table 11.1). The factor loadings of all variables are different from those noted in earlier studies (Ashman *et al.*, 1981; Das, 1980) in that a separate planning factor did not emerge. Factor 1 is defined by the simultaneous tests, and in addition, each of the three planning tasks has a high loading on this factor. This supports the proposition that institutionalized moderately and severely retarded persons do not have the necessary coded information available to them to deal in an organized way with the more complex planning tasks. From the results, it ap-

TABLE 11.1
Principal Components Analysis with Varimax Rotation of Coding and Planning Tests ($N = 100$)[a]

Variable	Factor		
	1 Simultaneous	2 Successive	h^2
Visual Serial Recall	475	347	346
Auditory Serial Recall	247	919	905
Digit Span	250	901	874
Raven's Coloured Progressive Matrices	574	336	442
Figure Copying	846	234	770
Memory-for-Designs	785	315	715
Beery Test of Visual Motor Integration	889	285	871
Alternative Routes	728	171	559
Visual Search	661	294	523
Trail Making	−752	−115	578
Variance	4.330	2.253	

[a] Decimals omitted.

pears that retarded people of low ability may have a preference for simultaneous processing. This is supported by the loadings of the Visual Serial Recall task. Under different circumstances, the VSR is more closely related to successive than to simultaneous tasks. The visual nature of the planning and Visual Serial Recall tasks may enhance the contribution made by the subjects' visual–spatial approach, a finding also reported by O'Connor and Hermelin (1978). Factor 2 was the usual successive factor, with high loadings of the marker sequential processing tasks.

From this analysis, it can be concluded that deficits exist in the most basic areas of information gathering—namely, the scanning of stimuli and the organizing of incoming information in terms of already existing cognitive structures. This may be inferred from the failure of the subjects to perform in the prescribed manner on the planning tasks.

Before developing an intervention program, it would be useful to consider some facets of cognition that are closely linked to the coding processes. One aspect of interest is language and psycholinguistic abilities.

Researchers working with more severely retarded subjects have been concerned with the limitation imposed upon both tester and subjects by the low language skills. The moderately and severely retarded present speech and language proficiencies that range from little more than gutteral sounds, generally incomprehensible to others, to fluent communication. Studies of language provide an additional source of data from which inferences can be made about the information processing capabilities of retarded persons and that can guide the development of remedial techniques and programs. The following section deals with some of the issues and research.

LANGUAGE AND CODING DEFICITS

The examination of the language development of the mentally retarded has focused predominately on the mildly retarded. However, simply focusing on the acquisition of words would provide only part of the scenerio, as both the functions and the processes that facilitate communication are of equal importance (Carroll, 1967). Both areas are of prime concern to those who work with the moderately and severely retarded, as is evidenced by the early interest in the influence of language on behavior, the study of verbal and perhaps nonverbal language mediation in instruction, and the study of psycholinguistic abilities.

Luria (1961) reported that severely retarded children were much inferior to nonretarded children in their ability to regulate their motor actions by means of speech. On the basis of his findings, Luria argued that retarded children were characterized by an inertness of the verbal system and that in these children the verbal system was poorly integrated with the motor system. Additional research extended Luria's work on the language-based deficits of the severely retarded child and concluded that the deficits in acquisition and coding of information were more marked than deficits in retention and transfer. It was found that retarded children often failed to focus attention on relevant features of stimulus display, and this failure was attributed largely to the lack of verbal encoding and labeling. When verbal encoding was made an intrinsic part of the task, performance improved (O'Connor & Hermelin, 1963).

Within an institutional setting, the development of receptive and expressive language is viewed with particular interest, as the development of language or communication skills has the effect of changing the power base within the institution. This occurs by providing not only quantitively more interactions but qualitatively higher communication between staff and residents, and between residents. From another perspective, training in cognitive skills might progress more rapidly if the language capabilities of the retarded were more advanced.

Exploring the language comprehension of severely retarded subjects has shown that these children were strongly influenced by semantic constraints operating in sentences. They tended to rely on semantic expectations more than did the mental age matched, nonretarded group, and they responded in simple active-voice sentences. For example, Dewart (1979) claimed that such performance in younger mental age retarded children indicated such an extremely low level of skills that one could argue that they have no mastery of the syntactic aspects of language. The lack of a preference or the ability of moderately and severely retarded persons to encode verbally has prompted researchers to investigate the value of manual signs as an encoding category. Sign language has been taught successfully to nonverbal retarded people, but the underlying mechanisms are not fully understood (Kiernan, 1977; Reid & Kiernan, 1979). The interesting feature of sign language is the use of what might be considered a "preferred input modality" for the retarded (visual) that would facilitate the communication of both syntactic and relational information, two aspects of language discussed by Luria (1975).

Luria argued that each linguistic function depended upon one of two processes. Sequential, or serial, processing underlies the reception and expression of contextual grammatical structures (syntax), whereas comprehension of quasi-spatial relational thought depends upon the processing of information in simultaneous units or groups. Research that supported Luria's proposal regarding sequential processing and syntactical complexity was reported by Cummins and Mulcahy (Note 8). Later Cummins (1979) showed a relationship between successive and simultaneous coding and both logicogrammatical structures. Several studies have examined language in mildly and moderately retarded children (e.g., see O'Connor & Hermelin, 1978), and others have compared resident versus nonresident samples.

Differences between institutionalized and noninstitutionalized moderately retarded children have been examined using tests of structure and complexity of sentences, and measures obtained from the Illinois Test of Psycholinguistic Abilities (ITPA) (Kirk, McCarthy & Kirk, 1968). Institutionalized groups generally perform more poorly than the noninstitutionalized sample on most ITPA measures, notably those associated with auditory reception, auditory sequential memory, verbal expression, and auditory closure (McNutt & Leri, 1979). Grammatical structure appears not to be affected by the environment, although Phillips and Balthazar (1979) suggested that communication may decline during prolonged institutionalization. In addition, residents transferred from a large institution to a smaller residential setting showed slight language improvements and some positive changes in ITPA scores, notably on Auditory–Vocal Sequencing (similar to the WISC Digit Span) (Gilbert & Hemming, 1979).

Institutionalized retarded persons, especially those of low ability, may be divided into several subgroups based upon the cause of the retardation. While much of the research on the mildly retarded appears to accept the assumption that such groups are homogeneous, presumably familial retardates (Jensen & Rohwer, 1970; Zigler, 1967), the same assumption is not tenable when dealing with retarded people at the lower levels. There is no basis for assuming that a young adult with Down's syndrome would have the same deficiencies or use similar cognitive functions as another person with mental retardation resulting from infantile meningitis. Differences between subgroups based upon etiology of retardation can be expected.

Early research drew attention to differences between Down's syndrome and brain-damaged retardates. Notably Down's children appear to have difficulties with sequential memory tasks (Bilowsky & Share, 1965) and with tasks requiring visual–spatial skills—for example, matching and copying figures (O'Connor & Hermelin, 1963). More recently, a study of differences between Down's and non-Down's syndrome subjects was reported. Using the ITPA, Rohr and Burr (1978) found that distinction patterns of psycholinguistic abilities were associated with specific etiologies. Down's syndrome subjects were affected more than other subjects in all processes in the verbal–auditory domain. Rohr and Burr, however, argued that auditory sequential memory is the most significant deficit for all etiological classes of mentally retarded children, expressive channels being affected least. Subjects with identifiable brain damage, either biologically or environmentally produced, and subjects with unknown cause did not in general perform differently on the ITPA.

In considering retardation caused by brain damage, it might be useful to refer to Luria (1966). While localized lesions in the brain may produce quite different disabilities depending upon the focus, in moderately and severely retarded groups, brain damage leading to mental retardation appears to be of a more general nature. For example, brain damage through perinatal asphyxia, anoxia, or meningitis would generally be of a more diverse nature than damage in localized areas through war injuries as reported by Luria and his co-workers. The question of differences between subgroups of the moderately and severely retarded is one that needs further clarification, notably if there are implications for the development of educational programs specific to groups with identified deficits.

In the present study, it was necessary to evaluate the utility of measures of performance. Several methods of language assessment were considered (e.g., Cummins, 1979; McNutt & Leri, 1979; Miner, 1969; Montague, Hutchinson, & Matson, 1975); however, because of the wide range in communication skills across the 100 volunteers and the low performance level of the group, none were considered appropriate. An alternative procedure was sought.

Three members of the hospital staff who have regular and intensive interactions with residents were asked to rate the language use and understanding of subjects. A questionnaire was devised using 12 Likert-type scales, and raters responded on a five-point dimension of 1 (not at all) to 5 (with ease or very well). Three questions referred to residents' receptive-relational thought—that is, the *understanding* of terms referring to space (*in, on, around, above, top*), time (*before, now, then*), and other dimensions (*big, full, alone*). These ratings were summed for a receptive-relational score (RREL). A further three questions asked for raters' perceptions of the residents' *use* of the relational concepts. Ratings were summed for a total expressive-relational score (EREL).

Three questions related to the degree of *understanding* subjects had of syntactically complex statements ranging in difficulty from a single word, to simple sentences, to complex sentences. These questions gave a total receptive-syntax score (RSYN). A further three questions asked for ratings of subjects' *ability to express* themselves; the scores of the last three questions gave an expressive-syntax score (ESYN). The reliability between raters across scores was 0.77; however only 72 ratings were available because the staff was unfamiliar with eight subjects.

Intercorrelations between planning, coding, and language variables were found, and a principal components analysis with Varimax rotation was performed. Three factors were extracted (see Table 11.2), providing a solution that was easily explainable. Factor 1 contained loading of the successive markers (ASR and DS) and both syntax and relational language variables. Factor 2 was a conglomerate of variables supporting the interdependency of

TABLE 11.2
Principal Components Analysis with Varimax Rotation for Coding, Planning, and Language Variables for the Moderately and Severely Retarded Sample ($N = 92$)[a]

	Factor			
Variable	1	2	3	h^2
Visual Serial Recall	201	153	737	607
Auditory Serial Recall	689	443	024	672
Digit Span	692	498	−105	737
Raven's Coloured Progressive Matrices	193	290	708	623
Figure Copying	129	698	508	762
Memory-for-Designs	202	636	539	736
Beery Test of Visual Motor Integration	205	758	500	867
Alternative Routes	227	696	170	565
Visual Search	077	781	139	635
Trail Making	−021	−799	−115	651
Receptive Syntax	901	−104	164	850
Expressive Syntax	917	−019	226	892
Receptive Relational	815	188	314	798
Expressive Relational	848	251	262	851
Variance	4.224	3.860	2.162	

[a]Decimals omitted.

coding and planning with this group, and Factor 3 contained primarily simultaneous variables, with minor loadings on the relational language variables.

This factor solution was partly supportive of earlier research. The association between syntax and successive processing is notable, but in this case, a significant relationship was found between successive processing and relational thought, although the minor loading of RREL and EREL on Factor 3 does suggest that simultaneous processing may underlie the comprehension of relational notions.

To further examine the relationship between coding and language, the group of subjects was divided into four groups on the basis of median splits of simultaneous and successive factor scores—namely, a low simultaneous–low successive group ($N = 23$); a low simultaneous–high successive group ($N = 21$); a high simultaneous–low successive group ($N = 24$); and a high simultaneous–high successive group ($N = 24$) (see Das & Kirby, 1978). Differences between the groups on the language variables were analyzed using two-way analysis of variance. The means of the four groups and F values for simultaneous and successive main effects and the interactions are presented in Table 11.3.

The successive main effects on the syntax ratings are consistent with the

TABLE 11.3
Means and F Values of Processing Groups in Language Measures, Age, and Months Resident in the Institution ($N = 92$)[a]

	Low simultaneous low successive	Low simultaneous high successive	High simultaneous low successive	High simultaneous high successive	Simultaneous main effect	Successive main effect	Interaction
Receptive Syntax	10.78	11.07	9.52	12.81	0.16	8.80**	6.19*
Expressive Syntax	7.46	8.31	7.23	11.79	0.93	17.48***	8.20
Receptive Relational	8.02	9.17	9.40	12.19	13.16***	10.56**	1.85
Expressive Relational	6.07	8.05	7.29	11.19	10.85**	19.66***	2.08

[a]From A. F. Ashman, Strategic behavior and linguistic functions of institutionalized moderately retarded persons. *International Journal of Rehabilitation Research*, 1982, 5, 203–214. Copyright © G. Schindele Verlag. Reprinted by permission.

*$p \leqslant 0.05$.
**$p \leqslant 0.01$.
***$p \leqslant 0.001$.

findings of Cummins and Das (1978) and Cummins (1979), indicating the relationship between sequential processing and the subject's ability to link together the elements of a statement with a single discrete whole. An examination of the group means shows that individuals with high successive factor scores outperformed those with low successive factor scores. Simultaneous processing, therefore, can be an advantage or a disadvantage, depending upon one's successive processing capabilities.

The simultaneous and successive main effects on the relational language ratings are also consistent with the Cummins and Das (1978) results. The significant differences found between the groups on both simultaneous and successive scores reflect the importance of both processes for relational thinking.

These analyses demonstrate the involvement of successive processing in the comprehension of verbal language by the retarded, first in understanding the stream of language, and second in the production of language. The significant successive main effects also point to a relationship between serial processing and relational thought at both receptive and expressive levels. The results appear to confirm the relationships between the coding and language ratings using very low ability subjects and gives further support to the value of the Das *et al.* model in understanding the information processing capabilities of more severely retarded persons.

It has been argued that the language deficit manifested by moderately and severely retarded people stems from low-level performance primarily in the analysis of the linear structure of language. The successive main effects and interaction suggest that improvement could be expected in expressive language if residents were trained in successive processing.

One other body of literature has relevance to the training of sequential processing—namely, studies that have examined differences between subjects with varying etiological backgrounds. To evaluate the differences between etiological groups and to clarify whether successive processing is more important for one subgroup (e.g., Down's syndrome) than others, the sample was divided into four groups based upon the categories set out by Rohr and Burr (1978). Group 1 consisted of 20 subjects with Down's syndrome. The mean age of the group was 20.3 years ($SD = 5.38$) and the mean IQ was 24.2 ($SD = 15.13$). Group 2 consisted of 20 subjects with known environmentally caused brain damage—for example, from anoxia, meningitis, and motor vehicle accidents. The mean age was 19.9 years ($SD = 5.55$) and mean IQ was 30.5 ($SD = 20.1$). Group 3 contained 19 subjects with biologically caused brain damage, such as Turner's syndrome, Lennox–Gestaut syndrome, and microcephaly. The mean age of Group 3 was 19.0 years ($SD = 5.15$) and the mean IQ was 30.8 ($SD = 18.09$). Group 4 contained 29 subjects with no documentation available regarding the etiol-

TABLE 11.4
Group Means for Coding, Planning, and Language Variables

Variables	Group			
	Down's syndrome ($N = 20$)	Environmental brain damage ($N = 20$)	Biological brain damage ($N = 19$)	Unspecified causation ($N = 29$)
Visual Serial Recall	3.57	4.00	3.73	3.29
Auditory Serial Recall	4.50	11.55	11.68	12.66
Digit Span	3.90	6.50	6.89	6.28
Raven's Coloured Progressive Matrices	7.40	8.70	8.84	10.52
Figure Copying	3.90	4.45	5.37	5.45
Memory-for-Designs	4.75	7.15	10.00	11.21
Beery Test of Visual Motor Integration	5.35	5.05	5.74	6.03
Alternative Routes	11.20	12.00	11.58	12.97
Trail Making (latency)	164.85	208.30	217.89	179.03
Visual Search	732.68	781.50	782.23	836.29
Receptive Syntax	10.28	11.03	12.05	10.71
Expressive Syntax	7.73	9.10	10.87	9.02
Receptive Relational	8.23	9.85	10.61	9.78
Expressive Relational	6.10	8.15	9.37	8.52

ogy or onset of their retardation. These subjects had a mean age of 21.0 years ($SD = 5.42$) and a mean IQ of 29.8 ($SD = 17.84$).

The group means for the coding, planning, and language variables are shown in Table 11.4. In general, the Down's syndrome subjects performed more poorly than other groups on all but three measures—namely, Visual Serial Recall, the Beery Test of Visual Motor Integration, and Trail Making. Also, it appears that the biologically brain-damaged group was more successful than others. To examine the extent of the noted differences, one-way analyses of variance were performed on all variables. Four significant effects were found, on Auditory Serial Recall, Digit Span, Expressive Syntax, and Receptive Syntax, and it is apparent that the scores of the Down's syndrome subjects were the primary source of the effect.

While several writers have suggested that Down's subjects perform more poorly than others on serial processing and on measures of expressive language, no examination of linguistic performance has been made in respect to successive and simultaneous processing. Examining the composition of the groups with low successive factor scores showed that the Down's subjects comprised less than half—that is, 16 out of 47 subjects. Clearly, others have very low serial processing capabilities, and to assume that the Down's subjects form the homogeneous group of low successive processors would be false.

REMEDIATING INFORMATION PROCESSING DEFICITS

The results of the work to the present time provide some insight into the performance of moderately and severely retarded persons on the coding and planning tasks, and these in turn provide a basis upon which training programs may be devised for institutionalized persons. Specifically, the subjects used in the study outlined in the preceding discussion showed significant deficits in successive processing and used predominately simultaneous strategies when faced with problem situations. This disposition may result from the largely visual nature of the simultaneous tasks, and some support for this position may be found.

The apparent difficulty the subjects experienced in tasks related to successive processing (e.g., Digit Span, language measures) draws attention to the importance of both processes in the development of cognition. While Das and colleagues (e.g., Das, Kirby, & Jarman, 1979) have argued that simultaneous and successive processing are not hierarchical and that one does not depend on the other, the analyses reported here indicate that both simultaneous and successive coding processes play important roles in effective cognition. With low-ability retarded persons, it appears that successive processing has not developed comparably with simultaneous processing.

While an element of the "chicken and the egg" argument prevails in any discussion that attempts to disentangle processes from performance using samples of retarded persons, one must consider the cumulative effect of retardation. Is the poor performance on the subjects on the successive tasks a result or the cause of retardation? Similarly, is the apparent language deficit a function of institutionalization and the lack of interactive communication, or a function of poor cognition resulting from retardation? Does the emphasis on simultaneous processing indicate an attempt by the organism to compensate for inadequate successive processing, or alternatively, the only way to communicate with others in the environment? The success of the use of sign language in institutions provides some support that retarded persons can learn to communicate through a visual modality, and the comprehension of a sequence of signs indicates that retarded persons can develop more advanced successive processing skills. This may provide some direction in program development.

The work to date is the foundation for a continuing research program aimed at (a) delineating the cognitive capacities of the moderately and severely mentally retarded; and (b) effecting improvement in their information processing capabilities. With the current emphasis upon the normalization of retarded persons, it has become important to take into consideration those aspects of cognition that may influence the life experiences of individuals, especially those who are residents of hospitals or institutions and those who have very low levels of ability.

While it is recognized that it is not possible to make moderately retarded people function as their nonretarded peers in many tasks, it is valuable to develop those skills that will enable retarded persons to function more proficiently inside and outside their homes or institutions. Consequently, it appears legitimate to focus on training that will develop self-help skills, such as dressing and other activities relative to daily routines; vocational training skills, such as the development of safety practices; sequencing activities; attention to details and relevant cures; and academic tasks related to language skills, numeration, and identification of recognition skills. Underlying many of these life experience tasks are identifiable cognitive processes, such as simultaneous and successive synthesis, and organizational, integrative, and decision-making processes that are fundamental to efficient planning. Research directed toward the identification of coding and planning aspects of daily lives is one important thrust. A second is the training of the processes that will lead to improvement, not only in the use of the related strategies, but in the skills dependent upon these processes.

REFERENCE NOTES

1. Brown, A. L., Campione, J. C., & Barclay, C. R. Training self-checking routines for estimating test readiness: Generalization from list to prose recall. Unpublished manuscript, University of Illinois, 1978.
2. Friedman, M., Krupski, A., Dawson, E. T., & Rosenberg, P. Metamemory and mental retardation: Implications for research and practice. Paper presented at the Fourth International Congress of the Association for the Scientific Study of Mental deficiency, Washington, D.C., August 1976.
3. Kessel, F. S. Meta-this, meta-that, meta-the-other. Paper presented at the meeting of the Society for Research in Child Development, San Francisco, March 1979.
4. Kirby, J. R. Towards a rational framework for remedial instruction. Paper presented at the annual conference of the Australian Association for Research in Education, Perth, November 1978.
5. Jarman, R. F. Final report—Early childhood program design: Assessment of a screening model—year 1. Unpublished paper, University of British Columbia, 1978.
6. Cummins, J. Systems of mediation in memory and reasoning. Paper presented at the meeting of the Canadian Psychological Association, Victoria, Canada, June 1973.
7. Klish, L. Z. Aboriginal learning styles. Paper presented at the second Newcastle Invitational Conference on Cognitive Studies in Education, University of Newcastle, April 1981.
8. Cummins, J., & Mulcahy, R. Simultaneous and successive processing and narrative speech. Unpublished paper, University of Alberta, 1978.

REFERENCES

Ashman, A. F. *The relationship between planning and simultaneous and successive synthesis.* Unpublished doctoral dissertation, University of Alberta, 1978.
Ashman, A. F. Planning—the integrative function of the brain: Empirical evidence and speculation. *Educational Enquiry, 1979, 2,* 78–94.

Ashman, A. F. Strategic behavior and linguistic functions of institutionalized moderately retarded persons. *International Journal of Rehabilitation Research*, 1982, *5*, 203–214.

Ashman, A. F., & Das, J. P. Relation between planning and simultaneous and successive
processing. *Perceptual and Motor Skills*, 1980, *51*, 371–382.

Ashman, A. F., Molloy, G. N., & Das, J. P. Coding, planning and mental retardation: Theory,
evidence and implications. Part II. *Australian Journal of Developmental Disabilities*, 1981,
7, 57–64.

Baumeister, A. A., & Kellas, G. Process variables in the paired-associate learning of retardates.
In N. R. Ellis (Ed.), *International review of research in mental retardation* (Vol. 5). New
York: Academic Press, 1971.

Beery, K. E. *Developmental test of visual-motor integration: Administration and scoring manual*.
Chicago: Follett Educational Corporation, 1967.

Bilowsky, D., & Share, J. The ITPA and Down's syndrome: An exploratory study. *American
Journal of Mental Deficiency*, 1965, *70*, 78–82.

Bilsky, L., & Evans, R. A. Use of associative clustering techniques in the study of reading
disability: Effects of list organization. *American Journal of Mental Deficiency*, 1970, *74*,
771–776.

Blackman, L. S., Whittesmore, C. L., Zetlin, A. G., & McNamara, B. Use of constraint-seeking
questions by retarded and nonretarded individuals. *American Journal of Mental Deficiency*,
1977, *82*, 19–25.

Borys, S. V. Factors influencing the interrogative strategies of mentally retarded and nonretarded students. *American Journal of Mental Deficiency*, 1979, *84*, 280–288.

Bray, N. W., & Ferguson, R. P. Memory strategies used by young normal and retarded
children in a directed forgetting paradigm. *Journal of Experimental Child Psychology*, 1976,
22, 200–215.

Brown, A. L. The role of strategic behavior in retardate memory. In N. R. Ellis (Ed.), *International review of research in mental retardation* (Vol. 7). New York: Academic Press, 1974.

Brown, A. L. The development of memory: Knowing, knowing about knowing, and knowing
how to know. In H. W. Reese (Ed.), *Advances in child development and behavior* (Vol. 10).
New York: Academic Press, 1975.

Brown, A. L., & Barclay, C. R. The effects of training specific mnemonics on the metamnemonic efficiency of retarded children. *Child Development*, 1976, *47*, 71–80.

Brown, A. L., Campione, J. C., Bray, N. W., & Wilcox, B. L. Keeping track of changing
variables: Effects of rehearsal training and rehearsal prevention in normal and retarded
adolescents. *Journal of Experimental Psychology*, 1973, *101*, 123–131.

Brown, A. L., & Lawton, S. C. The feeling of knowing experience in educable retarded
children. *Developmental Psychology*, 1977, *13*, 364–370.

Bryant, P. G. Verbal labelling and learning strategies in normal and severely subnormal
children. *Quarterly Journal of Experimental Psychology*, 1967, *19*, 155–161.

Burger, A. L., & Blackman, L. S. Acquisition and retention of a mediational strategy for PA
learning in EMR children. *American Journal of Mental Deficiency*, 1976, *80*, 529–534.

Burger, A. L., & Blackman, L. S. Digit span estimation and the effects of explicit strategy
training on recall of EMR individuals. *American Journal of Mental Deficiency*, 1979, *83*,
621–626.

Burger, A. L., Blackman, L. S., Holmes, M., & Zetlin, A. Use of active sorting and retrieval
strategies as a facilitator of recall, clustering, and sorting by EMR and nonretarded children. *American Journal of Mental Deficiency*, 1979, *83*, 253–261.

Burger, A. L., & Erber, S. C. Effects of preferred stimuli on the free recall of moderately and
severely mentally retarded children. *American Journal of Mental Deficiency*, 1976, *81*,
391–393.

Butterfield, E. C., & Belmont, J. M. Assessing and improving the executive cognitive functions of mentally retarded people. In I. Bialer & M. Sternlicht (Eds.), *Psychological issues in mentally retarded people.* Chicago: Aldine, 1975.

Butterfield, E. C., Wambold, C., & Belmont, J. M. On the theory and practice of improving short-term memory. *American Journal of Mental Deficiency,* 1973, *77,* 654–669.

Byrnes, M. M., & Spitz, H. H. Performance of retarded adolescents and nonretarded children on the Tower of Hanoi problem. *American Journal of Mental Deficiency,* 1977, *81,* 561–569.

Campione, J. C., & Brown, A. L. Towards a theory of intelligence: Contributions from research with retarded children. *Intelligence,* 1978, *2,* 279–304.

Carroll, J. B. Psycholinguistics in the study of mental retardation. In R. L. Schiefelbusch, R. H. Copeland, & J. O. Smith (Eds.), *Language and mental retardation: Empirical and conceptual considerations.* New York: Holt, 1967.

Cattell, R. B. *Abilities: Their structures, growth and action.* Boston: Houghton, 1971.

Cavanaugh, J. C., & Borkowski, J. G. The metamemory–memory "connection" effects of strategy training and maintenance. *Journal of General Psychology,* 1979, *101,* 161–174.

Cavanaugh, J. C., & Borkowski, J. G. Searching for metamemory–memory connections: A developmental study. *Developmental Psychology,* 1980, *16,* 441–453.

Cohen, R. L., & Nealon, J. An analysis of short-term memory differences between retardates and nonretardates. *Intelligence,* 1979, *3,* 65–72.

Conroy, R. L. Facilitation of serial recall in retarded children and adults: Verbal and kinesthetic strategies. *American Journal of Mental Deficiency,* 1978, *82,* 410–413.

Cummins, J. Language functions and cognitive processing. In J. P. Das, J. Kirby, & R. F. Jarman (Eds.), *Simultaneous and successive cognitive processes.* New York: Academic Press, 1979.

Cummins, J., & Das, J. P. Simultaneous and successive synthesis and linguistic processes. *International Journal of Psychology,* 1978, *13,* 129–138.

Das, J. P. Patterns of cognitive ability in nonretarded and retarded children. *American Journal of Mental Deficiency,* 1972, *77,* 6–12.

Das, J. P. Cultural deprivation and cognitive competence. In N. R. Ellis (Ed.), *International review of research in mental retardation* (Vol. 6). New York: Academic Press, 1973.

Das, J. P. Planning: theoretical considerations and empirical evidence. *Psychological Research,* 1980, *41,* 141–151.

Das, J. P., & Jarman, R. F. Coding and planning processes. In M. Friedman, J. P. Das, & N. O'Connor (Eds.), *Intelligence and learning.* New York: Plenum, 1980.

Das, J. P., & Kirby, J. R. The case of the wrong exemplar: A reply to Humphreys. *Journal of Educational Psychology,* 1978, *70,* 877–879.

Das, J. P., Kirby, J., & Jarman, R. F. Simultaneous and successive syntehsis: An alternative model for cognitive abilities. *Psychological Bulletin,* 1975, *82,* 87–103.

Das, J. P., Kirby, J. R., & Jarman, R. F. *Simultaneous and successive cognitive processes.* New York: Academic Press, 1979.

Denney, D. R. Recognition, formulation, and integration in the development of interrogative strategies among normal and retarded children. *Child Development,* 1974, *45,* 1068–1076.

Dewart, M. H. Language comprehension processes of mentally retarded children. *American Journal of Mental Deficiency,* 1979, *84,* 177–183.

Ellis, N. R. Memory processes in retardates and normals. In N. R. Ellis (Ed.), *International review of research in mental retardation* (Vol. 4). New York: Academic Press, 1970.

Eyde, D. R., & Altman, R. *An exploration of metamemory processes in mildly and moderately retarded children* (Final Report). Columbus, Mo.: Department of Special Education, University of Missouri-Columbus, January 1978.

Fisher, M. A., & Zeaman, D. An attention–retention theory of retardate discrimination. In N. R. Ellis, *International review of research in mental retardation* (Vol. 6). New York: Academic Press, 1973.

Flavell, J. H. Developmental studies of mediated memory. In H. Reese & L. P. Lipsett (Eds.), *Advances in child development and behavior* (Vol. 5). New York: Academic Press, 1970.

Flavell, J. H., & Wellman, H. M. Metamemory. In R. V. Kail & J. W. Hagen (Eds.), *Perspectives on the development of memory and cognition*. Hillsdale, N.J.: Erlbaum, 1977.

Gilbert, K. A., & Hemming, H. Environmental change and psycholinguistic ability of mentally retarded adults. *American Journal of Mental Deficiency, 1979, 83,* 453–459.

Graham, F. K., & Kendall, B. S. Memory-for-designs test: Revised general manual. *Perceptual and Motor Skills, 1960, 11,* 147–188.

Guilford, J. P., Berger, R. M., & Christensen, P. R. *A factor analytic study of planning. II. Administration of tests and analysis of results*. University of Southern California, Psychological Laboratory Report, 1955, (Whole No. 12).

Hagen, J. W., Streeter, L. A., & Raker, R. Labelling, rehearsal, and short-term memory in retarded children. *Journal of Experimental Psychology, 1974, 18,* 259–268.

Haring, N. G., & Brown, L. J. (Eds.), *Teaching the severely handicapped* (Vol. 1). New York: Grune & Stratton, 1976.

Haywood, H. C. What happened to mild and moderate mental retardation? *American Journal of Mental Deficiency, 1979, 83,* 429–431.

Heal, L. W., & Johnson, J. T., Jr. Inhibition deficits in retardates learning and attention. In N. R. Ellis (Ed.), *International review of research in mental retardation* (Vol. 4). New York: Academic Press, 1970.

Hiskey-Nebraska test of learning aptitudes. Lincoln, Neb.: Union College Press, 1966.

Ilg, F. L., & Ames, L. B. *School readiness: Behavior tests used at the Gesell Institute*. New York: Harper, 1964.

Jarman, R. F. Patterns of cognitive ability in retarded children: A re-examination. *American Journal of Mental Deficiency, 1978, 82,* 344–348.

Jensen, A. R. How much can we boost IQ and scholastic achievement? *Harvard Educational Review, 1969, 39,* 1–123.

Jensen, A. R. A theory of primary and secondary familial mental retardation. In N. R. Ellis (Ed.), *International review of research in mental retardation* (Vol. 4). New York: Academic Press, 1970.

Jensen, A. R. The role of verbal mediation in mental development. *Journal of Genetic Psychology, 1971, 118,* 39–70.

Jensen, A. R. & Rohwer, W. D. *An experimental analysis of learning abilities in culturally disadvantaged children*. Office of Economic Opportunity Final Report. Washington, D.C.: U.S. Government Printing Office, 1970.

Kaufman, D., & Kaufman, P. Strategy training and remedial techniques. *Journal of Learning Disabilities, 1979, 12,* 416–419.

Kendall, C. R., Borkowski, J. G., & Cavanaugh, J. C. Metamemory and the transfer of an interrogative strategy by EMR children. *Intelligence, 1980, 4,* 255–270.

Kiernan, C. C. Alternatives to speech. *British Journal of Subnormality, 1977, 23,* 8–26.

Kirby, J. R. Individual differences and cognitive processes: Instructional applications and methodological difficulties. In J. R. Kirby & J. B. Biggs (Eds.), *Cognition, development, and instruction*. New York: Academic Press, 1980.

Kirby, J. R., & Ashman, A. F. *Strategic behavior and metacognition* (Final Report). Newcastle, N.S.W.: Department of Education, University of Newcastle, 1981.

Kirk, S. A., McCarthy, J. J., & Kirk, W. D. *Illinois test of psycholinguistic abilities* (Rev. ed.). Urbana: Univ. of Illinois, 1969.

Kreutzer, M. A., Leonard, C., & Flavell, J. H. An interview study of children's knowledge about memory. *Monographs of the Society of Research in Child Development,* 1975, *40* (1, Serial No. 159).

Krywaniuk, L. W., & Das, J. P. Cognitive strategies in native children: Analysis and intervention. *Alberta Journal of Educational Research,* 1976, *22,* 271–280.

Lawson, M. J. Metamemory: Making decisions about strategies. In J. R. Kirby & J. B. Biggs (Eds.), *Cognition, development, and instruction.* New York: Academic Press, 1980.

Leong, C. K. Spatial-temporal information processing in disabled readers. Unpublished doctoral dissertation, University of Alberta, 1974.

Luria, A. R. *The role of speech in the regulation of normal and abnormal behavior.* New York: Liveright, 1961.

Luria, A. R. *Higher cortical functions in man.* New York: Harper, 1966.

Luria, A. R. *The working brain.* Harmondsworth, Great Britain: Penguin Press, 1973.

Luria, A. R. Basic problems of language in the light of psychology and neurolinguistics. In E. H. Lenneberg & E. Lenneberg (Eds.), *Foundations of language development: A multidisciplinary approach* (Vol. 12). New York: Academic Press, 1975.

Luszcz, M. A., & Bacharach, V. R. List organization and rehearsal instructions in recognition memory of retarded adults. *American Journal of Mental Deficiency,* 1975, *80,* 57–62.

Lyle, J. G. Reading retardation and reversal tendency: A factorial study. *Child Development,* 1969, *40,* 833–843.

McBane, B. M. Rehearsal capacity and dimensional independence in retardates. *Journal of Experimental Child Psychology,* 1976, *22,* 216–228.

McNutt, J. C., & Leri, S. M. Language differences between institutionalized and noninstitutionalized retarded children. *American Journal of Mental Deficiency,* 1979, *83,* 339–345.

Miller, G. A., Galanter, G. H., & Pribram, K. H. *Plans and the structure of behavior.* New York: McGraw-Hill, 1960.

Miner, L. E. Scoring procedures for the length-complexity index: A preliminary report. *Journal of Communication Disorders,* 1969, *2,* 224–240.

Molloy, G. N. Age, socioeconomic status and patterns of cognitive ability. Unpublished doctoral dissertation, University of Alberta, 1973.

Montague, R. C., Hutchinson, E. C., & Matson, E. A. A comparative computer content analysis of the verbal behavior of institutionalized and noninstitutionalized retarded children. *Journal of Speech and Hearing Research,* 1975, *18,* 43–57.

Mosher, F. A., & Hornsby, J. R. On asking questions. In J. S. Bruner, R. R. Olver, & P. M. Greenfield (Eds.), *Studies in cognitive growth.* New York: Wiley, 1966.

Mulcahy, R. Memory deficits in the mentally retarded: Is this the real problem? *Mental Retardation Bulletin,* 1979, *7,* 123–131.

Neimark, E., Slotnick, N. S., & Ulrich, T. Development of memorization strategies. *Developmental Psychology,* 1971, *5,* 427–432.

O'Connor, N., & Hermelin, B. *Speech and thought in severe subnormality: An experimental study.* New York: Macmillan, 1963.

O'Connor, N., & Hermelin, B. *Seeing and hearing and space and time.* London: Academic Press, 1978.

Payne, J. S., Polloway, E. A., Smith, J. E., Jr., & Payne, R. A. *Strategies for teaching the mentally retarded.* Columbus, Ohio: Charles E. Merrill, 1977.

Phillips, J. L., & Balthazar, E. E. Some correlates of language deterioration in severely and profoundly retarded long-term institutionalized residents. *American Journal of Mental Deficiency,* 1979, *83,* 402–408.

Porteus, S. D. *Porteus maze test: Fifty years' application.* Palo Alto, Calif.: Pacific Books, 1965.

Raven, J. C. *Guide to the coloured progressive matrices.* London: Lewis, 1965.

Reid, B., & Kiernan, C. Spoken words and manual signs as encoding categories in short-term memory for mentally retarded children. *American Journal of Mental Deficiency*, 1979, *84*, 200–203.

Richie, J., & Butler, A. J. Performance of retardates on the memory-for-designs test. *Journal of Clinical Psychology*, 1964, *20*, 108–110.

Reigel, R. H., Danner, F. W., Johnson, L. S., & Kjerland, L. K. *Improving organization and memory*. St. Paul, Minn.: Research, Development and Demonstration Center in Education of Handicapped Children, University of Minnesota, 1973.

Riegel, R. H., & Taylor, A. M. Comparison of conceptual strategies for grouping and remembering employed by EMR and nonretarded children. *American Journal of Mental Deficiency*, 1974, *78*, 592–598.

Rohr, A., & Burr, D. B. Etiological differences in patterns of psycholinguistic development of children of IQ 30 to 60. *American Journal of Mental Deficiency*, 1978, *82*, 549–553.

Rossi, E. L., Development of classificatory behavior. *Child Development*, 1964, *35*, 137–142.

Simon, H. A. Information processing models of cognition. *Annual Review of Psychology*, 1979, *30*, 363–396.

Smirnov, A. A., & Zinchenko, P. I. Problems in the psychology of memory. In M. Cole & I. Maltzman (Eds.), *A Handbook of contemporary psychology*. New York: Basic Books, 1969.

Spitz, H. H. Evolutionary processes and mental deficiency. *Journal of Special Education*, 1973, *7*, 343–356.

Spitz, H. H., & Nadler, B. T. Logical problem solving by educable retarded adolescents and normal children. *Developmental Psychology*, 1974, *10*, 404–412.

Spitz, H. H., & Winters, E. A. Tic-tac-toe performance as a function of maturational level of retarded adolescents and nonretarded children. *Intelligence*, 1977, *1*, 108–117.

Turnbull, A. P. Teaching retarded persons to rehearse through cumulative overt labelling. *American Journal of Mental Deficiency*, 1974, *79*, 331–337.

Wechsler, D. *Wechsler Intelligence Scale for Children—revised*. New York: The Psychological Corporation, 1974.

Zeaman, D., & House, B. J. The role of attention in retardate discrimination learning. In N. R. Ellis, *Handbook of mental deficiency*. New York: McGraw-Hill, 1963.

Zigler, E. Mental retardation, technical comment. *Science*, 1967, *157*, 578.

12

The Effects of Intervention on
Deep and Surface Approaches to Learning

JOHN B. BIGGS
BERNARD A. RIHN

In this chapter, we describe an intervention program with university students and show its effects on two basic approaches to learning, deep and surface. These approaches are at the level of meso strategies (see Chapter 6) and operate within the "study process complex" (see Figure 6.1).

DEEP AND SURFACE APPROACHES TO LEARNING

Previous Research

In the field of complex human learning, say at senior high school or university, many writers have referred to basically two different ways that such learning may be approached. The distinction reflects that of Ausubel (1968) between *meaningful* and *rote* learning, and there are various elaborations around those two modes of learning: generic and surface coding (Biggs & Telfer, 1981); understanding and reproductive (Entwistle, Hanley & Hounsell, 1979); deep level and surface level (Marton & Sälsjö, 1976a, 1976b); deep processing and fact retention (Schmeck, forthcoming); internalizing and utilizing dimensions (Biggs, Table 6.1 this volume); and so on.

These distinctions are based on syndromes, the boundaries of which are

*Cognitive Strategies
and Educational Performance*

Copyright © 1984 by Academic Press, Inc.
All rights of reproduction in any form reserved.
ISBN 0-12-409580-1

drawn to achieve different purposes. Entwistle, Marton, and Biggs, for example, include affective factors, whereas Schmeck does not. Again, while Marton and Schmeck use very similar terminology, in the deep–surface distinction, both their conceptions and applications are different; Marton being interested only in reading text, Schmeck in a range of tasks. Schmeck also makes a distinction between "deep" and "elaborative" (personalized) processing—reflecting Craik and Tulving's (1975) reference to "depth" and "spread" of coding—whereas Marton does not.

The history of these terms starts with Craik and Lockhart (1972), who proposed that the depth of active processing, or thinking, that goes into the original learning would determine the nature and extent of subsequent memory of the episode. They proposed a continuum ranging from processing the physical attributes only at the shallow end, to semantic encoding at the deep end. Marton and his co-workers (Marton & Sälsjö, 1976a; 1976b) have taken this notion and used it to help construe the relationship between the process used by students in reading text and the ensuing level of complexity of the students' comprehension of that text. Marton also emphasizes that the student's intention is crucial: What the student intends to get out of his or her learning in large part determines the student's approach to learning (deep or surface), and that in turn determines the level of outcome. This distinction between intention and approach corresponds to that between motive and strategy, as outlined in Chapter 6.

Schmeck (forthcoming) has also pursued the depth of processing analogy and proposes four factors in complex learning: Deep Processing, Elaborative Processing, Fact Retention, and Methodical Study. These factors are measured in his *Inventory of Learning Processes.* Deep processing is represented by both "vertical" and "horizontal" aspects. Horizontal or elaborative processing is a "personalization" of knowledge, reflecting the extent to which the individual relates material to his or her own knowledge and interests; vertical or deep processing refers to depth of conceptual understanding. Shallow processing appears to be either a low score on one or the other, or both, of the Deep and Elaborative Processing scales, or a high score on Fact Retention, or some combination of these.

The work of Biggs has already been referred to in Chapter 6. The utilizing and internalizing dimensions, with the reproducing and meaningful strategies, relate closely to surface- and deep-level processing, respectively. Entwistle et al., (1979) refer to *orientations* toward learning that include understanding and reproducing. In a later version of their questionnaire, they specifically include items referring to deep- and surface-level processing.

While there are clear differences in conception between these accounts, there is, as Schmeck (forthcoming) makes abundantly clear, a great deal of overlap. If we place all these different approaches together, in the university context, we get the strong impression that two basic approaches to learning may be adopted by students, depending on the nature of the task, their own predispositions toward one style of learning or another, their motives for engaging the task (Marton's "intent"), institutional demands, and so on.

In sum, it would be generally agreed that a student who adopts a deep approach:

- Is interested in the academic task and derives enjoyment from carrying it out
- Searches for the meaning inherent in the task (e.g., if a prose passage, the intention of the author)
- Personalizes the task, making it meaningful to his or her own experience and to the real world
- Integrates aspects or parts of task into a whole (e.g., relates evidence to a conclusion), and sees relationships between this whole and previous knowledge
- Tries to theorize about the task, and forms hypothesis.

And a student who adopts a surface approach:

- Sees the task as a demand to be met, a necessary imposition if he or she is to reach some other goal (e.g., a qualification)
- Sees the aspects or parts of the task as discrete and unrelated either to each other or to other tasks
- Is worried about the time the task is taking
- Avoids personal or other meanings the task may have
- Relies on memorization, attempting to reproduce the surface aspects of the task (e.g., the words used, a diagram, or a mnemonic).

One question remaining concerns the *generality* (and hence teachability) of the strategies involved in processing the task (see Chapter 6). Marton emphasizes that the level of processing is situation determined; it is task specific and can be switched on or off as fits the student's perception of the current task. Schmeck, on the other hand, refers to depth of processing as a learning "style," which is a predisposition of some students to adopt a particular learning strategy regardless of particular task demands. Both facets can be demonstrated: Ramsden (1979) showed that students switch strategies to suit students' perceptions of course demands, whereas Thomas and Bain (1982) showed that deep- or surface-level processing was consistent in many students across tasks.

In line with what appears to be an emerging usage, we refer to "deep approach" and "surface approach" to learning, and we show that, while students do have a predilection for a deep or surface approach, appropriate intervention can induce a deep approach in surface processors.

Relation to the Study Process Complex

As mentioned in Chapter 6, the "study process complex" (see Figure 6.1) consists of three motives and three associated strategies, derived by second-order factor analysis of 10 scales, suggested by theory and previous research to be relevant to student study processes (Biggs, 1978a). As their intercorrelation shows (see Table 6.2), however, motives and strategies do not correlate at unity within dimensions or at zero between dimensions. There is therefore some sense in carrying out a further factor analysis, in effect a third-order analysis. Accordingly, a principal components analysis, with Varimax rotation, was carried out across two large samples of Australian institutions, comprising students from 10 colleges of advanced education and five universities. An identical two-factor solution appeared within and across institutions. The combined analysis is given in Table 12.1.

Two factors account for 64% of the study process complex. Both factors have affective and cognitive components. In the first factor, the affective component comprises intrinsic and achievement motivation, and the cognitive component, the adoption of a meaning strategy (wide reading, relating to previous knowledge, checking for one's own understanding) and an organizing strategy (keeping good notes, undertaking required reading, etc.). This looks very like a generalized deep approach to studying.

The second factor implicates both instrumental and achievement motives in the affective domain, and in the cognitive domain, it implicates the reproducing strategy, with no significant recourse, despite the presence of

TABLE 12.1
Principal Components Analysis, with Varimax Rotation, of Study Process Complex in 2141 Australian College and University Students

		Factor		h^2
		1	2	
M_1:	Instrumental	.010	.801	.64
M_2:	Intrinsic	.792	−.134	.65
M_3:	Achievement	.517	.542	.56
S_1:	Reproducing	−.171	.805	.68
S_2:	Meaning	.860	−.131	.76
S_3:	Organizing	.728	.143	.55
	Eigen value	2.193	1.639	
	Percentage variance	36.6	27.3	Total 64%

achievement motivation, to organizing and planning. This in turn looks like a generalized surface approach to studying.

In short, there is considerable theoretical and empirical support for summarizing the affective and cognitive components present in the study process complex in terms of two independent approaches to learning, deep and surface.

Contrary to what may seem to be implied in the original distinction, these are not either end of a single continuum. Rather, they suggest quite independent ways in which students may become involved in learning: Students may adopt one, the other, or both, to varying extents.

In this chapter, we operationalize "deep" in terms of Factor 1 and "surface" in terms of Factor 2 on the refactored Study Process Questionnaire. What this means in effect is that, for students to adopt a deep approach, they need to be both intrinsically and achievement motivated (the "ambitious academic" referred to in Chapter 6) and to adopt both meaningful and organizing strategies. Students who adopt a surface approach are still motivated to do well (the virtual equivalence of the loadings of the two factors on M_3, the achievement motive, is interesting), but they intend to do this by reproducing class material.

The Desirability of Deep versus Surface Approaches to Study

At first sight, there would appear to be a strong prima facie case for arguing that the deep approach to learning is preferable. The derivation of the term *depth of processing* strongly implies meaningfulness in learning material, and for its part, *surface* implies skipping across the top, picking up the epiphenomena of the content rather than its latent or potential meaning.

The empirical evidence would support these implications. A deep learning strategy, based on wide reading, relating new knowledge to what is already known, etc., results in better learning, whether *better* is defined as complexity of outcome (Biggs, 1978b; Marton & Sälsjö, 1976a, 1976b), satisfaction with performance (Biggs, see Chapter 6), self-rated performance in comparison with peers (see Chapter 6), or examination results (Schmeck, forthcoming; Svensson, 1976; Thomas & Bain, 1982; Watkins & Hattie, 1981). Not only does consistency exist over such varied ways of defining good quality learning, but the measures of depth of processing are also quite diverse, including individual interview in the case of Marton and Svensson, and self-report questionnaire (the Inventory of Learning Processes, by Schmeck, and Watkins and Hattie; the Study Process Questionnaire, by Biggs; and a short seven-item questionnaire by Thomas and Bain).

Notwithstanding the overall trends, it might be asked if some tasks are indeed better performed by a surface approach. For example, when learning for a short-term purpose, or when learning facts and details, a surface, reproductive approach might appear to be appropriate. The evidence bears this out. When the student's intention is to learn the surface facts, either by inclination or because he or she is instructed to do so, a surface approach works well (Biggs, 1978b).

In the undergraduate years at university, much learning required in science is necessarily surface or reproductive, and indeed science students tend to score higher on the attributes of a surface approach than do liberal arts students (Biggs, 1982; Watkins & Hattie, 1981; also see below). Nevertheless, as Watkins and Hattie also point out, science students, especially in the senior years, who *do* use a deep approach obtain better examination results than those who do not.

Biggs (1982) compared Australian college and university students' responses on the subscales of the Study Process Questionnaire (see also Chapter 6). In interpreting the results, it is important to note that colleges offer 3- and 4-year terminal courses for specific professional careers; course units are organized laterally, to cover the spread of knowledge from a variety of disciplines judged to be necessary for expertise in a particular profession. University courses, on the other hand, are hierarchically organized so that students will know more about their chosen discipline as they progress, with the possibility that many of them will go on to research higher degrees. The distinction can be summarized by saying that college courses are utilitarian and instrumental; university courses (at least in arts and science) lead the student into increasing depth and presuppose an intrinsic interest in the subject matter studied, whether or not it leads to a particular profession (which hopefully it will, but that is a separate motivational question).

One would therefore expect that college students would tend to display the attributes of a surface approach (instrumental motivation and a reproducing strategy) and university students a deep approach (intrinsic motivation and a meaning strategy). Biggs found very strong evidence that this was the case; he also found some of the unwanted side effects of the surface approach, in that the proportion of college students expressing dissatisfaction with their learning was over five times that of the university students, despite the fact that college students did not rate themselves as *performing* any worse; also, achievement motivation declined sharply over the 3 undergraduate years in college students, but not in university students.

The data concerning faculty are summarized in Figure 12.1. It can be seen that all university students, irrespective of faculty, were higher than college students on the deep approach ($p < .01$). There were no faculty

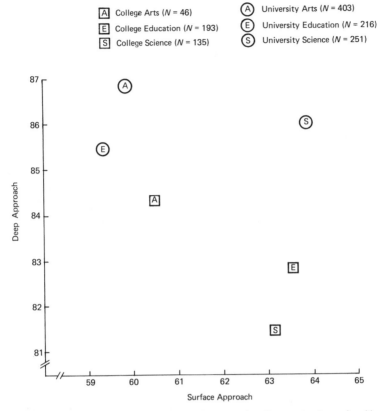

Figure 12.1. Deep and surface approaches in arts, education, and science faculties in 15 Australian colleges and universities.

differences on deep approach. On surface approach, however, there was an institutional main effect ($p < .05$), a faculty main effect ($p < .001$), and their interaction ($p < .001$). University science students are high on *both* deep and surface approaches, whereas college arts students are low on surface and moderately high on deep approaches. In other words, the surface approach is not all bad: It depends on the task, particularly when, as in university science, it is combined with a deep approach. It might be noted that teacher education students at university are high on deep and low on surface approach, but at college, the balance is reversed, being low on deep and high on surface. The implications of this finding as to the appropriate sector in which to prepare teachers are clear.

Collectively, then, these studies suggest that it is highly desirable that students adopt a deep-level approach to learning. Although there may be occasions, with particular tasks, when a surface approach is helpful, that approach should remain an *option* rather than a characteristic style.

The case for modifying a student's approach, if it does not already incorporate the deep approach, appears to be strong. Schmeck (forthcoming) reviews several studies of such intervention, but the results are not very encouraging. Many such attempts appear to address deep-level processing only tangentially, and when training was effective, it was often with high-ability students rather than with those who are most in need of deep-level strategies. Perhaps more importantly, the intervention programs concentrated on cognitive strategies, not on the motivational patterns of the students. As emphasized in Chapter 6, however, and as may be seen in Table 12.1, a deep approach necessarily involves the affective domain. To change a student's approach to study, in other words, may also involve changing his or her motivation to study, if the appropriate motivation is not already present.

In the rest of this chapter, we describe a program that was used successfully to decrease surface and increase deep approaches to the academic task.

AN INTERVENTION PROGRAM

Orientation

In 1979, one of the authors (Biggs) spent some time at Stanford University on study leave. He became particularly interested in the work of the Stanford Learning Assistance Center (SLAC), which provided a rehabilitation program for students who were dissatisfied with their grades.

By way of background, it needs to be noted that Stanford is an elite private university with a highly competitive entry and very expensive term fees. On graduation, about 40% of students go directly into graduate work, and as many again indicate their intention of doing so at some future stage. There is, then, enormous and continual pressure to maintain academic excellence in coursework. A student who perceives him- or herself "at risk" in this context, and seeks assistance from SLAC, is thus not comparable at all to the student who would present him- or herself at the student counseling service at most state universities. Personal and existential problems aside, the former would be bright and highly motivated to achieve but likely to be lacking an appropriate approach to study; some students are attaining a range of A− and B grades but spend too much time studying. These students seek assistance from SLAC to help them become more efficient in their study.

This picture was confirmed when the Study Process Questionnaire

(SPQ) was administered (anonymously) to two intakes of students into the SLAC program: 51 students in the fall quarter and 48 students in the winter quarter (1980). Two comparison groups are provided: a Stanford group (SU) enrolled in Psychology 1 ($N = 18$) and in Western Cultures ($N = 35$), and a group of Australian university students (AU) from five different institutions ($N = 883$). There were no differences on the six SPQ scores *within* each of the SU and SLAC groups, and so these were combined. The resulting profiles are given in Figure 12.2.

The major interest here is on the overall profiles rather than on the individual comparisons along particular scales. The AU and SU groups show comparable profiles, except that the SUs are (significantly) higher on M_3 (achievement motivation) than the AUs. Given the highly competitive ethos of Stanford, it would be something of an indictment of this scale if this were not so. The SLACs, on the other hand, show an incongruent profile in terms of the congruence hypothesis: They are consistently high on all three motives (cf. the "hogs"; see Chapter 6) but they are notably inferior on the two strategies embodied in a deep approach and high on the strategy embodied in a surface approach. In terms of the congruence hypothesis out-

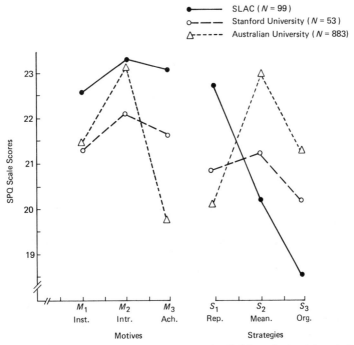

Figure 12.2. Motive and strategy profiles for SLAC students and controls.

lined in Chapter 6, the SLAC students are intrinsically motivated, but do not use the meaning strategy to any great extent, and achievement motivated, even higher than the SUs (as would be expected on the basis of their attendance at SLAC), but deficient in the cognate organizing strategy, S_3.

The picture is one of high motivation and incongruent strategy deployment; in other words, the SLAC students are attempting to succeed on the basis of a surface approach to learning. An intervention program (LAC 1) is described that was intended to encourage deep-level learning.

The Intervention Program (LAC 1)

LAC 1 ("Effective Learning Skills") is a course open to undergraduate students of any year or faculty and "is designed to help you become a more efficient learner" (from the course outline). The course is offered for credit toward a degree on a pass/no credit basis, and it takes 9 weeks to complete. It operates in each quarter of the academic year.

The course addresses the following topics: time management, goal and priority setting, self-management, understanding and remembering what one reads, effective listening and note taking, concentration and memory, test preparation and prediction, decision making, problem solving, nutrition, relaxation, and reading speed. Most important, the course stresses utilization of these skills through demonstrated changes in behavior on particular study goals. Peer counselors act as mediators. The students are required to interview with peer counselors after each important specified period of selfguided work of about 2 weeks each. Pauk (1974) is the basic text, together with recommended readings, tapes, assignments, and exercises. Students are required to set up a contract and time schedule, write progress reports, and evaluate their own progress.

The affective domain is addressed more implicitly. Stanford students learn quickly that surface strategies alone will not work as they did in high school. There is simply too much material to learn. It is stressed from the beginning (with research and practical examples) that isolated detail is difficult to remember unless placed in the context of the main ideas. Students are taught first to identify the major ideas and their interrelationships. Then they relate specifics to the whole. Also, students learn the absolute necessity of periodic (spaced) review as an aid to memory. This is judged to be an appropriate mix of deep and surface learning, with the deep preceding the surface. Thus, when students begin to see changes in objective terms (test scores, grades, etc.) they experience an accompanying feeling of satisfaction, of being "on top of it." This affective consequence motivates them to repeat the successful pattern.

Evaluation of the Program

A preliminary look at the pre- and post-SPQ scores for two classes (winter 1980; spring 1980) showed some degree of normalization from the pattern outlined in Figure 12.2. Intrinsic motivation increased and instrumental motivation decreased, but neither significantly , and both meaningful and organizing strategies increased significantly. This pattern seemed to give some evidence of a decrease in surface and an increase in deep approaches to learning, but these data were obtained on overall entry and exit means, and there had been a 20% attrition from pre- to posttest. As these data were gathered anonymously, it was not possible to check the degree of change for each individual student.

The fall 1981 and winter 1982 classes were therefore monitored directly. The SPQ was administered to each student before and after the LAC 1 courses. It was not possible to look at possible faculty differences, as there was a wide and uneven spread across faculties, but it was possible to set up Class × Sex × Occasion repeated measures ANOVAs. The dependent variables were Surface Approach and Deep Approach, these scores being constructed on the basis of Table 12.1. Each significant factor loading was given a unit weighting, and the scale scores added as follows (the correlation between unit-weight scores and factor scores was .94):

Surface Approach = instrumental motivation (M_1) + reproducing strategy (S_1) + achievement motivation (M_3)

Deep Approach = intrinsic motivation (M_2) + meaningful strategy (S_2) + achievement motivation (M_3) + organizing strategy (S_3)

The results are outlined in Table 12.2. There were minor differences by

TABLE 12.2
Significance of Effects of Class, Sex, and Occasion (Pre–Post) on Deep and Surface Approaches in Two LAC 1 Classes[a]

Factor	Deep	Surface
Class	.10	ns
Sex	ns	.05
Class × Sex	ns	ns
Occasion	.000	.05
Occasion × Class	.05	ns
Occasion × Sex	ns	ns
Occasion × Class × Sex	.10	ns

[a]ns = nonsignificant.

Class and Sex. Males tended overall to use a surface approach more than did females, and there was a slight tendency for the fall class to already have a deeper approach than the spring class. The most significant findings, however, are those involving the program: There was overall a significant drop ($p < .05$) in surface approach and a highly significant rise in deep approach ($p < .0001$), irrespective of Class and Sex.

These effects and the interactions are depicted in Figure 12.3. The length and slope of the arrows depict the degree of change from pre- to posttest. The increase in deep approach can be seen in the altitudes of the arrows, the negative gradients showing the decrease in surface approach. The fall 1981 females manifest only a small move toward deep approach (as seen in the interactions), but this is undoubtedly due to the high level they started with. All groups also showed a decrease in surface approach. The SUs are plotted for comparison, and it is seen that, relative to the post-SLACs, they are low on both deep and surface approaches.

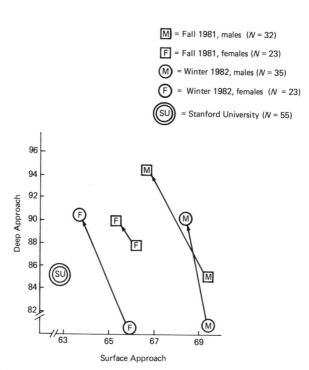

Figure 12.3. Movement from surface to deep approach by LAC 1 classes.

DISCUSSION AND CONCLUSIONS

While it is not yet possible to relate extent of movement from surface to deep approach with improvement in grade point average, previous research would certainly lead one to expect such a relationship; similarly, one would need follow-up data to check on the permanency of the movement.

Those two points aside, the present data would appear to have some important implications, both for the theory of student learning and for intervention programs for improving learning.

The question of whether a deep or a surface approach to learning is a matter either of situationally determined strategies or of relatively unteachable personality styles springing from the basic personality structure of the individual is simplistic. The study process complex (D and E in Figure 6.1) comprises motives and strategies that spring from *both* situational (B) and personological (A) components.

The factor analysis reported in Table 12.1 showed that 64% of the variance in the study process complex could be accounted for by two factors. The loadings of the motives and strategies on these factors suggest an interpretation in terms of deep and surface approaches to learning.

That analysis is important for two main reasons:

1. It demonstrates, yet again, that ultimate interpretations of student learning get back to these two basic approaches. Many authors, from many perspectives and methodologies, seem to arrive at this point.
2. It would seem to be mistaken to see deep and surface approaches as being determined by cognitive factors alone. As suggested by Marton, and as suggested in the factor analysis and in Chapter 6, the student's purposes and intentions are part and parcel of a deep or a surface approach.

The two factors are convenient for comparing institutions, faculties, and student groups on their learning approaches. Evidence was given, for example, that strong institutional differences exist when comparing colleges and university students. Given course structures, extent of vocationalism, emphasis on research, and self-selection of students, one would expect college students to score higher than university students on surface approach, and university students higher than college students on deep approach. These findings were confirmed with respect to deep approach, but there was a strong faculty by institution interaction with surface, due to the need in university science courses for *both* deep and surface approaches. Thus, college arts students used less surface approach than university science students, but they were not as committed to a deep approach as the latter.

Biggest differences between college and university students on both dimensions were found in teacher education students.

The major comparisons, however, involved students who were dissatisfied with their performance and sought assistance in study techniques by enrolling for a program on effective learning skills. It was shown in a pilot run with two intakes that these students were, compared to other students, very highly motivated all round but deficient in strategies involved in the deep approach, seeming to rely on surface rote learning.

The pre- and posttest results on deep and surface approach were compared for two further groups who were followed through an intervention program that was designed to capitalize on student motivation and to encourage a deeper approach to learning and discourage a surface approach. The program seemed to be remarkably successful in both objectives, in both years studied, and irrespective of sex (and as far as one can tell, of faculty).

This last finding is important, because it demonstrates clearly that adaptive strategies *can* be taught and maladaptive ones dropped. However, it must be pointed out that the Stanford LAC 1 students were the best possible material for intervention: They were highly selected academically in the first instance and very highly motivated. In terms of the congruence hypothesis in Chapter 6, the motivational context was "right" for deep-level processing and what they mainly lacked were the appropriate cognitive strategies. Under those conditions, the program was highly successful.

What the outcome might have been with students lacking the motivational context of the deep approach is unknown. It is likely that rather different intervention techniques would be necessary, specifically focusing on the affective domain. At the very least, then, this study might point the way for the general shape, structure, an content of intervention programs. Two generalizations are worth putting forward:

1. The concepts of deep and surface approach to learning appear to be useful in this context both diagnostically and for defining outcomes.
2. The prescriptions for treating students would depend upon their motivational and strategic profiles.

REFERENCES

Ausubel, D. P. *Educational psychology: A cognitive view.* New York: Holt, 1968.

Biggs, J. B. Individual and group differences in study processes. *British Journal of Educational Psychology.* 1978, *48*, 266–279. (a)

Biggs, J. B. Levels of processing, study processes and factual recall. In M. M. Gruneberg, P. E. Morris, & P. N. Sykes (Eds.), *Practical aspects of memory.* London: Academic Press, 1978. (b)

Biggs, J. B. Individual differences in study processes and the quality of learning outcomes. *Higher Education,* 1979, *8,* 381–394.

Biggs, J. B. Student motivation and study strategies in university and CAE populations. *Higher Education Research and Development,* 1982, *1,* 33–55.

Biggs, J., & Telfer, R. *The process of learning: Psychology for Australian educators.* Sydney: Prentice-Hall (Australia), 1981.

Craik, F. I. M., & Lockhart, R. S. Levels of processing: A framework for memory research. *Journal of Verbal Learning and Verbal Behavior,* 1972, *11,* 671–684.

Craik, F. I. M., & Tulving, E. Depth of processing and the retention of words in episodic memory. *Journal of Experimental Psychology,* 1975, *104,* 268–294.

Entwistle, N., Hanley, M., & Hounsell, D. Identifying distinctive approaches to studying. *Higher Education,* 1979, *8,* 365–380.

Marton, F., & Sälsjö, R. On qualitative differences in learning: I. Outcome and process. *British Journal of Educational Psychology,* 1976, *46,* 4–11. (a)

Marton, F., & Sälsö, R. On qualitative differences in learning: II. Outcome as a function of the learner's conception of the task. *British Journal of Educational Psychology,* 1976, *46,* 115–127. (b)

Pauk, W. *How to study in college.* Boston: Houghton, 1974.

Ramsden, P. Student learning and perceptions of the academic environment. *Higher Education,* 1979, *8,* 411–427.

Schmeck, R. R. Learning styles of college students. In R. Dillon & R. R. Schmeck (Eds.), *Individual differences in cognition.* New York: Academic Press, forthcoming.

Svensson, L. *Study skill and learning.* Goteborg Studies in Educational Sciences, 19. Goteborg: Acta Universitatis Gothoburgiensis, 1976.

Thomas, P., & Bain, J. Consistency in learning strategies. *Higher Education,* 1982, *11,* 249–254.

Watkins, D., & Hattie, J. The learning processes of Australian university students: Investigations of contextual and psychological factors. *British Journal of Educational Psychology,* 1981, *51,* 384–393.

Author Index

Numbers in italics indicate pages where complete references can be found.

Subject Index

EDUCATIONAL PSYCHOLOGY

continued from page ii

Ronald W. Henderson (ed.). Parent–Child Interaction: Theory, Research, and Prospects

W. Ray Rhine (ed.). Making Schools More Effective: New Directions from Follow Through

Herbert J. Klausmeier and Thomas S. Sipple. Learning and Teaching Concepts: A Strategy for Testing Applications of Theory

James H. McMillan (ed.). The Social Psychology of School Learning

M. C. Wittrock (ed.). The Brain and Psychology

Marvin J. Fine (ed.). Handbook on Parent Education

Dale G. Range, James R. Layton, and Darrell L. Roubinek (eds.). Aspects of Early Childhood Education: Theory to Research to Practice

Jean Stockard, Patricia A. Schmuck, Ken Kempner, Peg Williams, Sakre K. Edson, and Mary Ann Smith. Sex Equity in Education

James R. Layton. The Psychology of Learning to Read

Thomas E. Jordan. Development in the Preschool Years: Birth to Age Five

Gary D. Phye and Daniel J. Reschly (eds.). School Psychology: Perspectives and Issues

Norman Steinaker and M. Robert Bell. The Experiential Taxonomy: A New Approach to Teaching and Learning

J. P. Das, John R. Kirby, and Ronald F. Jarman. Simultaneous and Successive Cognitive Processes

Herbert J. Klausmeier and Patricia S. Allen. Cognitive Development of Children and Youth: A Longitudinal Study

Victor M. Agruso, Jr. Learning in the Later Years: Principles of Educational Gerontology

Thomas R. Kratochwill (ed.). Single Subject Research: Strategies for Evaluating Change

Kay Pomerance Torshen. The Mastery Approach to Competency-Based Education

Harvey Lesser. Television and the Preschool Child: A Psychological Theory of Instruction and Curriculum Development

Donald J. Treffinger, J. Kent Davis, and Richard E. Ripple (eds.). Handbook on Teaching Educational Psychology

Harry L. Hom, Jr. and Paul A. Robinson (eds.). Psychological Processes in Early Education

EDUCATIONAL PSYCHOLOGY